## PRAISE FOR *MEN WHO HATE WOMEN*

"The killing of women because we are women is not only the most common crime in the world—it is also the single biggest indicator of whether a nation is violent in its streets and will use violence against another nation. Laura Bates is showing us the path to both intimate and global survival."

—Gloria Steinem

"Laura has taken on a critical issue, one that society can no longer afford to overlook or trivialize: the reality of misogynistic extremism and the central role it plays today in family and social breakdowns, proliferating hate, terroristic violence, and political instability. This book touches on every aspect of our lives—personal, professional, political. It's unflinching, brave, and necessary."

—Soraya Chemaly, author of *Rage Becomes Her*

"A profoundly important piece of work."

—*The Observer*

"Brilliantly fierce and eye-opening."

—*The Guardian*

"*Men Who Hate Women* has the power to spark social change."

—*Sunday Times*

"If you only buy one book this month, then may we recommend Laura Bates's *Men Who Hate Women*."

—*Stylist*

"Compellingly argued and meticulously researched."

—*Evening Standard*

"A shattering read."

—*Irish Examiner*

"Laura Bates is a total powerhouse. This book is hard to read; triggering, unfiltered, shocking, and urgent. Laura has done again what she does best: gone there, all the way, to the darkest corners and brought all the research, anecdotes, and interviews to the surface for us all to see. This is how change is made: by looking at uncomfortable things directly in the eye and not turning away. This book is a rallying cry to end suffering, for both women AND men."

—Emma Gannon, *Sunday Times* bestselling author

"Laura Bates continues to be one of the most powerful, vulnerable, and incredible feminist voices of our time. She is unafraid of tackling the most complex, dark, and nuanced aspects of the patriarchy and shining a light on them in order to change the world. *Men Who Hate Women* is a fascinating, mind-blowing, and deeply intelligent book that should be recommended reading for every person on our planet. Laura Bates is my HERO and two chapters into this book, she will be yours too."

—Scarlett Curtis, curator of National Book Award winner *Feminists Don't Wear Pink and Other Lies*

"A book of courage and tenacity. Laura's humanity shines through. She is always a voice worth paying attention to. She continues to fight a battle that should have ended long ago, and she reminds us that we must be part of it."

—Robin Ince, co-host of BBC Radio 4's *The Infinite Monkey Cage* and the *Robin and Josie's Book Shambles* podcast

"In *Men Who Hate Women*, Laura Bates offers the alternative red pill to those who favor love, logic, and humanity over debilitating hate. Bates's exploration of the manosphere—from the monetized toxicity of social and mainstream media to Number Ten, the White House, and complacent law enforcers—should wake up and shame all of the above. If its brutally forensic honesty is sometimes painful to read, imagine what it was to live, investigate, and write. When once more, we award medals to our bravest feminist heroes, Laura Bates gets the Purple Heart. Young people, parents, teachers, journalists, and legislators should read this important book. All those keyboard warriors pounding away in the dark should dare to read it. The only thing to fear is fear itself."

—Shami Chakrabarti, lawyer and human rights activist

"Be prepared. This book is shocking. Just as we thought we knew all we needed to know about misogyny, here comes the bad news. Dark and menacing, this investigation of toxic masculinity is a wake-up call to men and women who want a better world."

—Helena Kennedy, QC, lawyer and human rights activist

"Laura Bates has written a fearless and unflinching account of how the most prevalent human rights abuse on the planet, the mistreatment of women and girls at the hands of men, is being given new energy and reach through contemporary technologies and the strategies of extremism. This is a vital and urgent book, detailing not just the growing threat of extreme misogyny and the mainstreaming of its message, but also how through allowing this to happen we are exposing girls and women to increasing levels of danger and abandoning countless boys and men to the coruscating damage of its influence. If the warnings of this book were to be heeded and acted upon, the world would take a significant step toward creating kinder, safer, better societies for all, men and women alike."

—Owen Sheers, award-winning author, poet, and playwright

"A book that is a challenging and sobering read but also brave, meticulously researched—and vital to anyone serious about tackling misogyny."

—Anna James, writer and journalist

## PRAISE FOR *EVERYDAY SEXISM*

"A pioneering analysis of modern-day misogyny."

—*Daily Telegraph*

"[An] extremely powerful book that could, and should, win hearts and minds right across the spectrum."

—*Financial Times*

"A game-changing book, a must-read for every woman."

—*Cosmopolitan*

"Admirable and culturally transferable. 'A storm is coming,' writes Bates. After reading this book, you'll hope so."

—*The Independent*

"If Caitlin Moran's *How to Be a Woman* is the fun-filled manual for female survival in the twenty-first century, *Everyday Sexism* is its more politicized sister."

—*Independent on Sunday*

"Following [Everyday Sexism on Twitter] will make most women feel oddly saner."

—Caitlin Moran

"We owe Bates a great debt of gratitude for her Everyday Sexism Project."

—*Los Angeles Times*

## PRAISE FOR LAURA BATES

"Laura Bates has given women of every age a frank guide to standing up for ourselves and each other."

—Gloria Steinem

"Mature, eloquent, and passionate, Bates is, in many ways, the voice of her generation."

—*HuffPost*

"Laura was one of the first women to harness the power of social media to fight sexism and misogyny, and give millions of young women a voice."

—*Grazia*

"[*Girl Up* is] another hard-hitting book, which exposes the truth surrounding pressures on body image, false representations in the media, and lots of issues very relevant to girls today."

—*Red*

## ALSO BY LAURA BATES

*Everyday Sexism*
*Girl Up*
*Misogynation*
*The Burning*

# MEN WHO HATE WOMEN

From Incels to Pickup Artists:
**The Truth about Extreme Misogyny
and How It Affects Us All**

## LAURA BATES

Published by Sourcebooks
P.O. Box 4410, Naperville, Illinois 60567-4410
(630) 961-3900
sourcebooks.com

Originally published in 2020 in Great Britain by Simon &
Schuster UK Ltd., an imprint of Simon & Schuster.

The Library of Congress has cataloged the hardcover edition as follows:

Names: Bates, Laura.
Title: Men who hate women : from incels to pickup artists : the truth about
    extreme misogyny and how it affects us all / Laura Bates.
Description: Naperville, Illinois : Sourcebooks, [2021] | Includes
    bibliographical references and index.
Identifiers: LCCN 2020047361 (print) | LCCN 2020047362 (ebook) |
    (hardcover) | (epub)
Subjects: LCSH: Misogyny. | Sexism. | Online chat groups. | Online hate
    speech. | Anti-feminism. | Internet and women.
Classification: LCC HQ1237 .B3827 2021 (print) | LCC HQ1237 (ebook) | DDC
    305.3--dc23
LC record available at https://lccn.loc.gov/2020047361
LC ebook record available at https://lccn.loc.gov/2020047362

Printed and bound in the United States of America.
SB 10 9 8 7 6 5 4 3

*For Nick, without whom none of this would have been possible.*

# Contents

# Introduction

Imagine a world in which millions of women are raped, beaten, mutilated, abused, or murdered every year because of the simple fact that they are women. Imagine a world in which the hatred of women is actively encouraged, with sprawling, purpose-built communities of men dedicated to fueling and inflaming the cause. Imagine a world in which such hatred blends seamlessly with racist rage: "whores" blamed for contaminating superior bloodlines; invading "savages," conjured from hate-fueled imaginations, framed as plunderers of the dehumanized commodity of fragile, white women. Imagine a world in which thousands of men band together, united by a common code of vitriolic rage, demonizing and railing against evil, soulless, greedy women, graphically plotting their rape and destruction in a glorious, bigoted uprising. Imagine a world in which some men actually enact such fantasies, killing women in mass murders, leaving behind manifestos explaining the ideology that drove them to commit these acts of terrorism. Imagine a world in which vulnerable men, lost boys, and confused, scared teenagers are swept up and preyed upon by such communities, which feed on their fears and push them toward hatred, violence, and self-destruction.

You don't have to imagine that world. You already live in it. But perhaps you didn't know, because we don't like to talk about it.

We don't like to risk offending men. We find it hard to think of straight, white men as a homogeneous group, though it comes so easily when we think of other types of people, because we are used to affording such men the privilege of discrete identities. These men are complex, heroic, individual. Their decisions and choices are seen to spring from a set of distinct and unique circumstances, because we see them as distinct and unique people. We don't mind talking about women as a group and about violence against women as a phenomenon, but we do so as though it is something that just happens. We do not, as a rule, talk about male perpetrators of violence against women. We describe a woman as having been raped; we discuss the rates of women sexually assaulted or beaten. We do not speak in terms of men committing rape or being sexual assaulters and violent abusers. That is what makes it so easy to focus on women's dress, behavior, and choices when we consider sexual violence. To warn women to take precautions to protect themselves and, implicitly or explicitly, blame those victims who do not. Because a rape is a shadowy, dark thing waiting to befall women who walk in alleyways wearing short skirts, not a deliberate, criminal choice made by real men. When we are forced to confront these men because high-profile cases hit the headlines, we describe them as "beasts" and "monsters" in order to separate them clearly from those other, ordinary, decent men among whom we walk every day. We do not count them, quantify them, or study them in any meaningful sense. In fact, we rarely think about them at all.

If we talk about masculinity, patriarchy, or male privilege, the conversations are immediately derailed by accusations of generalization and prejudice. "Not all men," rises the ubiquitous cry. It is too simplistic, too offensive, too broad. Yet we raise few such objections when the crimes of a man with brown or black skin are immediately assumed to be related to his race or religion. To speak ill of masculinity—to describe it, in its current societal iteration, as something problematic—is seen as an attack on men themselves. To question why some men behave in certain ways is viewed as an assault on all men and thus unacceptable.

Yet the opposite is true. Those who speak of "toxic masculinity" are not criticizing men but rather defending them: describing an ideology and a system that pressures the boys and men in our societies, in our families, to conform to unrealistic, unhealthy, and unsustainable ideals. Crushing gender stereotypes are damaging to men as individuals as well as to the society in which they live. Tackling this problem, dismantling these pressures, is a matter of life and death for our boys. They are toppling like dominoes into the chasm we leave behind when we tiptoe around and refuse to name the problem.

But we don't like to offend men. So we don't mention it. We do not use the word *terrorism* when describing a crime of mass murder committed by a white man with the explicit intention of creating terror and spreading hatred against a specific demographic group— even though that is the definition of terrorism—if the demographic in question is women. The man is just "disturbed," "deranged," a "lone wolf." We use language that designates him an outlier, an aberration. We do not call his online journey a "radicalization" or use the word *extremism* to label the online communities in which he has immersed himself, though we would reach for those words in an instant when describing other, similar types of crimes, committed by other, different types of men. We do not examine what led him to commit those acts or how he became so full of hate.

The majority of men are good and kind and would never dream of committing such crimes. But that must not prevent us from recognizing that those who do are not always acting in a vacuum. And if we don't see the connections, if we don't even consider masculinity and its toxic societal construction as a factor at play in these crimes, we will never effectively police or prevent them. This doesn't mean treating all men as the enemy—quite the opposite. It means embracing the legions of men working at the grassroots level, male activists and educators who are throwing their all into fighting the problem. There exists a real men's movement—founded in the late 1960s to complement the booming women's liberation movement and still active today—that encompasses communities truly fighting to tackle the many legitimate problems impacting men's lives as well as individual men fighting to defeat issues like relationship violence. It is a movement that seeks to question and dismantle toxic masculinity, realizing that it is as harmful to men as it is to women. But it is threatened and overshadowed by other, hateful male movements.

This is not just about women and girls. It is also a battle to protect the boys who are lost, who fall through the cracks of our society's stereotypes and straight into the arms of the communities ready to recruit them, greedy to indoctrinate them with fears of threats to their manhood, their livelihood, their country. While pretending that what threatens these boys is women or immigrants or nonwhite men, the real threat comes from the very forms of rigid "manhood" their so-called saviors are desperate to preserve and promote. Yet we'd rather stay ignorant of this misogynistic hate movement, actively grooming and radicalizing our boys, than be forced to confront it.

Maybe this all sounds very extreme, rather exaggerated. Perhaps you think there might be one or two men online with wild opinions and worrying views about women, but that's just the internet—they're just sad teenagers sitting in their parents' basements, whiling away the hours in a pair of grubby underwear, clutching a bag of Doritos under one arm. They don't pose any real threat. They're more to be pitied than feared.

Even the word we use to describe women-hating communities encapsulates this attitude perfectly. Beyond the occasional news report or small-circle conversations within feminist activist spheres, most of us do not know about the sprawling web of groups, belief systems, lifestyles, and cults that this book will unravel. Those who do know describe it as the "manosphere." Like *man cave, man flu,* and *man bag,* we use *man* as a prefix to denote a sense of gentle ridicule, suggesting something slightly pathetic, a deviation from traditional masculinity. The manosphere is seen as a joke and therefore harmless. But it isn't. It is an interconnected spectrum of different but related groups, each with their own rigid belief systems, lexicons, and forms of indoctrination. This book will explore the links in the chain, from incels to pickup artists, Men Going Their Own Way to Men's Rights Activists, and how they exist as a kind of living, breathing ecosystem in close, symbiotic relationships with other online communities like white supremacists and trolls. It will explore the ways in which these groups expand, a vast spiderweb of sites, blogs, forums, chat rooms, groups, and social media accounts, and reveal just how easily boys can blunder across the edges of this web and find themselves stuck, then gently rolled closer and closer to its center with smooth efficiency. These are communities that exist largely online, the massive underbelly of the iceberg going largely unnoticed and unseen, yet the tip extending into our "real" world and becoming bolder and sharper every day.

Perhaps you think we all need to calm down and remember that what happens online isn't real life—sticks and stones might break your bones and all that.

Maybe you've heard that freedom of speech is under threat, and if millennial snowflakes and PC warriors are allowed to have their way, nobody will ever be able to say anything critical about women or minority groups on the internet again. Or you might have heard that one of our vital freedoms is being undermined by pearl-clutching, humorless women taking offense at a few risqué jokes.

But what if there's more to it than that?

What if it's almost impossible to come to grips with the epidemic of violence facing women and girls when we're not able to clearly name and examine the problem? What if we can't begin to take a comprehensive and effective approach to policing acts of violence because we don't describe them in ways that acknowledge the connections between them? What if we are so inured to particular forms of violence that we consider them cultural, personal... inevitable? What if our ideas about men and women, about misogyny and hate crime, about what terrorists look like, are so trapped in stereotypes that we're making terrible mistakes? What if those mistakes have devastating consequences?

What if there was a kind of early warning system that could have alerted us to the possibility of tragedy in case after case of violence, but we never saw the red flags? What if legions of abused women were canaries singing in coal mines, their songs going unheard? What if violence against women has become so much a part of the wallpaper of our lives that it has blended in altogether? What if our desensitization to low-level, ubiquitous misogyny is preventing us from recognizing a fully blown crisis?

It's a little bit easier to see the signs if you are a woman. It's significantly clearer if you are a woman who has voiced her opinion online. It's blindingly obvious if you are a woman involved in feminist activism. Because then you don't have the luxury of continuing to look the other way. Then the hate comes to you. Then they get in touch.

For nearly a decade, men have sent me daily messages, often in the hundreds, outlining their hatred of me, fantasizing about my brutal rape and murder, detailing which weapons they would use to slice my body open and disembowel me, describing me as a dripping poison, sketching visions of lying in wait outside my home, letting me know which particular serial killers they'd particularly like to emulate as they end my life.

Why are these men so angry? Why do they hate me so much? Because I started a little website called the Everyday Sexism Project, through which people (of any gender) can talk about their experiences of sexism and inequality. I asked people to share their stories, and I gave them a space to do so. And that innocuous, simple act in 2012 was enough to unleash a torrent of abuse that continues to this day, spiking and redoubling every time I talk about the project online or in the media. It follows me to speaking events, where angry men hand out flyers calling me a liar, or into bookstores, where they leave handwritten notes in my books, warning readers that women lie about rape. It trails me from television studios, when men have seen me on the news, so I arrive home and open my laptop to find messages about using my hair as handlebars and raping me until I die.

Long descriptions about being abused and violated. Messages about my hypothetical future children being raped. Notes about destroying my genitals and vagina. Videos that depict me as the devil. Fantastical rants about my partner and threats to harm my family. Graphic details of how they will track me down, violate me using pieces of furniture, and film themselves raping me.

After that, it's even easier to see the warning signs. Easier to join the dots between the abuse that's hurled at women and ethnic minority politicians online, the lack of diversity in our legislatures, and the murder of a British female member of parliament in cold blood in her own constituency. Between the vitriol that faces girls who play games online, the sharp, cutting edges of their social media feeds, and the real cuts that litter their teenage bodies when half of them have self-harmed and a quarter have a mental illness.[1] Between the women who die silently, uncounted and unaccounted for, the articles that sympathize with the poor, heartbroken murderers, the stories that claim that wives withholding sex drive good men to rape, and the killers who murder dozens of women as "revenge" against the ones who wouldn't sleep with them. Because don't all men, really, have a God-given right to sex?

There are people who believe these groups do not deserve the oxygen of publicity, that to discuss them at all is to legitimize and elevate them. A few years ago, I would have agreed.

Almost every week for the past eight years, I have spoken to young people in schools across the UK about sexism. But over the past two years, boys' responses started changing. They were angry, resistant to the very idea of a conversation about sexism. Men themselves were the real victims, they'd tell me, in a society in which political correctness has gone mad, white men are persecuted, and so many women lie about rape. In schools from rural Scotland to central London, I started hearing the same arguments. The hair rose on my arms when I realized that these boys, who had never met one another, were using precisely the same words and quoting the same false statistics to back up their claims. Around the same time, I heard snippets of the rhetoric—the same phrases used in the online, woman-hating labyrinth I had occasionally encountered as a feminist activist—being repeated verbatim by respected politicians and mainstream news pundits. I could see the power of these online messages and communities starting to seep out and affect the everyday lives of people who had never heard of them. I realized that ideas that had previously been confined to the murkiest corners of the internet were taking on new life, hiding in plain sight.

I no longer believe depriving these groups of the oxygen of publicity is the best course of action, because we are kidding ourselves if we believe they aren't superb propagandists, already spreading their message like wildfire. And the spread of that message benefits from our careful silence, our choice to look away. So I don't think they should be ignored. Not because those who spread hatred and sow division deserve a "fair hearing"; not to legitimize the rhetoric of extreme prejudice by suggesting it is one side of a valid debate. But because we cannot confront the real threat these groups pose unless we are prepared to look it directly in the eye. Because right now, these groups have dug their claws deep into teenage boys across the country, and parents can't fight for their sons if they don't even know the problem exists. Because allowing the manosphere to remain shrouded in shadows lends a different kind of legitimacy—that of the scrappy, underdog outsider. It allows these groups to claim the mantle of righteous grievance, posing as alienated victims, when exposure to the bright light of day proves their ringleaders to be anything but.

So over the period of a year, I immersed myself in these communities to find out how all this is happening and to expose a powerful, hate-fueled force that is currently underestimated by the few who know about it while remaining invisible to everybody else altogether. I wanted to lay bare the reality of a hate movement, the very existence of which we have completely failed to acknowledge, and ask: What is attracting boys and men to this ideology? How does it spread? What will it take to fight it?

Some of what follows in this book will be very hard to read. I know lifting the lid on these communities is uncomfortable. I know the graphic and violent nature of some of the discourse will be shocking. I thought about paraphrasing or censoring the worst of it. But this is the world I live in. It is the reality of anybody daring to raise their head above the parapet and fight for change. It is the daily backdrop of teenage girls' lives. And half the problem is that nobody seems to understand how bad it is, partly because every time we try to discuss it, we euphemize, allude, and dance around its edges. I can go on the radio to discuss being abused online, but I can't actually say out loud what I am facing. Our collective squeamishness makes it a very slippery problem to tackle. We have to be brave enough to confront it. So I won't shy away from it in this book. I haven't amended or smoothed or changed the quotes taken from online forums; they appear, deliberately, in their original form.

Of course, it doesn't all look like terrorism, murder, violence, or even misogyny on the surface. It would be easier to catch it if it did. It has to be cleverer than that, because the only way it can become so wildly, phenomenally successful, the only way it can be so cleverly camouflaged as to be almost undetectable, is if its arteries creep outward from that black heart of violent hate, wending their way through online pathways and webbing out across social media platforms, splitting and dividing into finer and finer capillaries, infiltrating chat rooms, reaching out through message boards, sniffing tentatively at the air and taking the leap out of the dank realms of the internet altogether, slithering offline, penetrating our pubs and bars and sliding around street corners, twirling delicately up the wooden legs of kitchen tables, peeping into corridors of power, burrowing into institutions and workplaces, fanning out tendrils across talk shows and newsrooms, taking deeper and deeper root until they're part of the very fabric of our shared consciousness. Meaning that, eventually, when the shoots sprout, the fruits bud, and the flowers bloom, their taste does not disgust us and their colors don't surprise us, because they are familiar and known. Even though their roots lurk in the very darkest depths and the same poison drips through the entire network of veins.

# 1
# Men Who Hate Women

"Since they deserve to [be] raped, I cannot
concern myself with the pain rape causes them."
COMMENT ON AN INCEL FORUM

Most people have never heard of incels. The average person who asked me what I was working on as I wrote this book raised an eyebrow and asked "In-what?" One person thought they were a type of battery. Someone else expressed their surprise that I'm interested in microbiology. The people incels walk past on the street don't generally know they even exist.

That's why when incels do occasionally crop up in news reports or conversations, they are so easily dismissed as a tiny fringe group of online weirdos. What you hear about them sounds so strange, so extreme, so hard to believe, so laughable even, that it is easy to shrug off. That's a mistake.

The incel community is the most violent corner of the so-called manosphere. It is a community devoted to violent hatred of women. A community that actively recruits members who might have very real problems and vulnerabilities and tells them that women are the cause of all their woes. A community in whose name over one hundred people, mostly women, have been murdered or injured in the past ten years. And it's a community you have probably never even heard of.

A year before I started writing this book, it wasn't a community Alex had ever heard of either. Alex was a disillusioned young white man in his early twenties. He wasn't a hardened misogynist, just a bored guy surfing the internet. A bored guy with a vague awareness of people talking a lot about sexual harassment and the gender pay gap on the news and an uneasy sense that maybe that wasn't great for him. Alex was twenty-four and had never had a girlfriend. He didn't have a lot of money, and he felt frustrated and lonely. It didn't seem fair that people were complaining about women's needs when his lot in life, as a supposedly "privileged" white guy, didn't seem so splendid. Alex didn't feel privileged at all, so it annoyed him when people said he was. He spent nights browsing YouTube and bodybuilding sites, looking for tips on how to improve his looks. He discussed tactics in online forums dedicated to video games. He'd never come across the incel community until I did. But that's not surprising really, because I made him up, although there are countless real people like Alex online.

Under this identity, I came across an incel conversation one day on a generic message board. The idea of other men who felt similarly empty and frustrated appealed to Alex. He liked the idea of being one of many instead of the odd one out. He felt relieved to have the chance to discuss the feelings he sensed were unacceptable to voice anywhere else. So he visited some of the communities that were mentioned in the conversation he had stumbled across.

When Alex first joined an incel forum, he didn't know much about it except that it was a community of men who were unhappy being single. Alex was too. He posted a couple of pretty tame introductory messages, giving basic information about his age, single status, and frustration with women. Within a day, he'd been indoctrinated into the "truth." Told that the world was stacked against men like him. Advised that he might as well kill himself, that his life wasn't worth living, that nothing would ever change. Extreme and pornographic images were used in response to his posts. Other users were quick to tell him that his whole existence had been a lie: society had tricked him into believing men were in control, when really, they were at the bottom of the food chain. It was women who were privileged, who held all the cards, and who were given all the advantages. Men were the true victims. Above all, he was told, over and over again, women are the devil.

Initially, Alex felt confused, then intrigued, then angry. How was it possible that this was the world he had been living in his whole life without even knowing? But then Alex looked at his own experiences, and it started to make sense. It was appealing; until that point, he'd pictured himself as an underwhelming, very average man. But now he realized he was a survivor, part of a team of underdogs, fighting evil forces against the odds. Alex could be a wronged, avenging hero. This was a much more attractive version of himself than his previous reality.

After that, Alex didn't say much. He was a lurker. Like millions of other people on online platforms, his account appeared dormant as he just watched, listened, and absorbed. He saw a six-point thread titled "Why I Support the Legalization of Rape." At first, he was bewildered and a little overwhelmed by the messages on the thread. But they were persuasive. They used facts and historical examples to back up their case. It was seductive: a world in which nothing was his fault, in which he was an aggrieved martyr, not the privileged loser he felt society painted him as. Most of all, it was a community. Yes, some of the posts were extreme, and some of the replies were hostile and mean. But they treated him like a compatriot. Against the man-hating world they portrayed, he was their brother-in-arms. He was one of them, with a cause to believe in and an enemy to fight. Over time, it became easier and easier to see that women really were the enemy. When he had doubts, the messages he read reminded him that he had been deliberately blinded by the female-centric conspiracy designed to keep men docile and passive. He'd been tricked into allowing himself to be downtrodden and discriminated against. There were thousands of men who all believed the same thing. He quickly became a member of more and more forums, joining Facebook groups and private chat rooms, watching video after video on YouTube, and learning more and more. Every single day, he saw hundreds of messages like this: "I hate all women. They're the scum of the earth. If you're a woman and you happen to be reading this—I hate you fucking whore." Or this: "Women are disgusting vile parasites." The more he saw, the less extreme it seemed. Eventually, the ideas became normal. And I watched it all through his eyes, feeling physically sick.

In the mid-1990s, long before the advent of dating apps, Facebook, or even MySpace, a young Canadian woman, known only as Alana, started a simple website.

Alana was in her midtwenties and struggling to find love. Hurt by "lonely virgin" jokes and convinced she couldn't be the only one feeling this way, she started a mailing list and began posting articles to the website she called Alana's Involuntary Celibacy Project.

Over time, the project grew into a small and generally supportive online community where men and women shared their fears, frustrations, and unhappiness.

Gradually, Alana started having more success with dating and drifted away from the community she had started, no longer wanting to focus on her former lack of romantic success.

Over twenty years later, the little project Alana called "invcels" (a portmanteau of "involuntarily celibate") has morphed into something completely unrecognizable. What started out as a small support group has mutated into a nightmarish world inhabited—or so a significant proportion of its content would suggest—by men who hate women. Alana would later tell a *Guardian* journalist, "It feels like being the scientist who figured out nuclear fission and then discovers it's being used as a weapon for war."[1]

Now known as "incels," the community consists of a sprawling network of websites, blogs, forums, podcasts, YouTube channels, and chat rooms. The growth of the movement has, in part, coincided with the widespread adoption of the internet, but it has also seen a marked expansion over the past five to ten years, alongside a similar increase in the popularity and visibility of a progressive feminist movement, particularly in Europe and North America. Almost cultish in its development of a vehemently misogynistic ideology, this hydra-like incel subculture has spawned a detailed, often delusional, and violently antifeminist worldview.

New recruits find the incel community in a variety of ways. Some stumble across it while looking for answers to life problems or loneliness. Some segue into its path from other areas of the internet, like more general message boards or websites. Some are pushed toward it by algorithms, with video platforms such as YouTube recommending incel content, even though the user didn't go looking for it. Some are sucked in through more sinister means, groomed by messages in private gaming chat rooms or on forums frequented by teenage boys. We'll look at some of these routes in more detail later. But however you find the incel community, your

first initiation—in common with many other manosphere communities—is taking the "red pill."

Borrowed from cult film *The Matrix*, this refers to the scene
in which the protagonist, Neo, is offered a choice between taking
a blue pill, which will enable him to continue seeing the world
around him the way he always has, or a red pill, which will suddenly shift his perspective, enabling him to see the Matrix and, in
so doing, realize that nothing in his world is as he had thought. It's
ironic that I feel a little bit like I have taken a red pill after writing
this book. Once you know that there are hundreds of thousands of
people out there despising women to the point that many of them
believe we should all be exterminated, you can never unknow it.

Incels use the metaphor of the red pill to describe the moment
a man's blinkers fall away and he suddenly realizes he has been lied
to his whole life. The world he has been forced to believe works
in his favor is actually hopelessly stacked against him. Everything,
from our government to our wider society, is designed to promote
women over men. The myth of male privilege, so the story goes,
is perpetuated by a massive feminist conspiracy. Incels refer to
this man-hating world as a "gynocracy," a clever system designed
to keep men (the true victims of oppression) in their subordinate
place without them even noticing.

The red pill metaphor is a powerful and dramatic way of conveying an ideology, and it is immediately attractive to those with any
kind of grudge or grievance. Lost your job? What could be more
appealing than a whole new worldview in which it isn't your fault:
you've just been the victim of a power grab by women and minorities. Dumped or divorced? That lying bitch is part of a much bigger
attack on you and other men like you. Angry that you don't seem
to be lucky in love? It's not you, it's her. Every single "her," in fact.

Some of these are individual complaints, but many of them tap into wider forms of malaise that particularly affect men and boys. The burgeoning feminist movement is often seen as a threat. Our recent societal focus on equality is deliberately interpreted and framed by antifeminists as a criticism of all men, and the communities explored in this book spread the idea that there is no acceptable way to be masculine anymore. For many "good" men and boys, this can create a sense of injustice and attack, prompting a defensive knee-jerk reaction. And when you feel defensive, the first place you want to run to is somewhere you'll be told it's not your fault. The manosphere goes one step further: it subverts the narrative of the privileged and the victim altogether. It tells men they are suffering, and it blames women.

Many men, of course, are suffering, and suffering deeply. The male suicide rate is around three times that of women, men are vastly less likely to receive support for mental health problems than women, and men in particular are hard hit by issues such as unemployment and workplace injuries in a world that teaches them it is their duty and role to be a provider and protector.

Here we see the crux of the manosphere itself—its complexity and its heartbreaking irony. As we will discover, this sprawling web of communities encompasses well-meaning groups that tackle genuine problems affecting men, not just groups deliberately and systemically promoting physical and sexual violence against women. Its adherents range from naive teenagers to advocates of rape, vulnerable recluses to violent misogynists, nonviolent ideologues to grieving fathers, online harassers to offline stalkers, vocal propagandists to physical abusers. Clearly not every individual who has participated in this space is deserving of the same label or treatment; indeed, there may be a large cohort of these men and boys in desperate need of support. It is paradoxical, therefore, that the group at one end of the spectrum is responsible for the most acute harm done to the group at the other. Those most powerfully reinforcing rigid and patriarchal gender stereotypes are suffocating those who most need to escape them.

Superficial analyses of incel communities have sought to imply that class is the biggest factor driving new recruits to the cause: that this is about poor, white boys being left behind. Others have suggested it is a specific response to shifting labor markets, as manual jobs become increasingly scarce and women are employed in ever greater numbers in more powerful roles. But in the time I have spent immersed in these conversations and message boards, it has become apparent that the socioeconomic background of members is too diverse to wholly confirm any one of those theories. The membership of these groups spans from blue-collar workers, angry about immigrants "displacing" them at work and in the bedroom, to highly privileged private school graduates, furious that their "rightful" place at the top of the political food chain is being challenged.

What they do seem to have in common is a craving to belong, and this need is met in spades by a community that excels at conveying a tribal sense of cohesion. What better way to suck in new recruits and repel criticism than to borrow an origin story that immediately positions all acolytes as heroic, doomed visionaries and all critics or disbelievers as either pitifully ignorant or part of the oppressive system itself? (The fact that the *Matrix* trilogy was created by two transgender women or that its kick-ass female characters would revolt against the misogynistic ideology of any manosphere community is an irony apparently lost on incels.)

The foundational tenet of taking the red pill is at the root of almost all the major manosphere groups we will look at in this book, including pickup artists, so-called Men's Rights Activists, and Men Going Their Own Way. But it is a departure point from which different communities take dramatically different routes. In the case of incels, their prime focus is a feverish obsession with sex and anger at being "denied" it. Yes, this is a community of tens of thousands of men who claim that the world (and, in particular, individual women) is withholding from them the vital human right of getting laid. Amazingly, in the thousands of conversations and endless hours spent discussing their sparse sex lives, alongside lengthy rants about how women are evil, subhuman vessels, it never seems to occur to these men that their hatred of women might be related to their lack of romantic success. In fact, even to suggest such a thing is a banning offense in many incel forums. Instead, incels see themselves as innocent and tragic victims, creating a vivid portrait of a bleak society irreversibly stacked against them.

Tim Squirrell, a researcher studying social interaction in online communities, told me:

> The first thing you notice when you look at an incel forum is a mix of hopelessness and anger. These people genuinely hate and pity themselves, but, simultaneously (and almost paradoxically), they feel this righteous anger and vindication that they see the world for how it really is, even if they're at the bottom of the heap. That feeling of absolute certainty that they are *correct* is twinned with the fact that they're correct about their own misery, and that's a powerful and strange cocktail.

Visit any incel website and you are quickly indoctrinated into this worldview, pressed to accept that vapid, self-obsessed, greedy, promiscuous women are the enemy.

Women, so the story goes, are constantly hungry for sex, but they choose to sleep only with the most attractive cohort of men. Incels are obsessed with what they refer to as the 80:20 theory, which holds that the top 20 percent of the most attractive men enjoys 80 percent of the sex within our society. They lament that the "sexual marketplace" is brutally hierarchical, with women completely in control. They believe that when women are choosing sexual partners, looks far outweigh personality or any other attribute and that any man born unlucky enough to be ugly, short, bald, nonwhite, pimply, or a host of other perceived imperfections is cursed to a lifetime of unfair sexual frustration.

Young women are also accused of having huge amounts of sex with extremely attractive men before later settling down with less attractive men they don't really love but ruthlessly exploit as a means of financial support. These men (sometimes referred to as "beta cucks") are pitied, because they are forced to spend all their money on a woman whose virginity has already been taken, who is spent, used up, and sexually worthless, even if she does deign occasionally to allow her husband to sleep with her. Incels dub this alleged female sexual strategy "alpha fucks, beta bucks."

The self-ascribed physical shortcomings of incels are seen in such concrete terms that they have spawned a wealth of subcultures, including those dedicated to being *heightcels* (unacceptably short), *gingercels* (too redheaded), *baldcels* (irreversibly bald), *skullcels* (poor facial bone structure), or even *wristcels* (with a wrist circumference of 6.5 inches or less). Incels also have a rigid adherence to certain racist stereotypes, with terms such as *currycel, blackcel, ricecel,* and *ethnicel* used to denote men whose Indian, Black, or

Asian heritages are presumed to impact negatively on their romantic prospects.

A casual observer might surmise that those latter terms imply a certain intersectional perspective within the incel community, a surprisingly nuanced appreciation of racial discrimination within a group more broadly bigoted. But in reality, though there exists a small number of ethnic minority incels who describe interactions with women they believe have spurned them as a result of their skin color, these labels, often used by white community members, depict racist assumptions about the inferiority of men of color that fit neatly within a broader spectrum of racist elements of the incel and wider manosphere ideology. Much incel rage, for example, is focused on the temerity of white women to date nonwhite men, who many incels perceive to be inferior to themselves. Indeed, the majority of the community seems mainly to consist of straight, white, educated, middle-class men.

Dr. Lisa Sugiura, senior lecturer in criminology and cybercrime at the University of Portsmouth, told me:

> It's worth looking at the history and origins of [the manosphere]. If you go right back to the early Usenet groups in the 1990s and you think about the demographics of the sort of people [who] would have used these, they are primarily white, educated, tech-savvy men. And there was this thinking about it being their space, their ownership of the space, which is something else worth thinking of when we think of the manosphere and their vitriol—they are "claiming what is rightfully theirs"—and that demographic hasn't really changed. [It resembles] what we saw years ago in terms of race and gender—it really is white, western men—and in

terms of the education: it is very much the developed countries, very much the US, Canada, Australia, and the UK.
And what I've been getting through the data I'm looking at
is it links back to the alt-right; it's about white supremacy,
and there's very disparaging rhetoric coming out toward
Black and Asian men as well, which is where you get the
suggestion that this is a predominantly white space.

It is also almost exclusively male. So skewed is the gendered
bias of the sexual marketplace, according to incels, that almost any
woman in our society, no matter how physically undesirable, will
always be able to find somebody who wants to have sex with her.
So, incel logic dictates, it is almost impossible for a woman to be
an incel, which has led to today's incel communities being almost
entirely male dominated. (That the very term was invented by a
bisexual woman is a sad reminder of how ludicrously narrow subsequent incel beliefs have become.)

Dr. Sugiura's mention of the close links between the manosphere and the so-called alt-right is vital in understanding both
groups. A vaguely defined term, the *alt-right* refers to a network of
loosely connected movements, leaders, online communities, and
groups that are generally considered to represent far-right, white
nationalist, or white supremacist views. Many groups associated
with the term have been described by the Southern Poverty Law
Center (a leading U.S. nonprofit legal advocacy group) as hate
groups. Many of their members were represented at the now-
infamous 2017 "Unite the Right" rally in Charlottesville, Virginia,
where white supremacists marched carrying flaming torches and
Nazi symbols and chanting anti-Semitic and racist slogans. The
eventual violence that ensued culminated in a self-identified white

supremacist, named James Alex Fields Jr., deliberately driving into a crowd of counterprotesters, killing a young woman, Heather Heyer, and injuring almost forty others.

Like the manosphere, the alt-right represents the coalescence of a number of different groups that were until recently considered extreme, fringe movements but have to an extent been combined under the umbrella of the label. Like the manosphere, the movement brings together various communities, many of which originated online. The term *alt-right* was popularized on internet message boards and forums like 4chan, an English-language imageboard website on which users post usually anonymous messages, contributing to long, detailed conversations. Like the manosphere, the alt-right revels in masking vitriolic, violent, bigoted ideology with smokescreens of "irony," sarcasm, and deliberate provocation. The Southern Poverty Law Center describes how "chaotic" online forums have enabled white nationalist ideas, "most notably the belief that white identity is under attack by multiculturalism and political correctness," to "flourish under dizzying layers of toxic irony." And just like the manosphere, the alt-right takes a privileged group (white people) and sells them the comforting idea that they are really the ones facing discrimination at the hands of the group actually facing prejudice (people of color and immigrants), who are portrayed as the true oppressors.

Much has been written about the alt-right, and particularly its links to the rise of Donald Trump. But the deeply misogynistic beliefs that run through the movement and their role in many of its foundational tenets often go overlooked and unreported. In the same way, the racist elements of the incel movement are often omitted from commentary, suggesting that it is an exclusively misogynistic, sex-obsessed community. Rarely, too, do those writing about either group pause to focus on the extreme and sometimes violently heteronormative framing of their worldview, which depends on the idea that all men are (or should be) straight and that all women exist purely as sexual vessels, either to satisfy men or to bear (white) children. This may be expressed in different ways (from the total exclusion of LGBTQ people in many incel communities to the advocacy of murdering gay people by throwing them off buildings in some alt-right forums), but it is a far more significant feature of the groups than its common omission would suggest. At the root of manosphere communities and white supremacy is a shared belief that the core, sacred purpose of man is to have sex, to procreate, and to dominate. Thus, power and control are utterly central to both ideologies. The concept of a white man as a heterosexual, stereotypically masculine, utterly omnipotent figure is key, ironically representing both the hopelessly suffocating societal standard that drives many men to join these communities in the first place and the supposed solution they are indoctrinated to pursue with ever more extreme measures. So in both cases, the reality is far more complex than surface-level reports might suggest, and the lack of an intersectional lens leads to a common failure to recognize a complex, porous, and symbiotic relationship between the two communities online.

A simple example of what this looks like in practice? As Fields Jr. drove into the crowd in Charlottesville, he was chanting the same three words, over and over again: "White sharia now."[2] Though it started out as a satirical meme created by a white supremacist, the term *white sharia* has taken hold across alt-right websites. In a single concept, it blends the racist, Islamophobic, anti-Semitic, misogynistic, and heteronormative values of the alt-right. In a nutshell, white sharia is the argument that white men should adopt their own version of what they perceive as the Islamic practice of enslaving women. The aim would be to remove white women's sexual autonomy and force them (through brutal rape and servitude) to become "baby factories." This would enable white supremacists to ensure the "purity" of their race and create enough new recruits to their cause to overthrow the invading hordes of immigrants and the tyranny of the all-controlling, corrupt Jewish forces they believe dominate our society. "Our men need harems, and the members of those harems need to be baby factories," wrote Sacco Vandal, the white supremacist credited with creating the meme.[3]

Violence and abuse toward women of color goes hand in hand with this misogynistic doctrine. While the white supremacists of the alt-right dream of forcing white women to breed the future citizens of their ethnostate, they equally fantasize about denying reproductive autonomy to women of other races, on whom they would force abortions.

If all this sounds ridiculous, consider that one man was prepared to carry out an act of mass violence and murder in the name of this ideology on a night when he marched alongside hundreds of others chanting the phrase in question. Even if it started out as a sick joke, for many adherents to alt-right thinking, it has become deadly serious.

When you talk to anybody about the manosphere or the alt-right, they will often tell you not to take it too seriously. But who is telling that to the internet denizens who don't see the irony or pick up on the so-called humor? Just ask Heather Heyer's parents whether they think it's all a harmless joke.

This is not to suggest that the alt-right and the manosphere are always aligned or that members of one are necessarily affiliated with the other. But failing to recognize the complex connections between them or overlooking the racism inherent in the manosphere and the misogyny embedded in the alt-right will only tell half the story.

Take, for example, the case of two teenage boys who were jailed in London in June 2019 after penning criminal online propaganda encouraging terrorist attacks. Headlines across the media referred to them as "neo-Nazis" or "far-right extremists." No headline mentioned misogynistic extremism, yet their online campaign had repeatedly incited rape as a punishment for women. They had obsessed over Prince Harry's marriage to Meghan Markle, writing that he was a "race traitor," and said that white women who date nonwhite men should be hanged. The prosecutor told the court that one of the boys had run an "extremely violent and aggressively misogynistic" blog encouraging the rape, torture, and murder of women.[4] The headlines missed this.

Squirrell noted that many other online communities, often including alt-right figures, tend to mock and loathe incels, portraying them as weak and pathetic failures. Nonetheless, he said, there is a great deal of crossover exemplified by similarities in the groups' dense lexicon: "A lot of the vocabulary that has been adopted by the reactionary right over the past couple of years has really come from the incel community. They've been culturally enormously influential, even if they're not politically incorporated."

So extensive is the jargon used by the incel community, in fact, that an uninitiated outsider stumbling across one of its millions of message threads might struggle to decipher the conversation at all. When Alex and I first started exploring the incel world, I had to find a glossary on one forum that I could refer back to, slowly deciphering the conversations I was reading word by word, my heart sinking further with every new term I uncovered. I started to realize that incels have to create their own language, because there simply aren't existing words to express the extremity of many of the concepts they use on a daily basis. *Roastie*, for example, refers to a woman who has had "too much" sex, in order to suggest that this deforms her labia, causing them to resemble roast beef. *Foid* is a shortening of "female humanoid," a term incels use to refer to women, because the word *woman* allows too much of a sense of humanity. *Rapecel* (used sickeningly commonly online, to the extent that it has spawned its own forums and discussion groups) denotes an incel who simply resorts to rape to "resolve" his sexual frustration. The creation of a single, offhand word to describe this somehow makes it seem like a normal, even mundane notion. The exclusive terminology plays an important role in reinforcing the clandestine thrill of belonging to what adherents see as a superior and close-knit community, thus increasing the attractiveness of the group to potential recruits.

The saddest and most disturbing part of my year spent wading through incel forums, disguised as lonely Alex, was how differently the threads affected me toward the end. In the early days and weeks, I frequently lay awake at night, haunted by the graphic and disgusting things I had read. I winced as I painstakingly translated those early posts, understanding the violent meaning behind the jargon I was slowly beginning to decipher. But as time went on, I referred back to the glossary less and less. I became used to seeing women referred to as foids, barely registered the incitements to initiate misogynistic massacres, and skimmed over posts about rape, because they were just so common. Finally, one day, I read a post about giving a foid the violence she deserved in order to avoid being cucked, and I realized I understood every word. In short, I got used to it. Or, rather, Alex did.

The sense of a coherent worldview and a shared language may

be deeply appealing to those who hold extreme prejudices but don't feel able to express them offline in face-to-face conversations, warned Dr. Sugiura, who has studied incel and other manosphere communities. These forms of hatred, she noted, have long predated the internet, but

> online communities and virtual platforms provide the means for these ideas to take shape, take hold and spread. If people did hold these ideas and they didn't necessarily feel they could talk about them in person, they've now found a new way. Others [who] are likeminded can provide support and validation, which helps them to spread. It's just a hate movement that was previously fractured, but the technology allows them to come together, combine, flourish, find more people—that's the recruitment and radicalization part of it as well. These ideas have been able to take place on an exponential scale through the technology.

Almost all incels take as their starting point the idea of a feminist conspiracy and a deeply rigged sexual marketplace that is hostile to men. However, they divide into factions when it comes to deciding on the best solution to this situation. Some believe it is possible to overcome their celibacy ("ascend"), or at least improve their situation, by working furiously to better their appearance. This is commonly known within the community as "looksmaxing," and the practice has spawned enormous forums dedicated to sharing tips on how best to go about it. Websites reveal threads, thousands of messages long, in which men post their own photographs and plaintively ask one another for "ratings" out of ten, begging for advice on how to make the best of their looks or asking, "Is it over?"

The responses are a curious amalgamation of brutal honesty, ruthless mockery, and sympathetic support. They range from brotherly pep talks and grooming advice to cutting insults and recommendations to give up altogether. Some incels seem to view their online world as a genuine community, united in the face of their common struggles. Others see it as an opportunity to cause the greatest possible hurt to other men, perhaps as a means of easing their own pain. I am reminded, again, that this community is not a homogeneous group.

One large subset of this community focuses on physical exercise as a way of boosting their looks (men who pursue this option are known as *gymcels*), but there are also more extreme trends, with significant numbers of adherents, that promote everything from "mewing" (a kind of jaw exercise incels believe will change the bone structure of their faces, leading to more attractive jawlines) to plastic surgery, skull implants, and penis stretching. Such extreme measures are a reminder of the sheer desperation and self-loathing of some men who identify as incels. They are also a stark reflection of how few alternative options these men perceive for themselves in the outside world.

Another group of incels (by far the largest of all, comprising around 90 percent of the community, if one forum's internal survey is to be trusted) commonly refer to themselves as "blackpillers" or "blackpills." This group takes a more defeatist view, believing that the social and genetic lottery is so rigidly fixed that their inherent flaws doom them to a life of utter failure and celibacy that no attempt at self-improvement could possibly alleviate. These groups resort to railing violently against the unfairness of non-incel society (people they call "normies"), the selfishness of the most attractive men ("Chads"), the superficiality of beautiful women ("Stacys"), and the promiscuity of less attractive women who are still able to attract sexual partners ("Beckys"). These men often discuss suicide at great length, tagging their posts to denote material that is likely to encourage readers to take their own lives. They use specific terms as shorthand for suicide and often egg each other on to do it. These are clearly, in many cases, men in desperate need of help.

In such threads, you really feel the contradictions of the community: vulnerable, unhappy men mingling closely with men determined to wreak as much destruction as possible. You watch as people in urgent need of mental health support, who have somehow found themselves sucked into this whirlpool of misogyny, are met with vitriol, ridicule, and incitement to self-harm by other men getting their kicks from online hate.

When one forum user posted on an incel forum asking for the "best place to shoot yourself to guarantee lethality," there were around seventy responses, the vast majority urging him on and giving cold, technical advice.

Perhaps most disturbing of all are the frequent posts in which violent misogyny explodes off the page, from graphic fantasies about raping and murdering women to threads in which forum users goad each other to carry out the "incel rebellion," "beta uprising," or "day of retribution"—a sick fantasy in which involuntarily celibate men would punish the world by carrying out bloody massacres of the women who torment them and the Chads who unfairly monopolize the sexual marketplace. "All females deserve our utter hatred," wrote one user.

Incel logic seems to reveal a hopeless contradiction: women are simultaneously reviled for sleeping with men and for refusing to do so. One user, for example, described women as "greedy selfish evil

crazed sluts, who prevent decent hard working men, from achieving their biological purpose."

But things become clearer when viewed through the lens of the
most basic incel belief. At its simplest, the argument goes like this:
if women's sexual autonomy has given them wicked and tyranni-
cal control over men's lives, then women's liberation is at the root
of all male suffering. Therefore, the obvious remedy is to remove
women's freedom and independence and to use specifically sexual
means (like rape and sexual slavery) to do so. In other words, the
problem is not women having sex but women having the choice of
whom to have sex *with*.

Once this is understood, a number of repeated incel beliefs
become chillingly clear, illustrated again and again in countless
blogs, forum discussions, and YouTube videos.

First, there is the notion that women are dehumanized objects:
subhumans who are either too evil or too stupid to deserve to make
decisions about their own lives and bodies. This idea promotes a
complete disconnection from the idea of women as people who are
capable of suffering, grieving, enjoying sexual pleasure, or making
rational decisions. This dehumanization is essential to the justification of other incel fantasies, like the mandated redistribution of sex,
the keeping of women as sexual slaves, or the widespread massacre
of women and girls.

A thread titled "Should Women Be Considered Human?"
attracted lengthy debate, most of it coming to the conclusion that
they should not. This is a common area of discussion. "Women
are not sentient," wrote another user. "All women are whores." In a
conversation about whether women should have legal rights, a user
wrote, "I hardly consider them an alive body let alone entitled to
having human rights."

It's ironic that I battled, horrified, through reams of threads about the idea that women are robotic and unfeeling. We are discussed interchangeably with sex robots, which many incels feel could represent an end to their problems. "We can beat and torture them legally. I'm super hyped," wrote one forum member.

Second, this idea of women as empty sexual vessels without the right to sexual autonomy leads naturally to a feverish obsession with sexual violence, which ranges from assault fantasies and open advocacy of rape to lengthy, chillingly casual arguments about whether rape should be legalized. To boast about committing or planning to commit a sexual attack is not uncommon, and the response is unfailingly one of encouragement rather than censure.

On one forum, where users eagerly coalesced around a video of a man beating and kicking a woman, one frustratedly complained that there was no audio: "I want to hear her screams." One user wrote that he is tempted to "rape a bitch just so I can get a 10 page thread on here," and another said that he has "decided to become a rapecel," asking other users for "thoughts, advice, experience." His peer responded encouragingly: "Go nuts!... you'll find it's impossible to get caught if you do it properly... you have a 98.95% chance of getting away with it if you rape."

In one calm debate about the legalization of rape, most users were in favor (though some did argue against—on the basis that rape being legal would take the fun out of it for them). "Rape is natural and sluts should have no say in what dick they take when their holes get used up so much cock anyway," wrote one forum member. Other "rationalizations" included the argument that it is women's fault men are driven to rape in the first place (because they refuse to provide them with sex), thus absolving rapists of responsibility—a typical form of incel logic that reverses the positions of victim and perpetrator.

One user argued that rape should only be illegal if the victim is a widow, an unmarried virgin, or a nun. The rape of "sluts," he argued, "should be praised and is a healthy, hygienic measure for a good society."

Another typical post reads, "My concern for level of pain of rape would be greater if it weren't for the fact that most American women deserve to raped because they oppose prostitution as a sexual outlet for men. Since they deserve to raped, I cannot concern myself with the pain rape causes them."

If this sounds like a twisted kind of noble moral code, it isn't. It is simply another layer of misogynistic bullshit, designed to confer a sense of validation on the heinous argument that the vast majority of women deserve to be raped.

On other incel websites, users debate the type of woman who would make an ideal sex slave for the purposes of domestic servitude, rape, and forced impregnation.

Such statements are not shocking or confessional on incel websites though. They are simply bald, unremarkable statements of fact. There is very little evidence that any of the men involved in incel communities fear any recrimination as a result of these sorts of posts. Occasionally, websites will have rules that claim certain forms of hate speech are disallowed, but these are inevitably completely ignored. Occasionally, users might be blocked or banned from posting, but this happens far more frequently because they dare to suggest that incels aren't innocent victims than because they suggest women deserve to be raped. Occasionally, incel forums seem to be taken offline or rejected by the companies that host them, but they quickly find new routes to get back online. In all the time I spent perusing them, I saw no evidence that there was any effective external policing or monitoring of these sites at all.

Of course, we are talking about the internet here, and about a group with complex links and overlaps with online trolls, whose main self-stated purpose is to use the most extreme and socially abhorrent speech possible with the aim of shocking and provoking a reaction. (More about trolls later.) Among thousands of deeply misogynistic and violent messages, it is impossible to know where the dividing line lies between those who genuinely and fervently wish to incite such acts and those who choose to post online, either in anger or as a form of sadistic humor but without intent to carry out real harm offline. That's not to say that the latter groups are inherently harmless, rather that it is important to be aware of the complexity of the situation if we are to have any hope of effectively tackling it.

I'm not suggesting that we should carry out a heavy-handed blanket ban on these forums or that everyone who has contributed to them deserves to be arrested or jailed. But as I'll later consider in more detail, it is clear that there is some illegal incitement to real-life violence here that is able to flourish with absolute impunity.

There is an established hierarchy within incel groups, with "weaker" members seen as overly self-pitying, or those less well versed in incel lore relentlessly eviscerated by more established group members. In some forums, hierarchy is dictated by the number of posts a user has contributed; in others, users' comments might be "upvoted" by their peers. In each community, there exists a handful of legendary characters, well known to the rest of the group, who are idolized and revered by other users. These men, who often spend the best part of every day on the forums, are a bit like community elders or leaders, popping up to resolve disputes and declare judgment on less-experienced users. Their rebuke of forum members who don't appear to comply with incel ideology correctly is swift and ruthless.

Squirrell noted that the incel community comprises many young and impressionable members. "Most of them," he believes, "will ultimately grow out of it." But for a vulnerable minority, he raised the potential risk of them becoming radicalized by more entrenched group members. "Older members are often more extreme: they've experienced this frustration for a prolonged period and see little chance of their circumstances ever improving." He highlighted the dangers of a culture that "promotes saying more and more extreme things just for the 'lols' [an incel and internet expression for humor]" and "abhors expressions of emotional vulnerability," adding that

> [this culture] emphasizes mockery and the externalization of blame as the means by which one should cope with negative emotions. Posters can always claim that the things they're saying are ironic or jokes or meant just to provoke a reaction, but, with enough posts and posters, it becomes impossible to differentiate between those who mean it and those who don't.

Particularly chilling from the perspective of young and potentially vulnerable newcomers to such communities is the way in which posters' explosive rants are matched by long, faux-academic debates, relying on pseudoscience or math, in which the men who frequent these forums make detailed arguments to rationalize their sadistic fantasies. These posts are suggestive of recruitment, aimed at convincing and converting others to the same cause. They might include twisted versions of classical myths or deeply flawed references to ancient Greek culture to give a vague sense of academic weight to what are essentially exhortations to commit rape and abuse. The 80:20 theory itself is a sort of rough bastardization of the Pareto principle, named after a nineteenth-century Italian economist who noticed that around 80 percent of the land in Italy was owned by just 20 percent of the population.

In one post, for example, a user backed up his argument that rape should have much lower penalties by telling other forum users that rape was only punishable by a fine in ancient Greek cities. This automatic correlation of a past civilization with a sense of greatness and nobility fits with a much wider nostalgic yearning for ancient societal rules and stereotypes. It is a tendency that not only abounds within the incel community and wider manosphere but also provides a further link to the alt-right and white nationalists.

Another incel forum member wrote a passionate defense of rape and slavery:

> Taking female slaves has always been a normal part of human history, when enemies would fight each other the winning party would take female slaves and distribute them among the fighters. As an incel you were rewarded in history when joining an army, you would raid towns and villages and took female slaves for yourself and make babies with them. History had place for incels, incels in the Roman or any other empire had better options than we have today.

As early as 2003, this tendency to use "historical" arguments to support incel beliefs was becoming evident. A user on a now-defunct website wrote that women's sexual autonomy "was fine in the days when women did not have jobs."

Nature gave them a bunch of social and sexual advantage to compensate for their lack of resources. Now that they have resource and sex power, things are out of balance. We need that prevent females from going to university or taking family supporting jobs from men. Our prisons are full of men who could not feed their families. the rape laws should be repealed. Females are artifically restricting the supply of available females in their reproductive years. Rape is the answer. Societies go to war over lack of females and jobs. Females have become a threat to society and must be put back in their place.

Here you can see how the idea that women are encroaching on men's space in the labor market is a driving factor for some incels. But it is entwined with the strange logic that rape is the solution.

This worldview might sound ridiculous. But it is an ideology to which incels adhere with remarkable tenacity. This isn't just a group of websites on which men spout random profanities and abuse. It is a movement, cultlike in the loyalty and passion of its devotees. Incels are not just looking for a place to share rape fantasies and violent posts; they are invested in building and spreading an entire belief system to support and encourage such ideas.

As I swam through the murky depths of these communities, disguised as Alex, I realized that it isn't even as simple as just saying that some group members are vulnerable victims and others are extreme misogynists. It is quite possible, common even, for individuals to be both. Late one night, I sat in bed in the dark, reading a new post on a major incel forum. In graphic and painful detail, a man described the drudgery of his daily life, caring for a seriously disabled parent, unsupported by friends or wider family, frequently finding himself covered in urine and feces. He went back further, describing childhood abuse that left him with a permanent disfigurement and parents who covered up the situation for fear of being arrested instead of seeking medical help for their son. My heart ached for him. I felt that I could understand what had driven him to a community of online support and belonging and why he felt desperately lonely.

A few minutes later, I was reading a different discussion, in which the same user casually wrote, "I wouldn't feel like a real man if I had consensual sex. Rape is the alpha method of pleasure and procreation and foids know this, that's why they prefer to get raped."

This isn't a cut-and-dried situation of victims being preyed upon by ideologues. It is possible for one incel to be both.

Raise concerns about the vitriolic and misogynistic nature of these online communities among the minority of people who have even heard of them, and you are likely to encounter three different arguments to dismiss your fears. Each is common, and each undermines the notion that such networks pose any real offline threat. The first argument is that these groups are extremely small, comprising a few men with extreme and unusual opinions, like any other wildly out-of-touch, fringe internet community. The second, which follows logically from the first, is that these groups have very little offline impact or influence, so removed from society are their members likely to be. The third, on the basis of the first two assumptions, is that the groups pose no real, concrete threat and should be either ignored or pitied.

Each assumption is wrong, and together they lead to dangerous complacency.

It is almost impossible to estimate the size of the incel community with any great accuracy. There is neither an official database of all the different websites, forums, and subgroups nor any way to determine with certainty how many of the users of these various sites overlap. But it is possible to say with confidence that the movement is far bigger than the dismissive "just a few weirdos" theory would suggest. Looking at the numbers of members, active users, and posts on some of the most popular incel websites is very much a view of the iceberg's tip (it is not necessary to be a member or a registered user to browse and read the forums, so the sites are likely to boast far higher viewing figures), but it gives some idea of scale.

At the time of writing, one of the most popular incel websites boasts over 350,000 threads with more than three million posts and 9,000 members. Another site has 8,500 members, almost two million messages, and 87,000 threads. This site is the latest reincarnation of an earlier site that transferred to a new domain name in mid-2018, when it had around 6,000 members and 45,000 threads, which gives some idea of the fast pace of growth within these communities.

Reddit (a popular internet discussion forum with dedicated pages, or "subreddits," for specific issues) was one of the early breeding grounds for the incel community, though many members have now migrated to different websites and forums. One of the most active subreddits had 40,000 subscribers before it was closed in November 2017 for inciting violence against women, after a user posted a thread asking how to commit rape without getting caught. Other incel communities continue on Reddit, though, including one subreddit that has 100,000 subscribers at the time of writing. The largest incel group on Facebook has around 2,000 members and around 700 new posts added each month. Another large incel forum lists 10,000 unique posters and 730,000 posts. A site that focuses on incel discussions about improving men's physical appearance has 605 members, 83,000 messages, and 5,000 threads. Yet another site—which roughly approximates the now-defunct incel website PUAHate, thanks to its self-described focus on "bash[ing] the pick-up art community"—has almost 10,000 members and over a million posts.

Based on these numbers and taking into account the fact that there may be some crossover of membership between the different sites and forums, a conservative estimate would still put the size of the incel community into the tens of thousands of registered members before one even considers the lurkers and watchers who frequent such sites without officially signing up. And these are just the most well-known examples of a community that also encompasses countless smaller blogs, discussion groups, and web pages. We are, of course, talking about a tiny minority of men. But this is not a tiny number. It is not an isolated group of a few dozen outliers.

When I met Jacob Davey, a project manager at the Institute for Strategic Dialogue, who has studied incels and other manosphere groups, he stressed that this is a "transnational" movement. While he believes that the largest incel community is based in the United States, he estimates that the size of the manosphere in the UK alone (including incels and other groups explored in this book) may be as great as 10,000 people. Further proof that writing this movement off as a tiny group of weirdos is a mistake.

Next, let's consider the insistence that these men and their ideas have little offline impact or influence.

In March 2018, a website called Incelocalypse was taken offline after activists and journalists alerted its hosting company,

DreamHost, to some of the content on the site, including threads advocating rape and graphic descriptions of child pornography.

The tagline for the website, appearing prominently in a banner at the top of the homepage, read, "The day we make the jailbaits our rape slaves." Incels particularly fetishize virgins and teenagers, often using the term *jailbait* to describe them.

Some users in the forum, including its creator/administrator, who went by the pseudonym "Leucosticte," self-defined as rapecels. Leucosticte started threads titled "Even If You Could Get Pussy from a Willing Female, You Should Still Want to Rape Girls" and "Father-Daughter Incest Makes More Sense Now Than Ever," as well as a post called "Acid Attacks Are the Great Equalizer," which suggested that women should learn what it feels like to be "crippled with ugliness."

Incelocalypse also hosted a private area for pedophiles.

Members of these communities—and particularly the more enthusiastic or obsessive ones like Leucosticte, who once wrote a 3,300-word essay titled "How to Psyche Yourself Up to Feel Entitled to Rape" ("Don't forget: feminism is the problem, and rape is the solution")—are commonly dismissed as crazy, isolated losers who rarely participate in public life, let alone have the ability to influence it.

Except that Leucosticte was later exposed as Nathan Larson, a thirty-seven-year-old accountant and congressional candidate from Virginia.

Speaking to *HuffPost*, Larson confirmed his ownership of the Incelocalypse website and his authorship of articles about father-daughter incest. Far from distancing himself from what he had written online, he told the outlet, "A lot of people are tired of political correctness and being constrained by it. People prefer when there's

an outsider who doesn't have anything to lose and is willing to say
what's on a lot of people's minds." In other words, he argued that his
views might actively help him to attract votes. As well as praising
Adolf Hitler as a hero, Larson explicitly advocated for incels in his
political campaigning, claiming it was unfair for them to be "forced
to pay taxes for schools, welfare, and other support for other men's
children." He also called for the Violence Against Women Act to
be repealed, because "we need to switch to a system that classifies
women as property, initially of their fathers, and later of their husbands." Other online posts by the prospective politician included "A
Man Should Be Allowed to Choke His Wife to Death as Punishment
for Cutting Her Hair Short Without Permission, or Other Acts of
Gross Insubordination." When he was asked about how potential
constituents might respond to his views, Larson seemed encouraged by the success of Donald Trump, saying, "A lot of people who
disagreed with someone like Trump...might vote for them anyway,
just because the establishment doesn't like them."[5]

In a community of thousands of men, there will, of course,
be those who are unemployed or voluntarily withdrawn from
society. What scant media reports there have been on incels have
frequently centered on those people, portraying them as social out-
casts and hermits. But there are also likely to be many others in
gainful employment, with jobs and influence in our society, or even,
like Larson, running for public office.

In June 2018, American tech investor Ellen Pao, former CEO of
Reddit, warned in an article for *Wired* that "incels often work in the
tech industry and in engineering," enabling them to use "tech platforms and workplace communities to spread their ideas, onboard
new recruits, and train them on how to execute these ideas in their
companies." Technology, Pao wrote, "plays a central role for these

hate groups, as a career and as a weapon," adding that she received "daily" reports from tech employees and executives informing her of the ways in which these groups were infiltrating the industry. She also cited incels' own online postings as corroboration, noting, "On incel forums, they pride themselves on their tech contributions; they joke that the world would collapse without them to maintain network infrastructures, and that their companies would fail without them."[6]

But the offline influence of incels is not restricted to their physical presence and jobs, even in spheres as influential on our daily lives as technology and politics. It can also be felt powerfully in the ways in which their ideas and their lexicon have infiltrated and influenced other communities and ideological groups, both on- and offline. There is a trickle-down effect through these groups, whereby certain myths or prejudices that start as seeds on incel websites are incubated and nurtured through alt-right or Men's Rights Activists' networks before eventually filtering into the wider consciousness of mainstream society—a process that can be traced through the subsequent chapters of this book. So we cannot dismiss incel communities on the basis that their ideas never see the light of day either.

On to the final, and perhaps most common, defense of incels then: that they are frustrated men letting off steam online, that freedom of speech is paramount, and that misogynistic ideas on websites and forums do not cause real offline harm.

On May 23, 2014, twenty-two-year-old Elliot Rodger drove to the Alpha Phi sorority house near the campus of the University of California, Santa Barbara, and knocked on the door. When nobody answered, he started shooting at female students nearby. Rodger shot three sorority sisters, killing two of them (Katherine Breann

Cooper, twenty-two, and Veronika Elizabeth Weiss, nineteen) and wounding the third. It was part of a longer killing spree that saw Rodger both shoot victims and deliberately drive into them, killing six people in total and injuring fourteen.[7]

This wasn't a random or spur-of-the-moment decision. Before driving to the sorority house, Rodger uploaded a YouTube video titled "Elliot Rodger's Retribution."

"Hi, Elliot Rodger here," he began before declaring, "Tomorrow is the day of retribution, the day I will have my revenge." He went on to lay out his grievances against women and described his plans to punish them for rejecting him sexually. "I've been forced to endure an existence of loneliness, rejection, and unfulfilled desires, all because girls have never been attracted to me. Girls gave their affection and sex and love to other men, never to me." Rodger's tone oscillated between plaintive and angry—"I'm still a virgin. It has been very torturous... I've had to rot in loneliness, it's not fair"—but it became darker when he addressed women directly. He failed to ever turn the focus on himself or the role his own behavior might have played in his situation—a classic hallmark of incel ideology:

> I don't know why you girls aren't attracted to me, but I will punish you all for it. It's an injustice, a crime, because I don't know what you don't see in me, I'm the perfect guy, and yet you throw yourselves at all these obnoxious men instead of me, the supreme gentleman.

"I will punish all of you for it," Rodger declared, laughing. "On the day of retribution," he continued,

I am going to enter the hottest sorority house at UCSB and I will slaughter every single spoiled, stuck-up, blonde slut I see inside there. All those girls I've desired so much. They have all rejected me and looked down on me as an inferior man if I ever made a sexual advance toward them, while they throw themselves at these obnoxious brutes.

Rodger directly linked his act of violence to his misogyny and positioned it as a means to secure his status as an alpha male. "I take great pleasure in slaughtering all of you. You will finally see that I am, in truth, the superior one, the true alpha male." He laughed again.[8]

Although YouTube removed Rodger's original video, copies have been repeatedly uploaded to the site. One available at the time of writing has been viewed over 1.5 million times and liked almost 10,000 times.

Rodger, who turned the gun on himself at the end of his killing spree, also left behind a 107,000-word manifesto, which he emailed to various family members, former friends, and acquaintances. He titled it "My Twisted World: The Story of Elliot Rodger." In it, he attributed the majority of his unhappiness and loneliness to the fact that "the females of the human species were incapable of seeing the value in me."

After his death, it was revealed that Rodger had posted extensively on forums frequented by incels. In his manifesto, Rodger described the website as "a forum full of men who are starved of sex, just like me." Chillingly, he detailed his own experience of online radicalization, even though he did not recognize it as such:

Many of them have their own theories of what women are attracted to, and many of them share my hatred of women...

Reading the posts on that website only confirmed many of the theories I had about how wicked and degenerate women really are... It shows just how bleak and cruel the world is due of the evilness of women.

Rodger's online postings showcased classic incel ideology. In one post, he wrote that women's minds "haven't fully evolved." On the website PUAHate, he wrote, "One day incels will realize their true strength and numbers, and will overthrow this oppressive feminist system. Start envisioning a world where WOMEN FEAR YOU."

In his manifesto, it is clear that he had been heavily influenced by some of the most common arguments on major incel websites:

The ultimate evil behind sexuality is the human female. They are the main instigators of sex. They control which men get it and which men don't. Women are flawed creatures, and my mistreatment at their hands has made me realize this sad truth. There is something very twisted and wrong with the way their brains are wired. They think like beasts, and in truth they are beasts.

Rodger's online radicalization into extremist incel ideology led directly to his offline act of mass misogynistic violence.

In a small bookshop in Toronto a short time afterward, a woman named Alana would read an article in a magazine about Rodger's killing spree and realize, with a horrified jolt of recognition, what had happened to the community she had started fifteen years before.

Rodger was neither the first nor the last man to commit an

act of mass violence with an explicitly misogynistic motive, and he was not the only one to be directly involved in incel and other manosphere communities. In fact, the police report into the Santa Barbara massacre revealed that when officers investigated Rodger's laptop, his search history included material about George Sodini.

On August 4, 2009, forty-eight-year-old systems analyst George Sodini entered a women's aerobics class at the LA Fitness center in Collier Township, Pennsylvania. He turned off the lights, took out two guns, and began firing bullets, killing three women and injuring nine others.[9]

After the event, it emerged that Sodini had been a member of the pickup artist community, a group directly related to incels and part of the manosphere. According to ABC News, "Police found two typed notes in Sodini's bag at the scene, each reflecting his extreme frustration and depression with women."[10]

For the nine months preceding the shooting, Sodini had kept a blog, which started with the question "Why do this?? To young girls? Just read below. I kept a running log that includes my thoughts and actions." The blog revealed Sodini's deep misogyny, even as he lamented the fact that he had not had a girlfriend since 1984 or had sex since 1990. Like Rodger, Sodini fixated on young, attractive women who chose to sleep with other men over him, including "young white hoez" who were attracted to Black men. With twisted logic, typical of manosphere communities, he extrapolated from the number of years he had been single and his own "rough guesstimate of how many desirable single women there are" to reach the bizarre and exaggerated conclusion that "30 million women rejected me... I owe nothing to desirable females who ask for anything."[11]

Less than a month after Rodger's massacre, British teenager

Ben Moynihan began a month-long stabbing spree that saw him attempt to murder three different women in Portsmouth on three separate occasions over June and July 2014. After he was found guilty, a diary Moynihan had written emerged, in which he said, "I was planning to murder mainly women as an act of revenge because of the life they gave me, I'm still a virgin... I attack women because I grew up to believe them as a more weaker part of the human breed."[12] Precisely demonstrating the contradictions of incel ideology, Moynihan wrote, "I think every girl is a type of slut, they are fussy with men nowadays, they do not give boys like us a chance." During the period of the attacks, Moynihan also sent the police a letter that said "All women needs to die and hopefully next time I can gouge their eyeballs out." Closely echoing Rodger, a video found on Moynihan's computer saw him declaring "I am still a virgin, everyone is losing it before me, that's why you are my chosen target." When Moynihan was sentenced, the judge said, "The contents of your computers were as chilling as they were disturbing." But further details were not released publicly.[13] However, almost no British media reports seemed to make any connection between Moynihan and Rodger, though the cases occurred just weeks apart.

On October 1, 2015, twenty-six-year-old student Chris Harper-Mercer entered a classroom at Umpqua Community College and forced students to the center of the classroom before shooting eight people dead, including himself. A ninth victim later died in the hospital, and eight other students were injured.

Harper-Mercer left behind a manifesto in which he bemoaned the fact that he was a virgin with no girlfriend. He also named Rodger as somebody he considered to be "elite" and to "stand with the gods," adding,

It is my hope that others will hear my call and act it out. I
was once like you, a loser, rejected by society. When the
girls would rather go with alpha thug black men, we can all
agree that somethings wrong with the world. When good
individuals like myself are alone, but wicked black men get
the loot, like some sort of vaginal pirate, it's not fair.

He left the warning, "And just like me, there will be others... we
are your sons, your brothers, we are everywhere."

Unnamed law enforcement officials told *USA Today* that
Harper-Mercer "appeared to be involved in a loosely affiliated
online community known as the 'beta boys,'" a name that closely
reflects incel terminology about "beta males" and "beta uprising,"
used to describe the incel fantasy of a violent massacre of normies.[14]

On July 31, 2016, security guard Sheldon Bentley killed a homeless man he encountered sleeping in an alley in central Edmonton,
Canada, by stomping on his stomach. In a presentencing report,
Bentley tried to argue that his actions stemmed, in part, from
his frustration and stress, caused by four years of "involuntary
celibacy."[15]

On December 7, 2017, twenty-one-year-old gas station worker
William Atchison disguised himself as a student and entered Aztec
High School in New Mexico. Taking out a handgun, he shot two
students dead before killing himself. The *Daily Beast* reported that
Atchison had an extensive online presence, using Rodger's name in
one of his online monikers. According to a report by the Southern
Poverty Law Center, Atchison also praised Rodger, "the supreme
gentleman," in his online postings.[16]

On February 14, 2018, nineteen-year-old former student
Nikolas Cruz opened fire at Marjory Stoneman Douglas High

School in Parkland, Florida, killing seventeen people and injuring seventeen more. The massacre sparked a huge student movement against mass shootings and gun violence. On a YouTube video about Rodger's manifesto, Cruz had commented, "Elliot Rodger will not be forgotten."[17] It would later emerge that Cruz had reportedly stalked a young woman at the school.[18] He was also said to have repeatedly threatened and harassed an ex-girlfriend after she broke up with him.[19]

On April 23, 2018, twenty-five-year-old software developer Alek Minassian drove a speeding rental van through the North York City Centre district of Toronto, Canada, deliberately targeting pedestrians. He killed ten people and injured sixteen. A post was uploaded to a Facebook account, later confirmed as Minassian's, shortly before the attack. It read, "Private (Recruit) Minassian Infantry 00010, wishing to speak to Sgt 4chan please. C23249161. The Incel Rebellion has already begun! We will overthrow all the Chads and Stacys! All hail the Supreme Gentleman Elliot Rodger!"[20] The majority of Minassian's victims were female, with eight women and two men killed in the attack. Police later released a video of Minassian's post-arrest interview in which he focused specifically on being an incel, saying he had been radicalized online and had acted in the name of the ideology as a form of retribution. Minassian gave details about women romantically rejecting him, saying "I consider myself a supreme gentleman" (another reference to Rodger) and "I was angry that they would give their love and affection to obnoxious brutes." He added, "I know of several other guys over the internet who feel the same way." Like Rodger, Minassian described his attack as "the day of retribution." When police asked how he felt about the deaths of the ten people he had murdered, Minassian replied, "I feel like I accomplished my mission."[21]

On November 2, 2018, forty-year-old Scott Beierle entered a studio at Tallahassee Hot Yoga in Florida and shot six women, killing two, before killing himself. In the aftermath of the shooting, *BuzzFeed* uncovered Beierle's YouTube channel, which was filled with misogynistic and racist bile, including videos in which he described women as "sluts" and "whores" and discussed the "collective treachery" of girls. Like many incels, he railed against women in interracial relationships for betraying "their blood." One video, titled "The Rebirth of my Misogynism," said of a girl who had canceled a date with him, "I could have ripped her head off." In another video, called "Plight of the Adolescent Male," Beierle referenced Rodger, claiming that being in "the situation...of Elliot Rodger, of not getting any, no love, no nothing," was an "endless wasteland that breeds this longing and this frustration."[22]

In 2019, twenty-seven-year-old Christopher Cleary of Denver, Colorado, was arrested in Utah on the same day that several women's marches were planned in the area.[23] On his Facebook page, according to authorities, Cleary wrote,

I'm 27 years old and I've never had a girlfriend before and I'm still a virgin, this is why I'm planning on shooting up a public place soon and being the next mass shooter cause I'm ready to die and all the girls the turned me down is going to make it right by killing as many girls as I see.

On June 3, 2019, Alex Stavropoulos, a man in his midtwenties, took a bus to a Home Depot store in Ontario, Canada, and bought a pack of utility knives. Outside in the parking lot, he took out the knives and waited until he saw a woman with a young daughter and a baby in a stroller. He attacked them, severing an artery in the woman's neck and injuring the baby. The woman survived, after bystanders subdued Stavropoulos and managed to slow the bleeding until she could be rushed to hospital. Stavropoulos later told police: "I was angry at white women. I like white women but they won't fuck me. So, I wanted to see what it felt like (to kill a female child)." He also told police "I don't get laid," informing them that he identified as an incel.[24]

On June 17, 2019, a man wearing tactical gear and carrying a rifle and multiple magazines was fatally shot by police in Dallas, Texas, before he could carry out what appeared to be a premeditated shooting. The gunman, identified as Brian Isaack Clyde, aged twenty-two, had shot at the door of a courthouse before police engaged him. Clyde's Facebook page apparently warned of an upcoming attack and was littered with incel references and memes.[25]

On February 24, 2020, a seventeen-year-old boy took a machete into a massage parlor in Toronto and used it to murder twenty-four-year-old Ashley Noell Arzaga, as well as stabbing another woman. Police discovered evidence that the suspect, who could not be named due to his age, had acted after being inspired by the incel community. Detectives were so convinced that incel hatred of women was the main motivator behind the murder that they upgraded the original charge of first-degree murder to also bring terrorism charges against the suspect. Shockingly, this is the only known example of an incel attack being treated by authorities as a terrorist offense. It represented a marked contrast to the Canadian authorities' treatment of the Minassian case in which there were similar clear indicators of extremist motivation.[26]

In June 2020, twenty-three-year-old Cole Carini attended a Virginia medical center with severe injuries, including an amputated hand and shrapnel wounds, which he claimed were the result of a lawnmower accident. But authorities found bomb-making equipment and blood spatter inside Carini's home, suggesting he had injured himself with a homemade explosive device. A hand-written note at his property read:

> He casually walked through the shopping mall, his jacket concealed deadly objects... He was doing it and was assured it must be done... Even if he died this statement was worth it!... He now approached the stage of hot cheerleaders... He decided I will not back down I will not be afraid of the consequences no matter what I will be heroic I will make a statement like Elliot Rodgers did, he thought to himself.[27]

These men were not the first to carry out (or attempt) massacres based on an explicitly misogynistic ideology, and they are far from alone in personifying the link between abuse toward women and mass killing—an issue I will explore in more detail later. But the murderers on this list—who killed a total of fifty people and injured sixty-nine between them—all (with the exception of Moynihan, whose internet history is not publicly available, though the judge's comments suggest a link) had some direct connection to the online communities of men who hate women that are discussed in this book.

This evidence firmly refutes the idea that we need pay no attention to incels. This is a radical, extremist movement, at least tens of thousands of members strong, that deliberately spreads a doctrine of hate-fueled misogyny and male supremacy and actively advocates for the violent rape and murder of women. It sucks in young men looking for answers about relationships, indoctrinates recruits with dogmatic ideology and an entire self-spawned lexicon, and exonerates and lionizes those who kill in its name. Most pertinent of all, it has produced a significant number of mass murderers who have committed what ought rightly to be described as terrorist acts in its name. That so few people have ever even heard of it is, frankly, outrageous.

One of the greatest barriers preventing us from taking this threat seriously is the stubbornness with which we are inclined to think of the online world and the real world as distinct and separate realms, with a solid dividing line between the two. What is online, the assumption goes, is virtual, unreal, and, implicitly, harmless. But the offline impact of the killers who have taken incel beliefs to heart, experienced radicalization online, and put their ideas into practice, using real bullets and blades, is the devastating proof that such an assumption couldn't be further from the truth.

But this is far from the only reason that the majority of people don't take incels seriously or even know about their existence. We are, after all, quick to recognize and take action against the threat of other forms of online radicalization, like that used by Islamic extremists to lure young converts into acts of violence in the name of a twisted and prejudiced set of beliefs. Part of the problem is that this is about women. And we don't even take violence against women seriously offline, let alone on the internet, where it is so easily written off as banter, jokes, and satire. When online radicalization results in a Muslim attacker driving into white pedestrians, media reports and political commentators immediately alert us to the connection, the word *terrorism* quickly filling the front pages and the ideology and online footprint of the killer highlighted for all to see. The same is not the case when men kill in the explicit name of misogyny. Even people who are aware of these underreported attacks rarely know about the stated intent behind them.

And meanwhile, incel communities quietly grow, recruit, and revel in their victories.

In the aftermath of Rodger's massacre, media coverage was mixed. While some outlets reported Rodger's affiliation with incel groups or acknowledged the explicitly stated misogynistic intent behind the murders, many played down or omitted this link altogether. It is no surprise that so few people know about the extremist intent behind killings carried out by men who hate women when you look at the way in which they are presented to the public. "California Drive-By Shootings: Elliot Rodger Kills Six Near Santa Barbara University," read one typical headline in the aftermath of Rodger's massacre.[28] "Seven Dead Including Gunman in 'Mass Murder' California Shooting."[29] "'Mass Murder' in California, 7 Killed by 'Disturbed' Man."[30] Even when headlines or subheadings explicitly quoted from Rodger's manifesto or videos, suggesting journalists were aware of his extremist misogynist content, this content was often completely ignored in favor of coverage of other factors. "*Hunger Games*' Director's Son, 22, Pledged 'Utter Annihilation to Those with a Better Life,'" read one example.[31] Newspaper articles quoted Santa Barbara County sheriff Bill Brown describing the shootings as "the work of a madman" and Rodger as "severely mentally disturbed." Even in news coverage in the immediate aftermath of the event, mainstream outlets ran quotes from Alan Shifman, an attorney for Rodger's father, saying that, when police had interviewed Rodger several weeks previously, they had "found him to be a 'perfectly polite, kind and wonderful human.'"[32]

Several media channels explicitly questioned or rejected the idea that there was anything gendered about the murders, such as an article in *Forbes* that claimed the idea was "severe oversimplification and an overly rapid rush to judgment," adding that

Rodger hated "both men and women."[33] Many outlets picked up on Rodger's mental ill health, which may also, of course, have played a significant role in his actions, though he had not been formally diagnosed with a specific mental illness, despite receiving psychiatric treatment. But arguments mainly focused on gun control, or on the fact that Rodger had killed and injured a number of men as well as women.

An article in *Time* acknowledged the existence of misogyny in our society but played down the potential influence such ideas may have had on Rodger, writing that "the very isolation that mass-homicide perpetrators feel makes them unlikely candidates to respond to societal trends." This is deeply ironic, as offline isolation is one of the biggest reasons driving many men to become members of online communities like incels. The writer, like so many others, tried to focus the piece on mental health, describing mass killers in general as "angry, resentful, mentally ill individuals." Muslim terrorists, in stark comparison, are rarely referred to as "mentally ill."[34]

This determined portrayal of Rodger's actions as not being explicitly driven by extremist misogyny requires a deliberate misreading or omittance of much of the evidence he left behind. So it is disturbing that the Isla Vista police report summary also makes very little reference to misogyny—quite extraordinary, given the extensive expression of misogynistic intent set out in the report itself, which quoted from Rodger's journal entries and his manifesto:

I will be a god, punishing women and all of humanity for their depravity... I cannot kill every single female on earth, but I can deliver a devastating blow that will shake all of them to the core of their wicked hearts. I will attack the very girls who represent everything I hate in the female gender.[35]

Yes, Rodger killed his male housemates—a fact used by many news outlets to suggest that his intentions could not have been purely gendered—but he himself described the decision to do so thus: "This First Phase will represent my vengeance against all of the men who have had pleasurable sex lives while I've had to suffer. Things will be fair once I make them suffer as I did. I will finally even the score."

Yes, Rodger later targeted groups of people, including men, but he again explicitly framed this within his anger at women for not having sex with him: "I will specifically target the good looking people, and all of the couples... How dare those girls give their love and sex to those other men and not me?"

The pattern holds true for coverage of other mass murders, where the killers made clear their extremist misogynistic motivations. When Minassian killed ten people and injured sixteen in the name of the "incel rebellion," headlines read "Toronto Van Driver Kills at Least 10 People in 'Pure Carnage,'" and quoted authorities as saying, "The driver's actions...appeared intentional, but did not seem to have been an act of terrorism. 'The city is safe,' said the Toronto police chief, Mark Saunders."[36] His words came after officers had interviewed Minassian, who had explicitly told them of his online radicalization and the incel motivation behind his attack.[37]

And reporting on Harper-Mercer's manifesto repeatedly described it as racist (and yes, racism was certainly a feature, as in many incel manifestos) but failed to make any reference to misogyny. A typical quote described his writing as "espousing racial and social hatred."

How are we supposed to fight against this terrifying wave of violence if we can't even point out the very obvious fact that these killings had a misogynistic motive?

Finally, in the aftermath of the Toronto van attack, some media outlets began to draw a direct link between Minassian's references to Rodger and the misogynistic intent behind the killings, leading to a spate of online "explainer" pieces about the manosphere and incels. But even these were often confined to left-wing online outlets, with much of the mainstream newspaper coverage referencing the issue briefly, if at all. And even then there was resistance. A *National Post* article accused those who were pointing out the link as being "premature" and "counterproductive," saying "the attack is no more or less horrific if it was based on the victims' genders."[38]

It is, of course, quite possible to argue that any large group may contain outliers and extremists. One person's violent actions do not necessarily represent the group as a whole and should not be assumed to have been directly influenced by membership in the community. Indeed, in most of the above cases, there were several other factors that may have contributed, to some extent, to the killers' actions, including mental health issues, childhood abuse, or family dysfunction. But it should go without saying that the vast majority of people who have faced mental health problems, survived childhood abuse, or experienced family breakdown never carry out acts of mass violence. And none of those factors explain the notably male demographic of perpetrators, when such circumstances are met by people of all genders.

It is also difficult to accept the argument that these murderers and their acts are entirely divorced from the online communities they frequented or referenced in light of the treatment of their legacies within those communities afterward. Across incel websites and forums, it is extremely common to see the names of killers lauded, canonized, and revered. They are worshipped with cultlike devotion, and community members actively and repeatedly encourage others to emulate them. "THE INCEL REVOLUTION CANNOT BE STOPPED... there WILL come a reckoning," reads one post.

After the Isla Vista massacre, a subreddit called "Elliot Rodger Fans" was quickly created, though it was banned by Reddit soon afterward. On PUAHate, the forum Rodger himself had frequented, comments praising his actions described him as a "hero" and a "king amongst incels," mourning his death with "goodnightsweetprince" and crowing "incel goes mainstream, incel rage, insel terrorism is LEGIT." The website was shut down when Rodger's links to the forum began to emerge.

But this hasn't stopped other incel communities from idolizing Rodger, to the extent that his name has become shorthand for the notion of becoming a martyr for the cause. To "go ER" is a common term used to denote carrying out an incel massacre, while the initials are frequently included in other words with the same inference. In many posts, forum members are exhorted to become "hERoes." A typical post about Rodger reads, "He lived the dream, he died a warrior." Over time, the exaltation of Rodger hasn't diminished either; if anything, the cultlike worship increases. A user wrote, "INCELS RISE UP, WE WILL TAKE THE PLACE OF THE CHAD AND WE WILL REIGN SUPERIOR, ALL HAIL ELLIOT RODGER." Other posts call him a "prophet" and a "martyr." A YouTube video, mainly consisting of soft-focus images of Rodger, fading in and out against gentle background music, has almost 50,000 views and 295 likes.

Rodger is not alone among mass murderers in attracting veneration across incel forums. When media reports circulated in the aftermath of the Marjory Stoneman Douglas shooting that suggested Cruz may have been stalking a girl who had rejected him, members of the Incelocalypse message board discussed the case.

"The bitch deserved it I'm glad he killed them," wrote one user. Another agreed: "Good. Dumb sluts either deserve to be raped for rejecting men or outright killed." In perhaps the starkest example I have seen of dehumanizing misogyny in all my months of research on these forums, one user wrote, "I just wish this poor guy had raped the girl before killing, that way she would die knowing that the boy she rejected had still been inside of her body."

Many members of incel communities were quick to celebrate and embrace Minassian, too, as a new hero, saying he had attained "incel sainthood." "I will have one celebratory beer for every victim that turns out to be a young woman between 18–35," posted one. "Alek Minassian. Spread that name, speak of his sacrifice for our cause, worship him for he gave his life for our future," added another.[39]

Meanwhile, memes about Harper-Mercer display pictures of him holding a gun, with the admiring caption "No Mercy from The Mercer." And after Bentley blamed his brutal murder of a homeless man on involuntary celibacy, forum users discussed the case with feverish excitement. Comments included, "Can you feel it boys? ITS TIME"; "It's time to go ER on them"; "Why couldn't hr have done it to a foid"; "He should have done it to a woman instead"; "Am I wrong for feeling excited about this?"; "TIME FOR THE BETA MALE REVOLUTION GO ER."

Even when a mass killing occurs that has no apparent connection to incels, the incelosphere collectively froths with delight and speculation that the perpetrator might have been one of them, veering between praise for the murderer, critiques of his method, and suggestions about how he could have increased the number of victims or ensured that more of them were female.

During the writing of this book, I watched again and again,

sickened, as this glorification of violence happened in real time. When news emerged of Arzaga's murder, I saw incel forum members describe it as "good news" and suggest that "nothing of value was lost," as they assumed "she may be a stacy since she works in a spa." Referring to her killer, one community member wrote, "And may he find peace with a gun in his right hand and a sword in the left and at his feet the countless unworthy whores he calls prey."

Given the fact that these are just a few examples of a widespread trend across various incel communities, with additional web pages set up for the express purpose of "honoring" incel killers, it is difficult to swallow the argument that the actions of these violent men bear no connection to the incel community at large.

Indeed, it emerged that the day before Harper-Mercer's shooting, an anonymous forum user had detailed plans of the attack online, writing, "Some of you guys are alright. Don't go to school tomorrow if you are in the northwest."[40] While it hasn't been confirmed that the anonymous account was linked to Harper-Mercer, there is strong evidence to suggest that this may have been the killer calmly giving his online friends a heads-up about his murderous intent. The responses from other community members are chilling. One user suggested that the original poster "might want to target a girls school" and gave advice on the best weapons to use. Another offered tactical advice, including "I suggest you carry a knife on your belt as last resort." One response simply read "Make us proud." Another added, "Kill them all for us."

Whether or not the account actually belonged to Harper-Mercer, protestations that not all of the incel community should be tarred with the same brush are hard to accept, given the way in which its members respond to somebody claiming he is about to commit such an act. Had any one of those who participated in the thread reported the threat to law enforcement, it is possible that eight lives might have been saved. So it is difficult to accept completely the argument that the community at large bears absolutely no responsibility for the acts of its individual members. Yet this is a common refrain. When a forum user realized Rodger was behind the Isla Vista massacre and suggested informing the police about his online postings, another poster replied, "Don't. Whatever happens. We didn't do anything so just let it happen if it does."[41]

It is also somewhat ironic for incels to indignantly make the argument that they should not all be lumped together in light of the gross generalizations the manosphere itself makes about women: the phrase "all women are like that" is so ubiquitous on incel forums that it has its own acronym, liberally peppered across thousands of posts—AWALT.

Nonetheless, it is certainly the case that many members of incel communities are genuinely sad, lonely, or depressed men, seeking answers and support. Their usernames, for example, range from "uglycreep" to "uglyasfuck" to "fatvirginguy."

Many posts simply read as a cry for help. One thread, titled "Sometimes I Feel Like a Freak of Nature," points to the ways in which societal stereotypes of virile, dominant masculinity might contribute to feelings of inadequacy and shame: "Having Sex is part of being a man, and being a human being. Sometimes I feel like I'm not even human, because I rarely get laid." A group of users also bonded over the fact that they rarely wash their hair or clothes, because their self-esteem is so low that they don't see the point. Another man wrote that the only reason he hasn't "roped" (incel terminology for death by suicide) is he didn't want to ruin his family's Christmas.

An incel who made a YouTube video for his peers to describe

his experience of losing his virginity to a sex worker said softly, "It was kind of nice to feel like I was being hit on...even though I wasn't... It was kind of nice to feel that for the first time ever." He added, "It wasn't just about sex, I wanted to learn intimacy there."

There is also a small minority of incel community members that actively attempts to go against the flow. "Elliot Rodger is a murderer. He is a bad person. Violence is always wrong," wrote a user in one forum in response to posts praising Rodger as a hero.

And former members of some of the earliest incel communities from the late '90s describe their sites as mixed-sex forums, where dating advice and coping strategies were shared and problems aired. Even today, there are some small corners of the community that retain the same sort of character initially intended by Alana. A "femcel support group" on Facebook, with over 800 members, offers a safe space for women who self-define as involuntarily celibate, and a subreddit called "incels without hate" prides itself on promoting a "positive and helpful community." But they are dwarfed by the rest of the so-called incelosphere.

The most frustrating part of my experience of incel immersion, surfing these websites as Alex, was seeing posts from men who were vulnerable or in pain, many of them young boys going through the typical tumult of adolescent hormonal angst and looking for some guidance to help them through it, and then watching as these men and boys collided catastrophically with deeply twisted and misogynistic views, supported by pseudoscience and fake statistics, at precisely the moment when they may have been most impressionable.

In the small flurry of online articles that has emerged about incel groups, particularly in the wake of mass killings, there are two clear, polarized groups. The community is either characterized

as darkly violent and misogynistic, dangerously promoting violence against women, or as a mischaracterized and disadvantaged
group of lonely men, widely smeared by association with a tiny
number of bad apples who could exist in any movement. The reality, which almost nobody seems to have confronted, is that both
stories are true. That extended exposure to the violent rhetoric of
the most extreme ideologues slowly desensitizes and draws in the
other members too. And it is this combination that is perhaps most
explosive of all.

Unfortunately, once young men have attached themselves to
a community that gives them a sense of belonging and identity, it
can be a powerful draw that is difficult to renounce, particularly
as they become more radical in their ideas and online speech. As
Squirrell explained,

> they end up *defining* themselves by their incel status, mean-
> ing that to transcend incel would be losing the only com-
> munity they feel offers them support. They say things that
> are so extreme that they're difficult to take back or to move
> away from. They are, for all intents and purposes, a cult,
> rather than a community.

Dr. Sugiura, too, warned of the risks of radicalization and is
deeply concerned at the potential harms such communities pose
to boys:

> The messages that are being spread and disseminated,
> and the discourse... They are trying to recruit, they are
> trying to turn people to their way of thinking, their ideol-
> ogy. That is very suggestive of grooming—the talk of being

"red-pilled"—they have a whole vocabulary of waking up to the reality of what society has done to cis straight white men.

In some ways, genuine naivete (and gradual acclimatization) can prevent young people from recognizing the reality of the communities they are becoming involved in—a risk epitomized by the experience of Jack Peterson, a young American who found himself unexpectedly catapulted into the international media spotlight in the wake of the Toronto van attack.

Peterson was just eleven years old when he first started browsing internet message board 4chan in 2010. Over the course of several years, he gradually became immersed in online culture, discovering a range of different communities and ideas, until finally, in 2016, he stumbled into the incel community via Reddit and felt like he had found a group that understood him. "The term incel," he told me during a long phone conversation, "as soon as I read it, I realized it applied to me." He wasn't shocked by the misogynistic rhetoric, he explained, because he had already spent six years gradually immersing himself in similar websites:

I think, after you're involved in communities like that for so long, you're desensitized to that kind of misogynistic rhetoric, because it's just a normal part of what you're reading online, whereas some random guy who doesn't go on websites like that might find the incel community and be shocked, but for me, it wasn't that. It wasn't a big surprise.

Believing he had stumbled into a community that understood and supported him and somewhat inured to the violence of the rhetoric he encountered there, Peterson was shocked when the Toronto van attack took place and he realized that Minassian, the killer, had been a member of the incel community. Seeing some press begin to draw a connection between the murder and the online philosophy incels espoused, Peterson reacted with anger, speaking up to defend his community, and he suddenly found media outlets falling all over themselves to interview him. It was a heady and overwhelming experience for a lonely and fairly isolated young man with low self-esteem. The reality, of course, as Peterson says today with a wry, rueful tone, is that "I was the only person stupid enough to go on camera."

So Peterson's quotes were picked up and spread across internet articles and blogs. He condemned the massacre but also accused the media of "misrepresenting the incel community," claiming that "being an incel is not about violence or misogyny." Most of the extreme posts highlighted in the media were just sarcasm and dark humor, Peterson insisted. Instead, he spoke about camaraderie, mutual support, and a sense of community. So what happened next came as a nasty shock.

Abuse and anger started raining down on Peterson. But it didn't come from the mainstream media or members of the public who had seen the interviews, as he had anticipated. It came from the incels themselves. They were furious that Peterson had misrepresented them and undermined the very real hatred of women many of them claimed to feel. "The incel community was mostly pretty angry at me, because they claimed what they were saying was not dark humor and that it was genuine...so they were angry that I was watering down their message."

This, said Peterson, "was definitely not something I expected." And neither were the many posts he began to see from people praising Minassian, "saying it's a good thing that the message is getting out there." Meanwhile, as Peterson tried to defend incels from the accusation of vitriolic misogyny, the angry backlash continued. "What they were saying was, 'No, the media is portraying us 100 percent accurately. You're wrong.'"

For Peterson, the story had a happy ending. The experience jolted him out of his comfortable relationship with the online community, and the surprisingly supportive reaction he received from the media, feminists, and the general public drove him to brave more social interaction than he had experienced in years. Suddenly, the exact groups of people—feminists, women, and normies—he had spent the past six years being indoctrinated to fear and revile were providing him with a warmer reception than the community he'd thought of as home. Within a short period, Peterson left the incel sphere for good.

In the intervening time, Peterson, who is just twenty years old now, admits shyly that he has "had some success with women" and generally feels better about himself. But his experience is rare, and it underscores the risks of inexperienced young men being drawn into a community that becomes a safe haven without genuinely realizing what they are signing up for. Were it not for the surprising twist in Peterson's story, the gradual desensitization he underwent could have sent him ever deeper down the rabbit hole.

"I think the biggest thing that I've gained from now being distant from the community," he mused thoughtfully, "is that I can see it for how a normal guy on the street would see it... When you're not seeing that kind of stuff every day, you go back to it and then"—he paused—"yeah, it becomes apparent how far off the normal path the incel community is."

For most members of incel groups, their experience is likely to lie somewhere in the murky middle ground between Rodger's or

Minassian's explosions of offline violence and Peterson's redemptive moment of realization. Those with misogynistic leanings are likely to see their leanings solidify; those who have never considered sexist ideas about their inherent masculine "right" to sex will be introduced to such ideas; those who have tentatively entertained carrying out certain real-life acts might find themselves emboldened by the encouragement of others.

And in some ways, this might be one of the greatest threats posed to our society by the incel community. What about the behaviors toward which the incelosphere is gently nudging its tens of thousands of members and followers—behaviors that might not make the headlines or the front pages or even be linked back to incel forums at all but that nonetheless spring from ideas hatched, or impulses incubated, on those hate-filled websites?

One man wrote on an incel forum about the apparently banal experience of seeing a woman looking over her shoulder at him as he walked behind her at night.

"You should have raped her," came the immediate response.

Another forum member wrote, "I enjoy walking behind women in the parking garage after work. The sheer terror gives me a massive erection."

Again and again, users write about the impact membership in incel groups has had on their ideas and attitudes toward women, only to find their deeply misogynistic and violent impulses praised, normalized, and seized upon by their peers.

"Has your inceldoms caused you to get strange and dark sexual fantasies?" a user asked on one forum. "Once I realized that foids hate me and that my chances of a relationships were near to zero I began getting dark and violent fantasies. I get excited of women in pantyhose getting choked...and wetting themselves in fear."

Another user agreed that since becoming part of the incel community, his sexual appetites have changed dramatically, with fantasies about foids "getting choked and slapped." Yet another user chimed in with "foids should cry and beg for mercy." Yet another wrote, "All of my sexual fantasies are hostile and predatory in nature now... I only understand sex as being a form of violence."

As I spent hours poring through these posts, I realized just how much offline impact it can have when men are immersed in incel forums day in, day out. And I started to register just how many of the stories men told about manifesting incel ideas in their daily lives echoed and matched the thousands of stories I receive every year from women who are being harassed, assaulted, and abused.

If the questions we ask about incels only extend as far as the likelihood of them committing mass acts of violence, we are missing the point. But the biggest problem is this: at the moment, we aren't asking any questions at all.

# 2

# Men Who Prey on Women

"No means no—until it means yes."

**DARYUSH VALIZADEH ("ROOSH V"), FORMER PICKUP GURU**

"Is your father a thief? Because he stole the stars from the sky and put them in your eyes."

"Have you got any raisins? How about a date?"

There aren't many women I know who haven't experienced one or two clichéd come-ons from strangers in bars at some point in their lives, usually followed by awkward laughter and very little romantic action. The most memorable and least appealing in my own recollection went like this: "Have you just farted? Because you blew me away." Of course, I ripped off his clothes and we were married a week later.

When you hear the term *pickup*, it is this kind of silly example most people automatically think of. The buffoonish guy hiding his shyness behind a cheesy joke, or the slightly sleazy womanizer whose confident one-liners are supposed to render him charmingly irresistible. (Think Joey in *Friends*.) So the first thing to explain is that when we talk about pickup artists (or PUAs), we aren't talking about a jokey line here or there. This isn't about stopping men from approaching women, or complimenting them, or asking them out on dates.

What I'm talking about is a booming international industry that has repeatedly been valued, according to media reports, at an estimated $100 million.[1] It is a community that, at first glance, might seem a world away from incels: while it occupies a fairly enormous online space, it also has a major real-world presence, from boot camps to books to personal trainers. The community's veneer of public acceptability enables it to operate much more brazenly in plain sight than incels, protected by those "cheeky womanizer" pop-culture stereotypes. And as incels despair of ever having sex, PUAs pursue it relentlessly. Yet the two groups have more in common than immediately meets the eye. Both groups depend on the separation of men and women into narrow, highly stereotypical categories. Both cast heterosexual sex as the pinnacle of male achievement and portray women as little more than objects whose sole purpose is to provide sexual pleasure to men, like some kind of pornographic slot machines. The difference is that incels regard the machines as rigged, paying out only to a few predetermined, societally superior elites, while other men are doomed to feed endless coins into the machines without reward or are denied access to them altogether. For some incels, the obvious solution is the destruction of as many of the machines as possible. PUAs, on the other hand, believe it is possible, for a high enough price, to learn the secret combination of buttons to push and levers to pull to trick the machine into paying out every time, regardless of the customer. Both worldviews rest heavily on the perception of women being without humanity, individuality, or souls. Like incels and other manosphere groups, PUAs have their own lexicon, including a large number of acronyms, which can seem bewildering to the uninitiated. And both groups share a breathtaking sense of male entitlement to sex. "Awaken to your power as a man, and enjoy the success with women that is your birthright," blares one well-known pickup training website.

We are talking about an industry that exploits men's worst fears, preys on their vulnerabilities, and literally trains them in harassment, stalking, and even sexual assault. Targeting shy or romantically unsuccessful men as their disciples, so-called pickup gurus offer exhaustive, specific instructions for the entire span of a sexual encounter, from the approach to the minutiae of the conversation to the physical act of having sex. The problem is that much of their advice is, at best, deeply misogynistic and, at worst, can be described as a manual for sexual violence. Some of the pickup community's biggest rock stars are men who have openly admitted to rape or have advocated its legalization on private property. These are the "experts" charging thousands of dollars to pass on their wisdom to other men. What's most chilling is the fact that their courses are usually sold out.

The word *art* is a pretty rich way to describe this. In fact, pickup artistry can only be described as an oxymoron. Yet the so-called art and its self-proclaimed gurus have become a near religion, with millions of acolytes worshipping at its altars, sweating their way through its how-to manuals, and, in many cases, spending a fortune on everything from training camps to seminars dispensing supposedly life-changing advice.

The ultimate aim is to evolve from an AFC (average frustrated chump—comparable with a beta in incel terminology) to a MPUA (master pickup artist) or PUG (pickup guru). This is achieved by innumerable exercises, teachings, and tricks to improve their "game" (flirting technique). It mostly involves dressing in flamboyant clothing or jewelry to attract attention ("peacocking"), going on "sarging expeditions" (attempts to approach women), skirting FUGs (fucking ugly girls) and "warpigs" (ugly women), targeting HBs (hot babes, hard bodies, or hunny bunnies—often suffixed with a number out of ten), avoiding competition from AMOGs (alpha males of the group) and "cockblockers" (friends), and using techniques like "negging" (giving her a backhanded compliment to make her feel insecure) or FTC (creating a false time constraint to pressure her into a quick response). The aim is to achieve a "close" (a successful outcome, ranging from a "number close" to a "kiss close" to a "fuck close"). But to achieve this, you'll have to overcome her "bitch shield" (attempts to fend you off) and potential use of the UFEA (universal female excuse archive).

Confused? You'll get the hang of it. And the more accustomed you become to seeing women referred to as acronyms, the easier it becomes to forget that they are people too.

It's not a coincidence that so many of these terms literally describe women as prey; popular pickup techniques include BHRR—bait, hook, reel, release—and the most common word used to describe a woman in a pickup scenario is the "target." The act of tricking her into a sexual encounter is known as "gaming." The language creates a curiously detached and clinical tone when community members write "field reports" (sharing their experiences online), a classic example being "I opened a two set at the coffee shop—let's call them HB7 blond and HB9 blue eyes." If it all sounds a lot like hunting, that's because it is.

The most disturbing part of penetrating this community is the slow and uncomfortable realization that you have personally come into contact with its members. Suddenly, you remember the creepy guy in the weird hat who pursued you determinedly down the street in broad daylight, refusing to take no for an answer, bombarding you with sexualized "compliments" that felt more like an attack than a conversation. You remember your rising heart rate, the swift mental calculations as you tried to work out the nearest safe place, the carefully neutral facial expression you fought to maintain as you asked him to leave you alone. Politely, always politely, because of the fear that he might turn nasty, that the situation could escalate out of your control. The instinct to say anything, or even surrender your phone number eventually, just to get away. The sinking feeling later, when the harasser persisted and persisted, calling and messaging, continuing after you'd told him to stop.

For most women I know, this is not an unusual experience. It can make you feel scared, battered, weary, and unsafe. On a daily basis, I might receive as many as one hundred Everyday Sexism Project entries and emails from women all over the world who are sick to death (or scared to death) of the endless, draining battle with sexual harassment in public places. So to suddenly uncover a vast online world in which men are being actively trained in these techniques is deeply dispiriting. But it also rings true.

Men in the PUA community are repeatedly programmed to think of women as objects for pleasure, problems to be solved, children to be wrestled into obedience, or dogs to be trained. A woman's inconvenient resistance must be overcome to obtain mastery and control over her. This necessarily requires the infantilization and dehumanization of women as an entire gender, with men encouraged to see them as fickle and clueless. "I don't care what women say they want. I don't care what women think they want. I care what women respond to," says pickup guru Ross Jeffries in one instructional video. At one point in the PUA "bible" *The Game* (a multimillion bestseller), Neil Strauss describes a woman as "all holes: ears to listen to me, a mouth to talk at me and a vagina to squeeze orgasms out of me."[2]

Much PUA jargon plays on the increasingly familiar manosphere technique of using pseudoscience and psychobabble to generate an impressive and academic-sounding basis for what is effectively packaged misogyny, sold to men, in this case, as a fun, acceptable, and ultimately foolproof recipe for sex. One pickup guru, offering boot camp workshops for thousands of dollars, promotes his skills by citing his own transformation through intense study and devotion, which he claims "culminated in deep identity level change at the cellular level." And for just a few thousand dollars, it is implied, he could transform your cells too!

The advice and techniques recommended by different websites and gurus range from self-improvement techniques, devoted to sprucing up male appearance and improving confidence, to mildly obnoxious instructions for inserting oneself into a woman's immediate environment to outright encouragement and detailed instructions for sexual assault.

Clearly, as in the incel community, there's a sliding scale here. Reading one pickup guru's "tongue sucking technique," it's easy to feel faintly sorry for the large cohort of pickup devotees who are clearly just insecure, shy men looking for a little advice to help them overcome their nerves around women. "When we meet attractive women, it's normal to feel anxious and overwhelmed. This typically manifests itself with us speaking faster than usual and perhaps with a higher pitch," he tells his followers. "The tongue sucking technique can be utilized when, instead of speaking, we internally suck our own tongue, which prevents us from speaking."

But it's depressing to think of the number of vulnerable young men who might approach these so-called experts in the genuine hope of improving their relationships with the opposite sex, only to find themselves immersed in a bewildering world of insults, negging, and dehumanization. Take, for example, one pickup guru's insistence that men should "interrupt what a girl is saying every 10 words," simply to throw her off-balance and undermine her confidence.

PUA techniques range from the technical-sounding "kino escalation" (finding any excuse to make physical contact, usually without a woman's consent, and trying to keep intensifying it to make it more sexual) to "going caveman" (aggressively escalating physical contact). "Some examples of cavemanning," advises one pickup website, "include grabbing a girl by the waist and pulling her toward you, or, in the bedroom, picking up a girl and throwing her onto the bed." All this is framed within the "alpha male" imperative of establishing command and control over women. Aspiring PUAs are instructed about the importance of "isolating" a woman from her friends, often in language reminiscent of a hungry lion separating the weakest gazelle from the pack. I'm immediately reminded of an Everyday Sexism Project entry in which an older university student told a female freshman, "I'm going to treat you like a dolphin, segregate you from the group until you give in to me." One website helpfully suggests, "If she resists, punish for a second by turning away, then repeat the instruction." This gives the impression of a training technique for particularly stubborn Labradors; the same site recommends the "trick" of gaining the upper hand by giving a woman's hair a "firm, commanding pull." The tongue-sucking cohort are looking more appealing by the minute.

At the more damaging end of the spectrum are the ideas

commonly known in pickup parlance as the "anti-slut defense" (ASD) and "last-minute resistance" (LMR). These teach (with copious pseudoacademic biological reasoning, of course) that a woman who decides she doesn't want to have sex with a man is not making a rational or valid personal choice but rather responding helplessly to a biological imperative. Her body, pickup gurus insist, is trained to panic instinctively to avoid sex in case she dies during childbirth or is abandoned by the father of her children. Yes, really. Anything rather than countenance the possibility that a woman might actually just not be that into you (a possibility most PUAs simply fail to acknowledge even exists). All it takes are some techniques to circumvent women's "resistance" (which is frequently described as "token" or "fake") and push them into sex. "Overcoming LMR" is one of the most common and popular topics across pickup forums, seminars, and boot camps. Does it still sound like harmless, charming fun?

Users of one popular forum exchange advice on how to "plow through" the resistance of a girl who explicitly asks not to be touched, adding, "A caveman takes what he wants." A common technique shared is simply to grab girls in public, without asking for permission, because "you want to overpower the woman you're after." One forum user boasted, "Many times I have just thrown the girls over my shoulder."

Other threads focus on the best ways to manipulate or coerce women in sexual situations: in one thread, titled "How to Convince a Chick to Swallow," users swapped fake news articles about semen being good for women's health in the hope that they could use the information to put pressure on sexual partners to swallow their sperm or accept being "sprayed in the face." Others advised more direct methods that simply override a woman's consent, like "'forget' to pull out in time and just blast inside." Another user suggested, "Hold her mouth and nose shut. Just like when you have to get your dog to take medicine." There's that dog-training comparison again.

For a community that claims to be invested in romance, with members who often protest their distance from incel groups, there is a tellingly high level of violent and misogynistic content here.

A thread about "banging pregnant girls" discusses the best ways to trick a woman into thinking you will provide for her unborn child to manipulate her into sex before never contacting her again. The "benefits" of "gaming" pregnant women, according to one forum member, include the fact that she will be "emotionally weak," making her easier to manipulate. Another forum user "joked," "I banged this pregnant chick one time and her baby came out a week later with a black eye."

Other threads encourage men to use PUA techniques in other spheres of life, like one that advocates grabbing women by the hips in the workplace and brushing your penis up against them as you pass.

But because PUAs are one link up the chain from incels, because they are seen as charming or funny or harmless, they tend to receive a much more prominent hearing in the media. So the ideas that cross over seamlessly between the two groups, ideas that might never have seen the light of day from the depths of an incel forum, suddenly pop up in mainstream discourse by way of a PUA interlocutor. In an interview with the *Independent*, for example, one PUA explained that it is a woman's responsibility to avoid rape, because men are physically incapable of stopping during sex "with all that testosterone pumping through their system." Therefore, he argued grandiosely, "it would be prudent for them not to enter situations where the average man can't stop due to his innate weaknesses as an animal whose entire existence depends on him successfully mating."[3]

Common pickup advice suggests overpowering and controlling women, refusing to take no for an answer, and actively ignoring or circumventing their resistance. "What's the best way to assert dominance over someone? Initiating physical contact without asking permission," reads a typical forum post. "She's excited by displays of dominance and power," says a "master" PUA's blog. The entire narrative runs directly contrary to the tentative conversation about consent that is finally starting to penetrate the mainstream consciousness since the #MeToo movement. If we think we're making progress, then looking at these forums, with their hundreds of thousands of views, comments, and threads, makes you realize that the reality is, at best, one step forward and several steps back.

Often this is presented as something women actually want and need, almost doing them a charitable service (regardless of whether they are able to grasp the fact). One prominent pickup guru writes on his website, "Consider the possibility that pushing it, just a little bit, may be what she needs... A good hard fucking—connecting with a male—may be what she needs." He also suggests ignoring a woman's rejection of your approaches, again framing this as a magnanimous gesture for her own good: "I believe that not caving in to a woman's first 'knee-jerk' response is a good thing. I'm creating a space for her to have a new choice, to respond with more freedom and act differently." What a gent.

These are not just extreme, cherry-picked forum posts, misrepresentative of the wider pickup genre. Some of the men most famous within this international community, with thousands of online fans and followers, bestselling books, and sold-out "seminars," are the ones actively peddling the most violent and misogynistic messages.

For example, the self-proclaimed "international leader in dating advice," Julien Blanc, posted a video to YouTube in 2014 titled "White Male Fucks Asian Women in Tokyo (and the Beautiful Methods to It)." Presenting a seminar to a roomful of men in the video, Blanc tells his audience that, "in Tokyo, if you're a white male, you can do what you want," suggesting that men should approach women yelling "'Pikachu' or 'Pokémon' or 'Tamagotchi' or something." He boasts about his ability to go "romping through the streets" in Tokyo, "grabbing women" and shoving their faces into his crotch. ("Just grabbing girls' heads, just, like, head, *pfft*, on the dick. Head on the dick, yelling: 'Pikachu.'") He then shows the men video footage of himself forcing women's faces into his crotch on the street.[4]

Like much of the manosphere, the PUA community presents deeply problematic racist stereotypes, particularly through sweeping generalizations about the "types" of women in different countries, suggesting that they all conform to dehumanizing stereotypes. (Women from a particular European country are sex-crazed, Asian women are submissive to white men, etc.) One well-known pickup guru's website, for example, offers an "American Man's Guide to Seducing Oriental Women," which, after a disclaimer to reassure readers he's not a racist, goes on to promise it can teach men how to "get all the yellow and pink you can handle" by building their own "harem of willing, docile, obedient Oriental chicks." Topics include "Can't-miss approaches for picking up Oriental women that they gobble up like candy (or fortune cookies!)" and "How to use your vastly superior knowledge of American culture to appear as god-like superman in her eyes, who she is compelled to *obey, serve and satisfy!!* (Ha! Try that with an American girl!)." But thank goodness it isn't racist.

As with other ideas, these notions trickle down from the pickup gurus themselves to be clearly visible among their followers in the wider community. In one pickup forum thread extolling the virtues of having sex with "Muslim girls," a user crowed about the fact that they are "culturally *trained* to be cooks/good house keepers from teenage years," later comparing them favorably to "European girls and their whorish sexual adventures," which seems a tad hypocritical coming from a man writing long posts on a forum dedicated to sleeping with as many women as possible. But his biggest praise is reserved for the fact that he believes Muslim girls can't say no, because "refusing sex to husband...is considered unlawful in Islamic tradition/culture." The thread quickly descends into Islamophobia and racism, reminiscent of the prejudice on some incel forums. Some users warned the poster that he will become a terrorist if he sleeps with a Muslim woman. One wrote, "I want white or asian chicks. I want nothing to do with any muslim, hot or not."

The community is actively hostile toward LGBTQ people. One forum's rules, for example, casually state, "No girls, homosexuals, or transsexuals. Their opinions or comments are not welcome here." Pickup gurus present damaging and prejudiced stereotypes about lesbians (who are often portrayed as simply not having been "banged" by the right man yet, thus actively encouraging straight men to harass them) and bisexual women (who are presented as exotic, sexually greedy creatures whose main reason for existence is to spice up the sex lives of heterosexual men). Some pickup gurus even capitalize on these stereotypes to the extent of branding themselves "experts" in bedding such women. One promises to teach acolytes "How To Eagerly Get One Bi-Sexual Women To Recruit Others For Your Bed!" and "How To Validate Bi-Curious Women's Desire To Experiment And In Fact Position Anything Other Than

Her Exploring These Desires As A Terrible Restraint She MUST Abandon!"

The idea of pickup far predates the internet, as does its close relationship with misogyny. In fact, the term *pickup*, meaning a casual acquaintance formed with the aim of having sex, was popularized in the United States during the Second World War by propaganda posters that aimed to tackle venereal diseases among troops by discouraging them from having casual sex or visiting sex workers. "Loaded? Don't take chances with pickups!" said one poster on which a group of attractive young women clustered beneath an image of a gun. Another poster featured a pretty, dimpled young woman, smiling as three uniformed men looked on admiringly. Stamped across the image was the warning: "She may look clean— but pickups, 'good time' girls, prostitutes, spread syphilis and gonorrhea. You can't beat the Axis if you get VD."

Even in this early iteration, the term was associated with misogynistic assumptions. "A girl who would yield to one man has probably had relations with another. Very likely she is diseased," read one poster. "She may be a bag of trouble," said another beneath a suggestive picture of a dark-haired, heavily made-up woman in a beret, smoking a cigarette.

In the 1960s and '70s, as contraception, counterculture, and the sexual revolution took hold, the term *pickup artist* lost many of its sinister overtones when it was appropriated by psychologists who realized the potential profit to be gained from mixing self-help with therapeutic techniques, particularly with the alluring promise of helping readers to achieve sexual success. *The Art of Erotic Seduction* was published by psychologists Albert Ellis and Roger Conway in 1967, soon followed by Eric Weber's *How to Pick Up Girls!* in 1970. Those early guides might seem relatively tame compared to the modern iteration of the movement. Ellis, for example, who was one of the major forces behind the rise of cognitive behavioral therapy, famously described his own efforts to overcome chronic shyness and fears of public speaking, especially around women.

Of course, there is nothing wrong with helping people build up their confidence or even supporting those who are nervous about forming relationships in learning some techniques for striking up a conversation. That goes for those members of the modern community who are genuinely "confidence coaches" or who provide respectful, consenting relationship support too. Weber sets out the origins of his book in a way that sounds quaint and innocent, describing himself as "shy" around "the kinds of girls I always thought I should marry." But his book, which he sold through mail orders, brought in $10,000 worth of purchases after a single ad in *Penthouse* magazine, was far from wholesome, and foreshadowed the majority of the modern pickup industry in more ways than one.

Recounting the experience of seeing an attractive ("downright delicious-looking") woman on the street, he wrote, "You've just got to see more of her long lean legs. Her fine rounded breasts. Her high, firm behind. For an instant, you even consider rape."

Throughout the book, he promotes the same essentialist, heteronormative ideas about biology and gender that run deep through the modern manosphere:

Whether you know it or not, you already have one great thing going for you when it comes to picking up chicks. And that is you're a man... As a man, it's your right, your privilege, to approach a woman any time you want. But women—they've got to sit there and wait.

He even predicts the negging craze and the trend for intentionally treating women badly in a bid to attract them, evangelically describing the experience of a "friend" who berated a woman furiously on the street after she ignored his advances, only to discover that his tirade had successfully "broken through her defense."[5]

The book sold over three million copies and was translated into more than twenty languages. Even today, it remains available to buy on Amazon.

The 1970s and '80s saw pickup artistry slowly gain traction, with a smattering of independent writers and so-called teachers, plus a short-lived magazine, *The Pick-Up Times*, and a 1987 film, "The Pick-Up Artist," starring Robert Downey Jr. and Molly Ringwald. (Incidentally, James Toback, the film's director, was accused of sexual harassment or assault by thirty-eight women in a 2017 *Los Angeles Times* exposé, following which an additional 357 women contacted the paper to report that he had sexually harassed them, in accounts stretching over a forty-year period. Toback denied all the allegations and wasn't charged, in large part because the statute of limitations on the majority of the cases had already passed.)[6]

But it was arguably the aforementioned Ross Jeffries, a failed comedy writer, who created the beginnings of what we think of as the modern pickup community. Starting to teach pickup workshops in 1987 (the same year former psychotherapist R. Don Steele published *How to Date Young Women: For Men over 35*), Jeffries published a book, *How to Get the Women You Desire into Bed*, creating what he termed the "speed seduction" technique, which he claimed drew on neurolinguistic programming (NLP). This technique effectively promised to teach men how to hypnotize women into being attracted to them, with Jeffries making the bombastic claim on his website that his approach combined NLP with "Ericksonian Covert Hypnosis, Silva Mind Control, Huna, Magick, and more." As he became more successful and better known, Jeffries started offering home-study courses in seven languages and charging $3,000 for seminars, famously assuring men, "You don't get laid, I don't get paid."[7]

Among the products Jeffries has for sale online at the time of writing are his original book and his "Deluxe speed seduction home study course" (at a bargain price of $179.40), alongside a plethora of other content, like a guide to "Find, Control and Seduce the Women of Your Dreams." Priced at just $19.95, it promises to teach men how to "manipulate and control all of your women," "beat them at every game they'll try," "create a state of 'obedience in women,'" and "piss her off and get rid of her when you want to make room for some 'fresh meat' in your harem."

Here's the thing about pickup artistry: for something that claims to be all about making a connection with someone of the opposite sex, the advice given is extraordinarily focused on putting up barriers between men and the women they approach. Instead of being open to women's feelings and needs, acolytes are taught to ignore and deny them. Instead of mutual pleasure, the focus is all on the man's needs, at the cost of the woman's choice. Instead of finding a woman they like, pickup students are encouraged to find any woman and force her to change.

One $207 video package, for example, promises to teach men how to "induce permanent behavioral change in the women you desire, allowing you to mold them to the exact erotic specifications you require, demand and dream of." As the prices ramp up, so does the psychobabble: a set of videos costing the princely sum of $350 promises to reveal the mysterious techniques of "symbol fractionation" and the "apposition of opposites," as well as "hypnotic trance technique," and more. This all sounds very technical until you realize that Jeffries's psychic expertise extends about as far as advising men to use words and phrases like "below me" and "succeed" in conversation, in order to subconsciously trick women into sex, because they sound similar to "blow me" and "suck seed."

Nonetheless, Jeffries became enormously successful, featuring on high-profile shows from *Dr. Phil* to *The Daily Show* and inspiring Tom Cruise's character in the film *Magnolia*. Forty years on from the publication of his book, Jeffries's old website continues to peddle his original wares, with a slick new interface offering sleekly packaged online speed seduction courses that promise "rapid and total success with women."

As word of pickup techniques spread into the mainstream, an ecosystem of online forums, chat rooms, websites, blogs, and email lists began to spring up. It was the beginning of the modern pickup community. In 2005, the community penetrated the public consciousness for the first time in a major way thanks to *The Game*, journalist Neil Strauss's aforementioned book, which was framed as a kind of undercover exposé ("Penetrating the Secret Society of Pickup Artists," boasted the subtitle), though Strauss himself was, by this point, a genuine and well-known member of the scene himself. The book chronicled his transformation into a PUA (codenamed "Style") under the direction of mentor "Mystery," a real-life pickup master (actually named Erik von Markovik), and described his ascendance to the status of pickup guru—at which point he and a group of other gurus established themselves at a mansion base, nicknamed "Project Hollywood," to share their so-called expertise with other members of the community. Packaged in black leather with gold-edged pages and a red satin bookmark, the book was deliberately marketed to look like the Bible. It sold over five million copies, catapulting pickup artistry into the public imagination and introducing legions of men to its sexist principles.

"You just fucking push, push, push, and it can't not work," says one pickup guru in the book, describing a technique of sheer persistence to grind down a woman's resistance. ("I'll pummel their asses down.") Recounting the "tactics" of another pickup guru, Strauss writes, "I'd watch as a woman came over to his house for the first time and he'd throw her against the wall by her neck, then release her just before he kissed her, shooting her adrenaline level through the roof with equal parts fear and arousal." Some of this sort of material is forcefully reminiscent of the incel belief that women all secretly fantasize about being raped.

Strauss went on to write two follow-up books, including *The Truth: An Uncomfortable Book About Relationships*, which, to absolutely nobody's surprise, revealed his difficulties trying to form and maintain meaningful relationships after his exit from the "seduction community." He would later describe the techniques set out in *The Game* as "objectifying and horrifying":

> I got so deep into that community and was seduced by it that I completely lost myself in it... If you talked to me then about it, I would have defended the techniques as a way to learn courtship. If you ask me today about it, I'd tell you that anything that involves manipulation or needing to have a certain outcome is definitely not healthy in any way.[8]

In 2007, pickup artistry gained further prominence with the release of a television series, VH1's *The Pickup Artist*, which featured male contestants being tutored by von Markovik and then competing in the art of pickup. Following the show, von Markovik founded his own pickup company, Venusian Arts, and spent a decade traveling and "teaching." In October 2018, he returned to Hollywood, offering various seminars and mentorship programs, ranging in price from $997 for online training to almost $5,000 for a boot camp and $10,000 for a three-day residential course, where recruits learn everything from grooming and fashion tips to techniques for approaching women, persuading them to give up their phone numbers, and steering them into the bedroom. At the time of writing, courses are available to book throughout next year, from Las Vegas to Helsinki, with almost half already sold out, suggesting that pickup artistry is still booming.

As the practice grew in popularity and renown, both the community and the industry rapidly expanded. Internet pickup forums exploded, matched by a rise in real-life, offline spaces for men around the world to meet, discuss, and hone their techniques. These underground meeting groups, secretly coordinated online, are known as "lairs," and one online directory currently lists almost 200 worldwide, each with its own description and contact person, ranging from Dubai to Turkey, Israel to India, South Korea to Slovenia, Singapore to South Africa, by way of Romania, Peru, the Philippines, Mexico, and Japan. Broadly consistent with most estimates about manosphere hot spots, the list shows a markedly higher number of hangouts in Australia, Canada, the United States, and the UK, though several European countries, like France and Spain, boast a high number too.

A chilling window into the reality of so-called pickup boot camps was a recording that emerged in 2014 of famous pickup guru Owen Cook, who uses the pseudonym "Tyler Durden." Cook was caught on video telling a large group of men in one of his courses about an encounter with a woman who had stayed over with him the night before:

> She was a stripper... I fucking hated that fucking bitch. Fucking bitch... She's just a full slut, whore slut. I fucked the shit out of her, dude... The last way I fucked her, too, it was in the morning, she was taking a shower, and I didn't think she wanted to have sex again, but I just threw her on the bed and I put it in her, and I could barely even get it in, because she was just totally not in the mood. And I was like: "Fuck it, I'm never seeing this bitch again. I don't care." So I just, like, jam it in, and it's all tight and dry, and I fuck her, and I'm like: "I'll just make this quick, because she doesn't even want it."[9]

An encounter clearly amounting to rape can thus be boastfully positioned as a teachable moment for pickup "students" paying thousands of dollars for the privilege of such "inside secrets." As a woman in the world, likely to come into contact at some point with one of the thousands of men who are taking these classes every week, that's a pretty terrifying prospect.

Another infamous PUA, Daryush Valizadeh, who goes by the name "Roosh V," published a blog post called "How to Stop Rape" on his eponymous website in which he suggested that the real cause of rape was "women wholly unconcerned with their own safety," adding that many rape allegations arose from women feeling "awkward, sad or guilty for a sexual encounter they didn't fully remember" or scheming to get their "previous night's lover" imprisoned or expelled from college. He argued that the solution was to "make rape legal if done on private property," reiterating,

"I propose that we make the violent taking of a woman not punishable by law when done off public grounds." Rape laws should remain in place, he elaborated, "for seedy and deranged men who randomly select their rape victims on alleys and jogging trails... For all other rapes, however, especially if done in a dwelling or on private property, any and all rape that happens should be completely legal." Valizadeh has since claimed that the piece was intended as a "satirical thought experiment," but it revealed one of the very real ways in which ideas spawned in the manosphere have a massive offline impact. Because the idea that rape laws should only really apply to "seedy and deranged men" plays straight into the societal stereotype of rapists as extreme, violent strangers, crouching in the shadows, ready to attack women they don't know. It fuels the already significant problem that many young men don't think of rape in more nuanced terms, don't recognize the importance of ensuring enthusiastic consent from sexual partners, don't realize that if a woman changes her mind at the last minute or during sexual intimacy, it is still rape if he doesn't stop. Of course, this is pretty convenient for a community whose sole purpose is to get a woman into bed at all costs.

Valizadeh isn't the only member of the pickup community who has tried to distance himself from his own work when it attracts criticism, using the classic manosphere defense of "banter" or satire.

After his comments about Asian women sparked a public backlash, Julien Blanc appeared on CNN, where he was given a massive platform to excuse his videos as a "horrible, horrible attempt at humor," claiming his advice had been taken out of context.[10] Yet in spite of the international anger and the steps taken by several countries to expel him or refuse him a visa, Blanc continued to operate highly successfully within the pickup industry after the incident.

However, such backlash has led several high-profile pickup blogs and websites to run articles lamenting the death of pickup and the fact that politically correct madness has stigmatized and shamed men into silence. PUAs, like incels, frame themselves as the real victims of a world that denies them freedom and happiness. But the reality is that even those prominent PUAs who have been the subject of public outrage continue to practice, many of them still running profitable companies and carrying out regular expensive training camps. They maintain enormous online followings, continuing to influence large numbers of other men and boys, and, in many cases, even benefit from the media exposure the backlash causes. Describing the response to his article advocating the legalization of rape, Valizadeh wrote on his website, "Objectively, as a writer, that article was a raging success, a once-in-a-lifetime perfect storm. Writers can only dream of getting that kind of exposure." Valizadeh has over 100,000 followers across social media. Cook, who gleefully described his own assault of a woman to his "students," has over 400,000. At the time of writing, he is selling an upcoming tour, with boot camps and summits on sale across the United States. Places are going for up to $3,950.

These figures contrast comically with the attempts of PUAs to portray themselves as a persecuted, heroic group, driven underground and into ruin by feminazi attacks. "I'm sure many of you understand that we are in the early stages of a censorship wave that will sweep through society," wrote Valizadeh on one of his several websites. "Scoundrels like myself get banned first, and then soon the hammer will come down on anyone who dares to share the truth. Personally, I believe that I will suffer death by a million cuts, but, until then, you can continue to follow my work here." He went on to list the many mainstream sites, forums, audio outlets, and social media platforms that enable him to continue his career by prominently promoting his work and flogging his wares.

Valizadeh's choice of words is telling. By referring to himself as a "scoundrel," he very deliberately trades on the acceptable public face of pickup: the "charming rogue" persona. It's a convenient mask for somebody who has argued for the legalization of rape.

Regardless of whether any figurehead of the movement may or may not be censored or suffer legal action, it is important to recognize that these kinds of violently misogynistic sentiments, including the advocacy of rape and sexual assault, are not isolated to a few so-called gurus. They are, in fact, sentiments reflected by and spread widely across dedicated pickup forums, suggesting that they have pervaded the broader community as well. On one forum, a user wrote, "If they reject me i just grope them like i usually do." He later expanded, "i assault them because they deserve it and i take back what is mine and i dont care about anything other then my own needs... If i want to score a 10/10 and she rejects me i just rape her."

On another forum, a user wrote in a "lay report," "As I start to put it in she starts fighting me and saying no in a half ass sort of way. I could tell it was a rape fantasy so I pinned her arms down and kept going."

So we see how incel ideas, like the belief that women secretly want to be raped, begin to worm their way through the different communities of the manosphere and pop out into real people's lives. The woman who tried to fight off her rapist in the scene described above might never have heard of incels or PUAs, but they impacted her life in the most profound way imaginable.

If it sounds like an exaggeration to suggest that the men slavishly immersing themselves in the world of pickup ideology might end up actually assaulting women in real life, the evidence reveals otherwise. In 2016, three self-proclaimed PUAs were jailed after a woman they targeted tracked them online and found detailed "lay reports" describing her own rape on pickup websites.[11] Two of the men were so-called instructors for a company called Efficient Pickup; the third was their student.[12] One of the men, Jason Berlin, later had his sentence reduced by two years after arguing that "a recent autism spectrum disorder diagnosis made him unaware that his actions were wrong."[13] The man, whose psychiatrist argued that he had reduced emotional and social capacity, may be symbolic of the potentially disastrous influence of extremist misogyny on vulnerable targets, but the conviction of his two "instructors" is proof that for many of the men involved in these communities, their acts of abuse are deliberate and callous. Sentencing one of the gurus, the judge said that in eighteen years, he had not seen another defendant who was so "mean and cruel."

While it is rare for these cases to hit the headlines, it is not unusual to see them cropping up on pickup forums. When a user posted in another thread, asking for advice on persuading a virgin to sleep with him and his friend simultaneously, another man simply suggested "rape it." Yet another thread saw a man complaining that his girlfriend wasn't in the mood for sex, saying, "She says she hates me insisting... I am getting frustrated and horny, and could possibly rape her." A few hours later, he updated the thread: "Done, fucked her brains out till she cried." The emphasis on reporting back to the community, playing to the crowd, only promotes the escalation of such violence as members jostle and vie for each other's attention and respect.

What's more, such content is often not removed or tackled by the forums or organizations that own these websites. Indeed, in some cases, it is actively encouraged. In one example, quoted in the previously cited *Independent* article, a user on the Real Social Dynamics (RSD) forum started a thread titled "Lie Your Way Inside a Woman's Vagina," in which he advocated to other users that once they'd lured a woman back to their house, they shouldn't be "afraid to physically force her to do anything or to tell her no or shut up." He added, "ignore what she says and physically force her." Another user replied, "yeah, and then when you're done with her, you just like grab all her clothes and then throw 'em at her, then shout get out you fucking whore. Women deserve this because of what they've done to us." The article noted that one of RSD's coaches commented on the thread, encouraging, rather than disapproving of, the sentiment. "Loving the responses," he wrote.[14]

Although some forums have specific rules about not naming or identifying women, it is still not uncommon to come across pictures of men's sexual conquests, often in a state of undress and asleep or unconscious, apparently taken without the women's consent, for the general gleeful consumption of the community. These images are sometimes posted as "proof" of sexual success. Some men also upload explicit videos in which it seems highly unlikely the women knew they were being filmed or had consented to the video being shared.

There's evidence to suggest that pickup culture has particularly infiltrated university and campus communities. In one instance, at Ohio State University, a student started a Reddit thread warning others about a man who had stopped her six times, harassing her with clichéd pick-up lines and refusing to take no for an answer. The conversation spiraled into 359 responses, with dozens of other female students chiming in to say they had been approached, grabbed, groped, stroked, cornered, or harassed by a man matching the same description. Before the man (who wasn't a student at the university) was banned from campus, it emerged that he was a self-proclaimed PUA who was boasting about his exploits online, including posting videos of his "conquests" without their knowledge or consent, some of which were filmed using a hidden camera in his apartment. One student, writing on the Reddit thread, reported that the man had also created a secret Facebook group with other local PUAs in which they shared "creep shots" of local young women (once again taken without their consent) that they then divided up into photo albums, advising others about which students to target and which to avoid.

In a response on his Facebook page after his ban from campus, the man, Sean Larson, wrote, "LOL you guys don't seem to understand. You can't stop a player... campus isn't the only place with hoes."[15]

Despite all this—despite some of these men advocating what amounts to sexual violence and others boasting about having committed it, despite their open chronicling of illegal acts across online forums—PUAs seem to operate in a judicial vacuum. Yes, a handful of pickup gurus have found themselves banned from individual countries after enormous public outcry against their rhetoric, but a huge number of them merrily continued to flog their "products" on other shores. In fact, in researching this book, plowing through hundreds of examples of behavior that is either borderline or blatantly against the law, I came across only two instances of law enforcement ever engaging with pickup forums and the men who use them to boast of sexual violence.

The lesson for young disciples is clear: you can treat women illegally with impunity. And you can shout it from the rooftops. Nobody really cares.

In fact, many pickup sites and companies directly target young men and students, promising knowledge, advice, and power to the uninitiated and inexperienced. What's particularly sad about this is the number of young men likely to be swept into the PUA community with good intentions after googling tips on how to meet girls or nervously seeking out advice on flirting.

It is easy to imagine a slightly awkward student, with little experience of women, stumbling across some of these websites after a tentative Google search. Let's say he browses a few fairly mainstream pickup websites on which he is advised, in no uncertain terms, "First Date Rule #1: The Man Is In Charge. Period." He is also instructed that to improve a romantic relationship, a man must "be more assertive and take charge"; he should tell a woman "where to be," "what to wear," and to make sure she is "freshly waxed." A novice, who might start to feel a bit uneasy about this, is quickly assured that "all women want a strong alpha male" and is authoritatively told, as one PUA website bluntly puts it, that sex is "about urgency, anxiety and tension, not comfort, familiarity or rapport... Striving to make a girl feel comfort and trust [is] anti-seductive."

These are the kinds of attitudes many people would like to think were ousted decades ago. Yet here we see a whole new generation of men being drilled in techniques for mistreating women today.

Of course, if we were actively teaching young people about healthy relationships and sexual consent at school, such poor advice might not have such a catastrophic impact: at least boys would have something else to weigh against these suggestions. But the current provision of relationships and sex education is extraordinarily poor, with one recent study finding that just a quarter of young people were ever taught about consent at school.[16] This creates a vacuum that can be dangerously filled by disingenuous advice and pickup bile.

The internet allows widespread access to these ideas, and like the incelosphere, there are so many sites, forums, and message boards, all spewing the same sexist pickup ideology, that it is easy to become quickly desensitized to the skewed portrait of relationships they portray.

It is also easy to come into contact with the enormous pickup industry offline, thanks to the number of brands and businesses that have sprung up over the past decade or so to cash in on its success. In contrast with much other secretive, underground manosphere activity, these brands and businesses are often large, apparently respectable companies, very much out in the open.

RSD, one of the biggest such companies (which euphemistically describes itself as "The International Gold Standard of the Dating Industry"), boasts a website with 142,000 members, 72,000 Facebook likes, 180,000 Twitter followers, and over 100,000 YouTube subscribers. RSD alone has almost 200 global boot camps available for booking on its website, at the time of writing, ranging in price from $1,000 to $3,000. The company was cofounded by Nick Kho (PUA name "Papa") and the aforementioned Cook, both of whom featured in Strauss's The Game. Pickup guru Jeff Allen works as an "executive coach" for RSD, whose website proclaims that he has run programs "practically every weekend for the last 12 years in over 100 cities across North America, Australia, Africa and Europe." Allen is famous for boasting about his "rape van" and telling women to eat "a bag of dicks" when they reject him.[17] Until 2019, Blanc was another of RSD's "executive coaches," described by the website as a "super-star within Real Social Dynamics," who "has traveled to every continent teaching live programs on how to pickup girls and has successfully captured in-field video footage to share with clients on his successes." Which is a pretty euphemistic way to describe a grown man who has filmed himself screaming "Pikachu" while sexually assaulting strangers—but hey, you say "pot-ay-to," I say "pot-ah-to."

And that is just one site, though the options are endless. In most major cities across the world, it would be possible, on almost any given weekend, to sign up for an extortionately priced course in the "artistry" of "gaming" women, quite possibly taught by a man with a personal background of advocating or committing sexual violence. In Toronto, just $1,999 promises to "transform you into a master with women." In Sydney, just $497 will reveal the secrets to sweeping "any woman off her feet even while she's busy doing something else like working or shopping." In Tel Aviv, $2,500 will produce "fast results." In London, courses from £500 to £5,000 train you to pick up women in public, "at school or at work." So-called wingmen, who accompany PUAs to help them "close the deal," are also getting in on the act, with "professional wingmen" services available to hire internationally, with prices ranging from a few hundred to many thousands of dollars.

In other words, it's safe to say that a significant number of men are making vast sums of money every year from teaching others how to harass women more frequently and effectively.

Then there are the many websites, blogs, and social media accounts profiting from and promoting pickup artistry. At the time of writing, the YouTube channel Honest Signalz, offering "pickup, comedy and self development for the evolving man," boasts almost fourteen million views and 100,000 subscribers. In one of the channel's videos ("How to get sexual with girls"), the guru encourages viewers to find ways to insert physical touch and sexual conversation into interactions, saying to a woman, for example, "I feel like most girls enjoy getting choked during sex, am I right? Choked, hair pulled." Let me remind you that this guy's material has been viewed nearly fourteen. Million. Times. It's just one of many YouTube accounts dedicated to PUAs and so-called pranksters who film themselves haranguing women in public.

Beyond that, there are the forums in which individual men congregate to lap up the wisdom of the gurus and share their own experiences. The "seduction" subreddit, which is one of the site's biggest PUA communities, has 446,000 subscribers. Another forum, in which men offer advice, techniques, field reports, and tips as well as arranging real-life meet-ups, boasts 183,000 members and almost a million posts. The "Roosh V" forum has almost 20,000 registered members, with almost two million posts. A similar site has almost 300,000 posts and 20,000 members, with 2,700 simultaneously online at the moment I visited. One of the biggest UK PUA forums has 41,500 members, with over 75,000 posts.

So just as with incels, the pickup community is far larger than you might imagine. This is not some tiny internet backwater, populated by a few isolated losers. It's huge. Both on- and offline.

Becoming involved in pickup artistry is a decision likely lubricated for some men by the largely sympathetic and even admiring media portrayal of the community. One only has to look as far as the character Barney Stinson in the smash-hit television series *How I Met Your Mother* to see how widely the image of the pickup guru as a "charming rogue" or "cheeky womanizer" has penetrated. Stinson, part of the much-beloved core group of friends, was considered the show's breakout character, credited by critics for much of the show's success. Famous for his "playbook," "bro code," and attempts to cajole, trick, and manipulate women into having sex, Stinson deliberately targets women with "daddy issues" who he considers likely to be especially vulnerable. Reaching tens of

millions of viewers per episode and receiving thirty Emmy nomina-
tions, the show had a massive cultural impact, spawning countless
online articles with titles such as "Barney Stinson Tips to Pick Up
Chicks: Do They Really Work?" and "7 Plays Every Bro Should
Know, by Barney Stinson."

The UK's answer to Barney Stinson might be considered Dapper
Laughs, a character created by British comedian Daniel O'Reilly.
After O'Reilly rose to fame online, ITV commissioned a series called
*Dapper Laughs: On the Pull,* in which O'Reilly was seen offering tips
for "how to fucking pull," using classic pickup rhetoric like "Just show
her your penis. If she cries, she's just playing hard to get." Like many
PUAs, his content trod a blurry line between "banter," "flirting,"
harassment, and assault, with quotes from the show including "If
she's looking at me and playing with her hair, by the end of the night,
she'll need a wheelchair." But O'Reilly's rhetoric also played on classic incel and wider manosphere arguments, like his tweet claiming
that "it's only sexual harassment if she's more attractive than you"—
echoing the frequent (and completely inaccurate) incel refrain that
women only accuse ugly men of rape. Though O'Reilly's show was
eventually not commissioned for a second season, the airing of the
first series to an audience of hundreds of thousands helped to normalize and frame such ideas from the platform of a massive mainstream broadcaster. When women criticized the inherent misogyny
of the program, ITV responded, "Comedy is subjective and we realize the content of the show might not be to everyone's taste. We
regret that any of our viewers were offended. However, as with all
of our shows, the series content was carefully considered, compiled
and deemed suitable for broadcast." Which is not exactly reassuring.

These portrayals depicting pickup as a harmless or even highly
aspirational pursuit, carried out by attractive men and secretly

enjoyed by the vast majority of women, all helped to create a public image that does not line up with the darker reality.

But just like incels, members of the pickup community are keen to protest against what they see as unfair, broad-brush representations of them by feminists. And like incels, this rather ironically contrasts with the pickup community's own ideological standpoint when it comes to women. PUAs are, in fact, so confident in their belief that women are "all the same" that in their charming lexicon, the cure for a man feeling particularly attached to any one woman ("oneitis") is simply to GFTOW ("go fuck ten other women").

It is certainly true that there are individual examples of men in the pickup community pushing back against misogyny and violence. "Being sober and taking advantage of drunk girls is disgusting, it's rapey, you're a loser," wrote one user in response to a thread on a pickup forum.

"So you assault women who reject you? You suck," replied another forum participant to a post that seemed to advocate rape.

"Do you really want to go around groping girls that are scared of you? Or do you want to actually attract a woman that wants to rip your pants off and suck your dick?" another user briskly demanded of his peers.

But even though this community, like incels, is likely to include a broad spectrum of members and casual viewers, many of whom are just sad or nervous men, simply interested in improving their prospects with women, such posts cannot be described as the majority, or even the norm, and they contrast sharply with the more aggressive, misogynistic, and sometimes violent tone set by the leaders of the industry. Given the fact that they are such a minority, the risk remains, as in the incel community, that these moderate members are likely to be radicalized, squeezed out of the community, or gradually desensitized to the more extreme expressions of misogyny that are normalized and perpetuated around them. It is also possible, of course, that these messages are penned by irate forum observers from outside the community altogether.

And unlike incels, PUAs can hardly fall back on the argument that their ideology is confined to online, satirical speech and poses little risk of offline impact. PUAs form groups dedicated to training and instructing countless men in how to relentlessly pursue, harass, and, in some cases, assault women in real life. They run boot camps that take men out into the streets to "practice" their techniques on unsuspecting women. They get inside men's bedrooms and under their sheets, reminding them not to take no for an answer, to push past resistance, to persist and cajole and do whatever is necessary to force a sexual conquest to happen.

Like other purveyors of misogyny, PUAs are extremely adept at modifying and superficially rebranding their sexism in order to sidestep public criticism and project a veneer of transformation. In its simplest form, this has resulted in a large number of so-called gurus adopting euphemistic new titles like "social strategist," "life changer," or "transformational healer and thinker," all the while continuing to promote the same misogynistic ideas.[18] Part of the smokescreen is created by the dramatic articles on pickup websites that declare the art to have been vanquished—a sleight of hand that helps to deflect criticism while the industry continues to thrive. One such site, infamous for its lampooning of "hysterical" feminists, claims, "The pickup industry as we know it is DEAD... Those fat, red haired, nose ring wearing slut walkers took the pickup industry under their flabby hairy wings and disembodied it over several years." Well, who's being hysterical now?

In between the first and final drafts of this book, Julien

Blanc became the latest in a line of PUAs to turn his poor reputation into yet another money-spinning method. Abandoning his pickup boot camps with RSD, Blanc launched a new course called "Transformation Mastery." Openly linking it to the feminist campaign against his videos of sexual assault in 2014, the spiel on Blanc's new website seems, at first, to feign humility, saying that at the height of his pickup fame, he "still felt empty," and describing the public backlash as "a roller coaster of emotions." But he triumphantly concludes that the "media scandal" was actually the moment he "found everything," claiming to have transformed himself through "meditations, training and an INSANE amount of DEEP INNER WORK [emphasis Blanc's]." Confirming once and for all that even international opposition has little impact on the careers of men like Blanc, he describes how "new opportunities started to fly open, authors, entrepreneurs and business leaders started reaching out to me." And now? He's offering this transformational experience to others in a package with all the PUA hallmarks of "in-field footage" and psycho jargon ("reach deep inside your subconscious mind... drop the scarcity paradigm"), with online courses priced at hundreds of dollars each.

At its most breathtakingly hypocritical, the attempt to deflect criticism has led some prominent PUAs to attempt to rebrand their material as respectful and positive toward women, even theatrically setting themselves up as an evolved "alternative" to "creepy" guys. (Presumably those being the ones they formerly coached.)

Cook's older videos advocated physically grabbing women in public spaces and pulling them toward you (a "sloppy move" to "rip her in"). He recommended practicing on unattractive women first, to help his acolytes overcome their "this-is-not-the-behavior-I'm-supposed-to-be-doing block" (also known as their basic sense of human decency). And of course, in a PUA seminar, he also famously described raping a woman. Yet his more recent videos from 2019 boast about teaching men "how to approach girls respectfully without creeping them out," audaciously lamenting the fact that "women are often BOTHERED in the street by men who are unable to read their signals"! The brazenness of the attempt to capitalize on the era of #MeToo without actually changing the misogyny he is profiting from is incredible.

Then there's Valizadeh, the champion of making rape legal, whose previous book, *Game: How to Meet, Attract, and Date Attractive Women* (not to be confused with Strauss's book *The Game*), promised to teach men all aspects of pickup, including "tactics to try if a girl is refusing your sexual advances but you feel she truly wants to have sex" and "how to break up with a girl in a way that minimizes the chances she will successfully accuse you of domestic violence or rape."[19] That same Valizadeh, aware enough of the backlash against some of his work to have dramatically declared the death of pickup, then produced a new book, *Lady: How to Meet and Keep a Good Man for Love and Marriage*, promising to help "women find love, long-term relationships, and marriage in a modern environment where," he wrote disapprovingly, "most men seem to only want casual sex."[20] And in 2019, Valizadeh dramatically claimed to have had a religious awakening and banned all talk of "casual sex and hooking up" on his eponymous forum, withdrawing some of his books from sale and claiming, "I've realized that the majority of my published materials and online platforms lead men into sin or enable them to partake in sin." In fact, just like Blanc, Valizadeh continues to earn handsomely from the speaking circuit, with twenty-three events across U.S. cities in 2019, at which he expounded on "what I've learned about life" and offered acolytes the opportunity to have dinner with him for just $250.

In 2000, a new, anniversary edition of *How to Pick Up Girls!* was triumphantly released, the reference to rape quietly removed, and nine perfunctory lines on consent shoehorned in at the beginning. And in 2016, a year after Strauss remorsefully told reporters that the techniques described in *The Game* were "objectifying and horrifying," his publishers released a new paperback edition, which presumably continues to provide him with handsome royalties.

There is apparently no justice or reckoning for PUAs; there is only the flimsy disguise of "reinvention" to enable continued profit.

It is ironic that the exact techniques these snake-oil salesmen use to recruit hapless wannabe Romeos are the same as those they train their disciples to use on women: pretend to be possessed of some magical, transformative secret so as to con and manipulate your target into doing exactly what you want.

And PUAs are very successful at conning and manipulating—so much so, in fact, that they have, for years, been the most acceptable face of the manosphere. In this post-#MeToo era, we like to think that we have moved forward, that we no longer tolerate the mistreatment of women. But the trickle down is slow. In reality, the attitude that saw millions of male readers, fifty years ago, eager to learn about their "right" to approach a woman any time they want has barely shifted in the subsequent half century, as the booming pickup industry demonstrates. PUAs take misogynistic ideas and repackage them for sanitized public consumption. They are proof of just how quickly the ideas of the darkest and most obscure corners of the manosphere can pop up on our television screens or besiege us on the street.

# 3

# Men Who Avoid Women

*"I have never concealed my intense dislike*
*for this devolved creature, the 'woman.'"*

**COMMENT ON A MGTOW FORUM**

"THERE HAS BEEN AN AWAKENING. CHANGING THE
WORLD. ONE MAN AT A TIME." These are the dramatic
words that appear on the screen when you visit the homepage of
MGTOW.com, one of the largest MGTOW communities on the
internet. Looking something like an action movie trailer, the words
are soon followed by five more that appear to smash through the
screen, smoldering fiery red:

## MEN. GOING. THEIR. OWN. WAY.

Though MGTOW (pronounced "mig-tau" by adherents)
begins with the same "red pill" philosophy as other manosphere
groups, its proposed solution to the supposed gynocratic conspiracy and biased sexual marketplace is dramatically different from
other communities. While incels plot violent revenge and PUAs
deploy predatory "gaming" tactics, Men Going Their Own Way

choose to eschew relationships with women altogether. They are, literally, going their own way. Far, far away from any women. At all.

This manifests itself in various ways—some maintain platonic, but not romantic, relationships with women; some have one-night stands or visit sex workers; others prefer to abstain from sex altogether, a process referred to as "going monk"—but the general thrust of the movement is one of isolationism. For some, this extends to societal excommunication too: one MGTOW "manifesto" proclaims that as well as fighting to "instill masculinity in men," it is incumbent upon MGTOW to "work toward limited government." (In MGTOW circles, the concept of "limited government" seems to mean that men should be able to control their own lives and property, free from the interference of a government perceived as feminized and gynocentric or obsessed with women's needs and concerns.)

This self-imposed exile, in some respects, renders MGTOW less of an immediate threat to women than incels or PUAs. Unlike other manosphere communities, the majority of their energy is focused inward rather than outward. Obsessed with abstention from sex and relationships, they are more likely to cause hurt and harm to themselves than to the women around them. This doesn't mean that the MGTOW ideology is harmless, however; it underpins a wider notion of women as irreversibly toxic and dangerous, which we will later see has a real negative impact on women's lives and careers.

Unlike PUAs, MGTOW live out their philosophy individually in the real world and are unlikely to meet in person, instead sharing their techniques, successes, and failures in a large online community. Throughout the manosphere, it is common to see members expressing paranoia about normies who could be out to expose them, often leading to various forum users pointing the finger, accusing one another of being moles or spies. Nowhere is this fear more prevalent than in MGTOW communities, with any suggestion of meeting in real life usually receiving a swift and scornful rebuke.

A popularly repeated doctrine across MGTOW websites states that there are four essential "levels of MGTOW," starting from the base level zero, which represents taking the red pill. (Men who have not yet opened their eyes to the manosphere are described as "blue pilled.") Level one is summarized as a rejection of long-term relationships, and level two means avoiding even short-term relationships. Level three requires economic disengagement (reducing taxation as far as possible in order to avoid paying toward the support of other groups, from "elite alphas" to "single mothers"). Level four is described as "social rejection." As one MGTOW blogger, calling himself "The Observer Watches," summarizes this level:

> The MGTOW drops out of society altogether. He minimizes contact with the blue-pill world and seeks to further his own ends on his own terms. For all intents and purposes, he does not exist. A urbanite might keep to his own apartment, while someone further out may simply head into the wilderness and go off-grid.

Those who achieve this ultimate isolation are known as "ghosts" and treated as legends within the community. But they appear to be in a minority, and most MGTOW seem happy hovering somewhere around level two. The majority of MGTOW discussions online tend to center more on classic manosphere complaints, like the various evils of women and "misandry" (hatred of men).

Most of all, they discuss the dangers inherent in interacting with women—dangers apparently so great that the only possible means of self-preservation is total isolation.

"There is a lot of risk," said eighteen-year-old David Sherratt, a Cardiff University student and then-dedicated member of the MGTOW community, when asked to explain in 2015 what made him eschew the company of women. "We do not know how many false accusations there are. They could be the majority or they could be the minority."[1] The implication of this is twofold: the only meaningful relationship with a woman must be a sexual one, and there are so many women ready to lie about rape that any contact with them is simply too dangerous to risk.

What does it take for a young man, a teenager, to become so convinced that women are lying vipers that he would decide to completely cut them out of his life? It is a good indicator of just how powerful and persuasive these communities can be, even one, like MGTOW, that might attract sniggering derision from outsiders.

The (completely untrue) notion about false rape accusations that Sherratt mentioned is a central concern of MGTOW, identifying them more closely with another community, Men's Rights Activists (MRAs), than with incels or PUAs. Both MGTOW and MRAs envisage a world in which women pose an immediate threat to all men. MRAs believe that women are so unfaithful and untruthful that they often force men to raise other men's children, thus financially "cuckolding" them. MGTOW believe that women are extremely likely to make false accusations of sexual or domestic violence in order to damage men socially, steal their money, or even vindictively attempt to have them jailed. Of course, MGTOW celebrate avoiding women, while MRAs doggedly battle them; MGTOW revel in abstaining from sex, while incels and PUAs either mourn or pursue it obsessively at all costs. Nonetheless, there remains a wide range of common ideas and tactics underpinning these online manosphere communities. Just like incels and PUAs, men who choose to go their own way only do so on the basis of a foundational belief that all women are the same.

Sherratt went on to cite a checklist of manosphere concerns that would resonate particularly closely with MRAs but could also crop up across any misogynistic online community, including "Men are supposed to pay for dates and bow down to women... anything less than worship is hate" and "When it comes to marriage, the system is so stacked against men, it does not make sense." MGTOW and MRAs alike are particularly concerned with divorce, which they see as a deeply one-sided process, allowing women to rob innocent men of money, property, and, in some cases, children.

The MGTOW philosophy is elaborately and bombastically laid out on the MGTOW.com website, which summarizes it as "a statement of self-ownership, where the modern man preserves and protects his own sovereignty above all else." Drawing on snippets of quotes and newspaper clippings, the site claims that MGTOW dates back to great men, including Schopenhauer, Beethoven, Galileo, and "even Jesus Christ." (Suggesting that the son of God was primarily preoccupied with avoiding sexually deviant women seems like a bit of a stretch, particularly given his close friendship with Mary Magdalene, but that's an argument for another day.) The list of supposed MGTOW luminaries then veers from classical figures, like Chopin, Flaubert, and Proust, to Leonardo DiCaprio, whose name is followed by a tentative question mark, perhaps because of the actor's string of well-documented celebrity romances.

Women are essentially portrayed as parasites, simply riding on the coattails of men, who have, throughout history, been responsible for "far greater miracles of science, discovery and human endeavor." By shaking women off, it is explained, men will be free to pursue ever higher achievements.

Think women might have been affected by historic discrimination that barred them from those fields in the first place? Wrong. According to MGTOW philosophy, the truth is that women have simply never contributed much of real value to society and ought to be grateful for any scraps that superior men deign to throw, instead of having the cheek to demand equality.

MGTOW websites are, of course, keen to stress their historical pedigree as a means of bolstering the respectability of their movement. To an extent, they have a point: the movement does have a little in common, for example, with the mythopoetic men's movement, a fairly loose collection of self-help activities, spearheaded by various authors and organizations, particularly in the United States in the 1980s and '90s.

Closely associated with the poet Robert Bly, whose book *Iron John: A Book About Men* was published in 1990 and spent sixty-two weeks on the *New York Times* bestseller list, the general tenet of that movement was that men had lost their connection to one another and to the "deep masculine," so they needed to be supported psychologically and spiritually to reclaim their connection to their masculinity.

There were some elements of overlap with the modern MGTOW movement: advocates claimed that time spent at home and in intimate relationships with women had somehow eroded their connection to their innate masculinity and that all-male gatherings and rituals were key to restoring this. But the movement was not nearly as vitriolic, or as explicitly antifeminist, as the modern MGTOW community.

So where does the idea of avoiding women altogether come in? As well as the fear of false rape allegations, the MGTOW community is motivated by another concern: the risk that their male genius could be compromised by contamination with feminine mediocrity.

If you're unconvinced by this, you will surely be won over by the handful of past inventors and entrepreneurs—all great achievers, none of them ever married—who are offered up as proof positive that entering into a relationship with a woman is like chaining yourself voluntarily to a money-sucking, brain-cell-sapping leech. As MGTOW.com triumphantly concludes, "When a cost/benefit analysis reveals there is no benefit, it doesn't take a genius to remove himself from the equation." Well, they're right about one thing.

It is clear this philosophy has been welcomed with open arms by men already predisposed to misogynistic tendencies, who seem to appreciate the opportunity to validate their bias within a grandiose ideological framework.

In the testimonials section, a user wrote, "Thank you MGTOW for teaching me young and preventing me from the lies women and marriage bring. I can now live in peace."

"I have never concealed my intense dislike for this devolved creature, the 'woman,'" wrote another. "I love this! I feel like I found the secret to the universe," said a different user. Yet another wrote that his city has become so "ultra feminized" that "things are... mind-blowingly bad for men here, especially straight white men." Luckily for him, "the MGTOW community has made me feel like I'm not alone in this PC madness."

The MGTOW.com forums are extremely busy and teem with the same extreme misogyny common on incel websites, though the tone here tends to be more upbeat as men congratulate themselves and one another on escaping the claws of greedy, dangerous women, instead of commiserating over their failure to make sexual contact.

One user summed up the general philosophy when he wrote,

> Women are out of control and have been for a very long time. It's going to take a serious event to get them to behave like decent adults. Men aren't men anymore and have allowed women to walk all over them. So, as for the rest of us, we have no choice but to do what we're doing now and just go our own way.

The general vitriol aimed at feminism, or any kind of mainstream gender equality advocacy, remains the same. (Comments on a story about a woman who reported rape, for example, include "no one would rape that disgusting fugly cunt.")

Another website is focused on "helping" men who want to divorce. Modern marriage, it declares, is a form of "legalized slavery."

It is common to come across men on MGTOW forums sharing extreme and vitriolic descriptions of failed relationships with women, often bitterly denouncing ex-partners who have cheated on them or chosen to leave a marriage or relationship. From these individual examples, the movement encourages men to extrapolate a sweeping set of stereotypical assumptions about women, holding up one man's bad experience as proof of all women's wickedness and malice—a technique that, as we will see in the next chapter, is also copiously used by MRAs.

Of course, within such a framework, these men are influenced to conclude that the breakdowns of their relationships were entirely due to malicious women, thereby avoiding any introspection or responsibility and enabling them to perceive themselves as blame-less victims. It is easy to see what an attractive environment this is for an embittered, recently separated man, licking his wounds and looking for validation. Once again, a sense of belonging to a com-munity that understands and supports the true victim, set against the hostility of wider, bigoted society, is a powerful radicalizing cocktail.

I couldn't stop thinking about Sherratt, the teenager who so confidently expounded his core MGTOW beliefs in 2015, so I man-aged to track him down to ask him about his experience of becom-ing involved in the community. Now twenty-two, Sherratt is an engineering apprentice and says he has left the MGTOW commu-nity, as well as other manosphere groups, behind. Communicating via email, he explained the factors that helped to draw him into originally considering himself a man "going his own way." At first, he explained, being part of manosphere communities was "legiti-mately fun":

> I had lots of friends, which was new to me, lots of fans and
> positive reinforcement and, as we started to grow and build,
> it honestly felt like we were eventually going to start making
> some positive change. It wasn't just a community, but a new,
> growing movement that I got into "before it was cool," so, in
> a way, I felt like I was part of something progressive.

In Sherratt's description, the communities so often viewed from the outside as deeply dark, extreme, and violent are seen from the perspective of a teenage boy discovering an edgy and provocative group of rebels. It had never occurred to me to associate the word *fun* with the manosphere. Clearly present in Sherratt's account are other factors often cited by academics who study the attraction of extremist beliefs and communities: a sense of common purpose and belonging; of friendship, recognition, and encouragement; and of being part of something bigger that feels like an important or noble cause.

It is generally accepted within the MGTOW community that the movement was started in the mid-2000s by two men going by the pseudonyms "Solaris" (an Australian) and "Ragnar" (a Scandinavian, who described himself as "an old guy" and a former pilot), both of whom had been previously active in what they described as the "online men's movement." In a 2012 YouTube interview, claiming to be with the two founders, Solaris said, "A sense of alienation is where this whole thing starts... You realize, simply because you're a man, that you are considered a legitimate target for being the butt of jokes or being considered a class enemy." Originally, the founders explained, men with these grievances coalesced around a forum called Nice Guy, of which Solaris was a moderator, but more recently, other websites, blogs, and YouTube channels have seen the MGTOW concept explode in popularity.

Perhaps to an even greater extent than with incels, the vast majority of people have never heard of MGTOW, and a common assumption when it does come up is that it must be an extremely small fringe group. But just like other manosphere groups, the community is far larger and more active than one might imagine. The "MGTOW" subreddit boasts over 100,000 subscribers, with 1,500 online at the moment I visited in March 2019. (In 2016, it was reported to have 15,000, giving some idea of the movement's rate of growth and increasing popularity.) The MGTOW.com website has almost 33,000 members. Its forums ("for men only") contain conversations on over 50,000 different topics with over 750,000 replies, which range from advice on divorcing as cheaply

as possible to lurid stories about women who have found particularly inventive ways to murder their husbands. The site also lists
twenty-five video channels producing MGTOW content; between
them, these channels have over 730,000 followers, and the videos
have been viewed a total of 130 million times. It's a good example of
how much greater the audience on any given manosphere website
can be than its actual membership numbers might suggest. Another
popular MGTOW forum has 129,000 posts and up to 4,600 users
active on the site during busy periods. A single MGTOW Facebook
group has over 35,000 followers.

And though it is an even more obscure community, there is
one area, in particular, in which the online footprint of MGTOW
far exceeds that of incels. Members of the MGTOW community
are especially active vloggers (video bloggers). A Google video
search for "MGTOW" yields almost two million results, compared to a quarter of a million for "incels." On YouTube, one of
the best-known MGTOW vloggers styles himself "Turd Flinging
Monkey." His videos, on topics including misandry, loneliness,
and the "invasion of the femcels," boast over thirty-seven million
views. Typical comments on his videos include "I'm trying not to
hate women, but it's getting harder and harder" and "Further proof
that society not only neglects, but outright despises men." Another
major MGTOW vlogger, going by the pseudonym "Sandman," has
over sixty-seven million views, and YouTuber Howard Dare has
70,000 regular subscribers. His videos—such as "Top Ten Types
of Women to Avoid," "Why Good Men Choose to Remain Single,"
and "Five Lies That Women Tell"—have been viewed over twelve
million times, with over a quarter of a million views alone for one
titled "Treating Women Badly and Why It's Important." "Thinking
Ape," another MGTOW vlogger, has over six million views. These

are just a few of the most prominent names within a massive community of YouTubers vlogging on the topic of MGTOW.

Moreover, the community's output does not consist solely of philosophy and opinion; it is mixed in with a heavy dose of often deeply misogynistic advice, like this from the FAQs section of a MGTOW website:

> *My girlfriend is pregnant. What do I do?*
> Whatever you do, do NOT invite her into the hot tub with champagne to "celebrate." This can cause a miscarriage and she could lose the baby! Repeat: You should not under any circumstances do that...as quickly as possible.

Just as with the incel community, it is impossible to know how seriously or sarcastically a comment like this is meant. Perhaps more worryingly still, whether the original writer intended simply to shock or entertain, it is impossible to know how it might have been interpreted by the person to whom it was addressed.

The content is extreme. But this isn't a tiny, obscure internet cul-de-sac. It is a flourishing and highly active community.

Like most incel sites, the MGTOW community differs from some other areas of the manosphere in its decision to actively police its online spaces to exclude women. "MGTOW.com is exclusively a men's interest website—*for men only*," emphasizes the website. Of course, MGTOW philosophy gifts this community a particularly powerful rationale for the exclusion of women. As one typical site puts it, "The internet was...created by men (for other men), and it is only by our divine manly grace that women are permitted to use it." Tell that to Ada Lovelace and Grace Hopper.

MGTOW ideology has also spawned a number of spin-off and related online movements, including IBMOR (Introspective Black Men of Reform), an online movement with extremely similar aims but the additional desire to overthrow white supremacy.

"INTROSPECTIVE BLACK MEN OF REFORM (IBMOR)," declares the community page for the group in dramatic capital letters, "ARE BLACK MEN WHO ARE DEDICATED TO SELF-STUDY AND SELF IMPROVEMENT. WE DESIRE THE EVENTUAL REMOVAL OF BOTH WHITE SUPREMACY AND BLACK MATRIARCHY IN THE BLACK COMMUNITY. WE BELIEVE IN THE NECESSITY OF A BLACK PATRIARCHY." The site lists the official tenets of the movement, such as: "We believe in Heterosexual Black MAN Leadership. We understand that Females are only here for Sex and Reproduction. Females should NEVER be given authority in society over Men in any way. Men should NEVER cater to women in any way."

And if you thought it might be possible to enter into a debate about this somewhat extreme view, you would be sorely mistaken:

> We do not believe in arguing with females. Women "feel" the world. They don't "think" the world. So you cannot change a female's mind by way of entreaties or logical argumentation. The only action that will change a female's mind is Force. Denying a woman your attention is the most effective way to deal with females in the current gynocentric system of Caucasian supremacy.

By upholding the misogynistic assumptions of MGTOW but simultaneously opposing white supremacy, IBMOR create a curious and often inadvertently humorous conundrum for manosphere members. Conversations between MGTOW and IBMOR followers reveal the confusion that ensues when members of the deeply sexist, but also frequently racist, MGTOW community attempt to reconcile their support for half of IBMOR philosophy with their resistance to the other half.

"You really do sound like a typical, frustrated black male," wrote one man, attempting to navigate this dilemma, not realizing that his own arguments against the IBMOR community on the question of race might just as easily be leveled at his own group's treatment of gender. "This is why Black communities aren't taken seriously. Every speech becomes an 'Us vs Them' mentality. I'm not saying your argument against feminism is wrong, I just don't appreciate the 'it's fuckin' white people's fault!' vibe." The is clearly lost on him.

Within the IBMOR community itself, there are similar contradictions. While it recognizes and opposes inequality on the grounds of race, it also, like much of the rest of the manosphere, explicitly promotes other forms of bigotry and prejudice, with the website stating, for example, "We believe that Homosexuality and lesbianism, represent the death of people because no children are produced out of such unions and Bisexuality causes instability in society."

However, supporting experts' belief that the manosphere is a mainly white space, the IBMOR subgroup is much smaller than the MGTOW community at large, with most of its pages or online groups numbering in the hundreds, rather than the thousands. Though some IBMOR YouTube channels boast tens of thousands of followers and millions of views, these remain much smaller than the vast followings of the more mainstream MGTOW vloggers.

Again, like many other areas of the manosphere, it is difficult to pinpoint the location of most users of MGTOW forums and communities, though the majority communicate in English, and some reference their whereabouts in their comments or usernames, generally suggesting that the United States, Canada, and the UK are common locations. But there is no hard-and-fast data to tell us the exact number of active MGTOW community members resident in the UK. One forum participant uploaded a post titled "Hello from the UK," which drew enthusiastic replies from "fellow Brits" who claimed to be writing from various areas of the country, including the Midlands, Sussex, and Salford. They reveled in their shared ideology as much as their shared location, heartily agreeing with the participant's opening salvo: "fucking women, they are all snakes with t**s."

There is also a fairly regularly updated website specifically devoted to "British MGTOW," which rails against what it describes as the "Nazi-like behavior" of the British state in silencing and censoring non-PC views:

> If you say the wrong thing or believe against the norm, you are a danger... The UK is sick and it needs healing. The laws are in desperate need of a revamp but all I see around me are docile willing men led to the slaughter... go your own way and protect yourself.

But what MGTOW has in common with the majority of the other groups that make up the manosphere, perhaps best exemplified by MGTOW itself, is the special quality of being a group supposedly exclusively devoted to men whose near-total focus is women. In the case of MGTOW, this fundamental dichotomy builds inevitable self-destruction into the very core of the movement. It is, one imagines, very difficult for a man to release himself completely from the toxic and damaging impact of women and all they represent—blissfully freeing himself to live a life of simple, manly fulfillment—while remaining entangled within a community feverishly obsessed with, well, women.

This was even apparent to the teenage Sherratt, who told me, "I understood the skepticism of marriage and stuff, but, for men who were talking about trying to live lives that didn't center around women, they were talking about them an awful lot." When Sherratt tried to voice his disagreements with various elements of MGTOW ideology, he found himself accused of being "mind-controlled by a girl." Soon afterward, he left the community, having met a girl who (rather unsurprisingly) shared his criticisms. "So I guess the joke's on them," he mused.

In spite of all they have in common, many other manosphere communities are deeply scornful of MGTOW. Matt Forney, an infamous manosphere blogger, whose writing tends to straddle the divide between MRAs and PUAs, wrote that "men going their own way" is "no way for men to go," mockingly describing MGTOW as "a cult for lonely virgins" and claiming that it risks emasculating men by failing to acknowledge the defining masculine need for heterosexual relationships and sex. Forney claims that MGTOW was his original entry point "into antifeminist thought in general" but that he has since become deeply critical of the movement—an admission that gives an insight into the ways in which men might be drawn into the manosphere through one channel and then quickly progress through its different communities, settling their allegiance in other areas. Or, in many cases, going on to find a home in the ideology of the alt-right—a trajectory mirrored by the suffusion of manosphere terms and acronyms into the blogs and websites of white nationalists and other alt-right communities.

It isn't only within the manosphere that men who choose to go their own way are dismissed and ridiculed. Jacob Davey expressed concern that sensationalist and surface-level reporting about groups like MGTOW might prevent us from engaging with the real and serious issues underlying such communities.

I'd say there's a lack of nuanced understanding... I don't think there's necessarily been particularly responsible reporting around this—in my experience, a lot of the media interest has come from the fact that it's quite novel, quite unusual, it's seen as a story, first and foremost—and actually the questions you get as a researcher are: "Why do people believe this weird ideology?"

The writing-off of MGTOW as a weird group of goofy men is particularly easy, partly because of societal stereotypes that automatically mock the idea of men being "afraid" of women. But just as with other manosphere communities, the common assumption that this is a small group of online outliers with no offline or societal impact is extremely short-sighted. In fact, it is possible to argue that the MGTOW philosophy has had by far its biggest and most significant boost in support and membership over the past few years. MGTOW has, in some ways, successfully penetrated mainstream culture to a greater degree than any other manosphere community, even if its name hasn't been directly attached to much of the coverage of this phenomenon.

In the immediate wake of the #MeToo movement, which saw millions of women worldwide standing up to sexual harassment and assault by sharing their own stories, there was a swift and severe backlash. First, claims emerged that the women's testimonies were invented or exaggerated and that those speaking out against public figures were greedy gold diggers looking for five minutes of fame. There were accusations that the problem was being vastly hyperbolized by a feminist mob. These arguments, which exploded in the public sphere, were, of course, echoed and supported at a deeper level across manosphere forums and communities, where outrage was directed at the supposedly "cucked" liberal media for promoting the #MeToo lies and misandry of the controlling feminazi elite.

The backlash quickly intensified, criticism of individual women broadening into a wider rumbling that the whole movement was a pitchfork mob: a "witch hunt" designed to topple men from their jobs and lives without so much as an attempt at due process. Some commentators settled for writing vitriolic screeds, hounding women who had dared to share their stories of abuse, or denigrating the movement as a whole. But gradually another type of response emerged, deliberately calculated to play on the manosphere technique of turning the perpetrator into the victim. It was a response that spread like wildfire from the internet to the offline world, and it borrowed its essential ideology directly from MGTOW: *avoid women at all costs.*

It started with rumors: women reporting that men in their offices had suddenly started declining meetings with them or insisted on leaving the doors open. A human resources consultant reported executives telling her that they would no longer get into an elevator alone with a woman.[2] Suddenly, it began to snowball—story after story of men in different professions abruptly canceling business lunches or avoiding women they had previously mentored. The technique was MGTOW. Cut off from valuable contacts, denied important face-to-face meetings, the impact on women's careers was potentially disastrous. In exactly the same way that the

MGTOW movement turns the structural oppression of women on its head, claiming men are the true victims of gender bias, so, too, this spate of mainstream examples sought to cast men as the real victims of the #MeToo movement. Men, it argued, had little choice but to protect themselves from the all-powerful cabal of rampaging, vindictive women making up false accusations of harassment or abuse. Even if the solution is as extreme as total isolation.

An orthopedic surgeon in Chicago told the *New York Times* that he had ceased ever to be alone with female colleagues, saying, "I'm very cautious about it because my livelihood is on the line... If someone in your hospital says you had inappropriate contact with this woman, you get suspended for an investigation, and your life is over. Does that ever leave you?" His apparent implication that such accusations are simply random, based on no wrongdoing whatsoever, went unchallenged in the piece.[3]

In Austin, Texas, an events manager stopped having regular meetings with a communications consultant, saying, "I've been told it is not appropriate for a married man to have lunch with a single lady." He considered moving both her and another woman to different jobs in order to avoid any appearance of inappropriate "interactions," despite the fact that the woman in question bluntly informed him that "she was not interested in him romantically and only sought to have lunches with him for mentoring purposes."[4] You can only begin to imagine the scale of the eye roll.

At the 2019 meeting of the World Economic Forum in Davos, attendees told journalists that they were no longer mentoring women, as a direct result of the #MeToo era. By which, of course, they meant as a direct result of a deeply misogynistic and deliberate misinterpretation of the #MeToo movement. "I now think twice about spending one-on-one time with a young female colleague," an American finance executive said.[5] The issue, apparently, was just "too sensitive."

Not one of these men seems to have considered that they could have achieved the same effect by simply not sexually harassing or assaulting any women.

While such cases were shamefully portrayed across the media as anxious, even understandable precautions, taken by worried men in a hostile climate, it is nonsense to suggest that any nonabusing man need avoid the women in his workplace. There is no way to support such a stance that doesn't heavily imply an epidemic of false accusations. Because if women aren't making false accusations, then the obvious response to a spate of testimonies of sexual violence is simply to avoid committing sexual violence. Not to treat the women who do report it like they carry some kind of contagious, flesh-eating disease.

It is striking to realize that this core manosphere ideology, vaunted by tens of thousands of internet devotees, has even penetrated as far as the heady heights of the White House. Former Vice President Mike Pence told reporters that he will never eat a meal alone with a woman who is not his wife—a practice that female politicians, like his successor, Vice President Kamala Harris, have pointed out could have a massive detrimental impact on women's career trajectories in a fast-moving political world in which meetings over meals are common.

Pence's stance is a highly effective example of the many ways in which manosphere philosophy finds itself dressed up in a veneer of respectability and reasonable debate, pushed gently into the mainstream. We don't know whether Pence's habit arises from concerns about sexual harassment allegations or from a particularly conservative or religious outlook. It isn't unreasonable to suggest that the two are likely intertwined, given Christian gender and sexual doctrines. (The so-called Pence rule, as it has become known, is named after the Billy Graham rule—a similar stance adopted by Christian preacher Billy Graham, who refused to eat or meet alone with a woman other than his wife.) The trouble is it doesn't really matter. While Pence might not have explicitly echoed the MGTOW community's rabid obsession with rife false rape allegations, that is precisely the implication of his refusal to dine alone with women that was seized upon by men and media outlets alike in the wake of #MeToo—an interpretation Pence himself took no action to moderate or correct.

The impact of such a high-profile person adopting such a rule cannot be underestimated, and the sense of acceptability it confers quickly became apparent in media headlines. "Wall Street Goes Full Mike Pence to Avoid #MeToo Accusations," said *Vanity Fair*.[6] "Wall Street Rule for the #MeToo Era: Avoid Women at All Cost," cried *Bloomberg*, quoting a wealth adviser who claimed that "just hiring a woman these days is 'an unknown risk.' What if she took something he said the wrong way?"[7] The problem with this conspicuous support and subsequent mass-media coverage of manosphere ideology is that it legitimizes, and even sympathizes with, what is actually extreme misogyny.

Before it could be catchily dubbed the Pence rule, reporting on such ideas might have been seen as inflammatory or biased, requiring careful and robust presentation of opposing arguments. But as soon as the idea was attached to the U.S. vice president, it became untouchable—valid and respectable fodder for widespread coverage. Then other pundits weighed in, and far from a contested fringe idea, the "rule" became accepted as a mainstay of the public conversation, treated by some as simply good common sense. It became part of the dialogue and, as such, was quickly used by men to further pursue a sexist agenda. "THINK," tweeted Sebastian Gorka, former deputy assistant to Donald Trump. "If Weinstein had obeyed @VP Pence's rules for meeting with the opposite sex, none of those poor women would ever have been abused." Of course, if Weinstein hadn't been an abusive predator, the same outcome could have been achieved too. Just a thought.

Indeed, far from isolated examples, the mainstream discussion of the Pence rule as a reasonable precaution for men to take in an age of harassment allegations is reflected in the workplace behavior of a startlingly high percentage of men. According to a study carried out by researchers at the University of Houston in 2019, 27 percent of men avoid one-on-one meetings with female colleagues, and 21 percent are reluctant to hire women for jobs involving close inter-personal interactions with men (such as jobs involving travel). As writer and feminist activist Soraya Chemaly highlighted, this means that over a quarter of American men are committing workplace discrimination and violating Title VII of the Civil Rights Act, which bars differential treatment of people in the workplace on the basis, in this case, of sex. This illegality, Chemaly pointed out, was rarely mentioned in media reports "debating" the validity of the Pence rule, and moreover, "sex segregation and exclusion aren't legitimate responses to women's demands that we no longer, as a society, tol-erate sexual discrimination in the workplace."[8]

So the core belief of MGTOW, perhaps considered one of the most bizarre factions of the manosphere, is, in fact, being practiced to the detriment of women across American workplaces today. An extreme and misogynistic element of manosphere ideology is not only part of our international conversation, it is subtly making sexist assumptions more acceptable as well.

Lest we fear that the idea might not catch on more widely, a book has quickly been published to help spread the word. The book description on Amazon for *The Pence Principle*, by Randall Bentwick, boldly states that "every man in America could stand to learn a lesson or two from our Vice President. Be smart. Buy this handbook and learn to practice 'The Pence Principle.' Defend yourself, your career, your family, and your life from the false accusations of women today and into the future."

This did not go unnoticed by the MGTOW community online, whose celebrations were evident in gloating Reddit threads ("Why Feminists Fear the Mike Pence Rule") and YouTube videos ("We invented the Pence Rule"). It is direct evidence that the ideas we might think of as the shadowy, ridiculous concerns of the extreme internet fringes are actually being waved under our very noses from the White House front lawn.

# 4
# Men Who Blame Women

"As far as the state is concerned, males are pretty much subhuman, and they'll do anything they can to destroy men's lives."

**MIKE BUCHANAN, LEADER OF THE BRITISH POLITICAL PARTY JUSTICE FOR MEN AND BOYS (AND THE WOMEN WHO LOVE THEM)**

So-called Men's Rights Activists (MRAs) might more accurately be described as Women's Wrongs Activists. The name suggests something noble and important: a focus on the many issues affecting men today. The reality is very different. MRAs are about as focused on men's rights as defense contractors are invested in maintaining peace. There *is* a community of men's organizations focused on tackling issues like mental health, masculine stereotypes, and relationship violence. But this isn't it. Instead, MRAs are concerned, to the point of obsession, with attacking women. And their particular target is feminism.

Not only do MRAs do vanishingly little to tackle the many very real issues affecting men today, what's worse is that their efforts actually impede progress for many male victims. The efforts of men's rights groups to cling to outdated gender stereotypes and their crusade against the women trying to address those same stereotypes often mean that they themselves contribute to precisely the problems they claim to want to solve.

But for those not intimately familiar with the world of MRAs, their cause has a veneer of validity and respectability. Tackling issues affecting men, particularly when things like fathers' rights, cancer, and workplace fatalities are vaguely alluded to, sounds like a positive and important movement. Hence, MRAs are often able to slip through the net of public detection, their representatives finding fertile ground in news programs concerned with providing "balance." The gap between the community's purported aims and its actual activities enables it to act as something of a conduit, smuggling some of the misogynistic ideas of the wider manosphere into the public eye behind a false shield of credibility.

These are groups of men who share much common territory with other elements of the manosphere (sweeping, misogynistic generalizations about women; the assumption that a feminist conspiracy has created a world stacked against men; the idea that men are the true victims of inequality and abuse). To quote a typical summary of the movement from one men's rights blog, "From a feminist perspective 'gender equality' has come to mean female domination, and male subjugation. It has lead [sic] to a reversal of discrimination, where once women were marginalized, and disparaged men have now taken their place." Unlike other manosphere groups, however, rather than focus on individual sexual gratification or flee from interaction with women entirely, MRAs prefer to fight back. In the words of another men's rights website (Dads Against the Divorce Industry), they are battling "growing trends that impose a frightening number of legal and social sanctions against masculinity per se."

In a 1926 article in *Harper's* monthly magazine, writer John Macy complained that "the perversion of misandry...distorts the more querulous of modern feminist arguments." (By a curious twist of fate, Macy was married to Anne Sullivan, famous as the teacher and companion of Helen Keller, who, alongside her advocacy for people with disabilities, was a staunch feminist.) In the same year, the Austrian Federation for Men's Rights was founded, with the goal of combating "all the monstrosities that have come from the emancipation of woman."[1] Clearly, the central idea that fighting to give women rights must mean taking something away from men is hardly new.

But the sad irony is that the men's rights movement (MRM), as we know it today, grew from an initiative that began as a force for positive change and as a complementary effort to women's liberation. As a powerful new second wave of feminism gained momentum in the late 1960s and early '70s, it gave rise to a "men's liberation movement." Men's liberation actively supported feminist principles. It sought to deconstruct the harmful ways in which societally imposed masculinity both harmed men and led to women's oppression.

In the 1970 issue of the New Left journal *Liberation*, a young psychologist named Jack Sawyer published an article titled "On Male Liberation." He wrote passionately that

> male liberation seeks to aid in destroying the sex role stereotypes that regard "being a man" and "being a woman" as statuses that must be achieved through proper behavior... the battle of women to be free need not be a battle against men as oppressors. The choice about whether men are the enemy is up to men themselves.

Working along these lines, male consciousness-raising groups began meeting, particularly across the United States and in Britain. These groups gave men the opportunity to share their experiences and feelings and to explore the ways in which they might become part of the solution. Interviewed in *Life* magazine in 1971, a member of one such group explained, "Our enemy isn't women—it's the role we are forced to play." It's enough to make you want to cheer. And it is sobering to realize how novel these concepts still sound today.

Groups, resources, and men's centers began to spring up, with the Berkeley Men's Center releasing a manifesto in 1973 that reflected the ethos of the wider project:

> We no longer want to strain and compete to live up to an impossible oppressive masculine image... We want to be equal with women and end destructive competitive relationships between men... We are oppressed by conditioning which makes us only half-human... We want men to share their lives and experiences with each other, in order to understand who we are, how we got this way, and what we must do to be free.

The movement gained steam, with a slew of books, including Marc Feigen Fasteau's *The Male Machine* and Jack Nichols's *Men's Liberation*, adding a more theoretical framework in the mid-1970s.

So there began, as far back as the 1970s, a genuine movement— led by and concerned with men—that was able to tackle the problems men faced without demonizing and attacking women in the process. It was, in other words, a male feminist movement. But there was a devastating schism to come.

In the late 1960s, a doctoral student named Warren Farrell

was fast becoming a rising star of the men's liberation movement. Increasingly involved in feminist circles, Farrell joined the board of the New York City chapter of the National Organization for Women and was tasked with setting up a nationwide network of men's consciousness groups. Famed for his "role-reversal workshops," Farrell prodded groups of men to parade onstage in male beauty pageants, encouraging women in the audience to heckle and objectify them, with the purpose of forcing men to recognize the sensation of being treated as a piece of meat. In a similarly heavy-handed attempt to convey the pressures facing male breadwinners, Farrell lined up women according to their salaries, shouting at those at the lower end of the economic spectrum for being "losers." Farrell was widely lauded: he was profiled in a four-page spread in *People* magazine, featuring photographs of him cooking breakfast for his wife, in which he waxed lyrical about "learning how to listen rather than dominate...to be vulnerable rather than construct facades of infallibility." The *Financial Times* also named him one of its "top 100 thought leaders." "I was like a God to many women," Farrell later told one journalist, a sentiment that should perhaps have raised something of a red flag.[2]

But Farrell started to become concerned with the ways in which he perceived men to be systemically disadvantaged, and in the mid-1970s when the National Organization for Women staked its position against the presumption of joint child custody in divorce cases, he split from the organization. Farrell's personal journey was representative of a much greater tear in the fabric of the men's liberation movement, and by the late 1970s, it had ripped completely in two. One side, epitomized by groups like the National Organization for Changing Men (now the National Organization for Men Against Sexism), held steady to the course of profeminist, antisexist attempts to challenge men's roles within a patriarchal society, and this positive, constructive male-focused movement continues to exist quietly today. But a major separatist faction of antifeminist men's groups also emerged, encompassing organizations like the National Coalition of Free Men and the Men's Rights Association. Thus, the noisier, attention-grabbing MRM was born.

In 1973, sociologist Steven Goldberg wrote *The Inevitability of Patriarchy*, in which he argued, much like today's MRAs, that biology and human nature meant that the project of feminism was flawed and misguided, that male domination was natural, and that women's liberation would lead to dangerous cultural instability.

The National Coalition for Men (motto: "Freeing men from discrimination") was founded in 1977 and still boasts chapters or liaisons in Australia, Canada, Kenya, Israel, Sweden, and the Democratic Republic of Georgia. The organization has repeatedly entered lawsuits against women-only spaces—alleging discrimination on the part of sports teams, networking events, and groups seeking to increase women's participation in business and technology—and has often settled with the organizers for large sums of money. It has also filed court cases seeking to force the defunding of women's domestic violence shelters unless they admit men.

Over the years, other international organizations have sprung up, including the UK Men's Movement, the Save Indian Family Foundation, and a slew of organizations in Australia. Feminist academics have pointed out that the rise of the movement coincided with a period of significant social, political, and economic upheaval, as the post-1960s workforce became rapidly more diverse in both gender and ethnicity, and Thatcherism and Reaganomics caused seismic shifts in labor markets and union activity. Hence, the contemporary MRM has been defined, at least partly, as "a reaction to diminishing social status of cisgender white men, and the emergence of feminist and multicultural activism as a mainstream political force."[3]

The movement began opposing feminists and their efforts, arguing that men were the real oppressed gender, and focusing on issues it claimed revealed systemic antimale bias. In 1993, Farrell published *The Myth of Male Power*, a book that has become known as the "bible" of the MRM. In it, he raises issues such as the male suicide rate, the draft, male life expectancy, male-specific cancers, and other topics that have gone on to become mainstays of the MRM. But while these are, of course, very real issues (the UK suicide rate is three times higher for men than for women; male combat veterans continue to face poverty and mental trauma; male cancers are devastating for those affected), the movement distorted and exploited them, weaponizing them against women and feminist causes, instead of working to support the real victims affected by them.

In his book, Farrell tried to argue that women actually have greater economic capital than men because they are given money from their husbands' salaries to do the shopping. He suggested that women have only themselves to blame for unequal pay and that anti–sexual harassment protections simply make it unappealing for companies to hire women. In arguments that foreshadowed the incel and pickup communities as well as modern men's rights groups, Farrell claimed that women's "miniskirt power, cleavage power and flirtation power" gave them greater social advantages than men and suggested that women make fraudulent sexual harassment and rape claims, while "no one has taught men to sue women for sexual trauma for saying 'yes,' then 'no,' then 'yes.'" And he described the "murder, rape and spouse abuse" of women by men as "a minute's worth of superficial power to compensate for years of underlying powerlessness. They are manifestations of hopelessness committed by the powerless."[4]

In interviews, Farrell drew a direct comparison between male unemployment and the rape of women, suggesting that both lead to humiliation and the lowering of "self-concept," because, "when a man has unemployment forced upon him, he is humiliated...he feels violated, he feels imposed upon."[5]

As Farrell's ideas became foundational tenets of the nascent MRM, a sprouting crop of new organizations took up his battle cry, directing their fury and energy not against the patriarchy and its harmfully prescriptive version of manhood but against women and feminism instead. Farrell's book heavily criticized the American Violence Against Women Act (which significantly increased funding and legal redress for violent crimes against women), calling it unconstitutional and portraying it as sidelining and disadvantaging men. Men's rights groups subsequently went on to campaign to water down the act, calling for it to focus on victims of false accusations and to be rendered gender-neutral.

As the ideas of the MRM spread to the internet, a new network of websites, groups, and figureheads gave it fresh life, enabling it to reach a huge wave of new converts. Initial examples of internet men's rights discourse tended to coalesce on the early forum Usenet. A study into the use of language in the manosphere found evidence that the topic of "misandry" was frequently discussed on such message boards, as MRAs began online attempts to "discredit feminism," "make generalizations about feminists," and "create an equivalence between discrimination against men and discrimination against women, establishing both as equally valid." The authors of the study noted that both the original Usenet user base and the contemporary MRM were primarily composed of "white, educated, tech-savvy" men.[6]

The use of the term *misandry* and the online presence of MRAs went on to explode in the late '90s and early '00s as websites devoted specifically to the cause emerged. While hundreds of such sites now exist, perhaps the best-known and most influential is A Voice for Men (AVFM), founded in 2009 by truck driver Paul Elam, who claims to have been deeply affected by reading *The Myth of Male Power* and became a friend and protégé of Farrell.[7] The website's content and Elam's personal output are fairly good examples of the wider MRM, combining misogyny and violent rhetoric toward women and feminism with coverage of issues genuinely impacting men alongside inflammatory and misleading statements.

Elam has falsely claimed that "women are growing increasingly violent. They are matching men in domestic violence, blow for blow, and they are causing the lions share of injury and death to children in the home." He famously suggested that October, which is domestic violence awareness month, should be renamed "Bash a violent bitch month" and advised men "to beat the living shit" out of women who are supposedly physically abusive—"and then make them clean up the mess." He later claimed that this was intended as satire. Yet while the original attempt to launch "Bash a violent bitch month" happened in 2010, Elam has repeatedly doubled down on his suggestion in subsequent years.

Elam's YouTube channel, An Ear for Men, also provides a platform for him to release regular vlogs and audio recordings to over 100,000 subscribers, many of his individual lectures attracting more than half a million views. In a 2017 recording, he summarized the philosophy of the MRM:

Pussy is the only real empowerment women will ever know. Put all the hopelessly wishful thinking of feminist ideology aside, and what remains is the fact that it is men, and pretty much men only, who draw power from accomplishment, who invent technology, build nations, cure disease, create empires, and generally advance civilization.

In a 2010 post about rape on AVFM, Elam wrote that women who "dress and act provocatively" are "freaking begging" to get raped, adding that a lot of women are "stupid (and often arrogant) enough" to walk around with a figurative "PLEASE RAPE ME neon sign" above their "empty" and "narcissistic" heads.

In another blog, he boasted, "Should I be called to sit on a jury for a rape trial, I vow publicly to vote not guilty, even in the face of overwhelming evidence that the charges are true." (An editorial note on AVFM, where the post remains published, now claims that this piece was "deliberately inflammatory" and intended to force the reader to "confront brutal realities.")

Elam's portrayal of women as conniving is reminiscent of incels, and his obsession with false rape accusations aligns him with MGTOW, but his activist stance and determined attempts to attack feminists and undermine real-world protections for women and survivors are what set him firmly in the men's rights camp.

Even today, the deep schism between the two sides of the men's movement is clearly apparent. Thanks to the headline-grabbing antics of the MRM, the deeply misogynistic and often violent rhetoric espoused by the likes of AVFM completely overshadows the ongoing work of genuine men's organizations that actually address the problems the MRM pretends to be concerned with.

There is good work being done by and for men, some still in

the name of the men's liberation movement. In the United States, the National Organization for Men Against Sexism continues to hold annual conferences on men and masculinities and runs national task groups on issues such as fatherhood, child custody, eliminating racism, and men's mental health. In the UK, the Good Lad Initiative takes innovative workshops into schools and universities, where young men engage boys in discussions about gender roles, exploring the ways in which such stereotypes impact them and their mental health and teaching them skills and approaches to help them be part of a more equal culture. Yet these important efforts risk being smeared or buried by the reckless, violent damage inflicted on the public image of the men's movement by MRAs.

This damage is not just collateral. In 2014, Elam and AVFM took deliberate aim against White Ribbon, a male-led anti–domestic violence organization that seeks to engage men and boys in the battle against violence against women and girls. Elam set up a copycat website under the domain name whiteribbon.org, duplicating the original White Ribbon site almost exactly but replacing its content with antifeminist propaganda and false or distorted "facts." The fake website sought online donations for the cause, which might easily, at a glance, have been mistaken by visitors as donations for the real, highly respected White Ribbon movement. The funds, however, went straight to AVFM.[8]

While some of these examples may sound extreme, AVFM is by no means an outlying or fringe organization; rather, it is one of the biggest rallying points of the MRM, often cited as the largest and most influential website within the community. Its forum, which includes regional subforums in Africa, Europe, South America, and India, has over 13,000 members and a quarter of a million posts. But its readership and following is likely to be far greater.

Indeed, AVFM is certainly not the most violent or misogynistic men's rights community either. Alongside some content that is carefully polished and phrased to sound eminently reasonable, the movement also encompasses ideologies as violent as those of incels. Infamous blogger "Bardamu" (the pseudonym for Matt Forney), for example, ran an influential blog that combined elements of pickup artistry and the MRM. Forney has claimed that the site received 50,000 unique visitors a month.[9] The site is now defunct, though Forney continues to be an active and prolific member of the manosphere.

Bardamu described "the necessity" of carrying out domestic violence and claimed that smacking his then girlfriend led to "the most intense make-up sex I've ever had." Forney's website also blamed domestic violence victims for their own abuse, stating that "they are attracted to men who abuse them...because, unconsciously, that's what turns you on, what gets you wet." In a brief afterthought, clearly designed as a laughable attempt to preempt accusations of incitement to violence, the post concluded, "You should NOT hit women, not unless you want to end up in jail. But the principle still stands. Women should be terrorized by their men; it's the only thing that makes them behave better than chimps."

It's no small thing for arguments like these to be easily accessible and enthusiastically shared online in a country like the UK, where one in four women will experience domestic abuse, or, indeed, in a world in which one in three women will be raped or beaten in her lifetime. We'd like to be reassured that ideas this extreme don't make the leap from computer screen to real world, but they very much do.

These examples are part of a sprawling and interconnected web of social media groups, forums, and organizations visited, subscribed to, and participated in by hundreds of thousands of men worldwide. The main men's rights group on Reddit, r/MensRights, for example, now has almost a quarter of a million members who tend to be highly active and motivated, with several hundred, and sometimes even thousands, of new comments and posts each day. The page consists mainly of men highlighting news reports about false rape accusations and sharing their outrage at missions carried out by female astronauts (a waste of taxpayer money) or similar stories.

The movement also engages in the kind of targeted harassment more widely associated with the manosphere and, in particular, men who describe themselves as "trolls." When feminist author Jaclyn Friedman criticized AVFM, Elam published a blog about her, saying, "I find you, as a feminist, to be a loathsome, vile piece of human garbage. I find you so pernicious and repugnant that the idea of fucking your shit up gives me an erection." Others who have criticized the MRM have found themselves targeted with a mass harassment technique known as "doxxing," whereby their personal contact details are uncovered and posted widely online amid incitement to bombard them with abuse and threats. For one woman, this involved receiving hundreds of abusive messages from men who hoped she would "enjoy being anally defiled."[10] For other women, it has included the publication of details about their children's schools, with the implication that their children might be tracked down, or campaigns to contact their workplaces with misinformation aimed at getting them fired. One notorious MRA has targeted me so intensely and obsessively over a period of years that, as a *Guardian* journalist wrote, his behavior "might easily be mistaken for stalking."[11] His website currently hosts 164 individual articles about me, typically with titles like "Will Someone Change

Laura Bates's Diaper?," calling me "fucking pathetic" and "stupid." He writes again and again about my partner and private life, saying he would "gnaw off both feet without the benefit of anesthetic" to avoid the "grim fate" of marrying me (which makes it seem rather odd that he voluntarily devotes so much of his time and energy to keeping up with my romantic choices).

The MRM also goes some way toward attempting to rehabilitate its image from extreme and violent misogyny by copiously leveraging for propaganda a small but extremely vocal group of women who pride themselves on their rejection of feminist ideas. The biggest group, who call themselves "Honey Badgers," receive wild acclaim online from MRAs, with members like Canadian Karen Straughan attracting millions of views for her YouTube videos and others, like Janet Bloomfield, writing highly popular blogs dismissing female victims of sexual violence and lambasting women for single motherhood.

In one example, Bloomfield (who has claimed that her blog receives around a million hits per year) referred to the underage female victims of sexual abuse by British television star Jimmy Savile as "groupies" who "wanted all the benefits of hanging out with a big star" and "understood it came with a price and they paid it." She concluded, "And now they are claiming the MEN abused THEM? Looks to me like it was the other way around."[12] In the wake of the Steubenville rape case, in which two young men were convicted for the rape of a minor, Bloomfield wrote that it was "a tragedy for the boys" and described their female victim as "a stupid, drunk, helmet-chasing whore" who was not the victim of rape.[13] And in an Ask Me Anything discussion with mostly male fans in r/TheRedPill subreddit, Straughan said, "A rapist is a very damaged man (usually damaged by women) or a man who really

really really wants sex but can't convince a woman to willingly lie down with him."[14]

It is easy to see why such sentiments are likely to gain greater traction and attract less societal opprobrium when voiced by women. Indeed, the MRM is acutely aware of the beneficial optics of deploying this very small minority of its members as prominently as possible to provide the appearance that their views are reasonable and not deeply misogynistic. How could they be if women agree with them too? As Dean Esmay, former managing editor of AVFM, said, "People want to believe we're a bunch of sad, pathetic losers who can't get laid and are just bitter because our wives left us. The very presence of women in the movement creates cognitive dissonance."[15]

Like other manosphere communities, MRAs rely on questionable biology, patchily applied, to back up many of their arguments. But this can lead to hopelessly convoluted or self-defeating logic. Our descent from hunter-gatherer cavemen, for example, is often cited, without humor, to advocate for traditional gender roles in society. Many MRAs believe that women should stop clamoring for professional positions (particularly within traditionally male-dominated areas like STEM, for which our brains are apparently not well suited) and accept the biological imperative to stay at home, care for our husbands, and raise our children. These ideas are echoed in the castigation of women (and working women in particular) for the decline of family and moral values. Or the wistful hearkening back to days of strong, male breadwinners and nurturing, supportive, female spouses.

But this is deeply ironic, given the parallel focus of the movement on fathers' rights and custody disputes, which angrily declares that dads are routinely discriminated against by family courts, denied fair access to their children, and prevented from being granted sole responsibility for them.

There honestly seems to be no acknowledgment that this phenomenon—insofar as it is more common for women to be awarded custody of children (though the reasons are far more complex than MRAs would suggest)—is directly related to the same outdated gender stereotypes and assumptions propagated by MRAs. That's to say, it is precisely society's insistence that a woman's "natural" role is in the home—that she is biologically pre-disposed to be the nurturer of children and unsuited to the world of work—that has led to the unequal distribution of childcare and custody. But MRAs do not extend their outrage to the ways in which this unequal distribution negatively impacts women's lives: the maternity discrimination that sees mothers expelled from the workplace at a rate of an estimated 54,000 women a year, or the "motherhood penalty" that blights women's careers and curtails their salaries while working fathers see a corresponding finan-cial boost.[16] Perhaps most ironically of all, the one set of people staunchly fighting these stereotypes, battling to achieve better shared parental leave and split caring responsibilities, is the very group MRAs fight tirelessly against: feminists.

"Women are innately more nurturing. They are also generally better with children, the elderly and the infirm," pronounces the website of the Men's Rights Agency. On a different page, it claims, "The government proposes to roll back shared parenting provi-sions as if fathers are unimportant in their children's lives yet we know children raised in single parent matriarchal households are more at risk of harm." The movement is its own worst enemy.

Aside from using obsolete science and self-contradictory pseudo-psychology ("A woman has to be more emotionally stable than

85% of women to be as emotionally stable as the average man," Straughan confidently asserted in her Reddit Ask Me Anything Q&A), MRAs have a further tendency to cherry-pick, misquote, or deliberately fabricate statistical evidence to support their cause.

In the context of a discussion about MRAs' cherry-picking tactics, the case of Lorena Bobbitt is significant. In 1993, Lorena Bobbitt, who had suffered violent sexual and psychological abuse at the hands of her husband, John, cut off his penis with a knife after she said he had returned home in the evening and raped her. Despite the fact that she was found not guilty at trial (due to temporary insanity after years of rape, abuse, and terror and because both prosecution and defense attorneys agreed that Bobbitt had demonstrated a history of abuse), MRAs seized upon the case and continue to use it as evidence of the vindictive violence of women to this day. This is typical of the way in which the movement highlights individual, emotive, and often highly unusual cases and distorts them to try to imply a much wider pattern, or a gender-neutral problem, when there is overwhelming statistical evidence to the contrary.

The strategy of trying to create false equivalence in deeply gendered issues is not only deliberately manipulative but also undermines the cause of the real male victims who deserve help, support, and sympathy. If MRAs were genuinely focused on the needs and suffering of male survivors, their efforts might be more successfully directed toward advocating and fundraising for specialist shelters or raising awareness for the stigma surrounding male reporting of abuse, rather than attacking women's shelters, abusing women's sexual violence campaigners, and deliberately trying to distort statistics to suggest women are far more violent than men. On the urgent and taboo topic of male victims of sexually violent men, they remain resoundingly silent.

In other cases, groups go a step further and simply invent statistics altogether, as in the case of the high-profile and frequently quoted #21fathers campaign, created by the Australian Brotherhood of Fathers (ABF). Regularly cited in the mainstream media by politicians and journalists, the campaign prominently features the claim that twenty-one Australian fathers take their own lives every week because of family access issues. This statistic has subsequently been picked up and repeated widely, despite having no proven basis in fact. The web page about the campaign on the ABF website is subtitled "The statistics are truly shocking!" but then goes on to openly admit that the figure "came about initially as anecdotal evidence...together with a number of other sources." Numerous fact checks by media outlets and specialized organizations have demonstrated that there is no reliable source for the statistic, yet ABF and the wider MRM continue to use it liberally and emotively to argue that systemic family court bias exists and is ruining men's lives.[17]

This is not a single, cherry-picked example. The foundational arguments of the movement are overwhelmingly based on fallible or outright false assumptions.

In an investigation into the issue in the United States, fact-checking feminist outlet Skepchick analyzed national data and in-depth metadata, revealing that over half the time, fathers do not ask for custody at all, and only about 5 percent of all custody cases are contested to the degree that they end up being decided by a court.[18] Even in those cases, research from 2013 revealed that "the gender of the parent isn't significant, with the most important factors in gaining custody being mental stability, criminal history and financial resources."[19] Finally, the Skepchick analysis revealed that "when [men] do pursue custody to the point that it ends up in court, they stand a very good chance of getting it, *especially* if the mother tried to keep the child away from the father."

In the UK, family law lawyers have explained that the law includes no bias toward mothers, with the best interests of the child the sole basis for custody decisions. A comprehensive study by the University of Warwick concluded, "There is no evidence that family courts in England and Wales are discriminating against fathers because of gender bias... contact applications by fathers were in fact 'overwhelmingly successful.'"[20]

And despite a thriving portion of the men's rights community that focuses almost exclusively on the claim that women regularly make false allegations of abuse to win child custody, the facts suggest otherwise. In reality, according to one of the most thorough studies ever undertaken on false abuse allegations, in the rare cases that such allegations do arise, noncustodial parents (the vast majority of whom are fathers) make them most frequently, accounting for 43 percent of the total, followed by neighbors and relatives at 19 percent. Custodial parents (the vast majority of whom are mothers) are least likely to make them, at 14 percent.[21]

Of course, these refutations of entrenched prejudice against fathers within the justice system do not rule out the veracity of the many cases of individual men who have experienced either real or perceived injustice in specific cases, many of which are painstakingly detailed on men's rights websites. But where these cases exist, far from being the result of a man-hating feminist conspiracy within the system, as MRAs would have it, the opposite is likely true. Men are falling victim to the very stereotypes MRAs help to sustain.

Over and again, MRAs demonstrate a dogged and deliberately obtuse determination to lay the ills men suffer at the feet of those women who are often most invested in fighting to fix them, little caring about the harm they might do to the men they claim to support in the process.

We know, for example, that suicide and mental health concerns are a major problem among men, and statistics suggest that divorced and separated people, particularly men in that group, are at higher risk of suicide. Researchers who have studied this phenomenon have suggested that "resentment (toward the spouse and 'the system'), bitterness, anxiety, and depression" may all potentially contribute to suicide risk.[22] So the #21fathers campaign, for instance, represents a gross and irresponsible distortion of facts in the name of a genuine and serious issue. As writer Rebecca Watson pointed out, if researchers are concerned that bitterness toward "the system" may be a factor in suicide risk for separated men, then the fueling of an antifeminist conspiracy theory that vocally attempts to convince men that "the system" is biased and stacked steeply against them is, at best, unhelpful and, at worst, potentially devastating.[23] Of course, any man who carries out an internet search in need of urgent support for a child custody issue, a mental health crisis, or an experience of sexual violence and lands on one of the many manosphere websites likely to appear high up in the search rankings risks leaving with the impression that no support is available when, in fact, there are multiple groups and helplines they might be able to access. This is not to deny the MRM's claim that such services (much like those for women and girls) are often underfunded and insufficient, but exaggerating claims that they are nonexistent, to the extent that it prevents men from accessing what services do exist, is hardly the action of a group genuinely committed to supporting men in need.

In spite of all this evidence to the contrary, the efforts of the MRM to frame itself as a morally upright campaigning force enable it to take on the role of a conduit for some of the more extreme ideas of the broader manosphere, coating much of the same ideology that is rife on incel or PUA websites with a veneer of respectability and righteousness. In this way, if we are to see these different communities as part of a spectrum, the MRM is a crucial gateway through which arguments and beliefs that have originated in extremist spaces are able to gain somewhat respectable access to the public sphere, supported by the apparent scaffolding of legitimate grievances and concerns. "The men's rights movement lives in a pseudo-academic, seemingly respectable bubble," says the Southern Poverty Law Center, which classifies it as part of a male supremacy movement that "misrepresents all women as genetically inferior, manipulative and stupid and reduces them to their reproductive or sexual function."[24] Yet there remains a widespread tendency for mainstream media outlets to provide opportunities for MRAs to "debate" against women's rights spokespeople or to assert their case across national publicity platforms.

Take, for example, a BBC article in which ample space is given to Elam's ideas and quotes with relatively little rebuttal or examination, except to mention briefly that "women still face an array of serious issues." "Most of the discrimination is faced by men," Elam opines in the piece. "The fact of the matter is that men are suffering." The article, published on International Women's Day in 2017, was a largely sympathetic publicity boost for *The Red Pill*, a documentary by filmmaker Cassie Jaye that purports to show her unbiased exploration of the MRM. In the article, the BBC journalist described some of the men's rights content online as "deplorable," giving examples such as Elam's "Bash a violent bitch month," but immediately followed this with Jaye's "epiphany" that she was too "easily offended," going on to suggest that "equally shocking language is used by some on the feminist fringe." The impact of articles like this is to create a false equivalence between the violently misogynistic men's rights community and the feminist movement, suggesting that disagreements between the two are a matter of balanced debate. The author later suggested that there are "perhaps some similarities between MRAs and feminists," and the article uncritically cited Jaye's quote that "there are a lot of mirror opposites going on with these movements." It ended with a plug for the documentary.[25]

But what the article completely failed to mention is that Jaye's film was almost entirely funded by MRAs after her Kickstarter campaign attracted massive support from Elam, AVFM, and alt-right, antifeminist provocateur Milo Yiannopoulos, who boasted in the alt-right, antifeminist media outlet *Breitbart* that thousands of MRAs had backed the film in a matter of hours after its report about Jaye's funding struggles was shared "thousands of times on social media."[26] Spoiler alert: Jaye takes the red pill, sees the light, and denounces her wicked feminist ways.

That a major piece of men's rights propaganda, funded by hate groups, could receive such a boost from the BBC is a good example of just how well the MRM manages to portray itself as a reasonable and valid cause and thus receives mainstream exposure, which, in turn, helps to legitimize it further.

On popular Australian breakfast television program *Weekend Sunrise*, Elam was invited to air his views under the banner headline "Time for a men's movement—do men have fewer life-choices than women?" Highlighting the rise of the female breadwinner, the program sympathetically declared that the question of "where men fit in is more poignant than ever." On the program, Elam said that women have free choice over whether to work full-time or part-time or be full-time mothers and housewives, while men can only choose to work full-time. When asked about the increasing numbers of fathers doing childcare, he answered that stay-at-home mothers are referred to positively, bizarrely claiming that the only word for a father who stays at home is "gigolo." "Hmm," replied the female host, "there's a lot of merit in what you're saying there." When questioned about the claims on AVFM, Elam was then given airtime to expand on his website's notion that we need "an end to rape hysteria," allowing him to publicly claim that rape statistics cited by academics and politicians are "simply not true." While the male host did challenge Elam on some points, like his famous assertion that he would acquit a rapist if he were a juror, this gave Elam the opportunity to ramble about "prosecutorial misconduct... lack of due process" and false allegations, alluding to a government conspiracy and naming convicted men he believed were innocent. "I was so pleased to be here," Elam said at the end of the segment, which included no other guest to refute or rebut his claims.[27]

Like other elements of the manosphere, the MRM occupies startlingly large online spaces, but it also occupies more real-world space than many other misogynistic web communities, thanks to the presence of pressure groups, political parties, and campaign organizations, which hold meetings, protests, and conferences and engage more directly with the mainstream media and political structures than groups like incels do.

The penetration of the online hatred into everyday society is also facilitated by political activity. A prime example is Justice for Men and Boys (and the Women Who Love Them), a British political party that registered with the Electoral Commission in February 2013. By its very nature, the reincarnation of this particular men's rights community as an official political party has enabled the group, which formerly called itself the Anti-Feminism League and now goes by the acronym J4MB, to achieve a significant sweep of media coverage. From the *Telegraph* to *BuzzFeed* to the *Observer*, articles included quotes from the party's leader, Mike Buchanan, such as, "We hear a lot about misogyny, which is actually very rare, but a hatred of men is very commonplace... As far as the state is concerned, males are pretty much subhuman and they'll do anything they can to destroy men's lives." In his new status as a politician, Buchanan was also given free rein to opine unchallenged about the "myth" of the glass ceiling, stating, "Women just want to do other things with their lives... They're less driven and have less to gain from getting to the top of their professions, so they naturally don't put the effort in that a man would."[28] Although much of the coverage was critical, the very fact that such quotes appeared in the national press in the context of a political leader running for office helps to provide men's rights ideology with a sense of legitimacy and acceptability while also serving as a gateway for potentially susceptible converts, who might go on to access some of the movement's more extreme online spaces as a result. The impact can be subtle: one newspaper article, for example, described Buchanan as the author of three books, lending him an air of academic credibility, but failed to mention the fact that said books had been self-published—one of them being an antifeminist tome featuring a picture of a snarling vampire woman with bloodshot eyes on the front cover, which, at the time of writing, sits at number 602,916 in the Amazon charts. The party's YouTube channel, which it uses to record its members' radio and television appearances, features a large number of videos, including interviews with almost a dozen regional BBC radio stations, and many flagship UK primetime television news and politics programs.

This is an enormous amount of mainstream media exposure and airtime for a party whose two parliamentary candidates garnered a grand total of 216 votes between them in the May 2015 general election. A party whose website continues to promote articles such as "13 Reasons Women Lie about Being Raped" and "10 Reasons False Rape Allegations Are Common." A party whose election manifesto called for scrapping many of the elements of the 2010 Equality Act and suggested that women are as physically aggressive as men, if not more so, in intimate relationships. Large sections of the manifesto were reproduced without criticism in national articles—a prominence certainly not afforded to other similarly sized political outfits. Here we see another part of the problem becoming clear: MRAs capitalize on the media's thirst for "controversy."

In 2018, as I began to research this book, becoming a near-constant lurker on the platforms on which men fantasize about violently raping women, discuss the best ways to trick and force them into sex, and bitterly rail against their right to vote or have abortions, I stumbled across a video advertising an upcoming men's rights conference: Messages For Men 2018. The video caught my eye, primarily because it featured images of me. It seemed to the organizers that the best way to advertise this conference about "conveying positive messages for men" was to use a video of images of high-profile feminists, most of them crudely Photoshopped to include devilish red eyes or horns. Naturally. It seemed only fair to attend, given the lengths to which they had gone to make me feel included, so I purchased a ticket online. The event sounded right up Alex's street, so I booked my ticket in his name, in case mine rang any alarm bells, and immediately received several messages about the top-secret location for the conference, which could only be revealed after midnight the day before the event due to concerns about the potential disruption that might otherwise be caused by angry feminist protesters...

On the morning of the event, the long-awaited email with the details of the secret conference venue arrived. I anticipated a university venue or perhaps a generic conference space or meeting hall. But the address, which I checked twice, was for an O'Neill's pub in Chinatown, London. The email delicately described it as an "entertainment venue." A quick Google search of the pub website revealed that they don't particularly host events but helpfully offer to reserve a space in the pub for people wanting to arrange "drinks after work." This gave some idea about the real scale of an event that had been rather grandiosely referred to online as a major conference hosting academics, activists, and authors, with MRAs encouraged to snap up tickets before the event sold out. Nonetheless, I set off for Chinatown.

As I approached the venue, I saw a long line of people queuing eagerly ahead. An impressive turnout. But when I got a little closer, I realized they were waiting to get into a popular Chinese dessert shop, selling buns and pastries. Just beyond the queue, the entrance to O'Neill's was quiet, and the pub inside was trading as usual. I approached several confused staff members, most of whom seemed to have no idea that any event was taking place, before one disappeared to try to find out where the "conference" was being held. Eventually, he reappeared and directed me up two slightly sticky flights of stairs to a rather grim, low-ceilinged room with dark gray-painted walls in which some chairs had been set out facing a makeshift stage. In one corner, a Christmas tree, decorated with cheap red and silver baubles, drooped slightly to one side.

As I joined the dozen or so men waiting to be admitted, my

heart started to beat faster. I couldn't help wondering what overlap there might be between present company and those who had sent me graphic emails about eradicating me from the world like a dripping poison or waiting outside my house to rape me until I begged for mercy. I slipped quietly into a seat at the back of the room, sure that, at any moment, an angry hand would clamp down on my shoulder or a shout of recognition would ring out. But keeping my head down and allowing my hair to swing forward, partially shielding my face, seemed to work. After waiting a few moments for my heart rate to stabilize, I raised my eyes to take in my surroundings. A bar stretched most of the length of the room, and many of the assembled men were ordering drinks and greeting acquaintances.

There were perhaps sixty men milling around. I counted a handful of women, most younger than the men, and about seven men of color. There were no women of color present. The biggest single demographic seemed to be white men in their late fifties or sixties, but there were also a number of younger men who looked to be in their late twenties or thirties. One had brought with him a child of about ten. Most of the men were well dressed, with several in smart suits and ties. I saw a man wearing a black T-shirt emblazoned with "MALE LIVES MATTER." Another wore the slogan "This is what a gender equality activist looks like." The apocryphal underwear-clad pimply teenagers squinting at computer screens in their mothers' basements were not in evidence among this group of respectable-looking attendees. They were men you would pass on the street without thinking twice. Like the other inhabitants of the manosphere, they are men we all pass on the street.

One sat down next to me and introduced himself amicably. We chatted about the area of London he'd traveled from—how it's quiet on weekends, which allows him to decompress after a busy week. He asked me politely about my own neighborhood, and I sidestepped a couple of questions about what brought me there today, vaguely mentioning a desire to learn more about the movement. Technically true. He told me he'd attended previous events, including one in Birmingham, and found it convenient that "most gatherings of this sort" in the UK seem to take place in London. We exchanged a few further pleasantries before lapsing into silence. Later, he gave a speech about launching legal action against former Crown Prosecution Service chief Alison Saunders for the crime of championing victims of sexual violence during her time in the role.

A young woman took to the stage, welcoming the attendees to the conference. There followed an incongruous diversion to classical mythology as she drew our attention to the conference leaflets, which featured a muscular man clad only in a loin cloth, working at a fire with metal tools, surrounded by other crouching male figures. The homoerotic nature of the imagery was apparently not intentional. She explained that the image was supposed to represent Prometheus's sacrifice in defying the gods to bring fire to man; fire, she explained, represents so many important masculine qualities. A comment about Pandora bringing all man's problems was met with appreciative sniggers. The seemingly obligatory requirement of a vague classical reference to add a sense of authenticity was thereby duly satisfied.

We were then taken on a whistle-stop tour of the year's major events as perceived by an MRA. The Kavanaugh hearings (after which Brett Kavanaugh was confirmed as a Supreme Court justice in spite of claims he had committed sexual assault) were cast as the downfall of the #MeToo movement, much to the appreciation of the crowd. But the biggest cheer by far was reserved for the announcement that both Donald Trump and his wife, Melania, had made statements in support of "men and justice" following Kavanaugh's confirmation.

This struck me as the most significant moment I witnessed. Men all around me were cheering and clapping approvingly, nodding encouragingly at one another. It was the first tangible proof I had seen that the words and actions of Trump have had a direct evangelizing impact on the movements I was investigating. His statements are seized upon and held up as direct approval and encouragement for the manosphere and its ideology.

The conference was small and its attendees' arguments weak. But emerging from the pub into the bustling central London street reminded me just how real these communities are, in a way far more tangible than the easily closed tabs of the online forum hatred littering my laptop screen might suggest.

It is easy to ridicule these groups, but the breadth of their support, the foothold they have carved out in the media and political landscape, and the gateway they provide for the beliefs of other manosphere groups to slide into the mainstream narrative, greased with a sheen of respectability, all suggest that this is not a movement we should be laughing off.

Reports that do belittle and mock the MRM tend to rely on the idea that this is a dying, residual throwback to 1970s sexism that will eventually fade in the face of ongoing feminist progress. But this is not borne out by the evidence. If anything, support for the MRM only seems to be growing, galvanized by the powerful backlash to the #MeToo movement and the social acceptability engendered by Trump's vocal public assertion (in the wake of sexual assault allegations against Kavanaugh and others) that "it's a very scary time for young men in America."[29] *Mother Jones* reported that at a 2014 men's rights conference, Elam embraced Farrell on stage, describing him as a mentor, before Farrell emotionally declared that the positive response to his book was "finally happening...21 years later." In Australia, in 2018, a men's rights march attracted an estimated 500–1,000 people in Melbourne. At the march, Adrian Johnson, cofounder of the pressure group Men's Rights Sydney (which non-ironically uses the acronym MRS), proudly told a journalist, "People have been having these conversations around water coolers for a lifetime and now they are coming out into the open."[30] This is not a movement in decline.

Nor is it entirely devoid of the violence that characterizes the incel movement. Roy Den Hollander was a self-described "anti-feminist" lawyer and supporter of the MRM. He had, like many MRAs, spent years bringing spurious cases to court, suing universities for having women's studies programs, or challenging the Violence Against Women Act, which he described as the "Female Fraud Act." In a 2011 profile, after the Supreme Court dismissed his lawsuit against nightclubs for having "ladies' nights," Den Hollander told the New York Times: "The feminists have taken control over every institution in this country—they want to take control over men... I'm going to fight them to my last dollar, last breath."[31]

One of his most recent cases, challenging the male-only military draft, had come before Judge Esther Salas, whom Den Hollander had baselessly accused of delaying the case. In July 2020, Den Hollander arrived at the New Jersey home of Judge Salas, dressed as a FedEx delivery driver. When the door opened, Den Hollander opened fire. Judge Salas was in the basement at the time and was not injured, but her son was killed and her husband seriously injured.[32]

Perhaps to a greater degree than any other manosphere community, MRAs have identified a set of very real problems and grievances, from job safety for manual laborers to substandard mental health provision and parental rights. But when it comes to assigning blame, they have taken aim at precisely the wrong target. It is not women, or even feminists, who have limited, frustrated, diminished, hurt, and damaged men but masculinity itself or, rather, our society's constricting, toxic, self-defeating version of what it means to perform being a man. Yet every time anybody tries to make progress in tackling this particular version of masculinity, the MRM rises up as a united voice to condemn and undermine the attempt.

In January 2019, for example, the American Psychological Association (APA) took the unprecedented step of acknowledging publicly that "traditional masculinity is psychologically harmful and that socializing boys to suppress their emotions causes damage." Highlighting guidelines it had released the previous year for therapists working with men and boys, the association seemed to be tackling exactly the issues MRAs should have welcomed, noting that men are "the demographic group most at risk of being victimized by violent crime" and "they are 3.5 times more likely than women to die by suicide, and their life expectancy is 4.9 years shorter than women's. Boys are far more likely to be diagnosed with attention-deficit hyperactivity disorder than girls, and they face harsher punishments in school."[33] But despite the clear statistical evidence provided by the APA and the fact that it was directly addressing precisely the issues raised daily in the manosphere, MRAs and members of other manosphere communities were outraged, falling over one another to debunk, dismiss, and denigrate the APA.

Jordan Peterson, a Canadian clinical psychologist and author, dubbed the new guidelines "reprehensible, infuriating and disheartening," claiming that the APA was dominated by "political types" and "hard-left leaning political activists."[34] AVFM described it as a "war on masculinity," calling the APA "armed combatants in the war of ideas."

Their objection? That the guidelines acknowledged men as beneficiaries of privilege within a patriarchal society and suggested that certain forms of masculinity were harmful. But what they seemed to miss entirely was that that harm is damaging men and boys, not just women and girls. The male suicide rate is one of the genuine areas of serious concern most commonly cited by MRAs. Yet when a major organization with enormous potential influence on the treatment of this problem comes along with research suggesting it might be possible to address some of the problem's root causes, they angrily dismiss it. Men socialized to be stoic, competitive, dominant, and aggressive, the APA observed, have been proven to be less likely to engage in healthy behaviors, such as accessing preventative health care or looking after themselves—a tendency that extends to seeking out psychological help. However, even in the face of robust evidence that "men who bought into traditional notions of masculinity were more negative about seeking mental health services than those with more flexible gender attitudes," MRAs prefer to die on the hill of defending those very same "traditional notions of masculinity" than recognize that this could be a huge potential step toward tackling one of the greatest issues facing men today. They are, in other words, some of the most robust defenders of the precise problems they claim to want to eradicate.

In 1981, psychologist Joseph Pleck's *The Myth of Masculinity*, which might be described as one of the last major works of the men's liberation movement, included the line "How people continue to believe so fervently in values and norms according to which they can only be failures is an awe-inspiring phenomenon." Some forty years later, his observation remains an accurate summary of the MRM and is still as tragic—and as true—as ever.

# 5
# Men Who Hound Women

"I hope u get bashed, or get cancer,
you filthy man hating cunt"

**ANONYMOUS EMAIL, RECEIVED SUNDAY,
AUGUST 4, 2019, 3:42 P.M.**

"Shut the fuck up bitch."
*Just ignore it.*

"Fucking women should know their place, fucking skanks."
*Don't make a fuss.*

"The only reason you have been put on this planet is so we can fuck you. Please die."
*Don't take it so seriously.*

"KILL YOUR SELF."
*Turn off your computer if you can't handle it.*

"Laura Bates will be raped tomorrow at 9pm... I am serious."

*It's not personal.*

It's easy to tell people not to make a fuss when you're not the one on the receiving end. These messages all came through in the space of about half an hour. Just a single fraction of a single day.

Multiply them by forty-eight and then by 365 and you start to get a sense of what it feels like. Receiving these messages day in, day out is like drowning in slow motion, but nobody else can see the water. And even if you try to tell them, they don't understand.

Troll. It's such a silly little word. It makes it sound like a silly little problem. A ridiculous, pot-bellied, bright-haired '90s toy. Or a lumbering, stupid, green oaf, crouching slimily beneath a bridge. Neither one comes close to capturing the truth. But these two stereotypes are illuminating, because they accurately portray the most common ways in which our society perceives trolls. They are either seen as harmless, comical figures of fun or as nasty, mean, but ultimately dim-witted bottom-feeders, cringing away from sunlight, too stupid to do much real damage beyond giving people the occasional scare. The very word *troll*, much like *manosphere*, is a hopelessly benign euphemism for a much darker reality.

Trolls are distinct from other manosphere groups in that it can be helpful to think of the term *trolling* as more of an action than an identity. A verb rather than a noun. So a member of any manosphere group might engage in trolling while still retaining his identity as an incel or an MRA. Sometimes members of manosphere communities turn trolling tactics on one another, particularly in very hierarchical forums, where more experienced and respected members might abuse and harass newer recruits. Sometimes entire manosphere communities adopt trolling tactics en masse as a means to attack or disrupt a specific target, as we see when members of the AVFM community turn their wrath on individual feminist activists. But there are also large groups online that see themselves solely as trolls, distinct from other communities. Such groups are not confined to the manosphere. They're not even confined to men. Anywhere there are boundaries to be pushed and limits of human decency to be tested, trolls will appear. But we do know from several studies that men are more likely to engage in trolling or bullying behavior online than women.[1]

And while the victims of trolls might be anybody, from celebrities to politicians to grieving families, there is a particularly concentrated misogynistic element to much trolling, which places the majority of those who do it squarely within the bounds of the manosphere. Looking closely at trolls will also reveal the true depth and complexity of the overlap between the manosphere and the alt-right, not only because trolls appear in both spheres but also because those who spearheaded and sharpened trolling techniques in the manosphere went on to take their newfound skills and notoriety into the realm of the far right.

In classic internet terminology, the term *trolling* emerged in the late '80s or early '90s and was probably coined in reference to the fishing practice of trolling (or trawling)—slowly towing a baited hook to catch unsuspecting prey. In its earliest iteration, the term referred to the practice whereby seasoned and regular users of a particular forum or Usenet group would deliberately ask a very simple question, pretending to be extremely stupid or confused. Their inquiry would often be about a topic already discussed exhaustively on the forum, which would have the immediate effect of drawing out newcomers to the group, who would be the only ones to respond sincerely to the conversation and might then be mocked. As the internet expanded, the term spread. It started to include any activity that involved deliberately baiting other internet users into increasingly emotional, angry, or defensive responses. This was usually achieved by posting off-topic or inflammatory messages in a specific forum. The more sincere and earnest the targets, the better. The more passionate and indignant their responses, the more successful the troll.

As it has evolved, this particular form of trolling—derailing internet discussions with large quantities of poor quality, irrelevant, or ironic information—has become more specifically known, in internet parlance, as "shitposting." The aim is to trick respondents into taking trolls seriously and to draw them down a rabbit hole of pointless argument and escalating emotion.

It's a charge some would level at the whole manosphere itself. But manosphere communities are far more self-obsessed than that. Yes, there are some members who are playing to the crowd. But many more are genuinely invested in their perceived victimhood and their extreme misogyny. People who are just trying to provoke outrage with fake provocation don't go out and kill people in real life. Incels do.

The practice of trolling is widespread and established enough to have variants in many different countries and languages. My favorite example is the Portuguese expression *pombos enxadristas* (literally translated as "chess-player pigeons"), which refers to a Portuguese adage that describes a futile argument as akin to playing chess with a pigeon: "It poops on the table, drops the pieces, and simply flies off, claiming victory." The comparison is remarkably accurate—it captures the unequal playing field created when one party is prepared to engage in a genuine good-faith discussion and the other is simply invested in creating the greatest possible amount of chaos. But it also pinpoints another aspect of trolling that became increasingly significant as the term evolved and took on a darker meaning: the importance for internet trolls of claiming, and being seen to claim, "victory."

While our current terminology euphemizes and dismisses the work of online trolls, the terms *online abusers* or *harassers* might be more accurate, given the ways in which trolling has developed and mutated. Even now, in the media and public discourse, trolling is used to describe everything from fairly tame disagreement to sending rape and death threats or deliberately defacing memorial websites for people's deceased loved ones.

It is significant that of all the manosphere labels and identities, *troll* is the term that has penetrated most widely into the public discourse. Despite the fact that trolls have never been exclusively confined to the manosphere, for many a layperson, the word could encompass any of the groups and individuals referred to in this book. This is the extent to which our society has sublimated the threat posed by online misogynistic extremism into the perception of a small group of immature, annoying, sometimes funny teenagers, joking around and playing technological tricks. The most important element of this caricature is that it is perceived, above all, as *harmless*, or at least not genuinely harmful.

The reality is very different, partly because the tactics of trolls have now become far more organized and sophisticated than the label would suggest, partly because of the very real and enormously underestimated psychological consequences of trolling, and partly because of the ways in which online abuse has now begun to have deadly offline consequences.

It is impossible to understand trolls in their most modern form, which involves tactical harassment, mass participation, and a serious sense of competition, without understanding Gamergate. It was through this mass harassment campaign that many of the modern tactics and techniques deployed by large mobs of trolls with great precision and impact were honed and developed.

In August 2014, a programmer named Eron Gjoni wrote a revenge-fueled blog post about his former girlfriend, Zoë Quinn. Gjoni alleged that Quinn, an independent game developer, had cheated on him with Nathan Grayson, a video game reviewer for the website Kotaku. The implication picked up by readers, particularly male members of the online gaming community, was that Quinn had engaged in the relationship to win favorable reviews of her game, *Depression Quest*, which had been released in 2013, garnering positive responses from gaming media but a backlash from gamers, who saw it as overly concerned with politics and social justice (the game was primarily text based and encouraged players to explore the experience of depression). The episode should have been little more than the tiniest internet blip within a niche community. Kotaku investigated, finding no evidence of any wrongdoing—indeed, it transpired that Grayson had never even reviewed the game. But the story was picked up on platforms on which trolls congregated, including 4chan, Reddit, and other websites. Suddenly, Quinn began to receive a barrage of threats as well as the circulation of her stolen nude photographs. Her friends and family were subjected to extreme abuse; she was harassed and encouraged to kill herself; her online accounts were hacked; and eventually, after people threatened to cripple, maim, rape, and kill her, she left her home in fear for her safety.

The phenomenon swiftly began to spread. Shortly after the

abuse of Quinn began, Anita Sarkeesian, a prominent feminist media critic and blogger, started to receive a similar wave of threats. Sarkeesian was already well acquainted with online abuse: after she launched a video series examining the often sexist depiction of women in video games in 2012, she was intensely harassed online by gamers, who saw her commentary as an attack on the industry and an unwelcome attempt to sanitize or "feminize" it. The abuse included hacking and rape and death threats, and men sent Sarkeesian illustrations of herself being raped by various video game characters. It culminated in the creation of an online "game" in which players could virtually "beat up" Sarkeesian by clicking on an image of her face, watching as welts, bruises, and wounds appeared. A key feature of trolling, demonstrated by the rapidly escalating abuse Sarkeesian experienced, is the need to perform to and impress other trolls. The act of trolling itself is no more important than the process of documenting and sharing it on anonymous forums and message boards, collecting accolades and advice from other trolls, and competing to outdo one another in the extremity and obscenity of the abuse.

When Sarkeesian released a new video in her *Tropes vs. Women* series, the mob, already attacking Quinn, connected the two women, seeing them as part of the same "threat," and trolls began to abuse Sarkeesian as well. After her address was found and posted online, amid a mass of renewed death and rape threats, Sarkeesian, like Quinn, was forced to flee her home. As the harassment escalated, in October 2014, Sarkeesian traveled to Utah to give a planned address at Utah State University. But an anonymous threat was sent to the university, claiming that if Sarkeesian's talk was not canceled, an attack would be carried out against the attendees as well as students and staff at the nearby Women's Center:

I have at my disposal a semi-automatic rifle, multiple pistols, and a collection of pipe bombs... You have 24 hours to cancel Sarkeesian's talk... Anita Sarkeesian is everything wrong with the feminist woman, and she is going to die screaming like the craven little whore that she is if you let her come to USU. I will write my manifesto in her spilled blood, and you will all bear witness to what feminist lies and poison have done to the men of America.[2]

Sarkeesian was forced to cancel the talk after police refused to carry out searches for firearms in advance of the event because of Utah's open-carry laws.

Gamergate, as the controversy became known, continued to spiral, racking up thousands of posts online and on social media and sucking a significant number of other women into its vortex of harassment. Feminist writers who dared to speak out against the abuse of others suddenly found themselves experiencing similar threats, and other female game developers were forced out of their homes in the wake of threats describing their mutilated corpses and the deaths of their children.

The harassment continued for months, and as the campaign unfolded, trolls began to develop and hone increasingly crafted tactics to maximize and focus their attacks.

One tactic was ideological: the abusers quickly realized that they could defend, and even promote, the Gamergate "movement" if they portrayed it as a noble, ethical stance, using this as a smokescreen for trolling. Proponents began telling the story that this had nothing to do with Sarkeesian or Quinn. Instead, they said, it was an ideological battle over "ethics" in video gaming. They focused on the alleged (albeit debunked) relationship between Quinn and

Grayson, claiming to be gravely concerned about corruption in the industry and the closeness of relationships between some game developers and critics. Others suggested that the purity and very essence of gaming and the gaming community was under threat, at risk of erosion by Sarkeesian and other (mainly feminist) critics like her who wanted to destroy video game culture by forcing it to become stiflingly "politically correct" at the expense of high-quality game play.

Next, they tapped into the classic manosphere strategy of presenting themselves as the true victims, even while engaging in mass coordinated sexual harassment. In order to achieve this, the real victims had to be presented as the oppressors. Trolls put out stories on social media and gaming websites suggesting that the women were inventing and exaggerating the harassment they had received to attract attention and make male gamers (who were just trying to protect their culture) look bad. Others claimed that feminists themselves had sent the death and bomb threats to escalate the story. A narrative of the progressive left as "snowflakes," "social justice warriors," "feminazis," "professional victims," and the "perpetually offended" emerged; these became labels and claims that would be used increasingly in manosphere and also alt-right attacks over the coming years, especially when attempting to justify abuse in the eyes of the mainstream observer. Thus, coordinated harassment became justified as a form of moral self-defense. As one research paper into the subject concluded, "It is unsurprising that the men's rights movement pioneered and engages in weaponized harassment, given the centrality of the victim narrative to their ideology."[3]

Then the tactic of coordinating attacks emerged, with trolls using online message boards to designate specific women as targets at particular times, inundating them with mass campaigns of abuse in an attempt to terrify and overwhelm them into silence or with-drawal, making it difficult for them to report or take action against the abuse on social media platforms due to its sheer volume. This technique was honed to such a degree that it took on a specific name: "brigading." Two million tweets with the hashtag #gamer-gate were sent within the first two months of the controversy alone, and analysis of their content suggested that the campaign was far more closely focused on harassment than any discussion of ethics in video gaming.[4] During that same period, 35,188 tweets using the hashtag targeted Sarkeesian, for example, and 10,400 were directed at Quinn, compared to just 732 sent to Grayson, whose (falsely) alleged unethical reporting was supposedly the focus of the whole episode.

The rhetorical trick of presenting a campaign as nobly battling exactly the interests it itself personifies would go on to become central to future campaigns of the alt-right and the manosphere. Gamergate's proponents harassed, abused, and deliberately obfus-cated their real aims, all the while claiming to be acting in the name of ethics, transparency, and purity. In the same way, the mano-sphere calls for gender equality while indulging in extreme misog-yny, demands transparency of statistics while spreading false facts, and portrays itself as the champion of downtrodden victims while espousing the creation of greater gains and protections for the group already most privileged in our society. Similarly, the alt-right claims to have the noble cause of opening people's eyes to injustice and inequality, all the while attempting to revive some of the most deeply damaging hate campaigns of recent history.

So Gamergate introduced the idea of troll armies to the main-stream. Suddenly, what had previously been a solo pursuit could be harnessed as a mass activity for mass gain. And this would later be exploited by ideological leaders, who would build up great armies of "attack dogs," just waiting to be unleashed on unsuspecting targets.

Milo Yiannopoulos, for example, would finally be banned from Twitter in 2016 (after years of incendiary, bigoted tweets) for using misogyny, racism, and transphobia to play a major role in inciting a massive torrent of abuse against actress Leslie Jones for the crime of taking part in the all-female remake of *Ghostbusters*. Jones tweeted that she'd been sent images of apes' genitals and a picture of her own face covered in semen among thousands of other messages.[5]

The white supremacist website *Daily Stormer* has similarly continued to use brigading to horrifying effect, actively and deliberately calling for mass campaigns of terrifying abuse against specific (usually female) targets. Their "Filthy Jew Bitch Campaign" led to the bombardment of British politician Luciana Berger with 2,500 tweets, alongside blogs that called her an "evil money-grabber" with a "deep-rooted hatred of men," superimposing her face onto images of a rat.[6] The *Stormer* later set its trolls on Australian Muslim lawyer Mariam Veiszadeh, who founded the Islamophobia Register, which tracks instances of abuse against Muslims. The outlet called for its "troll army" to drown Veiszadeh in abuse, demanding that they "be as nasty, hurtful, hateful, offensive, insulting and 'vilifying' as you possibly can." One follower, who swiftly obliged, told Veiszadeh, "Leave now before we behead your mother and bury you all with pigs."[7]

Like many elements of the manosphere, it is perfectly possible to argue that there may have been a number of people involved in the Gamergate furor who had honest concerns, really did want to debate ethics within gaming, or genuinely didn't participate in the harassment and abuse of women and minorities online. But again in parallel with the manosphere, the vastly disproportionate focus of the Gamergate supporters and the enormous amount of vitriolic content associated with the movement belied the argument that misogynistic factors were nonexistent or a minority concern. And indeed, the very attempts by those who claimed they were above such behavior to belittle or dismiss its occurrence in their defense of the movement arguably amounted to a form of collusion with the very abuse from which they were trying to distance themselves.

Leaked chat logs revealed another tactic that has gone on to define both the alt-right and manosphere harassment campaigns for years to come. They showed that the trolls used "sock puppet" accounts: false online identities using fake names and photographs, often set up in large numbers and then employed to give the impression of widespread grassroots support for a movement or campaign that may actually be coordinated by a very small number of puppeteers. This is not to suggest that the number of trolls online is very small; rather that even just a few trolls can create havoc with the impression of a much broader base of support for a bombardment campaign. This technique has subsequently become known as "astroturfing": when a specific political, ideological, or advertising message is disseminated in such a way as to suggest it comes in the form of unsolicited comments and support from members of the general public when it is, in fact, orchestrated by design.[8] Use of this technique by the trolls was confirmed by later analysis of tweets posted using the #gamergate hashtag, which found that a quarter of the tweets were from accounts new to Twitter, most of them supportive of the harassers.[9]

Finding sympathetic media sources became another angle of attack, most famously achieved through an unholy union between Gamergaters, hungry for mainstream coverage to escalate and validate their harassment campaign, and Yiannopoulos, then an up-and-coming journalist trying to cement his reputation as a self-described "fabulous internet super-villain." He sensed that he could use this controversy to gain a foothold in the slippery world of online trolls, alt-right supporters, and manosphere followers who would go on to propel him to fame and success as a result. Sadly, he was right.

So Yiannopoulos waded into Gamergate with a deliberately inflammatory article on the influential and widely read *Breitbart* site, describing the victims of Gamergate abuse as "an army of sociopathic feminist programmers and campaigners...terrorizing the entire community—lying, bullying and manipulating their way around the internet for profit and attention." After repackaging the (already widely debunked) slurs about Quinn's sex life and making a string of other unsubstantiated allegations against her, Yiannopoulos went on to mimic many of the tactics already established by the wider campaign. "Let's be honest," he wrote. "We're all used to feeling a niggling suspicion that 'death threats' sent to female agitators aren't all they're cracked up to be."[10]

Yiannopoulos was not the only figure to capitalize on Gamergate as a stepping stone for self-promotion. In fact, the smorgasbord of manosphere, alt-right, and white supremacist leading lights who emerged from the controversy as internet legends makes it one of the clearest microcosms of how closely interrelated these communities are. It's no coincidence that provocations like "gamERs rise up" can be seen frequently on manosphere forums, combining the shorthand and jargon of incels (referencing Elliot Rodger) with a tip of the hat to the Gamergate mob. Or that forum users frequently use the term *alt-rightcels* to describe those with an allegiance to both movements.

Mike Cernovich, identified as a "male supremacist" and "one

of America's most visible right-wing provocateurs" by the Southern Poverty Law Center, initially rose to prominence through his role in Gamergate, during which he used his blog and social media platforms to elevate the controversy and egg on the harassers.[11] He described the incident as "the most important battle of the culture war this century" and offered to give Gjoni pro bono legal advice. He also, allegedly, obtained Quinn's legal complaint against Gjoni and passed it on to none other than pickup guru Daryush Valizadeh, who used it as the basis of a piece abusing Quinn on his own website.

Cernovich was later described as "the meme mastermind of the alt-right" by the New Yorker.[12] Though now perhaps best known for his associations with white nationalism despite extremely unconvincing attempts to distance himself from the label, Cernovich's journey to notoriety led him through the maze of manosphere misogyny. He has advised men to expose themselves and start masturbating in front of women in an attempt to harass them into having sex and published blog posts with titles like "How to Choke a Woman."[13]

As the Gamergate debacle spiraled out of control, offline abuse began to mingle with online. The harassers made liberal use of doxxing, with the express purpose of causing victims to fear for their safety. In the hands of online mobs, personal information revealed through doxxing has been weaponized offline in myriad ways: from ordering thousands of pizzas to targets' houses to covertly photographing them and posting the images online; from throwing bricks through victims' windows to making repeated threatening and abusive phone calls. Gamergate even saw a tactic known as "swatting" used against several targets: a form of harassment whereby hoax bomb threats are made to emergency services to provoke a SWAT team response at the target's home, something that risks putting them in very real physical danger.

Again, it's easy to think of these men as tiny minorities: a few sad and deluded individuals, clinging to obscure internet fringe groups as a way to feel a sense of belonging. But the reality, as with all the manosphere groups I have investigated, is that these are massive communities and internet spaces, populated by hundreds of thousands of people. When you visit the 4chan /b/ board, for example, widely acknowledged as one of the most infamous trolling platforms on the internet, posts flood in faster than you are able to read them. When I visited on an average Monday morning at 9:30 a.m., hundreds of pages of new messages, photographs, and links were added within the space of hours—a significant number of them showcasing extreme misogyny. In a hint at the sheer size of this community, /b/ is 4chan's single most popular and visited board, accounting for 30 percent of the site's total traffic, according to an interview with its founder.[14] The site claims to have almost twenty-eight million unique monthly visitors and around a million new posts every single day. Its user base, unsurprisingly, is heavily male dominated, and it claims that the most common demographic is eighteen- to thirty-four-year-old college-educated men, likely to be located in the United States, the UK, Canada, Australia, or European countries, which tallies precisely with what we know of the broader manosphere.

Intimate photographs of women are shared without their consent, rape fantasies are swapped, and "worthy" trolling targets are eagerly discussed. Women are referred to in derogatory and dehumanizing terms, alongside deeply anti-Semitic jokes and posts about the Holocaust. A user posted a picture of an actress and encouraged others to comment on how they'd "fuck [her] to death."

Within an hour, I had seen posts from men identifying as incels and MGTOWs ("I wish I didn't have to die a hugless virgin," wrote one), though the majority of contributors were more generically interested in trolling. The behavior spills offline: one user posted photos of a pair of lacy panties he claimed to have stolen from his best friend's little sister, while others incited him to steal more. Some shared private photographs they had taken without women's knowledge, using "creep cams," or pictures sent to them by their girlfriends. Users bartered among themselves, demanding sums of money to reveal more and more intimate images.

The uncomfortable truth is that communities of online trolls are far larger and more connected than public perception would allow. In fact, everything we know about people who have been prosecuted for taking part in online trolling suggests that these are members of our own communities: respected colleagues, fathers, partners, and active members of society.

Steven King, forty-five, for example, was found guilty in 2016 of sending a message to British Labor MP Angela Eagle the day after she announced a bid for party leadership. The message read, "You will die you Bitch, you will have too watch every step... evil witch... next time you see me I'll be with a real gun or knife cutting your life to an end... Leave the UK... or die." Far from being an unemployed recluse, it soon transpired that King, who was sentenced to an eight-week prison sentence, suspended for twelve months, had casually sent the message from his mobile phone while getting ready for work.[15]

Robert Ambridge, revealed in 2013 to be behind a notorious trolling account that had posted misogynistic, Islamophobic, and offensive tweets about dead children and mass deaths, was a middle-aged father of six and a recruitment consultant.[16]

In 2018, the *Sun* revealed that another troll, who had sent over 3,000 sexist, racist, and homophobic messages (including telling Jewish actress Sarah Silverman to watch out for gas chambers and asking model Katie Price, "Is your head as fucked as your caved in rancid cunt?"), was a junior football coach and father of two, working in design. He faced no charges.[17]

The Ligue du LOL case in France also revealed the extent to which trolling ideas can be embedded within respected professions and the enormous impact they can have on the careers of women in those areas. Ligue du LOL was the name of a private Facebook group, counting among its members around thirty highly successful, influential young journalists and media professionals. They were said to have used the group to organize campaigns of abuse and online harassment against other social media users (mostly women in journalism as well as feminist and LGBTQ activists and people of color) between 2009 and 2012. At the time, multiple victims tried to report the existence of the group and the severity of the harassment, both to the media and to the employers of those involved, with no success. In 2019, after a newspaper published an article about the group, stories began to pour out about similar private networking groups on services like WhatsApp, which were being used to circulate sexist and homophobic messages. The episode showcased the extent to which the tactics of online trolls might be adopted by internet-savvy young professionals in situations vastly different from what we might think of as typical troll territory.

Meanwhile, the complexity of internet anonymity, the importance of freedom of speech, the international nature of the troll population, and the trolls' technical skills at masking their locations and identities have all contributed to the fact that the problem is widely considered near unsolvable. This is convenient for tech companies and web platforms, many of which have simply admitted defeat or adopted a shoulder-shrugging "what can we do?" approach.

Trolls, and those using trolling tactics, can come for anyone they perceive as representing everything they hate—and anyone who expresses views they disagree with. But perhaps their most violent rage is reserved for those who dare to take a peek under their own rocks.

In 2014, Australian writer Brydie Lee-Kennedy was asked by a news and entertainment website to write a piece about incels and MRAs, "honestly, but in a light-hearted way."

Lee-Kennedy spent a few days researching MRAs and the sites Rodger had spent a lot of time on, learning about the red pill, scouring subreddits, and following links to some of the manosphere communities, before producing an article she summarized as "This stuff is ridiculous, but we have to take it seriously."

Unbeknownst to Lee-Kennedy, someone higher up the editorial chain made the decision to give the piece the headline "Let's All Have a Laugh at the Men's Rights Movement."

Within hours of publication, Lee-Kennedy's Twitter account exploded with abuse as messages poured in from angry members of the manosphere. Things quickly escalated. The criticism migrated to various manosphere subreddits, and, she told me, users had managed to dig up old photos of her:

> They found full-body shots of me and talked about how fat
> I was; then they found old columns, where I'd talked about
> sleeping with women, because I'm bisexual, and they were
> like: "Oh, this all makes sense now, because she's—insert
> derogatory term for lesbian here." The thing that freaked

me out was that they did research: they dug back over anything they could find about me online and used that, whether it was accurate or not.

Organizing swiftly, MRAs started to bombard Lee-Kennedy's employer with criticisms and complaints, trying to get her into trouble at work or even fired. Then the story was picked up on AVFM, and the Facebook abuse began. She felt firsthand the wrath of the manosphere via its well-honed mass trolling tactics:

I'd never wanted to become so aware of Men's Rights Activists as I became—I think I had it in my head that Men's Rights Activists were, like, the dads who think they haven't got fair custody arrangements, but then I learned all this other stuff and how quickly they can mobilize.

Later that year, Lee-Kennedy agreed to write an article for another online magazine—a year in review of sexism. She accepted the commission on the condition that she was allowed to make it a funny piece and wrote a lighthearted look at the year. But the editor reframed the piece and gave it a new headline: rather than "A Year in Review of Sexism," it suddenly became "Five Things Men Utterly Ruined for Me in 2014." "Of course," she sighed, "that drew loads of attention."

As the online abuse machine rumbled back into action and the piece went viral, Lee-Kennedy said she vividly remembers her management enthusing, "This is so great, we're getting so much feedback! God, people really hate you!"

Eventually, the abuse died down again. But four years later, a heavily pregnant Lee-Kennedy found herself commuting to work, standing on a busy London bus, when a man refused to move his bag from an otherwise vacant seat for her to sit down. Without thinking much of it, she fired off a quick tweet about the incident. "Well it finally happened in my 8th month of pregnancy, I just sat on a man's hand and bag when he wouldn't move them off the last spare seat on the bus. We're now sharing a very quiet ride." Then she arrived at work and put her phone away.

A few hours later, she looked down at her phone to learn that her tweet had gone viral, with almost 20,000 people liking or retweeting it. The "story" had been picked up by the websites of the *Daily Mail* and the *Sun*, despite Lee-Kennedy not approving the use of her content. With a sinking feeling, she realized the abuse was beginning all over again—this time, turbocharged by the attention of the national press.

The *Daily Mail* article attracted nearly 3,000 comments, many of them insulting Lee-Kennedy's appearance or lambasting her character, others accusing her of staging the incident or making it up altogether for attention, but most extrapolating from her specific complaint about a man refusing to move his bag to make wider points about feminism and equality that reeked of MRA rhetoric.[18] Somewhere in the manosphere, it seemed, a mass troll pile on had been orchestrated. None of the following comments were removed by the *Daily Mail*—they remain fully visible to anyone who Googles Lee-Kennedy's name to this day:

"Somebody actually getting her pregnant is an achievement."

"Women these days want equality and rightly so, yet they are the first ones to complain when they get treated like men. You can't have the cake AND eat it, you know."

"Women have sowed it and now are reaping it. Tough."

"Men now are in trouble whatever we do."

"They wanted emancipation. Well that's what it means."

"Keep telling us we are all misogynists and the epitimy of patriarchal tyrany and we may start believing you."

Lee-Kennedy continued her story to me:

Then I started getting Facebook messages. One of them said: "If I saw you in the street, I would punch you, I would beat you up." A terrible thing to hear anyway, but, when you're pregnant, I think you feel this extra physical vulner-ability, because you're sort of trying to protect two people... He said: "I will find you." Once again, they were digging.

Just when she thought things couldn't get any worse, the trolls began to focus on Lee-Kennedy's unborn child, suggesting she would be an unfit mother to a male child. Lee-Kennedy blocked harassing accounts on Twitter and upped her Facebook privacy settings, but trolls still managed to find and contact her. Suddenly, as she sat in the hospital waiting room, a message was received on her Instagram account. It said, "You should have aborted your baby, that's the right thing to do, feminists shouldn't have children."

For Lee-Kennedy, it was the last straw. She gave up journalism altogether.

Unfortunately, the prevailing public notion of trolls as isolated pranksters hurling insults is pervasive enough to color societal judgment about how victims should react. "They're just trying to scare you," a hundred people have told me after yet another email detailing the gruesome and bloody methods with which a man fantasizes about taking my body apart and molesting my corpse.

"You know you're not in any actual danger, right?"

"Have you thought about taking a break from the internet?"

But Lee-Kennedy's case, just one of thousands of similar stories, shows how these mass coordinated campaigns can have enough influence to end, or seriously affect, a victim's career. For a creative, a writer, an artist, a maker, among hundreds of other sectors, access to social media can literally mean the life or death of a career, so important a role does it play in professional promotion and visibility.

So when we tell women to simply switch off, spend less time online, or stop visiting certain websites, what we are really saying is that they, not their harassers, should suffer the negative consequences of trolling. They, not the trolls, should be excluded from hostile spaces. Like Lee-Kennedy was compelled to, we are suggesting women should sacrifice their careers as the price for escaping online abuse.

There is also a real lack of public understanding of the psychological impact such abuse can have, even in the absence of physical harm.

Lee-Kennedy recalled people telling her, during the bombardment of abuse and messages about aborting her unborn child, to "just ignore it... You've got a lot of other things to think about." She'd reply, "Yeah, but I'm not thinking about them; I'm thinking about this." Advice that we shouldn't "feed the trolls" implies that the problem is simply inevitable: that men will always harass, abuse, and degrade women, so we must inevitably take steps to protect women rather than trying to tackle the problem at its root. The next assumption is that if this is an ingrained and unavoidable issue, it is the victims and potential victims who should be corralled, en masse—their freedom compromised, their choices restricted—for their own safety. Yet suggesting treating men en masse or implementing preventative solutions that would have a similar impact on their own enjoyment of free movement inevitably provokes a swift and angry backlash.

The chilling impact of online abuse on women's internet speech and participation is not just anecdotal; research carried out with 4,000 women across eight countries found that almost a quarter of women aged between eighteen and fifty-five had experienced online abuse or harassment, with the figure at 33 percent for women in the United States. Over a quarter of those who'd experienced such abuse had received threats of physical or sexual assault, and one in six had been doxxed (a number that rose to almost one in three for women who had been harassed online in the United States). Respondents reported an enormous psychological impact, including stress, anxiety, and panic attacks, as a result of the effectively gendered form of censorship. Over three-quarters of the women who had experienced harassment or abuse on social media made changes to the way they used such platforms, and a third stopped posting content expressing their opinions on certain issues.[19]

If we accept that online abuse is simply part and parcel of public space, we risk alienating an entire generation of young women from the very spaces they need to occupy to become full citizens of tomorrow. We are ostracizing them from the online arenas young people are using to organize politically and to cut their teeth in debate. This is a silent time bomb that we will not see the effects of until it is too late.

Without needing to wait to witness the potentially devastating results this might have in the future, we already have evidence that reveals how it affects our serving politicians, with the women, people of color, and LGBTQ individuals who take on public-facing roles experiencing a deluge of abuse and harassment online. A 2017 evidence paper on the issue of violence against women in politics concluded, "Online abuse, intimidation and harassment leads to women's self-censorship and withdrawal from public discourse and correspondence, and represents a direct barrier to women's free speech, undermining democracy in all its key elements."[20] A 2016 survey conducted by the Inter-Parliamentary Union (IPU) of fifty-five female parliamentarians from thirty-nine countries across five regions revealed that over 80 percent were subject to some form of psychological violence. And 45 percent had received threats of rape, beatings, death, or abduction.[21] And further research by Amnesty International starkly laid bare the intersectional nature of such abuse, revealing that Diane Abbott alone received almost half of all abusive tweets sent to female UK members of parliament in the run-up to the 2017 general election. Even when Abbott was excluded from the total, the research still showed that Black and Asian female MPs received 35 percent more abusive tweets than their white colleagues, suggesting that those voices already most underrepresented in public conversation and politics are also the ones most at risk of silencing by online abuse.[22] In the United States, similarly, politicians like Alexandria Ocasio-Cortez and Ilhan Omar have been bombarded with hundreds of death threats.[23]

Beyond the psychological harm, the professional disruption, and the political damage, online abuse also has a real, offline impact.

In 2013, a men's rights group uploaded to the internet images and identifying details of a university student, claiming she had made a false rape allegation. The claim was completely untrue, but it quickly led to details of her family, friends, and social life being spread like wildfire across social media by trolls. Abuse began to flood the young woman's online accounts, terrifying her and leaving her parents devastated. She eventually gave up her university email address, deleted all her social media accounts, and stopped attending classes.

When women's addresses are leaked to violent mobs or bomb threats force them to cancel events, online abuse melds with offline harm. When their education is compromised or halted altogether because of deliberate campaigns of mass harassment and misinformation, the impact goes far beyond the internet. When highly armed police teams are directed to targets' homes under the impression that they are confronting a terrorist threat, or when trolls' use of swatting has led to real-life deaths, we are no longer talking about "sticks and stones."[24]

In the UK, the overwhelming majority of female MPs have received online and verbal abuse, and it is the norm to see women who dare to voice their views online excoriated and harassed by mobs into silence. These online norms create a powerful precedent. They suggest that the sheer impertinence of a woman daring to have a political opinion is unendurable and that the best way to deal with those who get ideas above their station is to silence them. And to do so violently. When we see rape and death threats bandied across social media in such extraordinarily high numbers, when we watch and take note as social media companies actively refuse to suspend the accounts of those who send the threats, we receive the message that this behavior, this discourse, is acceptable. Subsequently, a large number of female MPs have begun to experience real-life abuse, from being screamed at on the street to having their windows smashed. During the 2017 election campaign, when one female MP was out canvassing, a man walked into her constituency office and told staff he was there to kill her.[25]

In the run-up to the December 2019 UK general election, nineteen female MPs announced that they would be stepping down from politics—a higher figure than expected.[26] A significant number of them specifically cited abuse as part of their reason for quitting.

Labor MP Jo Cox was a passionate feminist and humanitarian, speaking out in parliament about the Syrian refugee crisis, immigration, and women's issues and serving as chair of the Labor Women's Network. In the period leading up to her death, Cox had been targeted with a wave of abusive messages and harassment, causing additional security to be considered at her home and office and a man to be cautioned by police for sending her "malicious communications."[27] She was, in other words, a victim of trolls, months before she was shot and stabbed to death while leaving a meeting in her constituency. Thomas Mair, the fifty-three-year-old white man who killed her, was not the man police had cautioned for previously sending Cox online abuse, but he was a dedicated follower of far-right organizations and obsessed with neo-Nazi ideology.[28] His internet history revealed a fixation with white supremacy and searches for "matricide." It was also reported that Mair had "made direct contact with racist so-called 'alt-right' movements in the US."[29] In sentencing him, the judge said, "There is no doubt that this murder was done for the purpose of advancing a political, racial and ideological cause, namely that of violent white supremacism and exclusive nationalism most associated with Nazism and its modern forms."[30] But beyond pieces by a small number of feminist writers, it was rare to see the press coverage of Cox's death make any link with the culture of terror, intimidation, and violence leveled against female and nonwhite MPs more widely online. Like so many other crimes committed by white men, the incident was portrayed as a terrifying shock, coming out of nowhere—the work of a deranged lone wolf.

And yet in spite of all this, in spite of the real-life impact and the very real silencing and detrimental effect on victims, one of the most pervasive arguments in defense of online trolls is the most ironic: the noble cry of *freedom of speech!*

Perhaps the problem is that many in the manosphere, and further afield, seem to confuse freedom of speech with the right to be heard, to have an audience, never to face disagreement, and not to be called a violent, misogynistic, racist bigot? One prominent Reddit manosphere community, for example, explicitly lists total acceptance of red pill ideology as its first rule of participation: "We are not interested in debating or defending our experiences to those who disagree with the red pill, nor do we want to clog up our threads defending the morality of our choices."

Freedom of speech is, in many ways, a red herring when it comes to dealing with online abuse and trolling, since it doesn't apply on private platforms like Twitter and Facebook, which already have the right to make decisions about what content and behavior to allow on their sites as well as codes of conduct or community standards prohibiting things like racism, anti-Semitism, and other forms of hate speech (not that these are always effective or fully enforced). Part of the problem is that when we talk about hate speech, our definitions (and, therefore, the decisions taken by

such companies) are naturally colored by societal perceptions of
the various harms of different forms of prejudice. And sexism is a
particularly socially acceptable form of prejudice.

Much manosphere rhetoric, Dr. Lisa Sugiura said, "absolutely"
constitutes a form of hate speech, but it simply isn't taken seriously
by social media companies, in large part because "I don't think
misogyny as a whole is taken seriously."

And Ellen Pao, whose tenure at Reddit gave her an unprecedented insight into the difficulty of balancing freedom of speech
with the potential incubation and incitement of extremist movements online, wrote the following:

> Many large tech companies have unwittingly encouraged
> these groups in the name of unconstrained debate and "free
> speech." Misguided advocates quote the late U.S. Supreme
> Court Justice Louis Brandeis—"Sunlight is the best dis-
> infectant"—to argue that open platforms will expose and
> show the wrongness of hate and terrorism. Instead, though,
> what we've learned from platforms, ranging from Reddit
> and Twitter to GoDaddy and Cloudflare, is that public
> exposure consistently normalizes, encourages, and ampli-
> fies these beliefs.[31]

Yet some of the world's biggest social media platforms repeatedly throw up their hands and imply that the problem is too difficult
to solve, claiming to be taking extensive action against harassment
but also refusing to disclose detailed reports of their records or
procedures for tackling it. They release polished PR platitudes
about working hard to keep everybody safe online, even as women
reporting rape and death threats or graphic images of sexual

violence are receiving automated responses telling them that the content "doesn't violate our community standards." These are companies with an income equivalent to some small countries. The idea that they couldn't tackle this problem robustly if they wanted to or certainly make enormous improvements very swiftly is laughable. Where algorithms are patchy and fallible, they could hire thousands of human moderators and invest in properly training them, with input from specialist organizations, transforming the online experience of their most vulnerable users.

Victims have repeatedly suggested common-sense methods for improving online responses to trolling. On Twitter, for example, it has been suggested that the platform could take action, when a mass harassment event is reported, by checking all tweets mentioning the victim's account and suspending any that violate their terms so that a victim doesn't have to wade through thousands of messages of abuse just to report the harassment. This would be particularly pertinent in response to the troll tactic of brigading. Yet even when practical suggestions like these are offered, social media platforms remain resistant and recalcitrant, often refusing to enact any change at all or introducing weak, ineffective measures, seemingly designed to court maximum positive publicity while affording minimal disruption to abusive users.

The extra vulnerability of certain groups is only exacerbated by the response of social media platforms to online trolling, which can be described as patchy at best, woeful in the main, and deliberately, deceptively awful at worst. Studies repeatedly reveal that women, people of color, people with disabilities, and members of the LGBTQ community, in particular, face huge levels of harassment and abuse online. When a high-profile woman (particularly a privileged, white, middle-class woman who already has a platform) experiences online abuse, her case is disproportionately likely to be picked up by the media, often taking the full opportunity to splash photographs of her throughout the piece and describe her "ordeal" in titillating or sexualized terms. Because social media sites are so bad at dealing with abuse, the woman in question may have received little support until journalists start calling asking for comment, at which point the PR machine grinds into gear. Stringent action is suddenly and miraculously taken to ban the accounts that have been bombarding the victim with abuse with apparent impunity. For these women (myself among them), there tends to be an outpouring of public support and sympathy, and they are able to return to the platform with the abuse at least temporarily stemmed. What this means is that the lackluster and uneven response of social media companies, combined with the media's particular interest in "ideal" or photogenic victims, directly results in greater support and action in the cases of abuse targeting more privileged people online. Meanwhile, those with the least privilege, who experience even worse, intersectional abuse, are also, accordingly, less likely to see any action taken or to receive much attention or support. Thus, the voices we most desperately need to hear—the people whose participation on such platforms is most needed if we are to tackle the tide of harassment and intolerance—are also those most frequently driven offline by intolerable and unchecked abuse.

When Seyi Akiwowo was twenty-two years old, she decided to run for her upcoming local council election in an attempt "to effect positive change." Standing up to be counted was important to her after the murder of a school friend at a house party when Akiwowo was just fourteen. "I quickly realized that a lot of decisions were being made about my community, about young people, but [we] were not part of the decision-making process," she explained when

I spoke to her. At just twenty-three, she was elected as the youngest Black female London councilor and, soon after, was invited to the European Parliament to talk about youth engagement in politics.

At the event, spurred by seeing a Syrian refugee speaker booed and hearing other delegates shouting that immigrants and refugees should go home, Akiwowo attempted to redress the balance. Impassioned, she made an impromptu speech calling for reparations. For months, nothing happened. Then, one day in February 2017, she was at the gym, and her Spotify playlist kept cutting out. Stopping the treadmill, she looked down at her phone to see that her music was being repeatedly interrupted by an influx of hundreds of messages and notifications. Completely unprepared, Akiwowo suddenly found herself confronted with racist abuse and slurs like "n*gger," "n*ggerress," "negro," references to lynching and being hanged, as well as "monkey," "ape," being told to "die of an STI" and threats about "blacks being exterminated." The video of her appearance at the European Parliament had been posted on a neo-Nazi website. In the days and weeks that followed, Akiwowo contended with a wave of racist and misogynistic abuse across social media. She spent upsetting hours trawling through threats on YouTube and Twitter in order to report them but said she "did not receive feedback or acknowledgment." It was only after the story was belatedly picked up by local press that the social media platforms began to respond and take action. "If I didn't go into fighter mode and make media appearances and gain public support, I very much doubt there would [have been] any action from Twitter."

So the failings of social media to tackle online harassment only serve to further radicalize and homogenize the online echo chambers that produce it.

This is not the only way in which mainstream bodies

deliberately or unintentionally aid and abet online trolls. In fact, the relationship between trolls and the media is deeply problematic and mutually parasitic. The trolls delight in inventing stories and baiting mass media to pick them up, either benefiting their cause through publicity and respectability or simply providing them with the "lulz" (victorious humor) they crave from seeing their chaotic fakery taken seriously by the national press. Meanwhile, in a media landscape of increasing competition and exponentially growing online content in which outlets desperately vie for clicks, eyeballs, and advertiser revenue, there is huge benefit to be gained from covering the most outrageous and shocking content that trolls can produce. The spoils of controversy and clickbait often outweigh the risks of reputational damage by providing coverage of morally questionable or even outright false content.

The problem is exacerbated by the media practice of presenting feminism in a deliberately belittling light, focusing on the most apparently minor and deliberately controversial topics of debate. Editors and programmers are well aware that these are most likely to generate online outrage, attract trolls, and induce widespread sharing.

The practice is blindingly obvious in the daily media requests I receive: my phone will ring off the hook when a single, highly unusual case of a false rape allegation hits the headlines but remain stubbornly silent as funding for frontline sexual violence services is slashed yet again. Repeatedly and exhaustively, I attempt to persuade journalists to cover topics like period poverty or the detention of refugee women. Instead, my inbox heaves with requests like these real examples:

"Hi Laura, would you like to come on tomorrow to debate wolf whistling?"

"Looking to set up a discussion [about whether] the #MeToo movement has gone 'too far'"

"Do you think that a sign saying 'Men Working' is sexist? If so, would you be interested in putting that view forward in the debate?"

"I am looking for a comment from yourselves...regarding Kleenex ditching the 'mansize' branding from their boxes...about why the branding was sexist"

"We will be debating: are women destroying feminism?"

"Has feminism gone too far? TV interview"

"Could we entice you on to discuss man flu: fact or fiction?"

This might seem harmless, and, of course, there is nothing to prevent a media outlet from discussing any issue it chooses, but it is deeply frustrating when the balance of coverage skews so very heavily in favor of topics like these at the expense of coverage of the myriad more pressing and urgent issues feminists are actually engaged in tackling. In reality, this tendency borrows manosphere tactics of deliberate misinterpretation, creating straw feminist arguments and implying a sort of whining, privileged feminist hysteria about trivial issues. Editors also pay little heed to the fact that these are the topics most likely to incite vicious armies of trolls to abuse the women unlucky or courageous enough to be lured in to discuss them, as Lee-Kennedy discovered. Indeed, in some cases, the extra traffic trolls bring seems to be a reward for which media outlets are happy to allow their writers to pay the price. As feminist writer Jessica Valenti once powerfully pointed out, no employer would expect their employees to endure a barrage of angry people screaming personal abuse at them while they tried to do their job. Yet that is exactly the predicament in which many modern writers, particularly women and people of color, find themselves. The only difference is that the abusers are online.

Lee-Kennedy did not feel protected or supported by her editors. When the vitriol began to drive high traffic to her piece, she even recalls being eagerly told, "If you ever want to write anything like this again, we'd love to have it." She replied simply, "I don't."

In a different sense, the tabloid frenzy around her story also contributed heavily to the trolling: "The *Sun* and the *Daily Mail* knew exactly what they were doing and knew the kind of people it would draw out." For the first time, she connected the "click economy" with the "awful" people behind it, pointing out that if something drives clicks, the media doesn't really care where it comes from.

The idea that online abuse is something harmless that happens in a separate bubble that can't touch your real life is one that you can only really subscribe to if you haven't experienced such abuse. Unfortunately, that means it's an idea that makes sense to the straight, white, male, middle-class majority of journalists who are reporting on the problem, the tech bros who are responsible for building and policing the platforms where it occurs, and the male politicians and lawmakers legislating (or not) against online abuse. A fundamental part of the problem is that those whose lives are deeply, endlessly affected by it are not, by and large, those with the power to stop it. And in some cases, those with the power to stop it are the same people actually perpetuating it. While it is deeply concerning that a large majority of female MPs have received abuse online and verbally from the general public, it is just as worrying that almost two-thirds of BBC survey respondents have also received sexist comments from fellow workers or male MPs. How can we rely on these men to take any serious measures to tackle the problem?

The time I have spent investigating online trolls has started to make sense of the abuse that seemed incomprehensible to me when I first received it. Tracing the complex links between the manosphere and white supremacy explains the liberal peppering of racist epithets thrown in with the threats. The odd messages that repeatedly told me "you have the choice to have sex i have the choice to rape you" seem clearer in the context of the false equivalences around sexual violence with which manosphere forums are so enamored. It isn't just about rape threats; it's about rape threats as a direct consequence of daring to assert female sexual autonomy. The two cannot be unlinked.

Looking back at the first brigading attack I ever experienced, hundreds of messages pouring in within the space of hours, I now understand the oblique references to 4chan and 9gag "turf"—the allusions to troll armies and point scoring. I realize that my experience, my terror, was the game board between two warring groups of online abusers, each loyal to a different forum, glorying in the escalating fantasies of destroying my body, which represented the playing pieces of their game, with the ultimate goal being my destruction by withdrawal from the internet and from my job, victory sought at all costs, for honor and for lulz.

Above all, we must discern these patterns. We cannot stop

these crimes if we aren't prepared to confront and name the root ideologies and active online incitement that encourage them. And we can't deal with trolls in an effective way if we don't even understand what they are doing.

But it's not really about understanding the minutiae of current troll memes, shitposts, and secret symbols. It's about recognizing them so that we can see through them to the real problem. It's not really about the online part. It's about the part that isn't online at all.

On March 15, 2019, a twenty-eight-year-old Australian white supremacist walked into the Al Noor Mosque in Christchurch, New Zealand, and started shooting. Fifteen minutes later, he continued his massacre at the Linwood Islamic Center. Altogether, fifty-one people were killed and forty-nine injured, most of them worshippers ranging between three and seventy-seven years old.

Brenton Tarrant, who carried out the massacre, was a far right, white supremacist, misogynistic, Islamophobic extremist. It is not going far enough to say that he had links to the troll culture of the chans, the alt-right, and the manosphere. His entire act of hatred was planned, framed, and performed within that world. For Tarrant, the massacre took place as much online as it did in real life. He was carrying out a mass murder, but he was also trolling. Two days before the massacre, he posted images of the murder weapons on Twitter. Shortly before the shooting, he announced his intent on the 8chan /pol message board, including a link to his Facebook page. From Facebook, he livestreamed the massacre in real time in a horrifying seventeen-minute video. Apparently wearing a camera on his head, Tarrant created a first-person perspective of the killings for his online fans to enjoy, essentially gifting them a first-person shooter video game with real-life victims.

At the beginning of the livestream, before beginning his

rampage, Tarrant told his viewers, "Remember, lads, subscribe to PewDiePie!" It was a reference to YouTube star PewDiePie's recent campaign for more followers, Tarrant's way of alerting a certain audience that this video was for them by referencing an obscure internet meme. This was an in-joke, a remark that would only be understood by those deeply involved in the minutiae of daily internet goings-on and fluent in chatroom rhetoric—people referred to as "extremely online." But it was also a trolling technique in its own right. In the aftermath of the attack, just as Tarrant knew it would, the mainstream media scrambled to cover the story, some believing that Tarrant had been a genuine fan of the YouTuber and offering long, irrelevant explainers of his output. The *Daily Mail* hosted excerpts from the video of the massacre on its website and made his manifesto available to download in full, elevating it to one of the biggest news platforms in the world and affording reach beyond Tarrant's wildest dreams. (The *Mail* removed the manifesto and took down the video clips within three days, following widespread criticism.)

Tarrant's extremist online peers responded quickly and in character. The very first response to Tarrant's statement of what he was about to do, from another 8chan "anon" poster, egged him on and urged him to "get the high score," language horribly suited to the video game–style montage that was about to play out. In his last 8chan post, Tarrant asked the "lads" and "top blokes" to "do your part by spreading my message, making memes and shitposting as you usually do." In the wake of the massacre, his fellow extremists, trolls, and trolling extremists shared Tarrant's video virally across Facebook, YouTube, and other platforms, confounding the attempts of social media companies to remove it for days. (It still remains readily available on many extremist websites.) On the /pol board,

Tarrant's peers rushed to translate his manifesto into as many other languages as possible in order to spread his message further. They now repeatedly refer to him as "Saint Tarrant" in posts with praise like, "He fought the invaders. /pol Honors its heroes!"

The manifesto was a form of trolling in itself. It mixed Tarrant's genuine, abhorrent, violently extremist beliefs with typical examples of shitposting, including glowing references to conservative pundits and mentions of children's video games, viral dance trends like flossing, and 4chan memes. All this amplified his intention to blend his act of terror so seamlessly with his online world that outsiders wouldn't know how to tell the difference. And insiders would revel in every last word.

When the media referred to Tarrant's manifesto as white supremacist, racist, and Islamophobic, they were, of course, absolutely right. The massacre was a devastating hate crime; its focus was innocent people, targeted for their religion and the color of their skin. In the coverage, misogyny was rarely, if ever, referenced. Sophie Walker, ex-leader of the UK Women's Equality Party, tweeted about the attack, describing it as Islamophobic terrorism but also highlighting the need to recognize the threat of male violence. She was deluged with anger and abuse and accused of opportunistically hijacking a completely unrelated event to push her extreme feminist agenda.

But Walker was right. The U.S. Congress defines a mass shooting as a single incident in which three or more people are murdered. Of 114 U.S. mass shootings using this definition between 1982 and May 2019, 110 were carried out by men.[32] Should we really keep turning a blind eye to this overwhelmingly clear statistic because men get offended when we mention it? Even if it means missing a crucial opportunity to understand the problem?

Furthermore, mass killings cannot always be easily separated into different categories of misogynist or white supremacist hate crimes. The murderers who describe themselves as primarily motivated by inceldom or manosphere ideology invariably include deeply racist and homophobic rhetoric within their manifestos. The crimes pegged to white supremacy are motivated by a hatred and fear that includes ingrained misogynistic notions about immigrants "stealing" white women or a yearning to return to an age of white purity and sexual slavery. These are not separate problems. They are indelibly interwoven into the fabric of online far right extremism. To recognize that complexity is not to diminish the horror of any one form of prejudice.

The first three sentences of Tarrant's manifesto were "It's the birthrates. It's the birthrates. It's the birthrates." The major thrust of the sprawling document was an obsession with "replacement theory," a staple of white supremacist websites. It refers to the idea that immigration risks contaminating supreme white bloodlines as birth rates in certain nations decline and the "invaders" supplant white men's rightful place in impregnating white women, ultimately leading to what is absurdly positioned as a genocide of white men. This is not just a horrifyingly racist and xenophobic theory; it has its foundations in the deepest, most dehumanizing levels of misogyny. The manifesto features a slew of incel and manosphere ideology as well as being suffused with the "logic" of "extremely online" white supremacists. "Strong men do not get ethnically replaced," Tarrant ranted. "Strong men do not allow their culture to degrade, strong men do not allow their people to die. Weak men have created this situation and strong men are needed to fix it."

It is no coincidence that Tarrant named Norwegian mass murderer Anders Behring Breivik as a major inspiration. Breivik, too, is widely acknowledged as a white supremacist, having slaughtered seventy-seven people, most of whom were teenagers, in what he described as a strike against "politically correct" liberals enabling Muslim immigration. But his manifesto also mixed fathers' rights with Islamophobia, railed against political correctness, feminist thinking, and "race mixing," and relied on deeply ingrained misogynistic beliefs throughout. He echoed incel and MRA paranoia about omnipotent feminazis "transforming a patriarchy into a matriarchy." He voiced the classic MGTOW belief that our PC-mad culture is obsessed with denigrating "the intrinsic worth of native Christian European heterosexual males," emasculating them in the process. He derided women's supposed promiscuity, citing the PUA belief that women have greater "erotic capital," which they can use to their advantage over men. Breivik's introduction concluded with this urgent warning: "The fate of European civilization depends on European men steadfastly resisting Politically Correct feminism." Yet nowhere are these foundational misogynistic aspects of Breivik's motivation and extremist identity mentioned or discussed. He is thought of solely as a white supremacist, which, of course, he also is.

Tobias Rathjen, the German gunman who killed nine people in the town of Hanau in February 2020, was a far-right terrorist who left behind a racist manifesto calling for certain races and cultures to be destroyed. He also identified as an incel.[33]

Trolls are a bit like a virus. They act as one, yet consist of myriad particles. They cause chaos by infecting their hosts. Most worryingly of all, they replicate and multiply with dizzying speed.

On April 27, 2019, little over a month after the Christchurch mosque shootings, on the last day of the Jewish Passover, nineteen-year-old John T. Earnest walked into the Chabad of

Poway synagogue and opened fire with an AR-15 rifle, killing one woman and injuring three other people, including the rabbi of the synagogue.

Before committing the act of terror, Earnest left a farewell post on the same 8chan forum as Tarrant, with a link to a Facebook livestream and a 4,300-word manifesto.

It wasn't a coincidence.

Earnest's manifesto praised the Christchurch shooter and said that the massacre had been a "catalyst" for him carrying out his own. It followed Tarrant's rhetoric closely, similarly mixing "extremely online" memes and content with an obsession with declining white birth rates. And he, too, made reference to PewDiePie, falsely claiming that the YouTuber had funded his "operation." In other words, both murderers were also trolls. And their crimes were carried out with more than half an eye on performing for the troll community.

Just like Tarrant, Earnest was described in the headlines as anti-Semitic and a white supremacist. Clearly, these were the driving motivations behind his crimes. But misogyny barely featured in the reports, despite the fact that the 8chan post in which he announced his intentions referenced the male supremacist red pill movement.

Journalist Casey Quinlan, whose work has probed the intersections between gender, sexuality, and the far right, seemed to be the only writer to pick up on the connection, writing, "It's no coincidence the synagogue shooter posted about the 'red pill' movement." Keegan Hankes, a research analyst at the Southern Poverty Law Center, told Quinlan that the MRM "really does not get the lip service it deserves in the part it plays in the path down extremism."[34]

These were murderous terror attacks that saw themselves as video games. They bristled with rules, motifs, histories, and lexicons that were impenetrable to outsiders, reinforcing a sense of identity, belonging, and self-importance for the communities to which they signaled. The exact features that have, for so long, encouraged us to dismiss and belittle these online communities are now playing out offline.

What's most terrifying of all is what this means for a community in which winning is everything and there is only one way to win: escalation.

Once, I wrote back. I wrote back to a man who had called me a "whiny little bitch" and had suggested that furniture be shoved inside me, and I asked him this: "Can you tell me what it is that has made you feel so unhappy?" You're not meant to feed the trolls, I know, I know. But I was having a good day, a strong day, and I genuinely felt curious. I wanted to try to understand what had brought someone to the point of firing off a message like this to a woman he had never met. And when he wrote back, I started to learn who he was. The man was ex-military, an airborne infantry-man. He was furious that women had been allowed to serve in the army or, as he put it, that they had "got there little cunt ass's into my unit." He was religious. He believed that there "are rolls for tra-ditional men, and there are rolls for traditional women. That is the way God created us." But his definition of those roles depended on a huge power imbalance. "Men are stronger physically and men-tally. Women crack under stress at a far greater rate than men," he wrote. Somehow, somewhere along the line, those ideas had been harnessed into a vitriolic obsession with the feminist movement. He said that the movement was "doing GREAT damage to societ-ies all over the western world." Even though his original email had focused more on Muslims than on women, once we got down to talking, it turned out he was really focused on misogyny. He was livid at feminists for "feminizing the young male population" and warned that we were creating "mass carnage."

Everything he said was drawn straight from the manosphere: conspiracies about the UK Department of Defense lowering standards to kowtow to the liberal PC warriors by admitting women; fury at the "candy ass men" failing to protect traditional society.

But most of all, he was a family man. "God created men to care for and take care of his wife," he told me.

> Woman have babies and care for those children. They are a family unit that live in love and harmony. That unit is almost non existent in today's society. The way I see it the entire feminist movement needs to be crushed and destroyed. Eliminated out of society so the nuclear family can be rebuilt.

Trolls might be the crusading armies of the manosphere—the vitriolic guns for hire who'll take down anyone they see as a threat. But they are also the weakest flank, because they expose the utter hypocrisy of the movement for what it really is.

Women, my pen pal fervently seemed to believe, must be protected at all costs. Just not women like me. So I wrote back and asked him about his own family, since family was so important. And I asked him how he would feel if a total stranger was emailing his daughter, calling her a bitch and a cunt. After that, he never replied.

# 6
# Men Who Hurt Women

"She's weaker than you, beneath you, and if she crosses you again, you'll put her in the hospital."

**MATT FORNEY, MANOSPHERE BLOGGER, IN A POST TITLED "THE NECESSITY OF DOMESTIC VIOLENCE"**

We might think of incels, PUAs, MGTOW, online trolls, and MRAs as distinct and specifically online communities. We might consider them separate from the offline, common, or garden variety of men who abuse, terrorize, stalk, harass, and murder women, most frequently their own wives, girlfriends, and family members. We may perceive those men as completely distinct again from the ones who use weapons to inflict mass acts of violence and murder. This is a mistake. The issues feed closely into one another, and their root drivers are inextricably intertwined.

Men hurt women. It is a fact. It is an epidemic. It is a public health catastrophe. It is normal.

Over a third of all women worldwide have experienced physical and/or sexual violence (not including sexual harassment) at some point in their lives. One hundred and thirty-seven women across the world are killed by a member of their own family every day.[1]

We cannot discuss violent misogynistic extremism and male supremacy without contextualizing it in a world in which violence against women is at stratospheric levels. The manosphere is both a symptom of that inequality and a furious backlash against attempts to reduce it.

Everything we have seen so far from the rhetoric of incels, PUAs, and MRAs suggests that the primary goal of these reactionary groups, like much of the alt-right and other online supremacist groups, is to regress to an idealized state of white, heteronormative male control and power. They want to see women subjugated as vassals, objects to be used primarily for men's sexual pleasure and reproduction: pliant, obedient, and servile. The end—achieving this extreme, patriarchal utopia—is considered infinitely more important than the means, which may include everything from trickery to harassment to assault to mass violence.

In reality, this core manosphere ideology is not far from a definition of heterosexual male domestic abuse or rape, which are methods of establishing heteronormative male power and control over women through violent or abusive measures. Women's Aid, the UK's national domestic abuse charity, describes domestic abuse as "a gendered crime, which is deeply rooted in the societal inequality between women and men" and states that "domestic violence is deeply rooted in issues of power, control and inequality." Those who perpetrate domestic violence, it explains, "do so to get what they want and to gain control." All these are accurate descriptors that could also be used in the context of men like Elliot Rodger, obsessed with power and inequality and using violence to gain control over the women they feel have wronged them.

Respect, a UK charity working to end domestic violence with a focus on working with male perpetrators, offers a confidential and anonymous helpline and web chat for people concerned about their violence or abuse toward a partner. It informs them "Abuse doesn't just happen. Rather than being about loss of control, as a lot of people think, most of the time it's about you trying to be in control."

If terrorism is a means of attempting to exert control and wield power by creating fear, then at a micro or individual level, it precisely describes domestic abuse.

Michael Kaufman, Canadian author, educator, theorist, and cofounder of the White Ribbon Campaign, told me it is important to understand domestic violence "as a weapon to establish and maintain power, but also a mechanism to cope with fear of not being a real man. Which is not for one second to excuse it." Kaufman understands the link between domestic and public terrorism better than most. His campaign was formed in 1991 as a direct response to Marc Lépine's antifeminist terrorist attack at the École Polytechnique.

On the afternoon of December 6, 1989, Marc Lépine arrived at the École Polytechnique in Montreal, Canada, and entered a mechanical engineering class, forcing the men and women to gather on opposite sides of the room. After ordering the men to leave the room, Lépine told the remaining nine women that he was "fighting feminism."[2] Then, according to a witness, he declared, "You're women, you're going to be engineers. You're all a fucking bunch of feminists. I hate feminists."[3] He then opened fire on them, killing six and wounding three, before making his way through the school, shooting at students and staff members, then finally turning the gun on himself. In total, Lépine murdered fourteen people and injured another fourteen.

As well as Lépine's example, academic studies support

Kaufman's suggestion that there is a link between male violence and gender stereotypes. For example, a 2018 study on violence against women notes that "traditional ideas about marriage, the family and gender roles support male dominance," and "men, who hold these patriarchal stereotypes, tend to blame women and children for breaking expected dutiful, submissive behaviors, thereby validating violence as a legitimate form of social control."[4]

Positioning domestic violence as a means of exerting patriarchal control and ownership is a theory brought vividly to life by cases like that of Kayla Hayes, a nineteen-year-old student whose "controlling and manipulative" ex-boyfriend Seth Fleury bit into her face and half ripped her lower lip off after she broke up with him, because, Hayes said, "he wanted to leave his mark on me for my next boyfriend."[5] It also fits closely with the significant number of cases in which men murder their own children, framed by the perpetrators, in multiple cases, as an attempt to regain control over their family when their female partner threatens to leave—or actually leaves—the relationship.

Members of the manosphere explicitly advocate physical and psychological violence against female partners in order to create structure and discipline within the domestic sphere.

For example, Matt Forney, in a blog post titled "The Necessity of Domestic Violence," claimed the following:

> Slapping a girl across the face isn't just about hurting her, it's a kind of neg. It says "I can crush you like an insect, but you aren't worth the effort." It's a tacit acknowledgment that she's weaker than you, beneath you, and if she crosses you again, you'll put her in the hospital. You treat her like she's a child throwing a temper tantrum, not an equal.

Perpetrators of domestic abuse exhibit the same obsession with male control and power that members of the manosphere refer to, both directly and obliquely, when yearning for a society in which women know their place and male supremacist order is restored through violent means. They are essentially using violence and fear to try to impose traditional, stereotypical gender roles within their relationships in the same way that male supremacists desire the imposition of such roles on a mass scale. In other words, domestic violence *is* a kind of terrorism, just a quiet, unacknowledged, everyday terrorism.

But the parallel also works the other way, to a breathtaking degree. It is a striking fact—long unacknowledged but finally and belatedly starting to be discussed in the mainstream—that a significant percentage of terrorist attackers and mass murderers have a previous history of domestic violence or abuse.

Rachid Redouane, one of the assailants behind the 2017 London Bridge terrorist attack, was reported to have physically and emotionally abused his wife.[6]

Khalid Masood, the man who drove a car into pedestrians outside the Houses of Parliament in 2017 before stabbing police officer PC Keith Palmer to death, had punched a woman in the face and been charged with actual bodily harm on a former girlfriend.[7]

Mohamed Lahouaiej-Bouhlel, who carried out the 2016 Nice terrorist attack, was known to authorities for assaulting and abusing his wife.[8]

Omar Mateen, the terrorist attacker who killed forty-nine people and wounded fifty-three at Orlando gay nightclub Pulse in 2016, had repeatedly beaten his wife as well as controlling her finances and isolating her from her family.[9]

In 2014, Man Monis held eighteen people hostage during the

Sydney siege, leading to a standoff and raid in which two hostages were killed and four other people injured. He had forty-three sexual assault charges and a history of domestic violence and harassment.[10]

Devin Patrick Kelley, who killed twenty-six and injured twenty in a mass shooting at the First Baptist Church in Sutherland Springs, Texas, in 2017, had been convicted of domestic violence and had beaten, kicked, and choked his wife.[11]

Esteban Santiago-Ruiz had been arrested and charged with assault in 2016 after breaking down his girlfriend's door and choking her, less than a year before he carried out a mass shooting at Fort Lauderdale–Hollywood International Airport in Florida, killing five people and injuring six others.[12]

This is by no means an exhaustive list—it does not include any of the mass killers named in the chapter on incels, many of whom also already had a history of violence against women—but it reveals that such a history is strikingly common among other mass murderers and terrorists, even when it isn't mentioned in media coverage of the attack or its motivation. And these are not isolated examples. A 2019 investigation revealed that in at least twenty-two mass shootings since 2011, the perpetrators had a history of domestic violence, had specifically targeted women, or had stalked and harassed women. Those twenty-two shootings accounted for more than a third of the public mass shootings that took place during that eight-year period.[13]

And when gun-control campaign group Everytown for Gun Safety analyzed FBI data on mass shootings in the United States between 2009 and 2018, it found that in at least 54 percent of mass shootings, the victims included an intimate partner or family member of the perpetrator.[14]

The connection between terrorist acts and domestic violence is something that feminist academics and activists have long warned of—a pattern that has been pointed out over and over again. As Rachel Pain, professor of human geography at Newcastle University, wrote, "Everyday terrorism (domestic violence) and global terrorism are related attempts to exert political control through fear."[15]

For years, amid feverish speculation about the possible causes and motives of terrorist attackers, the most blatantly obvious connecting factors (not least the fact that upward of 96 percent of terrorists are male, according to FBI data) were studiously ignored.[16] It was not until the mid- to late 2010s that the connection between mass killers and past histories of domestic abuse really began to emerge in the mainstream media. And even now, too often, crimes of white male violence are excused, belittled, and isolated using the inevitable "lone wolf" and mental health narratives, with media outlets bending over backward to find plausible "reasons" to justify and explain such acts, despite other types of perpetrators (most notably Muslims) experiencing the opposite treatment.

This plays out initially in which attacks receive coverage. A 2017 study examining data and news coverage for all terrorist attacks in the United States between 2006 and 2015 revealed that, controlling for target type, fatalities, and arrests, attacks by Muslim perpetrators receive, on average, 357 percent more coverage than attacks by non-Muslims.[17] Another study in 2015 analyzed 146 U.S. network and cable news programs between 2008 and 2012, finding that 81 percent of terrorism suspects who were subjects of news reporting were Muslim, far greater than the percentage of terror attacks in the United States committed by Muslims during that period.[18]

Then there is the nature of the coverage. A 2011 U.S. media study revealed "a thematic pattern of terrorism coverage in which fear of international terrorism is dominant, particularly as Muslims/

Arabs/Islam working together in organized terrorist cells against a 'Christian America,' while domestic terrorism is cast as a minor threat that occurs in isolated incidents by troubled individuals."[19]

A comparison of media coverage of Dylann Roof's 2015 massacre at an African American church in Charleston, South Carolina, with Mateen's Orlando massacre revealed that mental health was discussed three and a half times more in coverage of the former, while the terms *terrorist* or *terrorism* were mentioned roughly three times more in coverage of the latter.[20]

So there is robust evidence to suggest that news media are already biased to portray certain types of attacker in very different ways and are reluctant to apply the term *terrorist* to white men with the same readiness that they do to Muslim attackers. All this before you begin to broach the fact that crimes rooted in misogynistic extremism are markedly less likely to be taken seriously as "terrorist" incidents, even in comparison to those carried out in the name of white supremacy or far-right ideologies.

Such coverage is mirrored by the ways in which the justice system treats violent extremist attackers. James Alex Fields Jr., who drove into a crowd of protesters, was not charged as a terrorist. Instead, he faced federal hate crime charges.[21] After FBI agents found bomb-making materials and the note referring to a "heroic" massacre of "hot cheerleaders" at Cole Carini's home, he was only charged, at the time of writing, with the crime of lying to FBI agents.[22] A 2019 analysis of U.S. federal prosecutions since 9/11 concluded that "the Justice Department has routinely declined to bring terrorism charges against right-wing extremists, even when their alleged crimes meet the legal definition of domestic terrorism: ideologically motivated acts that are harmful to human life and intended to intimidate civilians, influence policy, or change government conduct."[23] Critics have pointed out that this glaring omission results from a lack of any U.S. law covering domestic terrorism. But it is not only legal hurdles that impact our public idea of who does and doesn't qualify as a terrorist. In 2020, for example, Donald Trump, on a telephone call with state governors, described those involved in the Black Lives Matter protests that swept America in the wake of George Floyd's death as "terrorists."[24]

Media coverage of mass violence is similarly problematic. After Brenton Tarrant carried out the Christchurch shootings, the *Daily Mirror's* front page featured a photograph of him as a rosy-cheeked preschooler with the headline "Angelic Boy Who Grew into an Evil Far-Right Mass Killer," followed by an article describing him as a "likeable and dedicated personal trainer, running free athletic programs for kids."[25] The piece also reproduced portions of Tarrant's manifesto, including his own description of himself: "I am just a regular white man, from a regular family. Who decided to take a stand to ensure a future for my people."[26]

"Christchurch terrorist's grandmother says he was a 'good boy,'" read one *Daily Mail* article.[27]

The headlines contrasted starkly with British tabloid reporting on terror attacks carried out by Muslims, such as the Manchester arena bombing, following which the *Daily Express* headline read "Evil Beyond Belief. How Could a Jihadi Barbarian Murder Our Beautiful and Innocent Children?" And the *Sun* went for "Pure Evil."

Compare this to front pages following Darren Osborne's terrorist attack on worshippers outside Finsbury Park Mosque in 2017 in which one person was killed and at least nine injured. "Jobless 'Lone Wolf' Darren Osborne Held over Attack on Finsbury Park Mosque," read *The Times* headline. "Mosque 'Attack,'" read the

*Sun,* as if to imply it wasn't convinced the attack had even really happened. A *Daily Mail* headline attempted to link the mosque to Islamist extremism, even as it reported on the terrorist attack: "White Van Driver Injures at Least 10 People after Ploughing into a Crowd outside London's Finsbury Park Mosque Where Hate Cleric Abu Hamza Once Preached as Muslims Finish Their Evening Prayers."

And in the case of men who kill in the name of misogynistic extremism, in particular, the motive tends to receive very little attention and is rarely mentioned in headlines. "We certainly don't use the word 'terrorism' to describe their actions when they blossom into violence," said Kaufman.

Consider, for example, media coverage of Elliot Rodger, perhaps the best-known mass killer to have acted in the name of incel and male supremacist ideology. An extensive *New York Times* profile of him, written by four men and published little over a week after his misogynistic massacre, is titled "Before Brief, Deadly Spree, Trouble Since Age 8" and illustrated with a sepia photograph of an angelic-looking Rodger in the fifth grade.[28] In a series of quotes from people who knew him, Rodger is variously described as "lonely," "introverted," "emotionally troubled," "smart," "liked," and "very innocent, very soft-spoken." "He never even raised his voice," his former principal is quoted as saying. Teachers are repeatedly cited referring to him affectionately as "our Elliot," a phrase repeated three times in the piece. The article focuses extensively on Rodger's experience of bullying, presenting him as a victim. It quotes his parents' concerns about whether he could "be easily taken advantage of" or "an easy target for some kind of a scam" and reproduces sections of Rodger's manifesto in which he describes having food thrown at him at school and asks, "What kind of horrible, depraved people would poke fun at a boy younger than them who has just entered high school?"

Despite quoting extensively from Rodger's manifesto, particularly in describing his own perceived victimization at school, there is only limited reference to the overwhelmingly detailed misogynistic content it contained; there are no quotes from the sections in which he described women as "beasts," "twisted and wrong," "the ultimate evil," or his declaration that women should have all rights removed, with men deciding who they must "mate or breed with." No coverage of his belief that "there is no creature more evil and depraved than the human female."

The article does cover Rodger's association with various manosphere websites, though it euphemistically describes this period of misogynistic radicalization as "retreating into the internet" and labels the extremist websites he visited as hubs for "sexually frustrated young men." It reproduces some of his online postings but says nothing of the video in which he directly and explicitly addressed women, declaring his intent to "slaughter every single spoiled, stuck-up blonde slut I see... I take great pleasure in slaughtering all of you."

Never using the words *terrorism*, *extremism*, *misogyny*, or *sexism*, the article paints a very specific picture of the mass murderer who would go on to become a hero and rallying point for future manosphere killers.

A *New York Times* piece about Pennsylvania killer George Sodini is euphemistically titled "Blog Details Shooter's Frustration" and opens by describing him as "tortured by loneliness." Though no details are given about the dead women named in the article, the male writer quotes a neighbor saying that Sodini was "friendly... and he wasn't bad looking."[29]

It is informative to compare these and countless other media articles that report on incel and male supremacist killers without ever calling them extremists or terrorists with the definitions of terrorism in the countries in which such attacks were carried out.

In the United States, terrorism is defined in Title 22 Chapter 38 USC § 2656f as "Premeditated, politically motivated violence perpetrated against noncombatant targets by subnational groups or clandestine agents."

In the UK, the statutory definition of terrorism is contained in section 1 of the Terrorism Act 2000. It specifies that terrorism is the use or threat of action that is designed to influence the government or an international governmental organization or to intimidate the public or a section of the public and is made for the purpose of advancing a political, religious, or ideological cause. The action used or threatened must involve serious violence against a person, serious damage to property, endangering a person's life, creating a serious risk to public health or safety, or the intention to interfere with, or seriously disrupt, an electronic system.

In Canada, the definition of "terrorist activity" includes acts or omissions committed with two key intentional elements. First, the accused must have acted with "a political, religious or ideological purpose, objective or cause." Second, they must have intended to intimidate the "public, or a segment of the public, with regard to its security," or compel a government or organization "to do or to refrain from doing any act." The activity in question must also have violently caused death or serious injury, endangered life, or resulted in a serious risk to public safety (including a segment of the public).

While there is a complex and nuanced conversation to be had about the label of terrorism and its benefits and restrictions, it is clear that many of the perpetrators and acts described in this book meet the threshold to be described as terrorists and terrorism according to these definitions. Yet only once, in the case of Ashley Noell Arzaga's murder, have authorities ever brought terrorism charges in an attack or murder with incel motivation. That this repeatedly fails to happen is undeniable proof of three things: first, the lack of severity our society attaches to violent extremism motivated by misogyny; second, a widespread desensitization to violence against women; and third, a lack of awareness of the extent of the online male supremacist community.

Where some may argue that male supremacist acts have not met the threshold to fall into the category of terrorism, it is worth considering the closely related but separate category of violent extremism, generally defined as supporting or committing violent acts to achieve political, ideological, religious, or social goals. This term, despite precisely encompassing many such events, is also rarely applied to men acting in the name of misogynistic extremism.

The way the media frames these incidents is enormously important. There is repeated evidence to suggest that framing attacks as terrorism has an impact on public opinion, influencing individuals' political stances on issues such as funding for antiterrorism activities and support for various government acts and policies.[30] This swaying of public opinion can, in turn, influence politicians' priorities and actions or affect the perception of particular groups. So the fact that news media underplay and soften their portrayals of white male terrorists, never define explicitly extremist misogynistic attacks as such, and never reference violent misogyny as a form of terrorism contributes to our societal normalization of such ideologies and such violence and reinforces the weakness of our government and policy response to the problem.

What we are seeing when we witness the dramatically different reporting on incel mass murders in comparison to other similar crimes arises from the overlap of two major media blind spots. The first is its reluctance to classify white murderers as terrorists with anywhere near the same eagerness as Muslim or nonwhite perpetrators. The second is its tendency to downplay, excuse, and humanize men who commit violence against women in general, including (and particularly) in domestic settings.

This effect is often achieved through coverage that suggests sympathetic motives for domestic abusers' actions, often implicitly blaming their victims by suggesting that they somehow caused or provoked their own attacks.

A typical headline reads "BBQ Dad 'Killed 6 over Wife's Affair.'" This both immediately humanizes the "BBQ dad" and directly links the mass murder to his wife's alleged infidelity. Another reads "Wife Jibes about Penis Size and Lesbian Tryst 'Drove Hubby to Murder.'" And a third reads "Life for Husband Driven to Double Murder by Jealousy." After a mass school shooting in Santa Fe, Texas, one headline cried "Spurned Advances Provoked Texas School Shooting, Victim's Mother Says." (Indeed, this in itself is a media narrative that would play right into the ideology of an incel reader.) And as I wrote this chapter, a news article popped up in my Twitter feed: "Hen-Pecked Husband Killed Wife Who Called Him 'Limp and Useless' over His Erectile Dysfunction."

An article about a man who stabbed his two children to death described him as a "jilted father," "devastated," and "heartbroken" after his wife left him—the kind of content MRA blogs drool over.[31]

A 2019 article about a Welsh man who beat and stabbed his wife and two children to death included quotes from the killer's sister, who said that her brother "was not a violent man until he saw text messages from other men on his wife's phone." In reality, the article itself admitted that he had served a jail sentence for an extended assault on his wife in 2013.[32] The coroner was quoted as saying that the murderer had "demons in his mind" (there was no mention of any mental illness), and in spite of his previous imprisonment for domestic violence, "no one foresaw what was to happen. There were no explicit threats that would have enabled someone to intervene to prevent this tragedy."

In July 2016, a man named Lance Hart murdered his wife, Claire, and their nineteen-year-old daughter, Charlotte, in Spalding, Lincolnshire. An article about the incident, by a male writer with no personal knowledge of the case beyond media reports, read as follows:

> Of course, such men are often motivated by anger and a desire to punish the spouse. But, while killing their partner as an act of revenge may be understandable, for a man to kill his children (who are innocent bystanders in a marital breakdown) is a very different matter. I believe it is often a twisted act of love, as the man crassly believes that the crisis in their lives is so great that the children would be better off dead.[33]

The use of the word *understandable* to describe a man's murder of his wife and the phrase *act of love* to describe the killing of his own child is symptomatic of how far into victim blaming our news coverage of domestic violence has spiraled. And the description of killing "innocent" children as a "very different matter" from the murder of a spouse immediately framed Claire as partly to blame—her murder a gray area. Other UK newspapers painted a sympathetic picture of Hart, focusing on his "struggle" to cope with marital breakdown. The *Daily Mirror* quoted acquaintances who said he was "always caring."[34] The *Telegraph* ran testimonials from neighbors who described Hart as a "very, very nice guy" as well as including irrelevant details about his DIY skills.[35] Reports speculated about what "drove" Hart to murder his wife and daughter.

Charlotte's brothers, Luke and Ryan Hart, who were both abroad at the time of the attack, have since described their sister and mother in interviews as "selfless, caring" animal lovers, "obsessed with dogs." Sporty Charlotte loved horseback riding and volunteered to help the elderly. Claire adored her children and liked to grow her own vegetables.[36] None of these details were covered in the mainstream media articles that waxed lyrical about Hart's DIY skills and good nature.

In the aftermath of their mother's and sister's deaths, Luke and Ryan made a crucial connection. Shocked by the casual sympathy the press afforded their father, they slowly began to realize that the media portrayal of domestic violence was exactly what had allowed him to get away with it for so long in the first place. "The false imagery the media puts out about domestic abuse meant we never recognized it for what it was," Luke and Ryan told me. Stifled by the normalization of their father's behavior, the boys had never felt able to label it domestic abuse, leaving them feeling isolated and helpless.

Their account of their childhood and their relationship with their father also starkly reveals the overlap between domestic abuse and the ideology of the male supremacist manosphere:

Our father was a firm believer [in] rigid stereotypes. He expected us all to submit to him and serve him. His belief was that a man is entitled to power within the family unit;

that everything the family owns belongs to him, and we should be grateful for his generosity for him allowing us to stay there.

The brothers presented a deep and poignant understanding of their father's patriarchal belief system, describing his anger and bewilderment that Ryan preferred to spend Saturday nights at home with his mother and sister instead of out with other men in the pub. They described their father as "uncomfortable" around Charlotte, who was strong, confident, and opinionated, and noted that he was "confused" by her loving relationship with a respectful boyfriend to whom she was not subservient. When his wife or children didn't obey him, Luke and Ryan said, their father seemed to feel "humiliated, emasculated or castrated even"—his sense of self-worth was inextricably and dangerously tied to his dominance over his family.

Luke and Ryan also poignantly skewered the deeply damaging media tropes of implying perpetrators must have been mentally ill or out of control (they point out that their father purchased a parking ticket twenty minutes before the murders and had begun writing the note he would leave behind weeks beforehand) and the misleading practice of gathering sympathetic quotes from peripheral figures:

> Our father didn't lose control of himself, he had lost total control over us when we escape[d] him. To regain control, he had to kill us. The fact that our father was considered "a good man" to neighbors and outsiders showed the level of control that he had over who he abused. Control over us was central to his worldview.

As the quotes from coroners in some of the aforementioned examples reveal, this is not a problem solely confined to the media. The notion of justified or "tortured" abusers repeatedly crops up within the criminal justice system and elsewhere. In 2019, twenty-four-year-old Alexander Heavens, who punched his girlfriend in the face, bit her, and bent her fingers back, was spared jail after admitting to engaging in controlling and coercive behavior in an intimate relationship. The judge told Heavens "everyone deserves a second chance" and advised him to "put her behind you, there are lots more fishes in the sea."[37] Given the extremely high proportion of domestic abusers who go on to become repeat offenders, it might be preferable, in fact, if Heavens did not catch another "fish" at all.

So our mainstream media portrayal of male violence and our societal misconceptions about it risk having a devastating impact. When we sympathize with the men who commit domestic violence, we normalize and condone it, providing fuel to the fire of extremist online communities. And as long as we willfully ignore the connection between mass terror attacks and past convictions for domestic abuse, we continue to overlook a vital red flag.

Even when killers kill in the name of explicit misogyny, even when they spell it out for us in manifestos or scream it in the faces of their victims, we will still look somewhere—anywhere—else for explanations. In the wake of a 1991 massacre by George Hennard, a former merchant marine, an extraordinary article appeared in *People* magazine. Its second paragraph read as follows:

> With cold-blooded efficiency, he stalked the restaurant and chose those who would die—most of whom were women. "All women of Killeen and Belton are vipers! See what you've done to me and my family!" Hennard yelled, calmly

carrying out his executions, often at point-blank range with
a single shot to the head.

Later, the article observed that Hennard was "known for
his hatred of women." It described him "wondering aloud" to a
coworker about committing the murders. "He got to talking about
some of the people in Belton and certain women that had given him
problems," said coworker Bubba Hawkins. "And he kept saying:
'Watch and see, watch and see.'"

The article discusses two young women he had stalked to
whom he sent a letter saying, "Please give me the satisfaction of
someday laughing in the face of all those mostly white tremen-
dously female vipers." It quoted his former roommate, saying, "He
said women were snakes... He always had derogatory remarks
about women, especially after fights with his mother." It described
Hennard's last supper, in a restaurant the night before the shooting,
with witnesses reporting that when an interview with Anita Hill
came on the television, "he started screaming: 'You dumb bitch!
You bastards opened the door for all the women!'"

Then the article concluded, "Still, the mystery of George
Hennard Jr. persists." It ends with a quote from a survivor:
"Nobody knows why it happened, and they are never going to have
the answers."[38]

Imagine if we were to take domestic abuse seriously. Imagine if
we acted to prosecute such men, to remove them from the streets,
or, as the bare minimum, to take better legislative action in certain
countries to prevent them from accessing firearms. Women have
always been the canaries in the coal mines, quietly singing. But we
are so used to seeing them die at men's hands, so used to justify-
ing and excusing it as normal or "understandable," that it wouldn't

occur to us to consider this enough of an aberration to raise alarm. And so women continue to suffer and die in silence. And sometimes days, sometimes weeks, sometimes months down the line, men (or rather, as they are seen, "people") die too. Then how we shout and react.

# 7
# Men Who Exploit Other Men

"Tough shit...go fucking bother
someone else with your problems."

PAUL ELAM, MRA, IN A POST TITLED "AN
OPEN RESPONSE TO TROUBLED MEN"

If we are interested in the ways in which these shadowy online communities have managed to penetrate the mainstream consciousness, we must pay attention to the individual figures who manage to bridge the gap between internet and reality, those who stand with one foot in the murk of the forums, subreddits, and chans and the other foot firmly planted on the solid ground of media platforms, political influence, and prime-time television.

Jacob Davey at the Institute for Strategic Dialogue told me,

This mainstreaming component is something we're seeing with the extreme right—by having more central figureheads, who can present a slightly more sanitized version of an ideology in a way [that] is easily consumable and seems [a] bit more acceptable, that very much opens the door for more fringe members to advance [that] ideology.

But in order for them to successfully smuggle their cargo of division, fear, and hatemongering, a delicate balancing act is necessary. The men who help to usher trends from the fringes of internet extremism onto our airwaves and into our living rooms must at once continue to appeal to the denizens of online communities, hitting the ideological keynotes that will chime with trolls and members of the manosphere, yet simultaneously package their message behind a veneer of "reasonable" debate and respectable (if unpopular) opinion for public consumption. In short, dog-whistle rhetoric, coded language, and sometimes outright self-contradiction are required.

Some of these men are cashing in on trends driven by manosphere communities, perhaps without even realizing who they are appealing to. For others, the decision to appeal to certain groups seems to be more deliberate. For political figures like Donald Trump and his advisers, such as former chief strategist Steve Bannon, there are gains to be made by issuing dog whistles to the alt-right and manosphere communities. Such rhetoric, like Trump's derisive advice to four Democratic congresswomen of color and American citizens to "go back" to the countries they originally came from, is greeted with wild applause across the masses frequenting extremist websites.[1] But a buffer of plausible deniability is also important in order to avoid alienating a more mainstream base: a feat achieved by publicly disavowing racism and white supremacy, even while his own statements seem to send a very different message.[2]

For many of the other figureheads idolized, quoted, and supported by the foot soldiers of the manosphere, it is also richly profitable to maintain the sympathy and loyalty of these communities while actually holding them (either genuinely or performatively) in contempt.

There's Daryush "I don't presently identify as a PUA" Valizadeh, who embarked on a 2019 speaking tour about his religious awakening while simultaneously raking in the cash from his books *Day Bang: How to Casually Pick Up Girls during the Day*, *Game: How to Meet, Attract, and Date Attractive Women*, and *The Best of Roosh* ("featuring all the lessons I learned from my intensive pursuit of casual sex"). Perhaps aware of the optics, Valizadeh has since removed the books from sale. And Milo Yiannopoulos, darling of the alt-right, whose leaked emails showed that he had repeatedly solicited neo-Nazi and white supremacist figures on the alt-right for ideas and feedback on his work at *Breitbart* yet also claims, "The alt-right, as the word is used today... I have nothing to do with it, and no fondness for it, and no interest in being associated with it."[3] Then there's Ross Jeffries, one of the founding fathers of pickup artistry, whose website is headlined "Meet and Bed More Hot, Sexy Women," even as he earnestly tells journalists, "I've leveled up as a human, as a man. I've outgrown my own marketing... That kind of messaging just hasn't resonated with who I am as a human being for some time."[4]

Their disavowals are about as believable as Yiannopoulos's claim that as he belted out "America the Beautiful" in a Dallas karaoke bar one night in 2016, his "severe myopia" meant he simply couldn't have seen famous white nationalist Richard B. Spencer and others raising their arms in Nazi salutes just a few feet away.[5]

Many of the men who find themselves arriving at manosphere communities and forums are vulnerable, looking for support in often difficult circumstances. The communities' leading men, these "idols," promise them redemption, success, victory beyond their wildest dreams. But the reality is that these men are far more closely concerned with their own reputation and profit than with the actual needs of their followers or even the success of their causes.

Take, for example, Paul Elam, founder of AVFM. Elam's posts regularly upbraid and excoriate his readership for its failure to contribute enough financial support to what he loftily describes as a "cause that should include millions." One tactic for shaming website visitors into coughing up cash is to boast about the devotion of followers who have donated $100 of their meager unemployment checks to the noble cause. How awkward then, after having previously suggested that the money donated to AVFM by its loyal followers would be spent on technical platforms, servers, and licensing fees, that Elam was eventually forced to admit that an unspecified portion of the site's estimated $120,000 annual revenue went directly into his own pocket.[6] With no transparency or likelihood of it ("AVFM is not a charitable institution and the financial records are not a matter of public record, nor will they be," wrote Elam in a blog post), supporters were supposed to be reassured by Elam's dubious insistence that "of course my personal financial gain has never been the objective here."

These are the kind of men who would line their pockets with the cash of their most vulnerable supporters, all the while preaching that other people are the real oppressors of poor, unemployed men.

Then again, that men like Elam are happy to make money off their staunch supporters while simultaneously berating them for not sacrificing enough becomes less surprising when one considers the way in which they are prepared to speak to, and about, those same supporters. In 2015, Elam published a seemingly drunken video to YouTube showing a group of fifteen men drinking beer and talking about high-profile feminists in deeply misogynistic and violent terms. But when a number of his men's rights supporters apparently expressed their concern that the video could be used as ammunition by opponents of the movement, Elam took to YouTube to denounce and ridicule these men, accusing them of pearl clutching and describing his critics as "a particularly useless, burdensome and energy-draining kind of make-believe activist." He told his men's rights detractors that they have neither "spine nor intelligence" and that they are welcome to take his explanation and "shove [it] up your asses." The episode illustrated the extent to which Elam's own pompous, misogynistic showboating takes precedence over the reputation of the movement he claims to care so deeply about.

Another rather unsubtle clue about Elam's attitude toward the men on whose backs he has built his personal renown came in the form of a blog post titled "An Open Response to Troubled Men," which he addressed to the "hundreds" of men he claims regularly contact him after being "screwed over" or "dragged through the mud" or seeing their lives otherwise "ruined" by a "horrifically corrupt" antimale society. Elam's response to these men, suffering from exactly the ills he claims to abhor, representing precisely the "victims" he professes to devote his life to helping? "Fuck you... tough shit... go fucking bother someone else with your problems." Unless they are prepared to "cough up five fucking dollars to help us out," Elam wrote, they must expect no help from him. He went on to add that their situation is hopeless, that "they are fucked and that there is no help," a message that jars immediately with his claim that they ought to join him in the noble warrior work of fixing the problem.

The response makes more sense, however, in the context of

the benefits available to Elam and men like him if they can create a graphic picture of a harsh and terrible world, unfairly stacked against men, convince their followers that they are doomed, and portray themselves as the only hope for redemption. If these men are unable to escape their problems or find constructive ways forward, they are reduced to remaining in the bitter ranks of the manosphere, consuming ever more of Elam's content, and continuing to build up his profile with clicks, likes, and donations. There is no incentive for men like Elam to help their followers move on or solve their problems, because such figureheads are dependent on the slavish support of men who believe the systemic discrimination against them exists and is inescapable.

If PUAs admitted to the shy teenagers who stumbled across their websites that their lack of romantic experience was not due to ignorance of some complex psychological technique but simply a normal rite of passage likely to pass with age and maturity, no longer could those PUAs rake in thousands of dollars for imparting the "secrets" of tricking women into bed. If men like J4MB's Mike Buchanan and other manosphere heroes acknowledged that the real issue at the root of so many of the problems they rail against is the stringent societal stereotype of masculinity, they would be stuck. There would be a risk that their adoring followers might be liberated, able to constructively tackle the issues that have left them silenced or reach out for genuine support. Worse still, these forum idols and false prophets might actually be forced to do some work on dismantling gender stereotypes. Instead, they double down on the very problem hurting their followers the most. They encourage men to hold ever more tightly to outdated tropes of masculinity, suggesting that adherence to these tired and rigid constructs is a life raft when it is actually the very current dragging many men beneath the surface.

The same men who are vulnerable to the false promises of PUAs touting sex as a commodity and women as objects are equally easy targets for semispiritual waffle about personal transformation. In this context, the pivot of PUAs like Valizadeh and Julien Blanc from game boot camps to "self-help" seminars is easy to understand. It enables them to continue exploiting the same audience, just in a new way.

It benefits Jordan Peterson (who is the darling of many a reverent manosphere thread) to evangelize a return to traditional masculine values and for MRAs to hearken back to an imagined utopian age of outdated gender roles, because it is exactly these values and roles that have driven men in their masses to their figureheads' websites and seminars in the first place. By encouraging more and more men in the ultimately doomed attempt to live up to toxic ideals of performative masculinity, men's rights idols are driving forward the vicious circle, ushering another wave of disaffected, broken, ashamed men straight into nets of misogyny, blame, and bitterness. The process is as ingenious as it is self-serving. As an article in the *New York Review of Books* put it, Peterson is "a disturbing symptom of the malaise to which he promises a cure."[7]

The men who benefit from a more sanitized version of the same ideas swirling in the vitriol of the manosphere are exceptionally careful and savvy about what they say. They might dance with ideology that appeals directly to extremist misogynists, but they tread very precisely on just the right side of the line of acceptable speech, couching their theories in caveats and preemptive defense, always ready to argue that their words have been taken out of context or misinterpreted.

They are also extremely adept at the use of irony and purported "satire" as a means of masking and legitimizing what might be their true beliefs. This has an incredibly powerful effect. It neutralizes their detractors, thanks to the cover of freedom of speech. It positions them as hip, scrappy combatants against the disapproving progressives who can't recognize humor when they see it. It appeals to the hardcore far-right adherents, who take it at face value. And it works as a gateway for those not yet so far along the process of radicalization, for whom what starts off as humorous "irony" can slowly slide into genuine belief.

As Dr. Lisa Sugiura said,

They're incredibly clever. They present themselves as edgy, cool—it's that appeal of counterculture. And that's not new… That's always drawn in audiences, challenging the norm, calling out political correctness gone wrong, but then standing back, holding their hands in the air and saying, "Well, we never encouraged people to actually act on it!" Or people like Milo Yiannopoulos—he always says things like, "Oh no, I'm not interested in politics." So they're very clever not to affiliate themselves completely with these groups, with these movements, but at the same time, they play to their ideologies, because they want the audience, they want the attention, they want the support.

We don't have to speculate about this deliberate use of "irony" to obfuscate a hate-filled message. It has been clearly explained by misogynistic, white supremacist Andrew Anglin himself, who has openly described his approach as "non-ironic Nazism masquerading as ironic Nazism."[8] In fact, it is actually written down for us in black and white by misogynistic and racist online extremists. In September 2017, as they attempted to recruit new writers for their fast-growing website, the proprietors of the *Daily Stormer* released a "style guide," or set of directives, for people aspiring to submit articles. The *HuffPost* acquired and published the seventeen-page document in its entirety, giving an unprecedented insight into the tactics ruthlessly and deliberately used by online extremists to attract and indoctrinate new recruits, all the while tiptoeing around the definition of hate speech. As *HuffPost* writer Ashley Feinberg pointed out, this was not just a style guide, "it's a playbook for the alt-right."[9]

The techniques described include the direct instruction to mix hate speech with humor in an attempt to woo new readers just beginning to dip their toes in the bile ("It should always be considered that the target audience is people who are just becoming aware of this type of thinking," states the guide). A list of suggested racist, misogynistic, and homophobic slurs is offered, with the precaution that when using such slurs, "it should come across as half-joking—like a racist joke that everyone laughs at because it's true... It should not come across as genuine raging vitriol. That is a turnoff to the overwhelming majority of people."

Then there are specific instructions on how to incite violence without being seen explicitly to promote it:

> I'm extremely careful about never suggesting violence... However, whenever someone does something violent, it should be made light of, laughed at. For example, Anders Breivik should be forever referred to as a heroic freedom fighter. This is great because people think you must be joking. But there is a part of their brain that doesn't think that.

The calculated self-awareness is chilling. Anglin knows exactly what he is doing, and he is damn good at it. It is a naked admission that recruitment of young people is the aim and "irony" and humor the vehicle. "The reader is at first drawn in by curiosity or the naughty humor, and is slowly awakened to reality by repeatedly reading the same points... The unindoctrinated should not be able to tell if we are joking or not."

It is also ironic, given the extent to which manosphere leaders are prepared to hack, steal, and expose confidential information relating to feminists' families and private lives, that many are so coy about the realities of their own pasts. Men like Elam and Buchanan seek to present their antipathy toward the court system and the abject wickedness of women as a noble battle with pure, ideological motives. So it is strange that they remain surprisingly silent about their own multiple divorces or respond with fury when media reports mention strained relationships with ex-wives and biological children. (Though perhaps using the term *biological* is the sticking point, given Elam's attempts to disavow his paternity of his own daughter so as to avoid paying child support.)[10]

Beyond the leaders and evangelists of the male online masses, there is another group often celebrated by members of the manosphere and the alt-right. A group that has shifted manosphere views further into the mainstream than its inhabitants could ever have hoped. Politicians.

And the attention and influence these politicians command powerfully belies the argument that manosphere communities remain obscure and inconsequential.

The first and most obvious politician whose success has emboldened the manosphere and alt-right alike is Trump. From his description of women as "fat pigs" and "dogs" to his assertion that putting a wife to work is "dangerous"; from his own admissions of grabbing women "by the pussy" to his implication that women on their periods are unstable; from his description of Mexican immigrants as rapists to his tweets telling four ethnic minority U.S. congresswomen to "go back and help fix the totally broken and crime-infested places from which they came"—the president repeatedly voiced ideas and deeply misogynistic, racist statements that fit neatly within the worldview of male supremacists and the alt-right.[11] They, in turn, expressed delight at his election, and many continue to revel in what they perceive as his support of their cause and his influence in helping to push it into the mainstream.

Valizadeh was one of the first to crow about Trump's victory and was not alone in the manosphere in claiming to have rallied to the president's support during the election. "The celebrations have ended and we've all come to absorb the fact that Donald Trump is our next president, an outcome that many of us have aggressively worked for in the past several months," he wrote. He went on to say the following:

> A Trump presidency will improve our standing... We now have a s\*\*tlord for President who has insulted ugly women as "fat pigs," and whose private macho talk, which all masculine men have done, was relentlessly attacked by the press but not punished in the voter booth... This means that, when you talk like Trump, the first thought your listener will have is, "He sounds like the President of the United States."[12]

Valizadeh's thoughts were echoed across incel forums, in which a typical post at the time, referring to groping, rubbing up against women, and forced kissing, read, "If Trump can do these things without getting arrested, there is no reason an incel male should not be able to either." Another said, "America has spoken wenches, Trump is the president. Nobody cares about your cunt whine anymore. And it is now time to show them this truth."

At Melbourne's recent March for Men, where marchers bemoaned the meanness of words like *mansplaining* and man flu while shouting "mangina" and "soyboy" at counterprotesters, a "Trump 2020" banner proudly waved.

"Every time I feel no one likes us I realize we are defended by the most powerful people in the world. The Trumps support incels, Trump loves us and respects us," wrote one incel forum member in 2018, going on to add, "He never said anything after the Alek Minassian thing like he did with every muslim attack ever."

The choices Trump made when in office about when to comment or not to comment on particular events were a clear example of how he, as a figurehead several steps removed from the actual manosphere itself, was nonetheless able to mobilize its members without explicitly being seen to refer to them. It was not only that Trump's policies—from attempts to restrict abortion to his crackdown on immigration—aligned closely with their goals. It was also the way in which he justified and championed them, repeatedly including dog-whistle references to specific pet obsessions and ideologies of such groups. His defense of the need for a wall to keep out Mexican immigrants, with the racist assertion that many of them are rapists.[13] His use, when describing immigrants, of the phrase "These aren't people. These are animals."[14] His scaremongering descriptions of "caravans" of refugees traveling from Central America to the United States, in which he claimed, "women are raped at levels that have never been seen before."[15] His use of such rhetoric to excuse inhumane policies, like separating young children from their families and keeping them in cages. These were not just far-right policies. They were justifications rooted in the alt-right and the manosphere.

Of course, like MRAs, Trump's concern for female victims of sexual violence seems curiously limited to instances in which it can be weaponized against immigrants and minorities. He was pointedly on manosphere message in his mockery of Professor Christine Blasey Ford, the woman who accused then Supreme Court Justice nominee Brett Kavanaugh of having sexually assaulted her. Trump crudely imitated Professor Ford at a rally, drawing cheers from the crowd, before suggesting that her testimony was invented as part of a partisan conspiracy. "They destroy people, these are really evil people," he said, playing directly into the manosphere narrative of rife false rape allegations being used to destroy men's lives and careers.[16]

If we think of the various manosphere communities as a chain of interlinked but distinct groups, starting from the extreme of incels and inching toward more mainstream misogyny, we can see how rhetoric and ideas may be passed along the chain, gradually gaining a veil of normalization as they go. Each community can interact with the ones directly above or beneath it on the chain, thus maintaining the overall mobility of ideas but insulating the higher links from the public censure and criticism associated with those at the bottom. So someone like Trump may not directly endorse incels and white supremacists, though he can borrow their arguments, but he is able to communicate his apparent support by interacting with the middle men like Bannon, who are more explicit in their support of communities like the alt-right, thus enabling Trump to imply a direct connection to such communities through intermediaries without actually getting his own hands dirty.

For any observer familiar with Anglin's *Daily Stormer* playbook, these tactics are transparent: say what you must to avoid condemnation but continue to peddle your true message nonetheless.

Trump's implied support is revealed in the way in which his tweets and actions correlate with specific events affecting the darlings of extremist communities. In 2017, he publicly threatened to revoke federal funding from the University of California, Berkeley, after protests there led to the cancellation of a speech by Yiannopoulos. "If U.C. Berkeley does not allow free speech and practices violence on innocent people with a different point of view—NO FEDERAL FUNDS?" tweeted Trump. Immediately after Facebook closed the accounts of a number of racist, misogynistic far-right figures, including Yiannopoulos, Trump warned that he would "monitor the censorship of AMERICAN CITIZENS on social media platforms."[17]

Dr. Sugiura suggested that Trump has both emboldened and validated the views of extremist online communities: "Yes, absolutely, it's validation. When you have the most powerful man on the planet who is openly sexist—well, he's more than that, he's a misogynist—when he can openly talk about women in the way that he does, that obviously gives justification to others for their views."

And the manosphere has every reason to celebrate, because there is ample evidence that their views are, indeed, being validated.

According to research by political scientist Brian F. Schaffner of Tufts University, Trump's rhetoric during the 2016 election made sexism more socially acceptable among Republicans. Schaffner's research found that Republicans were both "more willing to express tolerance for sexist rhetoric when it came from Trump, rather than from another source" and "more willing to endorse sexist statements after the 2016 election, likely due to the fact that Trump's victory changed their perceptions about the prevalence of sexist attitudes in American society." Professor Schaffner also observed that "this increase in expressed sexism has persisted into 2018."[18]

Women, too, felt the impact of Trump's presidency on what is considered socially acceptable: one in six U.S. women surveyed in 2017 said that Trump's comments in the *Access Hollywood* tape (in which he boasted about grabbing women "by the pussy") made them feel more physically unsafe.[19]

So Trump is perhaps the greatest example of the ideas of the extremist fringes writ large in the political mainstream, but he is far from alone in spearheading the penetration of manosphere ideology into the halls of government.

In many cases, elected politicians, who are members of major parties, provide a conduit for such ideas, as in the case of Philip Davies, a UK Conservative MP who has repeatedly voted against measures to tackle violence against women and girls and tabled a private members' bill to repeal the Sex Discrimination Act.[20] While there may be many politicians with similar views, Davies deserves closer attention for two reasons: the closeness with which his tactics mirror those of manosphere trolls and his own personal relationship with members of the manosphere.

In 2016, Davies spoke at a men's rights conference organized by the UK political party and MRM mainstay J4MB. Speaking at the conference, which also featured men's rights bloggers who had likened activist Malala Yousafzai to Osama bin Laden and had called for the creation of a "Dumb Fucking Whore Registry," Davies (who sat on the House of Commons Justice Committee at the time) told attendees that the UK justice system discriminated against men and was biased in favor of women.

Davies's language closely echoed classic men's rights rhetoric as he declared that "feminist zealots really do want women to have their cake and eat it," railed against "the politically correct agenda," and lamented "all the benefits women have compared to men." And in a section of his speech that could have been lifted directly from a fathers' rights website, Davies said, "Many women use their children as a stick to beat the father with, either because they're bitter about the failed relationship, for financial reasons, or because they've moved on and it's easier for them if their new partner takes on the role of father to their children." He told the *Guardian* that his appearance at the conference was not an endorsement of J4MB.[21]

In August 2019, Davies gave a speech at the International Conference on Men's Issues in Chicago, an event founded by and organized in affiliation with AVFM. MRAs, including Elam and Karen Straughan, also gave speeches at the conference.[22]

Like most MRAs, Davies also demonstrates a marked failure to attempt any actual action to address men's and boys' issues. When one interviewer inquired as to whether Davies had ever considered introducing his own bill to address the men's issues he claimed to champion, Davies suddenly seemed to "run out of words."[23] And in 2016, Davies joined the Women and Equalities Committee with the explicit stated purpose of working to make gender "irrelevant." In media coverage of the appointment, Davies repeated false and misleading statistics, another common MRA tactic, claiming that one-third of victims of domestic violence are men.[24] But unlike the extremist rants confined to manosphere websites, these claims immediately reached far greater circulation when repeated by Davies, reported unchallenged by major outlets like the BBC.

At best, the antics of men like Davies contribute to the perception of MRAs as manipulative antifeminists. At worst, they risk actively undermining men's rights in legislatures by positioning them in aggressive opposition to women's advancement. Davies is a thorn in the side of the men he claims to care so much about.

What is particularly striking is the extent to which he appears to have adopted the tactics of the manosphere, essentially utilizing a form of real-life trolling or shitposting to advance his agenda, rather than democratic debate. When he objected to an anti-domestic violence bill, he did so by filibustering for more than an hour, forcing female MPs to cut their own speeches short to prevent the bill from being killed altogether.[25] And when he opposed a bill on LGBTQ-inclusive sex and relationships education, he did so not by mounting a counterargument or presenting any evidence to support his view but by speaking for over an hour about a maritime shipping bill instead, running down the clock until it was no longer possible to call a vote on sex education.[26] So the same strategies used by the trolls, who we see dismissed as powerless internet loners, are, in fact, leveraged to seize control of the legislative agenda of our parliament to misogynistic ends.

Though these men may be a minority in elected office, they are by no means alone. Other high-profile and powerful politicians have given voice to manosphere ideology in the corridors of power, elevating it to the level of national prominence.

In Australia, Senator Pauline Hanson of the populist One Nation party successfully called for an inquiry into the family court system, claiming (without providing evidence) that women routinely lie about abuse to gain advantage in court proceedings.[27] With the semblance of respectability provided by a mainstream politician, it is easy to see how outright falsehoods peddled by MRAs in the manosphere can penetrate widely into the public consciousness. In a 2017 study, 37 percent of Australians said that they believed "women make up or exaggerate claims of violence to secure advantage in custody battles."[28]

These links are not restricted to political rhetoric—they can influence policy as well. In April 2017, One Nation representatives met with members of an Australian Facebook group called Blokes Advice. The private, men-only group boasts more than half a million members and was temporarily shut down by Facebook in 2016 for glorifying rape and violence against women.[29] Six months after the meeting, One Nation announced a new domestic violence policy. Speaking to the national press, the party leader, Steve Dickson, repeated the completely debunked manosphere statistic that "there are up to twenty-one fathers killing themselves every week in this country, and people need to be aware of that."[30] Suddenly, a fake fact planted by MRAs was delivered to millions of citizens by a high-profile politician via the national media.

After being appointed to lead the U.S. Department of Education, Betsy DeVos arranged meetings to discuss campus sexual assault with men's rights groups well known for their misogynistic views and attacks on sexual violence survivors.[31] One of the groups DeVos invited to a consultation, Stop Abusive and Violent Environments (SAVE), has been singled out by the Southern Poverty Law Center for promoting misogyny and "lobbying to roll back services for victims of domestic abuse and penalties for their tormentors." The SAVE website states as a "key fact" that "female initiation of partner violence is the leading reason for the woman becoming a victim of subsequent violence."[32] DeVos also reached out to the National Coalition for Men.

The following year, DeVos proposed a major overhaul of college and university sexual misconduct procedures, including narrowing the definition of sexual harassment and increasing protections for students accused of misconduct.

So the link between elected politicians and manosphere groups isn't just a matter of conjecture. It is having a concrete impact.

British prime minister Boris Johnson has also regularly made apparent allusions to manosphere, alt-right ideology, once claiming that female MPs were flocking to the Labor Party for its "planned erosion of male liberty—such as ending the right to drink in public places" and suggesting that female voters were turning to the party owing to the "fickleness of their sex."[33] In a column, he also described Muslim women as looking like "letterboxes" and "bank robbers."[34] Johnson later claimed the column was "a strong, liberal defense of the right of women to wear the burqa."[35] Such misogynistic, anti-Muslim rhetoric was straight out of Anglin's playbook: get people to laugh along with the joke and they will begin to feel that the misogyny and Islamophobia at its heart is acceptable.

But I know what you're thinking. Just because Johnson voiced arguments aligned with manosphere thinking, that doesn't prove a direct link between the two. It's not like the case of One Nation representatives, who actually met with members of a deeply misogynistic, male-only online community. Where's the connection?

Earlier, I mentioned Steve Bannon, who forms one link in the chain between Trump and the worlds of the manosphere and the alt-right. Bannon was a founding member of *Breitbart* and became executive chair of its parent company in 2012. Under his leadership, the outlet hosted virulently misogynistic and white nationalist content, particularly spotlighting the work of alt-right, misogynistic provocateur Yiannopoulos, whose career Bannon effectively launched. During Bannon's tenure, *Breitbart* published articles such as "Here's Why There Ought to Be a Cap on Women Studying Science," "Would You Rather Your Child Had Feminism or Cancer?" and "Political Correctness Protects Muslim Rape

Culture." Well known for his Islamophobic sentiments, Bannon provided a platform for anti-Muslim extremist writers as well as encouraging Yiannopoulos to pen manosphere-pleasing screeds like "Does Feminism Make Women Ugly?"[36] In 2016, Bannon proudly told a reporter that *Breitbart* was "the platform for the alt-right."[37]

In November 2016, then president-elect Trump appointed Bannon his chief strategist. Bannon became both buffer and conduit between Trump and the alt-right, helping to usher in policies that may as well have been plucked straight from white nationalist and manosphere communities, such as the immigration ban on mainly Muslim countries. It was no surprise that Bannon's appointment was gleefully received by famous white supremacists and misogynists, from Spencer to former Ku Klux Klan grand wizard David Duke to the chairman of the American Nazi Party. Members of the alt-right and white nationalist communities crowed about the news online, with comments including "Bannon is *our man* in the White House" and "We're like one or two degrees of separation away from the fucking President."[38]

Two degrees of separation was, in fact, a very accurate description. Bannon provided the convenient barrier that allowed Trump to remain just far enough removed from such communities to dance around accusations of outright racism, even as he enacted the wildest dreams of the alt-right at national policy level. And while shielding Trump from direct association with such groups, Bannon had simultaneously guided Trump's election campaign to appeal to the groups' adherents with calculated precision. He was said to have masterminded the incessant attacks on "crooked Hillary," and even before he officially became part of Trump's campaign, he had bombarded journalist Megyn Kelly with twenty-five misogynistic and aggressive *Breitbart* articles in the space of three days after she dared to challenge Trump's treatment of women.

What does all this have to do with Johnson? Everything. Because as with Trump, Bannon is Johnson's link to the manosphere and the alt-right.

In September 2018, journalist Matthew d'Ancona wrote an article warning that Johnson had been in contact with Bannon and that Bannon had influenced Johnson's message, making it veer toward populism. In particular, d'Ancona suggested a direct link between Bannon's apparent strategic input and Johnson's Islamophobic and misogynistic newspaper piece. Soon afterward, d'Ancona later revealed, he was bombarded with angry calls from Johnson. "I stopped counting at 15—though the calls continued," he wrote in an article for news outlet *Tortoise*.[39] "Boris Johnson was furious with me for writing about his contact with Steve Bannon." Specifically, according to d'Ancona, Johnson was furious that the journalist had linked Bannon's advice to his column. In other words, he seemed desperate to avoid the inference that Bannon's input had led him to spout classic manosphere and alt-right rhetoric in the mainstream press.

Writing in his own newspaper column, Johnson bristled that claims of any association between him and Bannon were a conspiracy theory and a "lefty delusion."[40] "Of course I met Mr. Bannon a couple of times when I was foreign secretary and he was Trump's chief of staff," Johnson wrote, "but not since." In the following months, Johnson continued to insist he'd had no communication with Bannon, with his team telling journalists that the only contact they'd had was "one text—an invitation to meet that Johnson declined."[41]

But in June 2019, a smoking gun emerged. Alison Klayman, an American filmmaker who had been following Bannon for months for a documentary, released footage to the *Observer* that showed Bannon talking about his relationship with Johnson and boasting that he had directly advised him, helping to craft a pivotal speech. "I've been talking to him all weekend about this speech," Bannon declared, saying he had gone "back and forth" with Johnson, both by phone and text message. Klayman said Bannon had been "unequivocal" about his contact with Johnson. The footage was taken just three weeks before the infamous "letterboxes" column. A spokesman for Johnson said, "Any suggestion that Boris is colluding with, or taking advice from, Mr. Bannon or Nigel Farage is totally preposterous to the point of conspiracy."[42] But Johnson's team abruptly stopped denying that the pair had been in contact.

So in the UK, just as in the United States, the manosphere communities we think of as obscure and impotent might actually be able to take advantage of slippery intermediaries to catch the ear of some of the most powerful men in the country.

And their dog whistles are answered. Speaking in the House of Commons in 2019 amid inflamed tensions around Brexit, Labor MP Paula Sherriff pointed to the chamber's plaque of remembrance for Jo Cox. Sherriff said, "Many of us in this place [are] subject to death threats and abuse every single day, and let me tell the prime minister that they often quote his words—'surrender act,' 'betrayal,' 'traitor'—and I, for one, am sick of it. We must moderate our language." Johnson's response? "I have never heard so much humbug in my life."[43] In the days following the exchange, Sherriff told ITV that she had seen a "significant escalation" in the number of death and rape threats she was receiving. In other words, there was a clear link between the dog-whistle rhetoric used by the prime minister and the abuse from online misogynist extremists targeting a female MP. And it was not an isolated incident. Another Labor MP,

Jess Phillips, revealed she had received a death threat that not only quoted the prime minister but also mentioned him by name. And the day after Johnson dismissed female MPs' safety concerns as "humbug," a man was arrested outside Phillips's constituency office, shouting abuse and smacking the doors and windows.[44]

There are clues, too, that politicians may be aware of the enormous support they stand to receive from extremist communities when they tap into their ideology. One of the clearest such indicators is the way in which the politicians may subsequently refuse to apologize for their rhetoric or double down with messaging that will appeal to the same communities, even when challenged. We saw it when Trump responded to the deadly, white supremacist Charlottesville rally by saying that there were "very fine people on both sides." (He later refused to apologize, claiming that the utterance had been put "perfectly.")[45] And we saw it after Johnson's rhetoric was put in the spotlight too. In the days that followed, as numerous female MPs reported death and rape threats and escalating abuse, Johnson's chief special adviser, Dominic Cummings, gave an interview saying that the anger directed at MPs was "not surprising." He said, "serious threats" of violence should be taken seriously but added that if politicians did not respect the result of the Brexit referendum, "what do you expect to happen?" Finally, he concluded that "the situation can only be resolved by parliament honoring its promise to respect the result."[46] In other words, he responded to the fact that female MPs were facing an unprecedented bombardment of death threats and abuse with the veiled warning that they'd better deliver Brexit if they wanted it to stop. A sentiment driven by logic chillingly similar to that of the death threats.

Elsewhere, perhaps emboldened by the Trump effect, there has been a surge in extremist figureheads themselves standing for elected office, guaranteeing a slew of mainstream media coverage for ideas previously considered too extreme to broadcast, regardless of the outcome of their campaigns. No matter how extreme, inclusion of any argument in the manifesto of a running politician generates immediate respectability and normalization.

Repeatedly cropping up through my research for this book was a well-known and deeply misogynistic manosphere figure known by the online pseudonym "Sargon of Akkad," a misogynist who came to prominence by promoting antifeminist conspiracy theories on YouTube during Gamergate and took part in the campaign of targeted harassment against Anita Sarkeesian. In 2018, he was banned from the Patreon crowdfunding platform for using "racial and homophobic slurs," and in 2016, he tweeted Phillips after she spoke out about online abuse, telling her, "I wouldn't even rape you." In the wake of this tweet (and perhaps evidencing the weight of its poster's online following, with just under a million YouTube subscribers and over 280 million video views), Phillips revealed she had subsequently received 600 rape threats in a single night.[47]

After the Elliot Rodger massacre, Sargon of Akkad released a YouTube video in which he blamed women and feminists for Rodger's actions:

> You are responsible for perpetuating it, by disenfranchising these poor fucking guys who don't have any options left... The question you and all of your stupid fucking feminist cultists need to be asking is: why are these men becoming misogynists in the first place? What is this feminist-run society doing to them that is causing them to go insane?[48]

So it was a shock, in the spring of 2019, to hear the name

Akkad crop up on the evening news. Looking up, I watched in disbelief as Sargon, real name Carl Benjamin, was unveiled as the UK Independence Party (UKIP) candidate for South West England in the European elections. Benjamin's foray into national politics was perhaps the clearest example yet of the penetration of extreme misogynist manosphere tactics and ideology into the mainstream through political pathways. Suddenly becoming a household name, he immediately reinforced his comments about rape, releasing a new video "debating" raping Phillips in which he said that, "with enough pressure, I might cave," which was quoted across the national news.[49] Yiannopoulos quickly announced his plans to hit the campaign trail in support of Benjamin.[50] Phillips, meanwhile, immediately began to feel the increased real-world consequences as political legitimacy emboldened and expanded Benjamin's fan base. Leaving Westminster after work one day, she was chased down the street by a man asking her "why Carl Benjamin shouldn't be able to joke about [her] rape."

In some countries where far-right and populist parties have won seats, entered into government coalitions, or taken political control, it is clear to see how the ideology of the online extreme right and manosphere communities might have an offline impact on citizens. In Spain, for example, far-right party Vox entered into a right-wing coalition in Andalusia, giving real political power to a group that called for the repeal of domestic violence laws and attacked "psychopathic feminazis."[51]

Even if unelected, the veneer of respectability granted by the platform of a registered political party, no matter how small, can provide an entry point for extremist ideas into mainstream discourse, as Buchanan's repeated appearances across popular news outlets demonstrate.

Dr. Sugiura explained that manosphere communities are swift to capitalize on these associations with political office:

It's the face of respectability. From everything I've seen within these groups, they're very keen to do that. They quote academia, they quote theory, so having somebody who's in a hugely influential position, who can have direct impact on policies, this is absolutely part of their agenda. MRAs, for example, they want to effect change, so if you've got someone who is a direct link to policy and legislation, that's huge.

And of course, there are benefits to be reaped by the politicians themselves, who often become the swift recipients of accolades and outpourings of praise from the extensive online spaces of the manosphere, as Valizadeh's lavish praise of Trump revealed. When Australian senator David Leyonhjelm made crude comments in the senate about a fellow senator's sex life and started speaking publicly about "misandry" and "the blaming of men for the actions of individual criminals," he was hailed "a new hero" by AVFM, and one tweet declared him to have provoked "the unbounded delight of the silent majority." It's a silent majority many politicians may be calculatedly counting on for future voting support.

The idea of politicians deliberately courting the manosphere vote is not as surprising as it might sound once you factor in the enormously underestimated size of these online communities and the likelihood of vacuuming up the even larger, mildly sexist, non-incel bloc along the way.

In fact, in October 2019, Cambridge Analytica whistleblower Christopher Wylie (who revealed that the company had harvested the information of fifty million Facebook users and used the data to help drum up fringe voters for Trump's 2016 presidential campaign) disclosed that Bannon, who had enlisted the company's services, had deliberately and specifically targeted incels. Wylie said that Bannon highlighted the fact that engaging with such groups could have a massive impact in swing states.[52]

Ben Hurst is the project coordinator and lead facilitator at the aforementioned Good Lad Initiative, an organization that delivers programs and workshops on gender inequality, particularly focusing on talking to boys. "Although I think there's a strong case for doing it," he told me wryly, "we would never frame this work as preventative work against radicalization in terms of Men's Rights Activist movements." I was intrigued, and he had a ready explanation. "Because the people who are running the country are the people who are in those movements, so you're not going to get funding for that from those guys!" He laughed, knowing it is a controversial argument. Yet consider the extent to which the arguments and ideas of these movements have successfully infiltrated every level of international power, from the UK parliament to the White House. Hurst has a point. It's not just about the normalization and spread of the discourse through political credibility. It's about recognizing the impact these ideas, and the men who represent them, could be having on our politics, our policies, and our lives.

Consider r/TheRedPill, a particularly active and virulently misogynistic manosphere forum. In 2017, it was revealed that the creator and chief moderator of that forum was none other than Republican New Hampshire state representative Robert Fisher.[53] Offline, he was a respected, mainstream politician. Online, he had written that rape wasn't all bad, because at least the rapist enjoyed it. In another post, he wrote, "Feminists are obsessed with rape because we live in a rape fantasy culture, where feminists wish they were hot enough to be rape-able."[54] When an investigation linked r/TheRedPill domain records to Fisher, he initially refused to resign, giving testimony to a public inquiry at which he claimed, under oath, that he had not been active in r/TheRedPill forum for years, despite this being directly contradicted by the evidence that had been revealed. Fisher did eventually resign under public pressure.[55]

Of course, politics is not the only sphere with the ability to lend respectability, normalization, and a sense of tacit approval to extremist ideas. Manosphere ideology is also increasingly gaining a foothold in the world of academia. Here its traditional tactic of using botched statistics and scholarly sources is given newfound clout by association with impressive-sounding titles and positions.

Take, for example, Jordan Peterson, the Canadian psychology professor whose YouTube videos about everything from the Bible to the "Marxist lie of white privilege" have driven him to international celebrity. A handful of Peterson's quotes reveal the ways in which his philosophy feeds into traditional gender stereotypes. "Men have to toughen up," he wrote in his international bestselling book *12 Rules for Life: An Antidote to Chaos*. "Men demand it, and women want it, even though they may not approve of the harsh and contemptuous attitude that is part and parcel of the socially demanding process that fosters and then enforces that toughness."[56]

"Healthy" women, so Peterson's book informs us, seek men who "outclass" them in intelligence, income, and status.[57] "If you're talking to a man who wouldn't fight with you under any circumstances whatsoever, then you're talking to someone for whom you have absolutely no respect."[58]

Some of what he says is simply outdated, biological essentialism. An article in the *New York Review of Books* described his twelve rules for life as presenting "some idiosyncratic quasi-religious opin-ions as empirical science." And Peterson repeatedly insists that men and women are biologically better suited to different roles. "Men and women won't sort themselves into the same categories if you leave them alone to do it of their own accord," he claims, arguing that men are inherently more likely to want to become engineers and women nurses.[59]

It's particularly ironic that men like Peterson should be seen as "edgy" and countercultural when their message couldn't be more regressive.

"The Queen is most anxious to enlist every one who can speak or write to join in checking this mad, wicked folly of 'Woman's Rights,' with all its attendant horrors, on which her poor feeble sex is bent, forgetting every sense of womanly feeling and propriety," wrote Queen Victoria in a letter dated May 29, 1870. "It is a subject which makes the Queen so furious that she cannot contain her-self. God created men and women different—then let them remain each in their own position." She might as well have been riffing on Peterson...150 years ago.

Some of what Peterson says is classic mainstream antifemi-nist rhetoric. He told the *Financial Times* that society should "stop teaching 19-year-old girls that their primary destiny is career." Which seems a bit rich, coming from someone heavily involved in teaching nineteen-year-old boys that their primary destiny is to toughen up and dominate. It's a message that is likely to do them far more harm than good.

Some of what Peterson says in his book sounds sweeping and vaguely academic but in a way that is so vague as to be pretty much impossible to disprove or, crucially, to dispute. "Consciousness is symbolically masculine and has been since the beginning of time."

"Culture is symbolically, archetypally, mythically male." Anything quite good, in fact, one begins to suspect, is somehow vaguely male in Peterson's book, but if you want an explanation of why exactly or who gets to decide, you're immediately rebuffed by the preemptive deflection: it's *symbolic*, okay? So what is *symbolically* female, you might ask? Chaos, Peterson claims, is associated with the feminine.[60] Thanks for that, Jordan. (Peterson defines chaos as "all those things and situations we neither know nor understand," so you can see why, for him personally, that might be quite a good description of women.)

And if you think evolution and societal shift might shake things up, you can think again. Certain gendered issues are immutable and cannot possibly change, Peterson argues, promoting a kind of pseudointellectual biological essentialism that closely mirrors the defeatist fatalism of incel ideology:

> You know you can say, "Well, isn't it unfortunate that chaos is represented by the feminine"—well, it might be unfortunate, but it doesn't matter, because that is how it's represented. It's been represented like that forever. And there are reasons for it. You can't change it. It's not possible. This is underneath everything. If you change those basic categories, people wouldn't be human anymore.[61]

It should be a bit of a warning sign that Peterson insists our modern lives can be deeply and accurately viewed through the lens of "ancient wisdom" and "the great myths and religious stories of the past," given the fact that very few of those surviving myths or religious stories were written by women or feature them much at all, beyond the roles of chattel or sex slave, or both.[62] (Not to mention the fact that Peterson repeatedly falls back on *The Little Mermaid* to back up his arguments.)

His style and approach are measured and genteel, and he uses the sort of intellectual sleight of hand that enables his followers to draw bigoted assumptions from arguments he frames as structural rather than personal. His initial rise to prominence, for example, came in 2016 after he repeatedly protested a Canadian bill banning discrimination against people on the basis of gender identity or expression, saying he would refuse to refer to transgender students by their preferred pronouns. "I'm not using words that other people require me to use. Especially if they're made up by radical left-wing ideologues," Peterson said in one interview.[63]

For somebody who is so supportive of freedom of speech, Peterson has a funny way of showing it. In 2017, he announced plans to create a campaign aimed at reducing enrollment by 75 percent in university classes he considered to be "indoctrination cults," including "women's studies, and all the ethnic studies and racial studies groups."[64] Peterson referred to his project as a kind of "nonviolent warfare" (though he has since described it as "on hiatus"). And he seems less of a fan of the principle of freedom of speech when it applies to his own critics and detractors. He regularly threatens to sue writers he feels have mischaracterized his viewpoints or takes to his personal blog to pen angry screeds, railing against the ways in which his words have been taken "out of context." Which is to say that he gets defensive when the smokescreen of reasonable, rational debate risks shifting enough for people to peek at the reactionary, sometimes deeply prejudiced content underneath. Like Trump, he also benefits from a dual-pronged publicity approach. Both men wield the power of a massive online following and use internet platforms to speak directly to their followers, circumventing the mainstream media. They both claim to be ostracized and shunned by news outlets while actually benefiting from the enormous profile bestowed on them by a media desperately keen to cover their output for its shock value and clickbait-worthy controversy.

An article in the *New York Review of Books* described Peterson as "remarkably in tune with contemporary prejudices," and indeed, many of his arguments do seem to present a sanitized version of distinctly recognizable manosphere refrains. "The masculine spirit is under assault."[65] Feminism (as represented by the Women's March) is, according to one tweet, a "murderous equity doctrine." "We're alienating young men. We're telling them that they're patriarchal oppressors and denizens of rape culture... It's awful. It's so destructive. It's so unnecessary. And it's so sad."[66]

All these are arguments beloved by MRAs: men are under attack; feminism is an evil, vindictive movement, literally capable of killing men; we are in the midst of a witch hunt against all men.

Then there are the crossovers with alt-right thinking. "White privilege," he says in a speech on YouTube, is a "Marxist lie," and feminists support Muslim rights, one tweet reads, because they have an "unconscious wish for brutal male domination." The argument is a whisker away from the deeply misogynistic, white supremacist obsession with birth rates and white women defiled by invading men. But Peterson seems to know exactly how to dance just on the right side of that line.

"Human female choosiness is also why we are very different from the common ancestor we shared with our chimpanzee cousins," he wrote in *12 Rules for Life*. "Women's proclivity to say no, more than any other force, has shaped our evolution." In other words, like incels, Peterson places a huge amount of weight and power on the idea that the sexual marketplace is dominated by women, who have the upper hand when it comes to making romantic choices. And like them, too, he describes the "devastating force" of rejection when women deny men a date.

The links he draws between animal biology and human behavior provide a neat sense of academic gravitas to manospheresque arguments about the inevitability of male dominance. "We were struggling for position before we had skin, or hands, or lungs, or bones," Peterson wrote on Facebook. "Dominance hierarchies are older than trees." Biology, of course, is not Peterson's academic area of expertise, but this seems of little consequence to his millions of online fans. In fact, it is usually when Peterson is furthest from his own area of academic focus that his academic credentials are most sensationally leveraged to lend weight to arguments about spheres in which he actually has little or no specialist knowledge.

The risks of this are self-evident. Under one interview in which Peterson talked about "female insanity" and suggested that it's impossible to "control crazy women" because men are not allowed by societal convention to get physical with them, a male reader shut down the objections of women with this comment: "The guy has a PhD. I think he knows what he is talking about."[67]

Sometimes, amid the vagaries and the careful distancing, the veil seems to lift briefly, and the similarities between Peterson's rhetoric and that of the citizens of the manosphere are much more clearly visible. This happens most notably when Peterson discusses misogynistic mass murderers. In a recent interview with the *New York Times*, he echoed incel attitudes about state-sanctioned "sex redistribution," appearing to imply that mass murderer Alek Minassian might have been pacified had he not been rejected by women.[68]

"He was angry at God, because women were rejecting him,"

Peterson said. "The cure for that is enforced monogamy. That's actually why monogamy emerges." The interviewer added, "Peterson does not pause when he says this. Enforced monogamy is, to him, simply a rational solution. Otherwise women will all only go for the most high-status men, he explains, and that couldn't make either gender happy in the end."

"Half the men fail," Peterson added. "And no one cares about the men who fail." In situations in which there is too much mate choice, "a small percentage of the guys have hyper-access to women." This is pure incel ideology. The 80:20 theory writ large.

Amid a moderate backlash, Peterson was quick to defend his comments on his website, claiming that "enforced monogamy" is a well-known anthropological and scientific concept and that he was referring to "socially promoted, culturally inculcated monogamy," not the "arbitrary dealing-out of damsels to incels." But this does nothing to redeem the implication that it was women's sexual autonomy, not Minassian's murderous intent and actions, that were to blame for the deaths. Nor does it cancel the inevitable boost of vindication that incel communities will have drawn from the voicing of their logic on so mainstream a platform, in the guise of academic rigor.

Of course, it is important to say that Peterson may be entirely ignorant, or even critical, of manosphere communities, and his tendency to give oxygen to some of their foundational tenets may be entirely coincidental.

Peterson did address MGTOW, calling them pathetic weasels in a lecture and lamenting the undue influence they have on embittered young men—before unusually walking the criticism back, claiming he had been too hard on them and that they "have a point."

But it is certainly clear that he has an acute understanding of the dynamics of misogynistic, right-wing online mobs. "I shouldn't say this, but I'm going to, because it's just so goddamn funny I can't help but say it: I've figured out how to monetize social justice warriors," Peterson said in a podcast interview. "If they let me speak, then I get to speak, and then I make more money on Patreon... if they protest me, then that goes up on YouTube, and my Patreon account goes WAY up." Patreon is a platform that allows fans of a content creator's work to become subscribers, paying regular sums of money to access that creator's artistic or intellectual output. On YouTube, Peterson has over two million followers—a group he himself admits is 80 percent male.

But Peterson and his fans are quick to excoriate accusations that he is a conduit for alt-right ideas. In his book, he calls the rise of far-right political parties "sinister." He has even claimed to play a role in moderating the political views of young men, saying he draws them away from extremism, though his evidence for this seems to be purely anecdotal.[69] Yet there are some suggestions of an eager following among the male supremacists and trolls of the manosphere that are slightly trickier to explain away. YouTube videos of Peterson attract a wildly high view count when they are framed as brutal takedowns of feminists or transgender people. And whether Peterson actively courts them or not, thousands of discussion threads reveal that he has a vast fan base across male supremacist communities like Reddit's r/TheRedPill. A typical post, praising Peterson for "melting the snowflakes," says, "I'd honestly be surprised if most people on TRP [TheRedPill] weren't familiar with him by this point." More pertinent still is the deluge of threats experienced by Channel 4 News anchor Cathy Newman after she dared to challenge Peterson's views in an interview. Newman described a "torrent of abuse" involving "literally thousands of abusive tweets—it was a semi-organized campaign. It ranged from the usual 'cunt, bitch, dumb blonde' to 'I'm going to find out where you live and execute you.'"[70] Her employers were forced to hire security experts, and the police became involved. This suggests something more than an entirely neutral relationship between Peterson and the online trolls, even if it might very well be completely one-sided.

When Newman's abuse hit the headlines, Peterson himself tweeted, "If you're threatening her, stop." But his tweet took on a subtly different meaning in light of comments he made about the abuse in an interview soon afterward: "They've provided no evidence that the criticisms constituted threats. There are some nasty cracks online, but the idea that this is somehow reflective of a fundamental misogyny, and that's what's driving this, is ridiculous."[71]

It is significant that Peterson has become such a symbol of antifeminism, given the fact that not a great deal of his actual personal output has been specifically devoted to gender issues. His *12 Rules for Life* is full of slightly banal, almost folksy quotes that read like something off a self-help poster decorated with a picture of the beach at sunset. "You have some vital role to play in the unfolding destiny of the world." "Compare yourself to who you were yesterday, not to who someone else is today." Some of his most famous pieces of advice urge his readers to tidy their rooms and stand up straight.

That his antifeminist philosophy has become his best known is perhaps evidence of a media obsession with creating clickbait controversy. The media deliberately pits feminists (who would much rather be discussing how to secure sustainable funding for rape crisis centers, say) against the very men who will gamely spend twenty minutes telling them that the patriarchy doesn't exist. This leads to a classic manosphere "Jordan Peterson Destroys Nose Ringed Feminist Pig" video (the creation of which Peterson himself has nothing to do with), which, in turn, is boosted by YouTube's algorithm and churns out several million likes, clicks, and ad views.

Peterson himself may not be entirely unaware of the publicity benefits of courting controversy, however, given the way in which he shot to fame after very publicly inserting himself into the debate about gender pronouns.

Doing so is lucrative too—enormously so. While Elam is reduced to alternately lambasting his followers and pleading with them to donate a few dollars to his personal pocket, Peterson was, at one point, reportedly earning $80,000 per month from fan donations via Patreon, and his book has sold millions of copies.[72]

Men like Peterson are not alone in lending a veneer of academic authenticity to the sort of misogynistic arguments beloved of the manosphere, deliberately or not. In some instances, a writer's academic credentials are leveraged to imply that their argument is robust, even when no scientific evidence is actually offered to support it at all. Consider, for example, a *Daily Mail* article in which the use of this technique is so blatant it is revealed in the title: "Academic Who Says Wives Who Deprive Husbands of Sex Are Wrecking Society."[73] From the headline alone, it would be natural to assume that the unnamed "academic" was speaking from the perspective of his or her research, inferring that some scientific study had made the case for this particular claim. But while the article contains sensational and deeply misogynistic claims by its author, Dr. Catherine Hakim, it provides no scientific research whatsoever that actually backs those claims up, apart from some references to Dr. Hakim's book, which the piece promotes. Recalling incel ideology, Dr. Hakim wrote,

Sexually starved men are more likely to visit prostitutes, view pornography and, in the worst cases, even molest other women... Men, as we know in our heart of hearts, will have affairs, or perhaps even worse, when faced with sexual starvation and the inevitable resentment that causes.

As well as accusing "negligent wives" of "calling chaos into their lives" if they do not have enough sex with their husbands, she also blames them for the rapes of other women: "More worryingly, there is little doubt, in my view, that sexual frustration can lead to assaults on women, though I am in no way excusing this behavior."

Dr. Hakim repeatedly uses scientific language to present incel logic behind precisely the respectable academic facade incels crave. She cites statistics that might sound vaguely connected to the matter at hand but actually have no bearing on her argument. "One sex survey in Britain found a fifth of women, aged from 45 to 59, had been celibate for more than a year." "In fact, a quarter of men in one survey said that, given the chance, they would like sex daily." "Perhaps for the first time ever, there are 6 percent more men in the world than women." None of this has any bearing at all on Dr. Hakim's claims that men who have less sex than they want are more likely to commit assault, and neither does her causal link blaming other women's sexual autonomy for these acts of sexual violence.

Gary Barker, founder and CEO of gender justice NGO Promundo, feels that the normalization conferred on such views by the grandiose association with academia is an even greater threat than incels themselves. "I probably lose more sleep over how Jordan Peterson makes his discourse normal," he told me.

And how he dresses it, and others like him who dress it in pseudoscience. So it feels like it draws on evolutionary science (and, in his case, it draws on Judeo-Christian tradition, as if that were science). I worry about how mainstream that's become, not that I don't worry about incels and what a few can do, but it worries me more that guys... who might look like our friends' brothers, and are polite company and don't look misogynist in public, are finding that he nudges them toward a space that says, "Yeah, I don't have to deal with this feminist whatever." That discourse worries me more.

There are things in our lives that we question. And there are things we just accept. We live in a society in which we're encouraged to accept what's written in the newspapers as fact. In which we assume that academics are the authority on any given topic. In which many people simply wouldn't question the wildly misogynistic idea that frigid wives are causing men to rape other women, because it comes from a source we have learned to trust. And there is so much more that spirals from that, unsaid. The idea that rape is something men can't help doing. That women are the ones to blame when it happens. That we should look for ways to understand and sympathize with rapists.

This can affect anybody. Even people who haven't heard of Peterson or any of the other men who stand as idols to manosphere communities. They're being drip-fed the same ideas, carefully filtered through mouthpieces we have all been taught to believe. And the very lowest-level sexism that has been the backdrop to all our lives absolutely primes us to accept those ideas without challenge. The tiny things, from gendered toy aisles to words like *fireman*.

The issues that lead women to be labeled "rampant feminazis" for daring to discuss them. Those all make it that little bit easier for us to trust that when a national newspaper or a person with an academic title spouts something deeply sexist, it is probably just an uncomfortable truth. Often it's those very same newspapers leading a preemptive charge against any criticism, calling us feminazis, and clearing the way for such ideas to be accepted.

Barker also expressed concern about the potentially chilling effect on freedom of speech when an academic like Peterson is able to underscore his arguments with the clout of an online fan base, several million strong, with a penchant for misogynistic abuse. How many female journalists might seriously consider declining to challenge Peterson after witnessing the rape and death threats endured by Newman? And what kind of an impact could this also have on other academics who might otherwise seek to publicly challenge Peterson's ideology? Barker pointed to a recent interview he gave for the *Washington Post* for a piece about Peterson. "The reporter who did the piece said, 'I've not found anybody else who wants to critique him with their name associated with it.'"

Finally, there are media commentators who sanitize these issues and bring them into the mainstream, both in the choices they make about whom to host on their programs and how to interview them and in their own rhetoric. Piers Morgan is the name that crops up repeatedly in my interviews. He exemplifies both issues: the former most famously evidenced by his fawning softball television interview with Trump; the latter by his own repeated comments, on social media and on air, about women, feminism, and masculinity. For a TV host to voice the sort of arguments traditionally confined to the manosphere gives them a newfound acceptability and a new lease on life.

"Whiny PC-crazed snowflake imbeciles who will be horrifically offended by absolutely everything I say or write" is a very typical extract from a Morgan tweet. Missives to his more than seven million followers are likely to contain references to "fragile snowflakes" and "manning up" and are disproportionately likely to focus ire on feminists. He tweeted 163 times on the day of the Women's March. The general gist of his tweets followed this one: "I'm planning a 'Men's March' to protest at the creeping global emasculation of my gender by rabid feminists."[74]

Morgan's social media output is bolstered by a regular tabloid column, which he tends to devote to topics like "Don't Let Hypocritical Radical Feminists Turn Men into a Bunch of Neutered, Groveling, Blubbering Doormats" or "I'm So Sick of This War on Masculinity and I'm Not Alone." Then there's his platform as presenter on the ITV breakfast program *Good Morning Britain,* a role Morgan deftly leverages to escalate and publicize the "controversies" and spats he deliberately creates on Twitter. In other words, Morgan plays squarely into the rich online demand for reactionary, "PC-gone-mad," antifeminist rants, carefully couched in the preemptively defensive rhetoric of reasonable debate and moral superiority.

For Morgan and his employers, the benefits to be reaped are mutual, as is evident from the formulaic nature of the cycle. Morgan tweets something incendiary and sexist to his millions of followers, waits to see who takes the bait, and then whips up the controversy to the greatest possible peak. The next morning, the Twitter spat is framed as "newsworthy" on his program, which deliberately highlights the most mundane and minor issues in order to present feminism and other social justice movements as ridiculous and extreme. The show capitalizes on the clickbait outrage of the subsequent segment, tweeting out the most inflammatory clips to entice people to visit their website and watch more. Wash. Rinse. Repeat.

This is fertile ground, and Morgan knows the territory like the back of his hand. Typical areas of focus include wolf whistles, criticisms of individual women who claim to be feminists but have dared to have their bodies photographed, and bombastic attacks on individual men for terrible crimes like parenting: he famously lambasted Daniel Craig for daring to carry his baby in a sling, tweeting that James Bond had been "emasculated."[75]

The game is transparent, painfully so, with Morgan frequently crowing with glee as his faux feuds reach wider audiences: "First the *Washington Post*, now BBC News. Papoose-Gate is growing bigger than Watergate," he tweeted during the Craig controversy.

But beneath the surface of whipped-up outrage, which is invariably light on substance, there are dog-whistle cues that engage a more sinister following.

"I'm sick of this war on masculinity," wrote Morgan in his column in January 2019. Morgan was bemoaning the release of an advertisement by razor company Gillette, which encouraged men to step in if they saw sexist behavior or sexual harassment. Morgan described the ad as emasculating, saying it suggested that "ALL men are bad, shameful people."[76] Soon afterward, one of the women behind the creation of the ad revealed that she had received a barrage of horrific abuse, specifically, she said, since Morgan's article was published. The tone of some of the messages, of which she posted extracts, suggested that those seemingly called to arms by Morgan's column were classic manosphere denizens. "Keep pushing us filthy whores and i will make you and the likes of you (ginocentric men-hating feminists) prey for hell," read one message, clearly suffused in the rhetoric of online extremism. It continued, "We white men treat women the best in the whole goddamned world, yet you treat us as shit... You want to see some 'toxic masculinity'? Just ask bitch (there will be no way back)."

At times, Morgan's rhetoric has echoed manosphere conversations with eerie accuracy; for example, he claimed to be launching a "campaign for men to seize back their country," saying that "the future of mankind depends on it."[77]

Ben Hurst of the Good Lad Initiative observed the following:

> I think people like Piers Morgan...are really careful about what they say and how they say it... Those men [are] also what other men would perceive as successful. That means what they're saying isn't [seen] as aggressive or offensive. [The] position and level of power that they hold in society means those messages become palatable for men. There are some kids [who] are really paying attention to stuff that Piers Morgan is saying—he's probably the most acceptable face of men's rights activism in the UK, even though I don't think he would even necessarily identify himself [in that way], but he definitely shares those sentiments and projects those kinds of opinions and views.

When accused of misogyny, Morgan tends to tweet protesting that he "loves women" and is simply "not a big fan of rabid feminists."

So manosphere ideology is shepherded into mainstream discussion by politicians, academics, and media figures, who seem to recall and signal to the underestimated online masses. It is a mutually beneficial relationship. For these unofficial spokespeople, the manosphere represents a powerful force, whether boosting voter turnout, book sales, or viewing figures. And for manosphere communities, it elevates their rhetoric far beyond the online echo chambers, sneaking it into wider conversation.

"If you look in fringe forums," Davey noted, "people say, 'He's actually quite useful, because he can bring people further on to our cause'... There's definitely an awareness that you can use these [people] to push the parameters and to open the window out further."

His use of the term *window* is not a coincidence—manosphere and white supremacist forums alike are obsessed with the concept of the "Overton window," a term describing the range of ideas tolerated in public discourse. When figures like Morgan use rhetoric that might previously have been considered radical or unacceptable, or politicians like Trump express ideas that might have seemed unthinkable for a former president to utter, alt-right and incel forums cheer at their perception that the Overton window has shifted, opening a wider gap for their even more extreme ideas to nudge their way into the mainstream.

So you end up with a chain, which starts in the most extreme online forums: men like Matt Forney explicitly advocate beating women, and incels discuss keeping women as sex slaves. Then there are the direct leaders of those communities: men like Valizadeh, who have egged their followers on, and Elam with his "Bash a violent bitch month." Next, men like Yiannopoulos, who sing their hearts out while Nazi salutes rain down around them but maintain a wide-eyed innocence if they get caught; who repeat some of the most outrageous ideals of the online mob but always claim they're "just being ironic"; who tread the line between online icon and offline provocateur and sometimes get their toes burned. Then there are the go-betweens, men like Bannon, who are familiar with this territory and with the groups behind them on the chain—even perhaps in direct and close strategic communication with them—but who distance themselves further, using more muted rhetoric. Or men like Peterson, who produce sanitized versions of very similar ideas. Finally, you reach the top of the chain: politicians and powerful media commentators, who are yet another step removed and will use that removal to maintain plausible deniability at all costs, but whose rhetoric and watered-down policies are socially acceptable versions of the same messages. The men in the middle are capable of alerting and mobilizing support further down the chain and, at the same time, are just respectable enough to attract new, more moderate thinkers to begin their own journey of exploration. And the people at the top of the chain don't need to repeat the ideology from the bottom verbatim. Indeed, if they did, it would ruin everything: exposing them to criticism against which the existing pattern cleverly protects them, disgusting new recruits before they've had time to be radicalized.

The men at the top of the chain don't need to gut the fish. They just need to hold out the bait and wait for a little nibble. People who are attracted enough to swallow the hook will find their own way down the rest of the line. And those holding the rod are able to capitalize handsomely, reeling in the benefits of their money, their online adoration, or their votes. The Overton window has shifted far enough for those who have newly discovered the manosphere to convince themselves that there's nothing too outrageous about what they are doing until it's too late. Until they reach the point at which being outrageous is exactly the point. And even those who don't reach that point of eventual radicalization are not lost causes. The moderates who are swayed a little further to the right, who take on just a little more tolerance of misogyny or racism (because after all, if the president says it, it can't be far wrong), are still part of a turning tide of social acceptability that allows greater influence and widespread impact for the beliefs and policies being passed up from the bottom of the chain. Not that mainstreaming incel ideology is necessarily the endgame for everybody involved. Simply leveraging enough support to inoculate their campaigns against what they see as the creeping tide of political correctness might be a big enough payoff for some. That extremist ideas might slip quietly into the public discourse is simply an acceptable side effect.

That leaders of online extremist communities are aware of and deliberately capitalize on this chain is indisputable. Whether or not the men further up play their roles deliberately or entirely unknowingly is far less clear. But the real victims are the men who become enmeshed in the vitriol and rigid, outdated stereotypes in which their idols traffic for personal gain.

The end result is revealed with terrifying clarity in a *New Yorker* interview with male supremacist Mike Cernovich. It describes an incident witnessed by the journalist and planned by Cernovich with military precision in which Cernovich used a video on social media platform Periscope to rally thousands of his followers to a narrative he had crafted about Hillary Clinton's emails, using the hashtag #HillarysHacker. Before Cernovich had finished filming, the hashtag was trending on Twitter. Within a day, more than 42,000 tweets had been posted with the hashtag. The topic was widely discussed on Reddit, which resulted in coverage by media pundits, and then a congressman alerted prosecutors in Washington to investigate. The chain was complete.[78] But crucially, before it penetrated the mainstream, it had been touched by enough pairs of semirespectable hands to carry an air of factual robustness to the casual media consumer. And by the time it reached the influential closed doors of Washington prosecutors, there was almost no remaining trace of its origins on the iPad propped up on misogynist Cernovich's kitchen table.

# 8

# Men Who Are Afraid of Women

"Is this a 'witch hunt'?"

**JOHN HUMPHRYS ON #METOO, *TODAY*, BBC RADIO 4**

Men today are terrified. They're living in a world in which they are persecuted and threatened within an inch of their lives. Any one of them, regardless of his past actions or relationships, is at risk of seeing his happiness destroyed, his career decimated without a moment's notice.

Angry, deceitful, manipulative women are on the warpath, and no man is safe. No scalp is off-limits, no history so unblemished to be safe from deliberate warping and destruction.

There are hysterical overreactions that paint perfectly innocent interactions as sordid acts of abuse. There are gold-digging professional victims who'll conveniently "remember" a brush of the hand three decades later in a shameless bid for attention, compensation, and "five minutes of fame."

And that's before you even start on the morally bankrupt women out there who'll invent a story out of thin air, torpedoing an innocent man's entire reputation and livelihood, just because they can.

"What about 'innocent until proven guilty'?" I hear you cry. Oh no. Not in today's world of feminazi Twitchfork mobs and PC snowflake hysteria gone mad. Not in this environment in which #MeToo has become so powerful that companies are jettisoning their most senior employees left, right, and center with no due process, based on little more than the whisper of a rumor circulated online.

This is a witch hunt, make no mistake. And any man might be next...

This is a not-inaccurate summary of the recent backlash following the #MeToo movement, a campaign started by Tarana Burke in 2006 and popularized on social media in 2017 following accusations of sexual abuse against Hollywood producer Harvey Weinstein. The campaign led to millions of women around the world sharing their stories of sexual harassment and assault, initially in the workplace but also further afield.

If the above representation sounds like an exaggeration, consider the following headlines and quotes about the #MeToo movement, taken from some of the most prominent and highly respected media platforms in the world:

"#MeToo Run Amok" —*The Week*

"When #MeToo Goes Too Far" —*New York Times*

"Is This a 'Witch Hunt'?" —*Today*

"Millennial Women Are Too Quick to Shame Men" —*The Times*

"A Clumsy Pass Over Dinner is NOT a Sex Harassment"
—*Daily Mail*

"What Will Women Gain from All This Squawking about
Sex Pests? A Niqab" —*Mail on Sunday*

Then consider the following comments, made online by men
who are members of the manosphere community:

"I think it's scary for men. It's the story of the fear of it
all. Where you get punished for something that you didn't
do." —Erik von Markovik ("Mystery"), commenting on
#MeToo to *BuzzFeed*[1]

"Every woman on this planet, regardless of her education or
background, is a bitch, a cunt, a slut, a gold digger, a flake, a
cheater, a backstabber, a narcissist, and an attention whore
that is dying to get out... this, I'm afraid, is the true nature
of women. This is the true nature that will come forth if
society doesn't put constraints or limitations on a woman's
behavior and choice." —Daryush Valizadeh ("Roosh V"), in
a blog post titled "The True Nature of Women"

"Ever since #MeToo came out and all these allegations
of harassment and rape and what not, I'm afraid to even
approach a woman... the harassment claims scare the shit
out of me. Also, the idea of a woman playing hard to get vs
No Means No... this has been all very confusing, as I wasn't
great with the girls to begin with." —Manosphere forum
user, in a thread titled "Is MeToo Making [Men] Weak?"

Notice the similarities?

The hysteria and panic whipped up in the furthest corners of the manosphere has spread online like wildfire, reaching its tendrils so quickly and effectively through the forums, blogs, websites, and platforms that it has extended far beyond the individual domains of incels, MRAs, and PUAs. It has spread so comprehensively, in fact, that it has emerged into the mainstream consciousness, almost becoming "common knowledge." In spite of all the evidence to the contrary: in spite of the fact that you would be hard-pressed to name high-profile men who have experienced a sudden downfall based on an unfounded accusation without due process; in spite of the fact that a relatively small number of high-profile men have faced consequences at all, compared to the millions of women who have recounted their experiences of abuse without ever having seen justice; in spite of the fact that many high-profile men accused of sexual violence by dozens of women continue to walk free... Still this idea of it being fake news has become an accepted and acceptable narrative. And it is no longer a fringe or extreme narrative. It is the norm.

These are the ideas of the manosphere. Of the woman-hating fringes that thrive beneath the radar, undiscussed, unstudied, and unchecked. When their ideas are repackaged and brushed up for a mass audience—threaded carefully into mainstream dialogue through quasirespectable figures who act as human conduits, through social media algorithms that give their content undue prominence and make it appear more widely accepted, through media outlets seeking controversy and clickbait and the appearance of "balance"—they don't emerge looking exactly the same. What starts out as hatred is subverted into something else: fear. Men who hate women make other men afraid of women.

The tactics and hallmarks of manosphere logic and argument, however, remain clearly visible. There is the use of "whataboutery" to distract from valid argument. The undermining of real statistics using pseudoscience or just outright lies to suggest a different reality. The focus on individual, emotive cases to try to create false equivalence or imply a wider trend. And the portrayal of those who are the most privileged and the most likely to commit acts of abuse as the greatest victims of all.

Let's be clear from the beginning that this misogynistic narrative is not rooted in truth.

Take, for example, the numbers surrounding the #MeToo movement, portrayed repeatedly as a witch hunt. According to a *New York Times* analysis, it is estimated that around 200 "prominent" men in the United States lost jobs, roles, professional ties, or projects after public allegations of sexual harassment, with just "a few" facing criminal charges.[2] Compare this to the fact that over twelve million tweets were sent using the #MeToo hashtag within its first four months alone, not including the millions of women who took to other social media platforms to share their stories. Even if we assume that a significant portion of those using the hashtag were critiquing or commenting on the movement, rather than sharing personal stories, and that some of the hashtag usage took place outside the United States, it is still clear that the disparity between women who have reported sexual harassment or assault and men who have been seen to face justice remains stark and is certainly not weighted against men.

The idea that "the tables have turned," as has been dramatically claimed, with the movement "going too far" and tipping the balance of gender power in the opposite direction, is absolute nonsense. We have barely seen a blip. Then there is the notion that a single woman's spurious accusation is enough to torpedo an innocent man's livelihood. The reality, again, is very different. What we have seen over and over again, as the trajectories of high-profile men like Donald Trump and Brett Kavanaugh clearly demonstrate, is that even multiple accusers or dozens of correlating accusations are often not enough to derail powerful men's careers.[3]

In fact, the New York Times investigation revealed that at least 920 people had come forward with sexual misconduct allegations relating to the 200 men in their investigation, suggesting an average ratio of 4.5 accusers per single case. It further pointed out that "more than 10 percent of the ousted men have tried to make a comeback, or voiced a desire to, and many never lost financial power." So even among the tiny number of men who actually faced any kind of repercussions, many salvaged their careers and finances regardless.

Finally, though dramatic media reports about men's "execution without trial" have attempted to portray the loss of reputation or individual roles as equivalent to imprisonment or even death, the reality is that many of these men will go on to be quietly rehabilitated away from the public eye. They are often able to continue their careers in new positions, as the swift return to work of one of the most high-profile perpetrators, comedian Louis CK, demonstrated. Similarly, Uber general manager Eyal Gutentag left his job after reportedly being witnessed sexually assaulting a female colleague, yet he quickly went on to become chief operations officer at another ride-hailing service and then chief marketing officer at a billion-dollar company. And his is not an unusual case: it has been reported that, in the technology industry particularly, "a number of men who have been accused of, and admitted to, sexual misconduct have reemerged on the scene—sometimes within months of allegations surfacing publicly. Many have returned with new start-ups or venture funds backed by investors well aware of their past behavior."[4]

When it comes to criminal charges, the justice gap yawns even wider. Some men are facing short-term professional consequences. The vast majority have faced no long-term sentences or criminal justice. The explanation for this is a complex cocktail of statutes of limitations, victim shaming, and the failings of our justice systems. But for many women who have been victims of sexual violence, it is not an exaggeration to say that the impact—psychological, physical, or professional—really is a life sentence.

Yet in spite of all this hard evidence, the narrative surrounding #MeToo in the mainstream media leaned far closer to manosphere hysteria than to actual facts.

During the rise of the #MeToo movement, I was inundated with requests to speak about the issue on the radio and television. A few of the invitations seemed to be made in good faith, with the desire to highlight women's experiences and explore the issue of sexual harassment and assault. But in only one interview, out of all the press requests I accepted during that period, did journalists steer completely clear of casting doubt on women's testimonies, asking about false accusations, or generally suggesting that the whole issue was a balanced "debate" between men and women.

How does this happen? How do the antifeminist conspiracy theories of the myriad manosphere forums find their way into our national narrative about sexual assault? The truth is it happens in a number of ways. Manosphere ideas leak out of the forums onto popular social media sites like Twitter, often in a deliberately orchestrated push by trolls, causing hashtags like #HimToo to trend worldwide. This gives journalists the excuse to seize upon a Twitter trend and describe it as a hard news story, sprinkling their copy with quoted tweets as "proof." They write articles portraying the issue as a "raging online debate" rather than a legitimate movement being hounded by a few hundred fake sock puppet accounts controlled by a group of extremists. Once in the national press, the story becomes fair game for discussion on mainstream radio and television programs, on which the concept of "balance" is often misinterpreted to portray urgent issues like climate change (or, in this case, sexual assault) as one side of a genuine debate.

Many commentators catch on to the rewards of playing to the manosphere crowd, finding that this "extremely online" audience will come out in great numbers to share and comment on pieces that repeat their rhetoric and worldview. So we see deliberately extreme and obfuscating articles in our national newspapers that present a barely sanitized version of the commentary found in men's rights or MGTOW forums.

*The Times* published a piece by columnist Giles Coren under the headline "A Couple of XX's Could End My Glorious Career," suggesting that putting an innocent kiss on the end of a text message could, in the current climate, be enough to destroy a man's livelihood. Giving high-profile, platformed voice to the murmurings and fears of the online masses, Coren wrote (without corroboration or examples),

> Over the last few years, man after man in the public eye has met his downfall when a woman came forward and made claims against him of sexual aggression of one sort or another... And then without any cross-examination of the stories, the man is finished. No trials or second chances... Time to stop being "charming" to waitresses. Time to stop

trying to make women laugh... One misfired flirt and I could be out of a job, publicly shunned, end up in prison. The women are out there who could make it happen. The historical crimes, real or imagined, are waiting to tumble upon one wrong move.[5]

It is, of course, possible that Coren would seek to defend this column as ironic. But given how closely he echoes the concerns and attitudes of a great swathe of men who have responded to the #MeToo movement with similar sentiments both on- and offline, it is likely nonetheless that his comments might be taken by many readers at face value, despite being nonsense in reality. The idea that completely innocent men are being laid off willy-nilly by employers making absolutely no attempt to verify allegations of workplace misconduct is simply false. What we do know—thanks to hard, statistical evidence—is that thousands of women experience workplace sexual harassment and assault, that their employers regularly fail to take any action over it, and that the vast majority (far from the specter of conniving, manipulative accusers conjured up by the media) never report what has happened at all. Most are too scared, terrified that they won't be believed, that they'll be blacklisted or seen as a "troublemaker," or that their careers may suffer as a result.

These fears are well founded. A 2016 UK poll of over 1,500 women, conducted by YouGov for the Trades Union Congress and the Everyday Sexism Project, found that over half of all women and almost two-thirds of young women have experienced workplace sexual harassment and that 80 percent did not feel able to report it to their employer. Of those who did report it, nearly three-quarters said that there was no change, and 16 percent said that they were treated worse as a result.[6]

That Coren's argument utilized the manosphere tactic of reversing the positions of victim and perpetrator doesn't mean he is a secret member of an incel or MRA group. It doesn't even mean he is necessarily aware of such communities.

But it does reveal how closely aligned manosphere logic has become with mainstream rhetoric around sexual harassment and violence. It reveals a symbiotic relationship whereby such rhetoric in the mainstream media risks emboldening and encouraging online extremists, and extremist communities' enthusiastic responses reward editors with clicks and shares.

Invited to discuss the outpouring of allegations of sexual violence in 2017 on the BBC Radio 4 program *The Moral Maze*, I found myself, on a highly respected national media platform, faced with arguments explicitly attempting to blame and undermine the victims who had come forward with their stories of abuse—in this case, the women who had accused Weinstein of sexual assault, for which he has now been convicted. The questions I was asked included:

"In the case of Hollywood, isn't it reasonable to assume there were some actresses involved in this who saw an opportunity to advance their careers?"

"Don't you think that, probably, young actors played along with this? It's understood, even by people at the bottom who have come to Hollywood...that they're entering a situation that they understand."

"Do you think, having arrived in Tinseltown, they'd be surprised by this?"

It is my belief that we will look back on these narratives and be shocked and appalled that this was our national response to the stories of women who gave chilling evidence at trial that they were raped by a sexual predator.[7] And when we do, we will ask ourselves a question: where did these attitudes come from?

Men (particularly those influenced by the manosphere or its ideology) are not only afraid of women who make sexual assault allegations. They are terrified of women's advancement in the workplace as well. Specifically, they have been led to believe that women's gains can only come at their own expense. In 2017, Google engineer James Damore famously wrote a memo, which he shared on an internal mailing list before it appeared in the media. In the memo, Damore criticized Google's diversity and inclusion program as "arbitrary social engineering of tech just to make it appealing to equal portions of both men and women." Damore's ten-page memo focused on "biological" differences between women and men (and their brains), which he claimed made men simply more naturally predisposed to be interested in tech roles like software engineering. He described the existence of mentoring or programs for women and ethnic minorities at the company as "discriminatory practices," suggesting that the bar was lowered at hiring for "diversity candidates" and accusing the company of promoting "veiled left ideology" that could cause irreparable "harm."[8]

There were several telling factors that seemed to link Damore's memo to the manosphere. It included rambling references to communism and "Marxist...class warfare," railing against a conspiracy to portray the "white, straight, cis-gendered patriarchy" as "the oppressor." After he was eventually fired, Damore went on to speak widely about his ideas and the belief that Google had discriminated against him as a white man. The interviews he gave were to Reddit and to the YouTube channels or platforms of men who would later be identified by one report as part of a powerful and influential net of high-profile figures, promoting reactionary, often misogynistic, antileft or alt-right views.

Within days of his firing, Damore had posed for a photo shoot outside the company's HQ, dressed in a T-shirt that read "Goolag" in the font and colors of the Google logo, a play on the word *gulag* (a twentieth-century Soviet forced-labor camp). The photographer was Peter Duke, a man dubbed the "Annie Leibovitz of the Alt-Right" by the *New York Times*, famous for photographing men like Milo Yiannopoulos and Mike Cernovich.[9] In a suggestion that Damore may have had support from people acquainted with trolling, fake anti-Google advertisements suddenly popped up around Google's LA offices, also featuring the "Goolag" pun.

Whether Damore was deliberately promoting manosphere ideology or had himself been influenced by the general terror it has whipped up beyond its own realm became largely irrelevant in the feeding frenzy that followed. The media latched on to the case with a vengeance, using it as an opportunity to debate the persecution of white men in the workplace. Such segments implied a legitimate correlation between the anecdotal experiences of individual men and the systemic, proven discrimination and disadvantages faced by other groups, such as women and people of color. It was another ideal opportunity for manosphere ideas to leak into the mainstream.

Damore's firing was portrayed as a politically correct punishment for his brave choice to speak truth to power. (Rather than the fact that his sweeping, sexist statements about women being less good at their jobs than men clearly contravened his employer's workplace policies.) And the overall result of the media maelstrom, which once again took Damore's outdated pseudoscience and misogyny at face value and debated it in good faith, was to create the impression that women everywhere were storming into workplaces, supported by PC-mad bosses, and stealing better-qualified men's jobs.

This is an ongoing pattern. We saw it in 2012, when two young men were convicted of the rape of a minor in the Steubenville case.[10] The media directed public outrage to focus not on the devastated life of the victim, whose ordeal was filmed and spread virally on social media, but on the "blighted" lives of the perpetrators, described by a CNN correspondent as "star football players, very good students." We were told live on air how the attackers were forced to watch as "their lives fell apart...when that sentence came down."[11]

We saw it in 2014, when *Washington Post* columnist George Will responded to a major Obama administration report into campus sexual assault by attempting to downplay the data and casting it as an attack on innocent young men. In a C-SPAN interview, Will said, "You're going to have young men disciplined, their lives often permanently and seriously blighted by this—they won't get into medical school, they won't get into law school, and all of this." Yet Will's own attempt to "reinterpret" the data, suggesting it was exaggerated and inaccurate, was itself shown to rely on a dubious analysis from a right-wing group with a long history of trying to undermine the public perception of the campus rape problem.[12]

We saw it in 2016, when a single, small BBC internship for Black, Asian, and minority ethnic candidates led to outraged headlines like "BBC Bans White People from Job," neatly portraying a corporation recently revealed to be struggling with a significant gender and racial pay gap as deeply discriminatory against white men instead.

Or when Jeremy Clarkson's comment that "men now just don't get jobs [at the BBC] at all" was widely reported in the news.[13] The most modest efforts toward equality are repositioned by angry white men as a potential threat to their own livelihoods. Thus, other men are encouraged to fear, rather than celebrate, progress.

We see it again and again in the media's willingness to whip up controversy and court the ire of online mobs by highlighting rare instances of false rape allegations and in the tendency to compare punishment of false accusers with sentences for sexual abusers in an attempt to suggest that the two problems are directly equivalent, creating the misconception that the crimes have similar prevalence rates. This false equivalency was breathtakingly widely touted in July 2019, when DJ Paul Gambaccini and musician Sir Cliff Richard launched a petition calling for anonymity for sexual offense suspects. Speaking to the *Today* program, Gambaccini said, "This is not a competition, who has been hurt the most. There are actually two crises—one is a sex abuse crisis and the other is a false allegation crisis."[14] Anonymity for those making accusations of sexual violence, he said, "does, unfortunately, encourage everyone from liars to lunatics to make some false accusations and get in on the action." It was a deeply damaging claim that completely belied reality. A man in the UK is 230 times more likely to be raped himself than be falsely accused of rape, so low is the number of false allegations.[15] In the meantime, 85,000 women each year in the UK experience rape or attempted rape.[16] And far from being hopelessly biased in favor of accusers, we have a justice system that sees a shamefully low 1.5 percent of all rape cases that are reported to police lead to a charge.[17] But did the media provide a robust examination of Gambaccini's claims? No. Outlets seized on the opportunity for more juicy "debates." And headline after headline suggested to the casual observer that there was, indeed, an epidemic of lying women feigning victimhood, including numerous examples that led with "Paul Gambaccini Warns of 'False Allegation Crisis.'"

In the year ending April 1, 2013, alone, the Daily Mail used the phrase cried rape in fifty-four separate headlines—a dramatic, manospheresque misrepresentation of the scale of the problem.[18] A Crown Prosecution Service review, undertaken over seventeen months between 2011 and 2013, found that just thirty-five prosecutions were brought for making false allegations of rape during that period.[19] In other words, the Daily Mail's reporting on false rape allegations outstripped the actual rate of such events occurring by almost double. "Wicked Women Who Cried Rape Trapped by Three-in-Bed Photos" is a standard example, which gives an idea of the titillating and vilifying tone of such reports.

Once again, all these are manosphere tropes and tactics.

Taking large-scale, representative statistics, demonstrating a systemic problem, and attempting to suggest that the problem doesn't really exist because women are "asking for it," then reversing the narrative by casting the perpetrators as the real victims of societal bias and oppression: classic incel ideology.

Using individual, rare miscarriages of justice to suggest that the whole system is unfairly stacked against men and that manipulation and lies by women are widespread: a tactic beloved by MRAs.

Suggesting that the climate is now so hostile toward men that even those simply enjoying their lives in the company of women risk seeing their careers and prospects decimated: MGTOW philosophy.

Focusing obsessively on false rape allegations and deliberately spreading fake statistics to whip up a climate of fear and undermine victims: a common stomping ground of PUAs like Valizadeh.

At the time of writing, Valizadeh's website contains more than one hundred articles about false rape allegations. They include pieces titled "All Public Rape Allegations Are False" and blogs advising men that the rate of false rape allegations may be as high as 90 percent before moving seamlessly into promotion of the PUA community, with the argument "Game can protect you from false rape accusations."

"PUAs do not hate women," Neil Strauss wrote in *The Game*. "They fear them."

Is it any wonder that men everywhere are so scared?

Sometimes the mainstream media picks up manosphere ideas through a less circuitous route, taking arguments that have originated in incel communities and helping to normalize them by debating them directly as valid propositions on national platforms. One recent example of this was the extended and high-profile discussion about so-called sex redistribution, a concept that originated in the manosphere as a supposed measure to prevent incels from engaging in mass violence.

The thrust of the argument, which has long been repeated across manosphere websites and blogs and is endlessly debated in incel forums, is largely summarized in a piece by Valizadeh on his website. The article—"How to Stop Incels from Killing People"— was written in direct response to criticism of incels following the Toronto van attack. Valizadeh completely absolves incel killers like Alek Minassian of responsibility, rationalizing acts of mass murder as a simple bid for attention by men "utterly forsaken" by society, writing that "incels are killing solely because they are failing to bond romantically or sexually with women... they resort to getting attention in the only way they know how: killing."

Valizadeh and other manosphere community members

extended this case by arguing that the state should provide sex workers to "service" incels. ("The whores that are a part of this program would be given special training to make the incels feel special by calling them 'handsome,' 'powerful' and 'confident.'") Single women, it is argued, should be forced to pay for this scheme through a tax on birth-control products. If a program like this isn't implemented and public attitudes don't shift to sympathize more with incels, he casually threatens, "there will be many more incel shooting sprees in the future."

This is clearly ridiculous and misogynistic. The very idea of redistributing sex, as it emerged within the manosphere, rests on a number of deeply sexist and harmful premises, each of which should have given mainstream media platforms pause before amplifying the concept or implying its validity. Yet the argument was picked up and widely discussed across major international outlets, exposing it to a far wider audience than the manosphere and communicating it to that wider audience with all the respectability and implied validity that these platforms confer. In the New York Times, opinion columnist Ross Douthat echoed incel forums, writing, "The sexual revolution created new winners and losers, new hierarchies to replace the old ones, privileging the beautiful and rich and socially adept in new ways and relegating others to new forms of loneliness and frustration."[20]

Douthat acknowledges the distinction between men who turn to incel communities through vulnerability and distress and those with violent intent, but then suggests that they should all be treated the same. This strengthens the idea that sexual deprivation is the true motive of murderers like Minassian and implies that violence against women is inconsequential. "I expect the logic of commerce and technology will be consciously harnessed, as already in pornography, to address the unhappiness of incels, be they angry and dangerous or simply depressed and despairing."

"At a certain point," Douthat suggests, we will all simply succumb to this sensible incel plan. "Without anyone formally debating the idea of a right to sex, right-thinking people will simply come to agree that some such right exists, and that it makes sense to look to some combination of changed laws, new technologies and evolved mores to fulfill it."

In a post on his blog, Robin Hanson, a conservative blogger and professor at George Mason University, wrote,

> One might plausibly argue that those with much less access to sex suffer to a similar degree as those with low income, and might similarly hope to gain from organizing around this identity, to lobby for redistribution along this axis and to at least implicitly threaten violence if their demands are not met.[21]

He went on to muse about possible practical implementation, adding, "Sex could be directly redistributed, or cash might be redistributed in compensation." Thus, women, as in incel culture, are equated seamlessly with inanimate commodities for possession and trade.

The *Spectator* ran an article by Toby Young under the headline "Here's What Every Incel Needs: A Sex Robot," in which he demanded, "Why is there so little compassion for the 'have nots' when it comes to the unequal distribution of sex? It must be because the 'victims' of this type of discrimination are nearly all male and, as such, classed as the oppressors not the oppressed."[22]

These mainstream media outlets and high-profile

commentators, intentionally or unintentionally, amplified incel ideology by taking it at face value and encouraging their millions of readers to do the same. The effect may have been inadvertent, but that makes it no less pernicious. Instead of examining the real misogyny and power dynamics at the root of incels' hatred of women, the deeply flawed premise of the manosphere's own arguments is adopted and debated.

What incel beliefs and the sex redistribution argument are actually about is terrorism. Manosphere figures such as Valizadeh, and many others like him, are effectively holding women hostage, claiming that more will die if the sexual demands of incels are not met. But somehow, seemingly, when it is "just" women at stake, all our societal norms about not negotiating with terrorists fly out the window. Suddenly, we seem quite willing to entertain the possibility that throwing a few women (particularly if they are "just sex workers") under the bus seems like a pretty good trade-off. Even entering into the debate, humoring it as a thought experiment, giving it the oxygen of publicity, sends the message that these terrorists are worthy of negotiation, whether their ideas are rebutted in the op-eds and blogs or not.

This is not just a vague comparison. Minassian, Elliot Rodger, and other incel killers like them weren't "akin" to terrorists. They *were* terrorists. So it can be argued that the mainstream media, in picking up the "debate" about sex redistribution, is engaging with the sympathizers and apologists for terrorist murderers. And just like the original media portrayal of these killings, which failed to identify them as acts of terror, these responses have a deep and lasting impact on our societal perception of the problem.

In light of this, it is mind-boggling that Douthat's column was published, especially given its opening words. "One lesson to be drawn from recent western history might be this: sometimes the extremists and radicals and weirdos see the world more clearly than the respectable and moderate and sane."[23] Imagine this (or the headline of a similar *National Post* article: "What Should We Do about Dangerous 'Incels'? Maybe Help Them") repurposed in the context of any other terrorist incident.[24]

What matters here is that the narrative becomes so persuasive and is eventually repeated by such reliable sources that it becomes extraordinarily convincing. And so it begins to convince good men. Kind, reasonable men who have never heard of manosphere communities and who genuinely believe in equality begin to become infected with a niggling worry. Men who really deplore sexual violence and want women to have equal chances in the workplace start to face the shadowy fear that the pendulum might be swinging a bit too far in the opposite direction. A seed of doubt is sown, and it whispers that perhaps they are paying a higher price than they realized for women's advancement. *Hang on a minute*, they might start to think. *I am all for equality, but is that really what's going on here?*

These are men who have not committed sexual violence yet still have a nagging sense of discomfort about the #MeToo conversation. They're the kind of decent, normal people who crop up again and again in press reports saying, "It just seems like you can't say what you think about anything anymore without a witch hunt." Or "This has all just gone a bit too far." The kind of men who might be looking back over their past relationships and sexual encounters and wondering with a nasty lurch of the stomach if they have ever acted inappropriately. And some of them may well have. But rather than reflect on that in a useful and uncomfortable way, they are urged, whether ironically or not, by Coren and his ilk to see themselves as persecuted potential victims instead. By far the most revealing line of Coren's article was this: "The historical crimes, *real or imagined*, are waiting to tumble upon one wrong move [emphasis mine]."[25]

Men who are afraid of women are actually afraid of other men. They are afraid of the myths that other men have created, which they have bought into without examination. They are afraid of an idea rather than a reality. They are afraid of the very cleverly fabricated, carefully disseminated notion that there is a shadowy danger floating somewhere out there, waiting to ensnare them. That their positions, their rights, and even their very identities are under threat in mysterious and powerful ways. That a movement of women seeking justice for transgressions puts all "innocent" men at risk. That somehow, without realizing, the tables of privilege have turned and men have become a persecuted minority, unable to defend themselves without being accused of increasingly worse crimes against progressive values. But this is not what women have asked for. We are asking for dignity, for justice, for an end to impunity. In short, many people have bought into the fear of a threat that does not really exist.

This was perhaps most clearly summed up when one American woman tweeted about her terror that her good, innocent son might have his life ruined by a false accusation coming out of nowhere, and she consequently encouraged him to videotape every encounter and invest in technology and software to monitor and record online interactions. This, another Twitter user responded, seemed like an awful lot of effort and expense, especially when the mother could achieve the same result by simply teaching her son not to assault women.

This is the same hysteria we saw whipped up by the media when the idea of recording misogyny as a hate crime was introduced.

Innocent men would be locked up in jail for having the temerity to pay a woman a compliment, the papers suggested. Wolf whistles would suddenly become criminalized. The world had gone mad. Except, in reality, the exact opposite was true. If we know one thing for absolute certain, it is that women are not falling all over themselves to report "minor" issues to the police. Every single available statistic we have proves the contrary: women shy away from reporting even the most major and devastating crimes. They are desperately unlikely to report being raped. What on earth makes us fear that they will suddenly be lining up in droves to complain about wolf whistles?

The interesting thing about this whole situation is that it is built on a tissue of lies so delicate that the faintest scrutiny brings it all down in shreds. The main thrust of the argument rests, after all, on the idea that innocent men are approaching, touching, or otherwise interacting with women in ways that are not really sexual or inappropriate but are just perceived to be so by the feminist mob. But this argument goes up in a puff of smoke when you point out the curious fact that these men, who claim to have no idea these behaviors are sexual or inappropriate, are nonetheless not acting in this manner toward other men.

Take another example: the cries of "not all men" and the repeated arguments, from the same crowd, that this moment of snowflake hysteria has created a PC minefield for modern men, who are unable to do so much as sneeze near a woman without triggering an accidental accusation of sexual harassment. That it isn't a man's fault if his colleague has a wildly different interpretation of a harmless "compliment" than his. That men are left desperately navigating a world in which one woman's "sexual assault" is another's friendly pat on the knee.

Except...those two parallel claims—"not all men" and "it's all accidental"—are directly contradictory. Either it's "not all men," in which case we must infer that it is only a small, specific group of men, deliberately committing acts of harassment and assault (a conclusion with which I broadly agree). Or this is all about poor, blundering men, making innocent missteps in a world in which behaving perfectly respectably risks being misinterpreted beyond one's control, in which case, presumably, we *are* talking about all men, since the specific implication is that it could happen to *anyone*. So once again, the logic falls apart.

That is because these arguments are not being made in good faith. They are simply attempts to dismiss and undermine the validity of women's complaints. The irony, of course, is that it is precisely these kinds of responses that risk tarring more than just a few men with the same brush. Yes, it might only be a small group of men who are deliberately committing the crimes of sexual harassment or assault in the workplace and beyond, but if the response of many men to hearing about this is to leap immediately to the defense of their gender and try to cast doubt on the validity of victims' testimonies, that doesn't exactly further the argument that not all men are implicated in the problem. No, of course, not all men are committing these acts. But those men who choose to respond to this moment of accountability by trying to discredit survivors remain complicit in the wider system that works, and always has worked, to silence victims and preserve the privileged status quo.

When men are encouraged to be afraid of women, the outcome is often most devastating to those women who are most vulnerable. In framing the problem as one of individuals, vulnerable to false accusations or losing prominent roles, the systemic nature of the issue is largely sidestepped, erasing from the narrative the importance of solutions and reforms that would have a much broader impact on women's workplace rights and safety.

The sensationalist focus on prominent cases renders invisible the women who actually make up the vast majority of workplace sexual harassment victims: those in public-facing, low-paid service roles. The victimization of women in unstable jobs with no human resources department to complain to. Those on zero-hours contracts, who stood out in the Trades Union Congress research as "a group which seems more likely to experience certain types of harassment and are less likely to report it."[26]

When the media narrative is wrested so firmly out of the hands of the women who are trying to discuss a serious and complex problem, we are reduced to firefighting: spending precious column inches or screen time defending the very premise that sexual harassment exists in the workplace at all or refuting the allegation that the majority of claims are false. Thus, the truly important aspects of the problem are edged out of the picture entirely. We never get around to discussing, for example, the migrant and refugee women who face shockingly high levels of sexual harassment in the workplace and are effectively barred from reporting it because of a failure to protect them from repercussions if they come forward to authorities.

The conversation becomes centered, again, on men's needs, fears, and rights.

When all this comes together, we see the perfect storm, with the internet, social media, mainstream media, commentators, and politicians all, wittingly or unwittingly, playing a part in a symphony that swells and amplifies basic tenets of manosphere ideology, resulting in the same aim: spreading fear. Fear of women, fear of feminism, fear of #MeToo, fear of progress, fear of change.

For those who oppose advancing equality, it is far more effective to make others terrified of it than it is to oppose it openly using logic or argument. People are motivated by fear. And it is fear of being under attack, of being vulnerable to a threat they hadn't even realized existed, that makes them most likely to succumb to hate and anger against others. It prevents them from sympathizing with those others, whether they are refugees or women in the workplace, because such support suddenly becomes positioned in direct opposition to their own best interests.

So men—even good, moderate men—become less likely to believe women and more likely to suspect them of malicious motives. In 2017, 47 percent of Republican men agreed that "most women interpret innocent remarks or acts as being sexist." A year later, after Professor Christine Blasey Ford's accusations against Brett Kavanaugh had been derided in the manosphere, painted across the media as a manipulative partisan conspiracy to topple an innocent man, and mocked by the president himself, the number jumped to 68 percent. Meanwhile, the number of Republican men who believe sexism is a problem in our society dropped.[27]

We become scared and preoccupied with problems that, in reality, are enormously unlikely ever to affect us. Consider the following, for example, in light of our societal obsession with false rape allegations. In October 2018, Channel 4 conducted a detailed investigation, using robust national statistics, and revealed that the average adult man in England and Wales has a 0.0002 percent chance of being falsely accused of rape in a year.[28] Most people, when I discuss it with them, find this statistic absolutely shocking. They believe the true figure to be far higher. This clearly demonstrates how insidiously assumptions about lying women and witch hunts have infiltrated our collective consciousness.

So the men who gradually become afraid of women are not just incels or hate-fueled online extremists, not mainstream commentators making a living out of provocative sexism that teeters just on the right side of socially acceptable. They are the nice, decent, ordinary men, just going about their daily lives, trying to make their way in the world, suffused with a thousand little hints subtly telling them that women are looking to take something away from them and they'd better watch out. These are men who would be devastated to be accused of being misogynists, who would quickly describe themselves in full favor of gender equality, who honestly want the best for their wives and daughters. They are not men who would commit sexual assault or shout at women on the street. But not being a misogynist doesn't mean that you can't sometimes behave in sexist ways. We all do it. When we make unspoken, unthinking assumptions about somebody's appropriateness for a particular role. When we praise our daughters for their looks and our sons for their strength. When we automatically reach for the word *bitch* to describe a woman who has acted in a way we don't like. This is not extreme misogyny, but it is there nonetheless, and it has an impact. Fifty percent of men are not extremist misogynists. But a recent survey found that almost half of all American men believe the gender pay gap is "made up to serve a political purpose."[29] That is what extremely successful fear-mongering looks like.

And so you find yourself sitting on a panel at a literary festival, faced with a male audience member who seems very nice and well-meaning, asking you, half apologetically, how men are supposed to support movements like #MeToo when there is "evidence" that thousands of innocent men have lost their jobs for no reason. And you want to ask him: "What evidence? Where did you get that idea? Where did it come from? How do you know?" But it is just something he knows. It is an idea born out of hate, slowly, slowly passed along a chain of communities and websites and interlocutors and commentators until it morphs into a shadowy fear that isn't easy to grasp or refute but suffuses our public consciousness. And you already know where it came from, even if he does not.

# 9

# Men Who Don't Know They Hate Women

"Loads of people I hear talk about things like women are getting our jobs now; before long, they're gonna have more rights than us."

**TOM, FIFTEEN-YEAR-OLD SCHOOLBOY INTERVIEWEE**

"But how do I know you're telling the truth?"

I blinked and looked into the eyes of the extremely polite teenage boy staring back at me.

"Why should I get involved," he continued, "when it's quite likely you could've just made the whole thing up?"

I didn't know what to tell him.

I'd just spent an hour talking to a group of boys about gender inequality, discussing everything from media sexism to street harassment, mental health, role models, political representation, and more. But I'd started the session by describing my own sexual assault, which happened on a bus, quite late at night, and was ignored by everyone around us, even when I said out loud what was happening. And at the end of the talk, I'd returned to the story, offering my hope that maybe some of the students listening would feel able to speak out if they witnessed something like that happening in the future.

Sometimes, when I talk to young people about being active bystanders or challenging things like street harassment, they ask very understandable and valid questions about safety and whether it's always sensible to intervene. The answer is that it isn't, not always, that their safety must always come first, and that there are other, nonconfrontational ways to take action, like reporting what has happened afterward or supporting a victim without engaging with the perpetrator.

But this was different. This boy wanted to know why he should go out of his way to support a woman who had just been sexually assaulted, because his first assumption was that she was probably lying. And it wasn't just any hypothetical woman. I was standing right there in front of him. I'd just talked to him for an hour, explaining how this experience had inspired me to take action against sexual violence, describing the lasting impact it had on me. And his calm, polite response was that I was probably lying. It felt very painful. It made me wonder where his assumption had come from. And I didn't know how to change his mind.

It wasn't always like this. Since starting the Everyday Sexism Project in 2012, I've visited roughly one or two schools a week, typically talking to several hundred students each time, either in small groups or whole-school assemblies, giving talks, running workshops, and having informal chats. For the first few years, the responses were varied and sometimes challenging, but they gradually settled into a pattern of predictability. For many pupils, this was the first time anyone had ever talked to them about sexism or gender inequality. Sometimes students were shocked or surprised;

often they were initially embarrassed and awkward, giggling at the pictures of bikini-clad women I used to demonstrate media objectification, gasping when I asked them to think about words like *slut* or *slag*.

Adults seemed to expect that I'd find a particular pattern of responses at a particular "type" of school. There was an assumption, for example, that sexism would be more overt at public schools or nonexistent at all-girls institutions. Instead, the problem seemed universal, with issues just as evident (sometimes more so) at private schools as anywhere else, mixed and single-sex schools struggling with similar problems, and teachers often stuck between a genuine desire to tackle sexism and a lack of training and resources to enable them to do so.

I gradually came to realize that the immediate responses from pupils were fairly strong indicators of the general atmosphere at any given school. At a school where an effort had already been made to deal with sexism and pupils had a sense that it wasn't acceptable, there would often be more open conversation, with boys and girls equally asking questions and participating in the discussion. At a school where sexism was rife, I watched boys jeering at female teachers, then snapping to attention when male staff walked in. In one particularly painful example, a female staff member left the room in tears as teenage boys joked disbelievingly about sexual assault victims.

At schools where there was a particular gender-inequality problem, girls would blossom in single-sex sessions, pouring out their experiences of harassment or assault, but clam up completely in a mixed group or fall all over themselves to denounce feminism, denying that the problem existed at all (all the while casting me apologetic looks). In such schools, boys would sometimes find quite deliberate ways to disrupt the sessions: once, I walked out on stage in front of hundreds of students, and all the boys, having organized themselves in advance, started wolf whistling in unison.

But over time, I discovered that even this level of resistance could be successfully overcome through honest conversations and respectful dialogue. If somebody wolf whistled at me on stage, I'd ask the other students to applaud them for giving us such an excellent example of sexism to discuss, and we'd talk about why it is that girls are more likely to experience wolf whistling and boys feel pressured to do it. When the topic of online pornography came up, instead of framing boys who watch it as "bad" or sexist, I'd talk about sexual pleasure and how a lot of the techniques we see in porn are unlikely to result in real-life arousal for women. I'd acknowledge the fact that nervously wanting to learn how to be a good lover is a more likely driver of many boys' online viewing than overt misogyny.

Boys who reacted in a resistant way at the beginning of a session usually did so because they were embarrassed, they thought the whole thing was a bit of a joke, or they worried that the word *sexism* meant they were going to be told off. We'd discuss the many ways in which gender stereotypes affect men and boys and talk about mental health and male role models, and as the boys came to realize that this was not an attack on them, they'd participate more and more fully in the conversation.

This phenomenon was most clearly illustrated when I visited an all-girls school where pupils from the neighboring boys' school joined us for the talk. The two schools often participated in shared activities, so the students knew each other fairly well. On the morning I was due to arrive, the girls started to notice belligerent comments cropping up on the boys' social media accounts. They demanded to know why they should be forced to sit through a stupid lecture about sexism and began planning to be as disruptive as possible, promising to jeer and snigger their way through the event. Instead of reporting the messages, the girls asked their teachers if they could leave their last lesson of the morning a few minutes early, giving them time to reach the assembly hall before the boys arrived. Fanning out, they sat in every other seat throughout the auditorium. When the boys arrived, they were stymied. Each of them stuck sitting between two girls and so stripped of the bravado of a disruptive bloc, they were forced to actually listen to the conversation the girls wanted to have. And the result was transformative. Genuine issues were raised and discussed. Misconceptions were gently corrected. Respectful debate ensued. Conversation works.

Sometimes, of course, there were still challenges. Boys who were determined not to be convinced would occasionally come up with increasingly wild comments to try to undermine the conversation, like the pupil who tried to suggest that "women in Saudi Arabia are better off not being allowed to drive, because they must be involved in fewer car accidents." But generally, these were isolated acts of bluster, intended to shock and disrupt, rather than deep-seated expressions of misogyny.

Over the past eighteen months or so, however, something has shifted.

It started at a particularly old and prestigious school, the kind at which weathered wooden plaques groan with the gold-lettered names of male Oxbridge candidates from centuries gone by, and austere portraits of past headmasters (not headmistresses) line the dining hall.

When I arrived to speak, a boy in the front row was waiting, pencil poised above a ruled notebook. He gazed at me intensely throughout the talk, scribbling furiously away. After I finished, he flipped back to the front page to read out a question that he'd prepared and brought with him. He cited false statistics about rape, claiming men were vastly more likely to be victims, and asking why I chose to ignore their plight. He seemed nervous but excited, confident he had caught me in a lie, with the air of triumphantly unmasking me in front of all his fellow students. He was wearing a red hat emblazoned with words in white: *Make America Great Again.*

Over the next few months, I started to notice something strange. There was always that one boy. Sometimes two or three. They watched intently, eyes shining with excitement. Then they asked the same questions. They gave the same statistics. Often they repeated one another, word for word. This was very different from the clumsily worded, badly thought-out jab about drivers in Saudi Arabia. It was coordinated, confident, and smooth.

Particular themes started cropping up again and again. Why should we listen to you when women lie about rape? Feminism is a man-hating conspiracy designed to let women take over the world when men are the real victims of gender inequality in today's society. Men are actually more likely to be victims of domestic violence than women. The gender pay gap is a myth.

The tone was breathless and defiant; the pose adopted was one of crusaders, speaking truth to power. The boy who quite calmly accused me of lying about my own sexual assault was not an outlier. He was part of something bigger.

Now, having spent many months immersed in the manosphere, the arguments and their wording are immediately recognizable. But at the time, I was baffled as to where these sentiments were coming from. Teenage boys are not inherently misogynistic or bad. Talk to them for a while and you soon learn that they have mothers, sisters, and female friends whom they love and respect. They aren't hard-wired to hate women. Something external was driving this.

Eventually, one boy referred to the "gynocracy" and another asked a question in which he directly quoted Milo Yiannopoulos by name. Everything started to fall into place. Instead of just answering boys' questions and gently providing robust statistics, I started asking them where they'd heard the quotes they were repeating. The answer was always the same: online.

According to a 2018 Pew Research Center study, 95 percent of U.S. teens have access to a smartphone, and 89 percent say they are online "almost constantly" or at least several times a day.[1] In the UK, a 2018 report from Ofcom, the British communications regulator, revealed that more than 450,000 children aged twelve to fifteen spend between six and eight hours a day online on weekends. The average time spent online for all children aged five to fifteen is just under three hours a day on the weekend and just under two hours a day during the week (almost double what it was a decade previously).[2]

Until a few years ago, one might have assumed that the majority of boys and teenage young men were unlikely to have heard much about feminism, an assumption borne out in my early experiences at schools. But talking to boys over the past few months, it became increasingly clear to me that their online world was giving them some very clear (and very misleading) messages about women, sexual violence, feminism, and sexism.

When I started writing this book, I put out a call for interviewees, asking parents if their teenage sons might be willing to talk to me about their experiences online and particularly their perceptions of feminism. One mother contacted me immediately, suggesting I speak to her twelve-year-old son. While he was playing video games, she had heard other players telling him, over the speaker system, that "feminism is cancer."

Her son, Alex, agreed to talk to me. "Yes," he said, "I've definitely heard a lot about feminism. A lot of the boys at my school, they don't usually class themselves as feminists, because they always think that feminism is man-hating and everything." When I asked him where this information comes from, he didn't hesitate. "It's mostly YouTube, definitely." As his peers find out about feminist activity, he said, "I think they may be worried that [it] could start to affect them in some sort of way."

Alex has a markedly different perspective from his friends. Growing up, his mom had already talked to him about feminism and inequality from a young age. So when he encountered the same online propaganda, it didn't have the impact on him that it did on his friends.

Another interviewee, fifteen-year-old Tom, said,

I think [antifeminism] comes from pretty much anywhere on social media really...mostly YouTube, Instagram, and Twitter, maybe Snapchat as well... [There are] quite a lot of memes and videos that are aimed as just jokes, but actually are quite nasty if you really think about it.

He added that he regularly hears boys at school discussing feminism and that they "often feel threatened." It would "definitely" be very difficult for a boy his age to publicly call himself a feminist, because of the peer pressure and "hate":

Loads of people I hear talk about things like women are getting our jobs now; before long, they're gonna have more

rights than us (I hear that quite a lot around school)...
Before long, women actually have more say in things, and
it's becoming much more equal, and I think it's just threatening... A lot of people are worried that they can't make
jokes any more...anything that they would have enjoyed
before, and they don't want it to change.

These are the kinds of comments most people would associate
with decades gone by. Yet here they are, coming from the mouths
of modern teenagers.

Adam, a twenty-year-old student, also told me that these attitudes and fears—messages picked up from online forums and from
memes on social media—are widespread among his peers:

I tend to hear it a lot—even stuff like if a woman's been
sexually assaulted she's lying, that sort of thing. With the
whole #MeToo movement...I see people saying the women
are just looking for their fifteen minutes of fame or why are
they saying this now? Or why do they want to send an old
man to prison for the rest of his life? Stuff that they think
makes sense but, when you step back and look at it, it's
incredibly poisonous.

All this also has to be understood in the context of the world
in which young people live their daily lives—a largely online one,
in which mainstream media messaging sets a loosely sexist and
stereotypical foundation upon which manosphere ideology can
easily build. It is also a world in which the majority of young people
have seen online pornography. A survey for the BBC found that
60 percent had viewed online porn by the age of sixteen and that a

quarter were twelve or younger when they first saw it.[3] It's a world in which the readily available videos they see contribute to the notion that sex is an aggressive, violent, humiliating, often racist act of dominance, initiated and controlled by men, while women submit, often in pain. If this sounds extreme, simply type the word *porn* into Google and click on the top link that appears—the most easily accessible, run-of-the-mill, free site you can find.

To give you a snapshot, when I followed exactly this process, among the very first videos offered were one about a "teen" with a "knife in pussy," one about sticking the biggest possible objects into the vagina of a "tiny teen," one about incest, one showing a woman looking terrified as a man covers her mouth with his hand and forces himself on her, one called "petite teen rough anal fuck and creampie" that shows a young woman with her face screwed up in pain, one that shows a woman crying with her face covered in semen, one whose title describes a woman being "throttled," one called "5 on 1 gangbang," and one labeled "black teen maid fuck the white man with her friend."

When I visit schools, extraordinary though it sounds, I frequently hear young people say that "rape is a compliment really" or "crying is part of foreplay." At one school, where they had had a rape case involving a fourteen-year-old boy, a teacher asked, "Why didn't you stop when she was crying?" The boy looked back at her, bewildered, and said, "Because it's normal for girls to cry during sex."

This is the backdrop against which manosphere ideology risks taking hold.

This is a generation for whom the boundary between online and offline is barely existent and for whom sexual violence has already become devastatingly normalized, in large part because of the way in which it floods the online world young people inhabit.

It is important to understand this if we are to appreciate how powerfully manosphere rhetoric might resonate with adolescent men. I spoke to Dr. Carlene Firmin, MBE, a British social researcher with particular expertise in the field of violence and abuse in young people's peer groups, schools, and communities. She explained that "young people will generally describe what happens online as being part of their peer group and their community, so, for them, it's very much integrated."

She emphasized the ways in which online portrayals of sexual violence impact offline behaviors:

> I don't think I've reviewed a case of sexual assault in school that hasn't involved wider harmful ideas that have circulated among the student body, and those ideas are ones that are informed by what they view online, as well as what they view offline. That assault has not occurred out of nowhere.

Dr. Firmin is particularly concerned with the "dehumanization of young women" online "and a lack of recognition of the severity of what is happening":

> I think that's what always struck me when I review cases: the casual nature of sexual assault in these cases, and the fact that it almost felt like young people were just kind of having a cup of tea. They were doing something so serious, but that severity was completely lacking from the accounts.

In other words, if young people are confronted with material online that minimizes or even glorifies sexual violence, it has a major offline impact on how they respond to it in the real world too.

The confusion and the harassment aren't always well dealt with by schools either. It is common to hear girls who have been harassed or even assaulted at school say that teachers told them to "take it as a compliment"—it's just "boys being boys." In this way, some teachers unknowingly normalize and reiterate exactly the sort of sexist ideas boys are starting to be exposed to online.

At one school I visited, the girls had been banned from starting a feminist society because the headmaster had deemed it divisive, unnecessary, and potentially sexist. The girls started meeting in secret anyway; it was only after the headmaster's daughter joined as an act of protest that the society mysteriously gained official approval.

And so hatred of women is ushered into young men's belief systems without them even realizing that that's what it is. It isn't hating women; it's standing up for men. It isn't hating women; it's asking for "real" equality. It isn't hating women; it's accepting biological difference. It can't be hating women if everybody is laughing about it online.

As messages and conversations like this increasingly cropped up on my radar, it began to seem like there was a gradual rise in the number of young people coming into contact with manosphere ideology.

The hostility reported by girls who identify as feminists at UK schools is enormous, with repeated stories of meetings disrupted with misogynistic chants, abusive slogans scrawled over posters, and long-term verbal harassment that has left girls devastated or even forced to change schools.

"Sometimes someone will start saying a teacher's a feminist and then saying nasty things about the teacher," Tom observed, suggesting that staff are not immune either. A young woman who identified

herself as a feminist in a school discussion I attended emailed me
after she was subjected to a campaign of harassment from her male
peers as a result. She showed me text messages she had received
from boys in her class, whose content read more like a manosphere
forum than a teenage text exchange. They informed her that feminism was "sexist," that men are simply biologically superior, and
that giving them better jobs is just the best way to progress the
human race. It's not their fault, they wrote. They're not trying to
be "mean"; it's just the way things are. And reading their messages,
I really think they believe it. These are the arguments that teenage
girls today—not a hundred years ago—are facing from their male
peers. Imagine having to try to confront those views among your
classmates. Imagine going to school and learning alongside boys
who genuinely believe they are simply genetically superior to you.
Imagine the impact on your academic endeavors. And imagine
being a teenage boy who has absorbed these ideas not as deeply
controversial opinions but as simple facts.

Not knowing whether my own observations were part of a
wider phenomenon, I decided to talk to Ben Hurst at the Good
Lad Initiative, who is ideally placed as a barometer of the ideas and
experiences of a diverse cross-section of boys.

As it turns out, Hurst's experiences are strikingly similar to my
own. Like me, he has repeatedly come across boys at schools who are
keen to discuss false rape allegations above anything else. And like
me, he has noticed a significant recent uptick in these conversations.

He said, "There are a lot of kids now who are really active on
YouTube and consuming a lot of mid-right to far-right men's rights
material." Also mentioning Reddit, 4chan, and Instagram, he added,
"There's loads of stuff that they can access really easily without
having to do any research or expand their worldview in any way."

When I asked Hurst to estimate the proportion of young people he works with who might have been affected by manosphere ideas, he was unequivocal: "I think it's more common than not—probably about 70 percent of the boys we have contact with have, in some way, come into contact with that kind of material, and I think it influences the way that they think to varying degrees."

Crucially, many of the young people Hurst works with don't seem to be members of the most extreme manosphere forums. Rather, they are accessing manosphere ideas further up the chain. Between us, we tried to pinpoint how the ideology of the manosphere is being translated and diluted across other platforms, and we agreed that the young people we've come into contact with have had differing levels of exposure, some of them going on an ideological journey that takes them from one platform to the next.

"So some schools you go into, kids will be like: 'I love Jordan Peterson'...and in those classrooms, you have conversations about 'feminazis,' or whatever the hot topic is at the moment around men's rights activism." But he believes that "there's a larger group of kids who are maybe a step or two behind that." These children aren't necessarily even aware of specific manosphere communities but nonetheless absorb aspects of their ideology, packaged in easily digestible and highly memorable memes and jokes or made palatable and respectable for mainstream consumption by prominent media figures.

Hurst estimates that at the school level at least, far more young people fall into this category than that of confirmed members of the incel or other communities. "They know [about incels]. But the thing about incels is [that] incels are not cool—that's one of the reasons they end up being incels, right?" He laughed.

They're involuntarily celibate. And so I think teenagers...
most of them, they haven't reached that point yet where
that material's relevant to them—at universities, we come
across that stuff a lot more. But still not loads. It's still more
common that it's lower level—people have been listening
to Piers Morgan or watching Jordan Peterson videos... It's
more like: "I'm scared that, if I have sex with a girl, she
thinks that I raped her."

He paused. "It comes with a lot of bravado, so they don't sound
like that," but that is the fear at the root of boys' concerted interest
in false rape allegations.

This notion of boys accessing manosphere thinking "further
upstream" of incel or PUA websites is confirmed by my young
interviewees. Neither Alex nor Tom had ever heard of incels or
Yiannopoulos (I envy them). It's also backed up by my own experiences in schools: a small but significant number of the boys I speak
to are clearly deeply immersed in manosphere message boards,
but the majority are not deliberately going looking for or are even
aware of this material. Instead, it is coming to them—the ideas filtered through anonymous accounts and meme factories.

At one school, a teenage boy agreed to show me some of the
Instagram meme accounts he says are most popular among his
peers. None of them mentions anything to do with feminism or
the manosphere in their titles—the accounts have bland names that
are most likely to include the words *memes* and *lols*. But as soon as
you click on them, the content is immediately familiar. Jokes and
images reference beating women up if they get too "uppity" about
equal rights, and feminist hypocrisy and false rape accusations are
among the most common topics. The hashtags are perhaps the

most revealing aspect of these accounts—they combine the reality of the content with the banality of the delivery system: #freshmemes #funniestmemes #schoolshootermemes #feminismiscancer #edgymemesforedgyteens.

The accounts typically have no visible face or persona, and they tend to attract hundreds of thousands of followers, with endless strings of comments beneath each image. Jokes about date rape and domestic violence mingle with transphobia and Islamophobia. Racism is rife, with the n-word appearing in around one in four posts I looked at. While explicit terms like *incel* or *men's rights* tend not to appear, the material is recognizable from the manosphere. A meme demanding users click "like" if they want Hillary Clinton to go to prison (10,434 likes) jostles for space with a doctored image of Anita Sarkeesian with a gun to her head. The boys who consume these memes might not have heard of Gamergate, and they may not even recognize who Sarkeesian is, but they are unwittingly becoming indoctrinated into the shared knowledge and groupthink of the misogynistic mob.

If the idea that misogyny is so accessible to young people comes as a surprise, it's likely because many adults tend to have very little concept of the sheer ubiquity and centrality of YouTube, in particular, to young people's lives.

First, think about those young people among whom almost 90 percent report being online multiple times a day. Then add the fact that Ofcom revealed a fifth of sixteen- to twenty-four-year-olds spend more than seven hours a day online every day of the week.[4] Now consider what they're doing during that huge amount of time online. Almost half of it is spent on social media, according to the analysis of their commuting phone habits. So which platforms are they most likely to be using? According to the Pew Research Center study, 85 percent of U.S. teens say that they use YouTube, compared to 72 percent who use Instagram, 51 percent Facebook, and 32 percent Twitter.[5] There are over 1.5 billion YouTube users in the world—a figure greater than the number of households that own a television.[6]

So while it might come as a shock to many grown-ups, it probably wouldn't surprise teenagers to learn that a recent report revealed YouTube to be responsible for a whopping 38 percent of all mobile internet traffic internationally.[7] (Netflix streaming, by comparison, accounts for just 2.4 percent.) This is particularly important for our purposes, considering that the teen demographic is significantly more likely to access the internet via smartphone.

This begins to make the picture a little clearer, insofar as it reveals the extent to which we might not be aware of the endless hours young people are spending on YouTube. But why is this of particular significance when it comes to alt-right and manosphere ideology?

For those adults who think of YouTube as the home of grumpy cat videos and movie trailers, it is unnerving to learn that the platform is heavily colonized by extreme right-wing thinking, represented by a vast number of channels with white supremacist, misogynistic hosts, pumping out thousands of hours of content in support of their worldviews.

"There are countless other forms of political expression on YouTube, but no bloc is anywhere near as organized or as assertive as the YouTube right and its dozens of obdurate vloggers," wrote John Herrman in an insightful *New York Times* article that compared YouTube to talk radio, suggesting that both platforms offered an opportunity for extreme, reactionary far-right thinkers to hold forth for hours at a time to a deeply engaged audience without challenge.[8]

But even for those who were already aware of the hefty influence of alt-right and manosphere influencers on YouTube, the publication of a 2018 report by New York–based research institute Data & Society created shock waves. The report, authored by researcher Rebecca Lewis, uncovered an "alternative influence network" of more than sixty academics, media pundits, and internet figures across eighty channels. They ranged from more mainstream, self-proclaimed libertarian and conservative commentators to extreme misogynists, white supremacists, and racists. "Many of these YouTubers are less defined by any single ideology than they are by a 'reactionary' position: a general opposition to feminism, social justice, or left-wing politics," Lewis wrote in the report.[9]

What she discovered was that the platform had become "the single most important hub by which an extensive network of far-right influencers profit from broadcasting propaganda to young viewers." Specifically, Lewis explained, these right-wing commentators were using similar branding, search engine optimization, and other tech-savvy techniques to create a powerful influencer network, allowing the more popular and socially acceptable personalities to boost the credibility of the more fringe figures and, in turn, benefiting from the cross-pollination and expansion of their audiences.

In other words, she wrote, "Social networking between influencers makes it easy for audience members to be incrementally exposed to, and come to trust, ever more extremist political positions." And far from the "dark corners of the internet," she warned that "much extremist content is happening front and center, easily accessible on platforms like YouTube, publicly endorsed by well-resourced individuals and interfacing directly with mainstream culture." Figures like Jordan Peterson represented the more socially acceptable end of the spectrum outlined in the report, while the other end featured recognizable names from the web's most extreme communities of white supremacy and misogyny, like Richard B. Spencer and Mike Cernovich. They also included influencers with "red pill" in their usernames. By hosting and sharing platforms with some of the more radical thinkers, even if they don't tend to subscribe openly to their views, the more mainstream personalities help to amplify "openly racist" or misogynistic ideas by treating them "as if they are perfectly normal."

The potential impact of these videos on young people's worldviews is enormous, not just because of their mass exposure but also particularly in light of the fact that repeated studies have suggested more young people now get their "news" from social media than from television or any other source. This risks leaving a deeply disturbing vacuum, ready to be filled by increasingly extreme YouTube content without the offsetting balance of any alternative or rigorously fact-checked information.

But the worst was yet to come. In 2018, sociologists and former YouTube employees began to speak out about the secretive algorithms that serve up recommended videos to YouTube users, trying to entice them to watch more content after the video they originally viewed has finished. These algorithms might not seem especially important, until you learn that 70 percent of all YouTube videos watched are recommended by the platform's algorithm.[10] So people spend significantly more time watching the content served up to them than videos they've actually gone looking for.

Remember that 38 percent of all mobile internet traffic is accounted for by YouTube? These two statistics combined mean that around a quarter of all mobile internet traffic in the world consists of people watching the videos YouTube has chosen for them to watch—a figure so mind-boggling it takes a minute to sink in. In that context, the sort of content YouTube's algorithm is directing us to suddenly takes on a whole new significance. Which is bad news when you learn what former YouTube engineer Guillaume Chaslot has to reveal about the algorithm and how it works.

Because YouTube makes its money from advertising, its greatest motive is to keep users watching videos for as long as possible, resulting in the greatest possible number of eyeballs to serve advertisements to. One major public misconception set straight by Chaslot when he voiced his concerns to multiple media outlets in 2018 is the assumption that the algorithm seeks to serve people the most relevant or highest-quality content. This, Chaslot said, is definitely not the case. Instead, it focuses entirely on "watch time." And research has shown that what makes people keep watching—and clicking for more—is increasingly extreme content.

Academics quickly picked up on the significance of this pattern. Writing in the *New York Times*, sociologist Zeynep Tufekci described how, no matter what average video she started out with, YouTube's algorithm would quickly send her down a spiraling rabbit hole of associated but far more hardcore content. "Videos about vegetarianism led to videos about veganism. Videos about jogging led to videos about running ultramarathons."[11] A *Wall Street Journal* investigation revealed the same phenomenon.[12] Of course, for those looking for videos about fun dance moves, say, or cooking techniques, this is a relatively harmless pattern. But for impressionable young people who start out looking at quite mainstream political content, it has much more serious implications. Chaslot told the *Daily Beast* he very quickly realized that "YouTube's recommendation was putting people into filter bubbles... There was no way out."

In a 2019 *New York Times* interview, YouTube's chief product officer, Neal Mohan, denied that the platform created a "rabbit hole" effect, saying that it offered a full spectrum of content and opinion and that watch time was not the only feature used by the site's recommendation systems. He acknowledged that the algorithm might queue up more extreme videos but claimed it might also offer "other videos that skew in the opposite direction."[13] But that didn't seem to be the case in my own experiments or those of other writers who have documented this phenomenon.

This doesn't mean that YouTube is deliberately setting out to promote and support these extreme racist and misogynist viewpoints. But it seems to be an inadvertent and powerful side effect of the way the site works. It is unlikely that these patterns were deliberately or maliciously written into the DNA of mainstream social media platforms, but it is also not a complete coincidence that none of these problems was foreseen, given the demographics of the people who tend to design, moderate, control, and profit from such platforms. The most recent annual diversity report of Google, which owns YouTube, revealed that its global workforce is 68 percent male, and in the United States, just 3.7 percent of its workforce is Black.[14]

Dr. Lisa Sugiura, who believes that social media platforms must take far greater accountability for the content they host, pointed to the very origins of Facebook, which was initially set up as a kind of "hot or not" platform, enabling Harvard students to rate and compare images of their female peers. Dr. Sugiura gave an exasperated laugh. "Sexism is embedded in the technology of something like Facebook—think about where it came from, how it started! So look at pickup artists and their agenda—they've got the validation from the very beginning with the tool that they're using."

There are several features of manosphere communities and

the types of videos they produce that play particularly well with YouTube's algorithm. The videos tend to be long, meaning they automatically rack up extended watch time, particularly if viewers watch the whole thing, which is more likely with a community as dedicated and invested as the manosphere. They pick up swiftly on current and trending news stories (taking any incident of a false rape allegation, for example, as an instant confirmation of their self-victimizing worldview) and are often able to produce content very quickly, free of the burdensome task of fact checking or balanced reporting. And there is enormous overlap between the ideological obsessions of groups like the alt-right and incels, white supremacists and MGTOW, PUAs and MRAs. This racist, anti-Semitic, Islamophobic, anti-immigrant, misogynistic, or homophobic crossover makes them a dream prospect for an algorithm looking for ways to create connections between "related" channels and content.

Jacob Davey, when I spoke to him, raised specific concerns about "the functionality of [internet] platforms" in enabling the spread of extremist views: "You can fall into an algorithmically supported rabbit hole on YouTube, which can very quickly put you in a situation where the only thing you're getting recommended is misogynistic vloggers... [It] needs to be addressed."

What does this look like in practice? To find out, I cleared my internet history, deleted my cookies, and opened a private browsing window to make sure that I was starting from a "neutral" point.

I opened YouTube, typed *what is feminism?* into the search bar, and clicked on one of the very first links (a profeminist speech by actress Emma Watson). From there, I let the algorithm take me where it would. The next video automatically started playing after the first finished. It was a video from *The Rubin Report*, which describes itself as a talk show about "free speech and big ideas."

Dave Rubin, host of the show, is one of the figures specifically cited in the Data & Society report about a network of alt-right influencers on YouTube. The video was an interview with Yiannopoulos in which he was given free rein, virtually unchallenged, to hold forth about modern feminism, which he described as "primarily about manhating...a very angry, bitter, profane, lesbianic sort of feminism," spreading a "constant message that men are evil and broken and wrong." He called campus rape statistics "nonsense" and said that figures cited by Barack Obama about sexual violence are "not true." The video has over two million views.

The next autoplayed video featured Peterson. Among the following ten recommended videos were Peterson (who appeared three times in the list) and Yiannopoulos (who appeared four times). What's fascinating is that they serve precisely to demonstrate the concerns Lewis raised. None of the videos comes directly from the channels of the more controversial figures themselves; they are all interviews with the commentators on the channels of more mainstream, "respectable" hosts, including Channel 4 News. For a young teenager who has started from a very simple, entry-level question, these are very specific and extreme answers to the question of "what is feminism?" And far from presenting a balanced spectrum of views, they all vehemently repeat the same misogynistic misconceptions about women's rights.

But imagine you are a young person who has just logged on and doesn't know much about the topic. The videos served up all have high production values. Their hosts are urbane and well known, the talk shows popular. It all suggests to the uninitiated viewer that these are widespread, valid views, not fringe or extreme ideas. The fact that YouTube's algorithm offers absolutely no positive or alternative content about feminism gives the impression that this is overwhelmingly the popular consensus. And between them, the next five recommended videos have thirty-six million views, indicating that it is not unusual for them to be served up as suggested fodder by the YouTube machine.

The young people I talked to gave accounts that strongly back up these fears. On the subject of YouTube and antifeminism, Alex said, "A lot of people with a lot of followers talk about [antifeminism]." These antifeminist videos, he said, are usually recommended to his friends by YouTube. "And from [online influencers] they look up to, it kind of creates a sort of opinion in their heads that this is how the world works."

Adam agreed.

I think, if you're in that community where everyone's validating everyone's views, they're not really getting any alternative outside influences and they'll obviously tend to assume that anyone else is a snowflake or a feminazi or whatever they want to call them, so they think their view is the only right view, because they're getting validated.

This essentially begins to create a space for online indoctrination—a problem, Lewis said, that is particularly acute with such a potentially vulnerable age group: "YouTube appeals to such a young demographic... Young people are more susceptible to having their political ideals shaped. That's the time in your life when you're figuring out who you are and what your politics are."[15]

These fears are only confirmed by a teacher of fourteen- to eighteen-year-old pupils at a mixed inner London comprehensive school who agreed to be interviewed on condition of anonymity, in order to protect her students' identities. She told me, "I've heard a lot of young people (mostly boys, but not always) make very radical statements about women and gender that, when I've questioned them, have come from watching MRA videos on YouTube." From overhearing student conversations, she said, it is her guess that they have come across these extremist videos at the end of an initially funny or silly YouTube video thread. In other words, she doesn't think they've gone looking for these types of videos, but the videos have been served up by YouTube instead.

While learning about Margaret Atwood's *The Handmaid's Tale* in high school, some of her students complained, saying there ought to be "a *Handmaid's Tale* for men." (Atwood's dystopian novel, set in an imagined totalitarian United States in which women are completely subjugated, is famously inspired by real-world oppression. Atwood has stated, "One of my rules was that I would not put any events into the book that had not already happened.") "When I asked them about this," the teacher told me, "they referred to a YouTube video, which said that men now have fewer rights than women and that women are always complaining, but now things are harder for men."

Just like mine, her suspicions were first aroused when she realized that students were parroting the same antifeminist bile she'd come across online from manosphere sources: "I've had several students make comments about feminism having gone too far and, when questioned, they'll use arguments that I recognize from men's rights activism, such as more men dying in wars, and child custody laws favoring women."

Having watched it affect her students, in spite of her efforts to intervene and challenge such views, she described the process of online radicalization as a deceptively slippery slope: "I think the initial videos can discourage empathy and encourage the 'othering' of women, and then this grows more extreme... I suspect there is a link between 'edgy humor,' 'fail' videos, conspiracy theories, and men's rights activism."

Of course, young people are not the only ones who can be affected by this kind of gentle, apparently random "nudging" toward more and more extreme content. Analysis by Chaslot and others of the videos recommended by YouTube's algorithm in the run-up to the 2016 American presidential election revealed that, even starting from a completely neutral point, YouTube was six times more likely to recommend videos that were anti-Clinton than anti-Trump, including many extreme conspiracy theories that suggested Clinton had secret severe illnesses or connections to satanic cults.[16]

Yet we have consistently underestimated and ignored YouTube as a source of potential political information and influence. Public attention on this issue has focused almost exclusively on Facebook, but as the *Guardian* pointed out, these findings are alarming in light of the fact that Donald Trump won the election by just 80,000 votes, and the videos in Chaslot's database of YouTube-recommended election fare were watched, in total, over three billion times before election day.[17] And of course, the algorithm plays straight into the hands of deliberate manipulation by trolls like Cernovich, whose conspiracy theories about Clinton's health created such a powerful ripple effect.

So is there concrete reason to be concerned that this could be having a serious impact on young people? Do we know for sure that simply being exposed to this content actually has an effect? In a word: yes. In 2018, investigative journalism collective Bellingcat published the results of an in-depth analysis into the extremist journeys of seventy-five fascist activists, exploring the ways in which they had become radicalized. The investigation used a database of hundreds of thousands of Discord server posts. (Discord is a chat platform primarily designed for gamers but often used by members of the alt-right and manosphere.) The investigation revealed conversations between fascists and white nationalists discussing their conversions to extremism. It found that the majority of the posters believed that they had been radicalized by online content and that "YouTube seems to be the single most frequently discussed website."[18]

Individual chats revealed how the journey to extreme white supremacy and fascism meandered between the tangled webs of the manosphere and the alt-right, with one classic example starting with being "redpilled on Feminism" on a blog, before going on to be "redpilled on Islam...in a youtube comments section," then via being "redpilled on GG [Gamergate]," reaching information about "rapefugees," and finally coming to believe in "racial IQ" (the false white supremacist belief that white people have bigger brains than people of color) and the notion "that 'we must secure the existence of our people and a future for white children.'" (This last phrase is a famous white supremacist, terrorist slogan.) The chats explicitly mention memes and jokes as ways in which converts were "eased" into the ideology—at first seeing it as ironic before "all of a sudden it stopped being a meme."

David Sherratt, who was in his teens when he began to adopt extremist manosphere rhetoric, told me, "I never went looking for these things, in all honesty... It was definitely mostly through YouTube's recommendations that I found these things."

If you never set out to find an extreme ideology, if you don't even realize that is what it is, then it is very easy to take on more and more radical views without even really knowing it. If everything you see online broadly reinforces the same viewpoint, if it is being suggested to you by a platform as reputable as YouTube, surely it can't be described as *hatred*, not really.

In 2019, a rare good-news story hit the headlines: scientists had, for the first time, managed to create a photograph of a black hole. The news was met with great fanfare, and attention quickly centered on Katie Bouman, a twenty-nine-year-old MIT graduate student who had led the team that made the historic achievement possible. But within hours, the manosphere had leaped into action. Thousands of comments, posts, and threads across multiple websites, including typical hot spots like Reddit, had sprung up, denouncing the praise of Bouman with extreme misogyny, conspiracy theories, fake news, and outright lies.

"Hi My Name Is Katie Bouman and I'm a Fraud," read the title of one typical thread, below which comments quickly descended into a cesspit of slurs about Bouman's appearance and vitriol about "feminazis" and "SJWs" (an acronym for the derisive manosphere term "social justice warriors"). As usual, the obsession spread like wildfire, with YouTube videos quickly materializing to criticize Bouman and (falsely) claim that her male colleagues had actually done the majority of the work for which she was being given credit. It was a good example of the kind of extreme, deeply misogynistic response many would think of as a fringe, minority activity.

But YouTube's algorithm had other ideas. Within a short space of time, the top result for searching Bouman's name on the platform was a deeply misogynistic and factually inaccurate video titled "Woman Does 6% of the Work but Gets 100% of the Credit: Black Hole Photo." Appearing more prominently than actual news from reliable media outlets, the video was recommended as the top source on the story by the algorithm, despite the fact that it came from a relatively unknown, little-followed account and had fewer views than other actual news videos about the story. And the "relevant" videos the algorithm recommended (and automatically played) for viewers to watch next? Videos of Peterson "debunking" the gender pay gap, of course!

YouTube is not alone in amplifying, normalizing, and enabling the spread of radicalizing and extremist ideologies by dint of its design. On Instagram, the thousands of accounts serving watered-down, digestible, meme-friendly versions of racism and misogyny to teens under the veil of humor and "banter" are able to operate with relative impunity due to the ability to reboot themselves or set up backup accounts in anticipation of any censure.

In an article published in the *New Media & Society* journal, communications professor Adrienne Massanari analyzed "the ways in which Reddit's karma point system, aggregation of material across subreddits, ease of subreddit and user account creation, governance structure, and policies around offensive content serve to provide fertile ground for anti-feminist and misogynistic activism."[19]

Writer Aja Romano observed how easy it is for Twitter to be manipulated by those wishing to use it for campaigns of sustained mass harassment:

> The ease with which anyone can make an account and begin directly tweeting at verified users may be a selling point for Twitter, but it also makes it extremely easy to populate "sock puppets" (that is, to create unconnected internet accounts all posing as different people) and proliferate harassment across the site.[20]

In short, social media has the capacity to be a tool for hate and harassment written into its DNA.

All these platforms have policies against hateful conduct, and all make attempts to police incitement to hatred and harm. But in their current forms, they still provide a lightning rod for certain ideologies to find their way to millions of young people.

All this means that a teenage boy can start out from fairly benign opinions—"gosh, feminists seem to be taking everything a bit seriously"—and then be ever so gently nudged from jokes and memes through to comedy video compilations and into the reaches of ever more extreme ideas and content without ever realizing the slippery slope he is on. Eventually, he assumes that a woman is lying about being sexually assaulted, even when she is standing right in front of him. He reaches a point at which he might begin to hate women without even knowing it.

While the ways in which social media companies end up aiding and abetting this process of radicalization may be entirely unintentional, the gears of the process are expertly greased by online extremists knowingly exploiting the social tools available to them to maximize new recruits. And they are deliberately and specifically focused on young men.

As Lewis observed, young people are particularly vulnerable to political and ideological exploitation as they start to explore their world and work out where they stand. The men of the manosphere and the alt-right understand this. They realize the opportunity that young, malleable minds present, and they are prepared to exploit them to the fullest possible extent.

In April 2019, Mike Buchanan published an article on AVFM in which he announced "a new strategy for J4MB, engaging with university students and academics, particularly those studying or teaching subjects close to our mission, such as Politics and History." Within months, he had booked a venue to speak at Cambridge University, then reaped mainstream press coverage when students protested.

One major PUA training organization boasts on its website that in order "to further cement" the organization's "massive credibility," it has "given talks at prestigious universities such as Yale, Harvard, Wharton, and more."

Andrew Anglin of the *Daily Stormer* wrote the following:

> Our target audience is white males between the ages of 10 and 30... I include children as young as ten, because an element of this is that we want to look like superheroes. We want to be something that boys fantasize about being a part of. That is a core element to this. I don't include men over the age of 30, because after that point you are largely fixed in your thinking. We will certainly reach some older men, but they should not be a focus.

In this spirit, popular manosphere websites host and share resources specifically designed as propaganda to attract young people to the cause. One example, "The Red Pill Primer for Boys," is described thus:

> By popular demand, the agents of the Red Pill Society have assembled an easy-to-understand guide to the Red Pill... for teenage boys and men who are intrigued by Red Pill concepts and practices. These are in Google Presentation format, presented free of charge for the betterment of young men everywhere.

The thirteen-part presentation includes categories like "Why feminism hates you" (a men's rights incubator) and, for budding PUAs, "Gaming girls: An introduction." It takes the form of a slick slideshow with catchy titles and images. It tells boys that feminists believe all sex is rape and teaches them that they ("younger white men") are feminists' primary "targets." And of course, incel ideology features too: "At center stage of this combat is the matter of young men who want to have sex. That is...you... Your Penis is their Enemy."

What this looks like, what this *is*, is radicalization. Extremist, ideological radicalization, deliberately aimed at vulnerable, young people. And we have seen its impact. Anglin has written about how he had no background in white nationalism before 2011 and became politicized "mainly on 4chan." His own journey to radicalization is painfully apparent in the online manifesto he wrote as a "public service announcement," instructing other white nationalists in how to win over new recruits. As well as stressing the importance of targeting young people, Anglin wrote, "Don't isolate yourself from mainstream culture... in order to be successful, you need to be able to connect to the culture at large." His next instruction is to

offer something to the people you are targeting... What resonates the most, in my experience, is issues surrounding the displacement and disenfranchisement of the white male which has taken place as a result of feminism. That is a gateway to all of this, much more than the race issue. So anti-feminism, anti-homosexuality, and the preservation of male identity and the man's role in society should always be a core focus of the brand.

In other words, male supremacist communities are not only directly targeting young men for radicalization but also seeing their ideology as a gateway to further white supremacist radicalization.

The ultimate aim for these groups, rooted in racist and misogynistic extremism, is to move from the internet to the streets, taking their violence and their recruits with them. The internet is seen as the recruiting ground for the physical acts to come. "All of the work we have done in these tubes is paying off, and the Alt-Right is ready to move off of the internet, into the real world," wrote Anglin on August 9, 2017. Three days later, the mass rally in Charlottesville saw the biggest physical manifestation of white supremacist sentiment on U.S. soil in decades, and a woman died.

Elliot Rodger's manifesto talks about the huge influence the internet and online culture had on him from the age of eleven, when he first started using the internet regularly. "Once I fully immersed myself in it, it really fascinated me," he wrote, describing his involvement with the manosphere forums that shaped and radicalized his beliefs.

When I spoke to Jack Peterson, the former incel who has since left the movement, he told me, "The incel community wasn't something I came across spontaneously." Starting with browsing 4chan in 2010, Peterson became gradually immersed in misogynistic discourse over a period of six years, coming across "numerous different websites with similar culture," until 2016, when he stumbled upon incels on Reddit. By then, he said, their views were more familiar than shocking.

This doesn't mean, of course, that every young person who comes across this kind of rhetoric will be radicalized or go on to carry out acts of violence. I'm struck again by the ease with which Alex was able to shrug off manosphere thinking, even when it was embraced by his friends, because he had already talked frequently to his mom about the issues. But so much of this flies beneath the radar. Most of us have never even heard of incels. How can parents start to have those vital, potentially life-saving conversations if they don't know what is happening to boys online?

This is particularly problematic when boys are being targeted with extremist ideas on platforms that might appear quite innocent to the outside observer.

As well as forums about inceldom and pickup artistry, Rodger also frequented websites like bodybuilding.com. Ostensibly communities devoted to fitness and strength, these bodybuilding forums appear to have little or nothing to do with the manosphere and men's rights communities. But it was there that Rodger ranted about seeing attractive women with less attractive men, and there that another user jokingly referred to him as a potential shooter, less than a week before he carried out his massacre.

It was initially surprising, when I started researching incel websites, to realize just how much crossover there was between the manosphere and the seemingly unrelated world of bodybuilding forums, websites, and social media groups. But as I started to trace the tentacles of incel ideology, reaching out to tickle the attention of those concerned about their muscle tone and chest size, it began to make more and more sense. The world of bodybuilding is packed with young men. They are often vulnerable or insecure. They are usually seeking advice on attaining a stereotypically masculine physique—the sort of boys who believe they have to look a certain way to be real men. This is fertile ground for the manosphere, whose doctrine is likely to have the greatest impact on people already concerned with traditional models of masculinity. A teenage boy who is so concerned about having big biceps that he is scouring the internet for advice on how to achieve them is perhaps more likely than others to fall prey to manosphere ideology, suffused as it is with outdated gender stereotypes.

Gradually, it became clear to me that the online network of the bodybuilding community is being used as a stomping and recruiting ground for male supremacist and white supremacist extremists, calculatedly targeting young men.

Within the online discussion forum of bodybuilding.com, teen bodybuilding is by far the most active and popular section, with almost ten times as many posts as the next most common subsection. These are young, impressionable users. The miscellaneous section of the forum, which features threads on gaming, relationships, and politics, contains over 93 million posts, compared to 382,600 under the category of sports training. It quickly begins to appear that bodybuilding is not actually the most popular topic on the bodybuilding forum, by a significant margin.

The average posts in the politics section might just as easily appear on an incel, men's rights, or alt-right website. On the day I visited the forum, the most recent post in that section featured six pages of abuse and attacks against U.S. politician Ilhan Omar, including Islamophobia, anti-Semitism, misogyny, and racism. Users suggested she go back to her "chit hole [sic]" country, while others discussed whether they would rape her. "Not gonna lie, I'd smash her, hijab and all." Little coincidence that she is one of the congresswomen Trump tweeted about, telling her to "go back" to where she came from.

There were threads about rape, on which posters declared, "There is no such thing as rape, rape is a fabrication of the female mind." "It's only rape once the chloroform wears off," wrote one user, typically disguising his misogyny and normalization of sexual violence as a harmless joke. Another user chimed in: "Fckin feminist government. When did rape become a crime? Men used to go around raping bishes all the time."

For a website with ostensibly no connection to extreme misogynist communities, such content initially came as a shock. But it didn't appear to surprise anybody posting there. The forum contained ninety-four separate discussions (with thousands of comments) about the red pill, ninety-four about incels, eighty-four about "false rape," seventy-one about MGTOW, and ninety-four about PUAs. There were eighty-seven threads about Rodger alone. While the average discussion thread might contain, say, twenty or forty posts, a thread about the identifying characteristics of Chads had over 5,000 responses. In the relationships forum, a single pickup thread has been viewed over a million times.

Another place in which young people are vulnerable to being groomed is the wildly popular world of online gaming. According to a U.S. study, 97 percent of teen boys and 83 percent of teen girls play video games—a fact that hasn't gone unnoticed by extremist online communities looking to extend their recruitment strategies.[21] While some games can be played online from a computer, even those played from a console at home are now often interconnected multiplayer games, where players are encouraged to form teams using an internet connection, either with friends or strangers. For many young people who want to play regularly and are not necessarily online at the same time as their friends, this leads to extensive amounts of time playing games with strangers they have never met. Team interaction is facilitated by in-game chat that can take place over headphones or text or in dedicated chat rooms where anybody can easily create a private chat. For those with ulterior motives for connecting with young men, it couldn't be a more fertile environment. And many parents are not even aware that the feature exists at all.

Joan Donovan, media manipulation research lead at Data & Society, said in an interview that online extremists have been using "gaming culture" as one of their "spaces of recruitment." And Christian Picciolini—a former neo-Nazi who went on to found the Free Radicals Project, a global prevention network for extremism— told the same interviewer that extremists can reach out to young people through their gaming headsets: "Typically they'll start out with dropping slurs about different races or religions and kind of test the waters... Once they sense that they've got their hooks in them, they ramp it up, and then they start sending propaganda, links to other sites."[22] I recall the dismay of Alex's mom when she overheard other players shouting "feminism is cancer" to her son as he played the wildly popular video game *Fortnite*.

The use of gaming as a recruitment tool is taken a step further by some who have realized the unique opportunity it affords to place young players directly into the shoes you'd like them to occupy, literally directing their viewpoint. In 2018, a PUA named Richard La Ruina created a video game called *Super Seducer*, which lets you play in character as La Ruina as he chats up women in parks, pubs, and nightclubs. (One review called it "the world's sleaziest game.") Widely available online, the game was successful enough to spawn two sequels, its budget increasing tenfold, with *Super Seducer 2: Advanced Seduction Tactics* described by massive gaming platform Steam as a "super massive hit." In a choose-your-own-adventure-style format, the games repeatedly present players with options that border on harassment or assault (do you "introduce yourself" or "look up her skirt"?). "I'm not trying to fuck you up the arse," the character yells angrily when a woman rejects him. The context quite literally allows for the classic manosphere defense: it's all just a bit of fun.

So we have a situation with all the hallmarks of grooming and online radicalization. Communities of millions of people in which young men are being deliberately earmarked for conversion to extremist, hate-fueled ideologies. In which mass murderers are lionized and others are actively encouraged to follow in their footsteps, often with detailed and specific advice about how they should go about it. Leaders of these communities actively boasting about targeting young men.

"Always include memes, funny gifs, Twitter embeds and YouTube videos in every post," says the *Daily Stormer* style guide. "This is very important." It adds, "Packing our message inside of existing cultural memes and humor can be viewed as a delivery method. Something like adding cherry flavor to children's medicine." The simile here, given the use of memes to radicalize actual children, is sickeningly accurate.

As Dr. Sugiura said,

What's very appealing about it is the vocabulary, the novelty of it, the videos, the blogs... They use things like memes and symbolism, things people can form an attachment to, an identity that is instantly recognizable, and it all goes back to being part of that community... They want as many people to come round to their way of thinking as possible, and the technology plays a significant part in how they are able to appeal to people. And, of course, when it comes to young people, this is where they're living their lives as well, so the audience is there ready for them to appeal to.

And yet in spite of all this, we don't talk about misogynist extremism. We barely talk about radicalization in terms of white supremacy and neo-Nazis, let alone misogyny. When we think of terrorist groups that radicalize young men online, we really mean

Islamic terrorism. We mean jihadism. Perhaps the clearest example of this is the UK government's controversial "Prevent" strategy, which places a duty on certain bodies, including schools, to have "due regard to the need to prevent people from being drawn into terrorism." But while the Prevent guidance claims it is "intended to deal with all kinds of terrorist threats to the UK," it is framed in such a way as to center clearly on Muslims. The extreme right also receives a number of cursory mentions, but incels and the manosphere do not appear at all. Islamist extremists are discussed in detail, and the strategy specifically cites threats from "terrorist organizations in Syria and Iraq, and Al Qa'ida-associated groups." The words *gender, boys, girls, women,* and *men* never feature, demonstrating a complete lack of gendered analysis of the problem. One example of the expectation placed on local authorities by Prevent is that they will "ensure children are safe from terrorist and extremist material when accessing the internet in school, including by establishing appropriate levels of filtering." But it is clear from the rest of the document that it wouldn't occur to anybody reading it that this should include filtering out misogynistic extremism.

The Prevent guidance describes "radicalization" as "the process by which a person comes to support terrorism and extremist ideologies associated with terrorist groups." It also refers to the current UK definition of "terrorism," which, as we have already seen, includes reference to "an action that endangers or causes serious violence to a person/people" and "must be designed to influence the government or to intimidate the public and is made for the purpose of advancing a political, religious or ideological cause." It is in no way an exaggeration to suggest that these definitions precisely describe the acts of violence and methods of radicalization deployed by extremist misogynistic groups, such as incels and other factions of the manosphere. But it is very clear that they are nowhere near the government's radar. They are virtually unheard of, while other forms of extremism are so highly monitored among young people that every teacher in the country is under orders to be on the alert for them.

Indeed, in 2016, a ten-year-old Muslim boy and his family were questioned by police after a spelling mistake in a piece of schoolwork. He wrote that he lived in a "terrorist house," instead of a "terraced house." Officials later denied the situation had been brought about by a spelling mistake and said that no further action was taken. The case recalled that of thirteen-year-old Ahmed Mohamed, an American Muslim teenager with a keen interest in engineering who was handcuffed and taken into police custody when he brought an alarm clock he had made into school to show his teachers, and they suspected that the clock resembled a bomb.

This is how hypervigilant we are about some forms of terrorism. Yet the weaponized, violent hatred of women engaged with by hundreds of thousands of men online and the process by which young men are being groomed to digest and normalize these ideas aren't even on the agenda. Adults who might be able to help and support young men with timely intervention don't even know the problem exists.

Ben Hurst of the Good Lad Initiative said, "It is almost completely under the radar. Teachers aren't aware. Staff in schools aren't aware of the kind of materials boys are accessing, or aware they're doing it."

My London teacher interviewee expressed similar fears:

I think there's a significant, dangerous lack of awareness from parents and teachers. If young people are watching videos on their phones in their bedrooms, their parents have no idea what they are engaging with. I'm concerned that our students' engagement with YouTube videos and conspiracy theories exists without any adult mediation whatsoever. The tone of the videos I've seen encourages distrust of authority figures and, as a teacher, it is particularly difficult to counteract that.

This is not a niche concern affecting a very small number of boys. There is a tendency to assume that younger generations will somehow naturally form more progressive attitudes, that prejudices we think of as old-fashioned will eventually disappear if we are just patient for long enough. The facts suggest this is not the case. Every year, the British Attitudes Survey asks the general public whether they think women are fully or partially to blame for being raped or sexually assaulted if they are drunk or have been "flirting heavily" before the attack. And every year, the results are deeply depressing. Not just because a quarter of the general public believe drunk victims are to blame or because a third believe those who were flirting bear responsibility. But because, among sixteen- to nineteen-year-olds, those numbers jump dramatically. Over a third believe a drunk victim bears blame for their own rape or assault, and for those flirting heavily, the number rises to almost half.[23] Perhaps sped by massive online exposure, such attitudes appear to be gaining traction with younger generations rather than diminishing.

The boys I meet at schools don't even know they hate women. They are mild-mannered and wide-eyed. They think it's only polite to point out the factual inaccuracies and lies repeated by feminists. They have seen misogyny online so often and heard it promoted so persuasively that they wouldn't even recognize it as a form of hate.

The total lack of awareness about this form of radicalization and the enormous impact it may be having on some young people is a missed opportunity to tackle the problem before it spirals out of control. But it is also a travesty for young men. We are letting down our boys if we don't acknowledge the deeply damaging and deliberately manipulative messaging they are being targeted with online. We fail them if we don't give them an opportunity to have open, robust discussions about these issues in a safe forum in which they feel supported and able to express their fears and anxieties. We are leaving them dangling, with no meaningful conversations or factually accurate information at all in the majority of cases, leaving them deeply vulnerable to the circling online sharks. And of course, the widespread fearmongering described in the previous chapter drives them straight into the waiting, open arms of internet extremists.

The more we underestimate the manosphere, the more we risk serving it our young men on a platter.

# 10

# Men Who Hate Men Who Hate Women

"If we don't help men and boys heal,
we don't bring them on board to be
the allies that they could be."

**GARY BARKER, FOUNDER AND CEO OF PROMUNDO**

There is a parasite called a Guinea worm that lays its larvae in water. The larvae are eaten by water fleas, and when a person drinks water that contains the fleas, they become infected with the larvae. Initially, there are no symptoms. But around a year later, a painful blister begins to form, usually on the lower leg. The blister causes a burning sensation, often leading the infected person to submerge their leg in fresh water, at which point the worm releases hundreds of thousands of larvae into the water, starting the cycle all over again. Over the course of the next few weeks, the worm begins to emerge from the blister.

Think of the manosphere like the Guinea worm. Its ideology, smuggled inside via other hosts, can infect you before you even realize it. Once inside, it spreads and grows, eventually causing great pain. In an attempt to ease that pain, hosts cause harm to others and accelerate wider infestation. And while only a small part of the problem is visible, a much greater portion lurks beneath the surface.

It isn't possible simply to pull the Guinea worm out of your leg. Though only the tip protrudes, the body of the worm might be up to a meter long, and it will not simply slide out with ease. Pulling too hard or too quickly risks breaking the worm, which can be disastrous, causing putrefaction. The only way to extract the worm is to wrap it around a small stick and to slowly turn the stick a little each day, pulling the worm out gradually over a period of weeks.

The same is true of the manosphere. It won't work to try to lop off just the visible tip. It isn't enough to try to yank it out in one go or to focus only on one part of the problem. Quick fixes won't do. The only method that will work must be slow and sustained, patient and thorough. We have to get the whole worm.

There is no single, simple solution to the complex problem outlined in the previous chapters of this book. But if we want to find ways to tackle it effectively, perhaps we should start by acknowledging where action is not being taken. Where the gaps are.

While we're finally beginning to wake up to the reality of white supremacy, white nationalism, and the alt-right as forms of online extremism, we're still lagging behind when it comes to recognizing the extremist strains of virulent misogyny. A 2017 *New York Times* article, "A Hunt for Ways to Combat Online Radicalization," examined the long-overlooked parallels between the use of the internet to radicalize young Muslim men and the ways it is leveraged as a grooming tool by white supremacists. The whole article explicitly focused on the ways some forms of extremism and online grooming had been disproportionately represented in the public discourse while others had been overlooked. Yet even within this context, the article repeatedly framed the issue as a dual narrative between Islamists and white nationalists—a perspective reiterated across the agendas of counterextremism think tanks and government task forces alike. Indeed, the article explicitly emphasizes this sense of duality:

> Several research groups in the United States and Europe now see the white supremacist and jihadi threats as two faces of the same coin. They're working on methods to fight both, together—and slowly, they have come up with ideas for limiting how these groups recruit new members to their cause.[1]

Nowhere is the virulent and deliberate dissemination of online hate against women and the widespread incitement to rape and harm them mentioned at all.

Unfortunately, evidence suggests that perhaps the weakest area of response to online misogyny and extremism, including the deliberate grooming of boys and men, comes from the very top. Looking at the major organizations and government groups tasked with tackling extremism, terrorism, and radicalization, it becomes clear that the threat posed by misogynistic communities is simply not taken seriously.

Published in October 2015, the UK government's "Counter-Extremism Strategy" is approximately 15,000 words long. Words and phrases with the root *Islam* (including, for example, *Islam extremism* or *Islamist extremism*) appear fifty-two times, and the word *Muslim* thirty-three times. The words *neo-Nazi* or *neo-Nazism* appear fourteen times. *White supremacy, white nationalism,* and *anti-Semitism* are all referenced. The phrase *extreme right-wing* appears ten times. The words *misogyny* or *misogynistic, incel,* and *masculinity* never appear in the document. In fact, it makes no mention at all of violent extremism that specifically and deliberately targets women.

A brief perusal of the document's introduction sets out fairly clearly what the government sees as the components of extremism: it discusses race and faith, refers directly to ISIL (another term for ISIS), describes the "fight against Islamist extremism" as "one of the great struggles of our generation," and references anti-Semitism and neo-Nazi extremism. It refers to faith communities and British Muslims and implies that these are the major loci for the stated aim of disrupting extremism and building "more cohesive communities." It makes absolutely no reference whatsoever to gender. This isn't only relevant to the gaping hole in which extremist misogyny should be. It also reveals a complete blind spot in recognizing the fact that those behind other forms of terrorism are overwhelmingly male. It totally misses the gendered angle of the issue—and, therefore, one of the important strands for tackling the problem.

The document "Tackling Extremism in the UK," a 2013 report from the prime minister's task force on addressing radicalization and extremism, presents a similar picture, again foregrounding Islamist extremism as the primary terrorist threat to the UK before mentioning "extremism of all kinds" and specifically referencing Islamophobia and neo-Nazism. It is completely devoid of any mention of male supremacy or misogynistic extremism.

The picture is similar in the United States. For example, a 2017 report on countering violent extremism from the U.S. Government Accountability Office begins by stating, "Violent extremism— generally defined as ideologically, religious, or politically-motivated acts of violence—has been perpetrated in the United States by white supremacists, anti-government groups, and radical Islamist entities, among others."[2] A further breakdown of those "others" includes "groups with extreme views on abortion, animal rights, the environment, and federal ownership of public lands." It is quite extraordinary, given the fact that the report spans the dates 2001–16 (a period including the massacres carried out by George Sodini, Elliot Rodger, and Chris Harper-Mercer, explicitly in the name of male supremacist and incel ideologies), that any misogynistic form of violent extremism does not even merit a mention. Meanwhile, environmental and animal rights extremism are included, even though the document states, "During this period, no persons in the United States were killed in attacks carried out by persons believed to be motivated by extremist environmental beliefs, [or] extremist 'animal liberation' beliefs."

The document includes a table showing "Violent Extremist Attacks in the United States That Resulted in Fatalities, September 12, 2001, to December 31, 2016," separated into two categories: far-right and radical Islamist. I wonder whether the male supremacist killings carried out during this period might be included under the category of the far right, given the broad overlap between the two ideologies. But neither Sodini nor Rodger's massacres appear in the table, and there is no mention of Harper-Mercer. A detailed breakdown of the characteristics of far-right violent extremist attackers is included, but while it includes factors such as nationalism, belief in conspiracy theories, white supremacy, and a belief that one's way of life is under attack, there is no reference to misogyny at all.

The report states that its list of violent extremist attacks is based on data from the U.S. Extremist Crime Database (ECDB). I investigated further. The criteria for inclusion in the ECDB require that an incident satisfies a two-pronged test: "First, an illegal violent incident or an illegal financial scheme must be committed inside the

United States. Second, at least one of the suspects who perpetrated the illegal act must subscribe to an extremist belief system."[3]

It seems confusing then that the three attacks carried out by Sodini, Rodger, and Harper-Mercer are not included, given the fact that this simple test would most certainly make them eligible. But then I reached the small print. Without reasoning or explanation, it simply reads, "The ECDB only includes violent and financial crimes committed by one or more suspects who adhered to a far-right, Al Qaeda-inspired, or extremist animal/environmental rights belief system."

So there it is, in black and white. The extremist ideology referenced by Sodini, Rodger, and Harper-Mercer does not qualify them to be included in the national government database of extremist crimes. In spite of the fact that these three men alone, explicitly acting in the name of violent misogynistic extremism, killed eighteen people and injured thirty-one more. Meanwhile, animal rights and environmental extremist ideologies are considered serious enough to be included, despite no killings in the name of these belief systems being carried out during the same period.

The knock-on impact of this is clear when data from this body is included in a report from the Government Accountability Office examining the government's response to violent extremism. It means that when the U.S. response to these forms of extremism is evaluated and recommendations are made for improvement, male supremacy and incel killers are not even on the agenda. How can we improve our response, or even begin to formulate a response to a major threat, if we don't even know it exists in the first place?

Violent extremist hatred of women, supported by an organized mass movement and online communities of thousands of adherents, leading to dozens of real-life victims and fatalities, simply doesn't count. Yet by almost every definition of terrorism and extremism, those who have committed atrocities in the name of manosphere ideology fall squarely into both categories.

The accuracy of the definition is also warranted by the fact that the extremist misogynistic communities described in this book have not just coincidentally spawned individual attackers: they repeatedly and deliberately goad other recruits toward carrying out similar acts of violence. This is not just a community whose numbers happen to include some mass attackers; it is a community that has actively driven and motivated those men to carry out their acts of murder. In the police interview immediately following his arrest, Toronto van murderer Alek Minassian used the word *radicalized* to describe his own experience in incel forums, described Rodger as a "founding forefather," and told officers he had been in direct contact with both Rodger and Harper-Mercer. Just as they had motivated him, he said, "I was thinking that I would inspire future masses to join me in my uprising as well."[4] On 4chan, Minassian posted before his massacre, "There will be a beta uprising tomorrow, I encourage others to follow suit." Minassian told police "quite a few" people congratulated him: "I suspect they probably knew what I meant by what I said." The release of the video and other documents relating to Minassian's case also revealed that another man had been arrested in Ontario, Canada, for threatening to cause death to others. It was thought that he may have been inspired by Minassian's attack.[5]

And still, in spite of all this, in each interview I carried out for this book and in all the background discussions I had with people involved in counterterrorism at the highest levels of national governments, violent misogynistic extremism simply doesn't seem to be on the radar. When I spoke off the record to one major UK government agency involved in counterextremism, there was the usual immediate mention of Islamist and far-right extremism, and the spokesperson also referenced animal rights extremist groups. When I asked about incels, there was a long pause on the other end of the phone before I was asked to repeat myself. I got the strong impression that the spokesperson had simply never heard of them. I was told they'd look into it and call me back. Several weeks later, a brief phone call confirmed that they had no data or evidence in this area as yet.

It goes without saying that investigating Islamist and white supremacist extremism, anti-Semitism, neo-Nazism, Islamophobia, and all forms of terrorism is of huge importance. I don't highlight these discrepancies to suggest that other forms of extremism shouldn't be urgently tackled. But it is striking that when it comes to the bodies specifically set up to protect us from extremist, terrorist threats, the notions of gendered hatred, overwhelmingly male attackers, and misogyny as a form of violent extremism are entirely missing from the conversation.

The experts I spoke to all agree that this is the case. Dr. Lisa Sugiura said,

> People are starting to talk about it, but it's not spoken about in the same sort of discourses as terrorism, unfortunately... I don't feel [the threats are] being taken as seriously as they should be yet, and certainly not in the same kind of consideration as, for example, Islamic extremism.

The same is true when it comes to any kind of effort to monitor or prevent the grooming and radicalization of young people online by manosphere communities, as the omissions in the government's own Prevent strategy reveal. When I spoke to Dr. Carlene Firmin, she noted, "It's not really discussed. I observe a lot of multiagency meetings, and I don't think I've ever heard this come up at a multiagency meeting that I've observed before. But there would be discussion about other forms of online grooming."

On a gray, spring afternoon, I visited the secret location of the Institute for Strategic Dialogue, a London-based "think and do tank" that pioneers policy and operational responses to violent extremism. The organization combines research and analysis with government advisory work and delivery programs and, as such, is at the forefront of our response to extremism and terrorism. In a glass-walled conference room, looking out onto a bustling open-plan office, I met with Jacob Davey, an associate in technology, communications, and education at the Institute for Strategic Dialogue and a communications coordinator.

Davey immediately confirmed that the antiextremist field is missing a focus on the issue of misogynistic extremism: "In terms of radicalization, extremism, and the role of toxic masculinity, that's something that I think there's not enough coverage on, as a sector."

Within the Institute for Strategic Dialogue itself, Davey does the most work on the manosphere and misogynistic extremism, with some of his colleagues carrying out separate work on "the role of women in extremist movements." But while he is extremely well informed, he was quick to admit that his expertise on specifically male supremacist communities is something "I sort of touch upon...tangentially" when it intersects with his "primary focus," which is the "extreme right wing." When I asked if there was any staff member at the Institute for Strategic Dialogue tasked solely with focusing on misogynistic extremism, he told me there wasn't, though the organization's website lists fifty-six members of staff. "I take the bulk of the men-specific research and the men's movement research, but there's no one who has that specific portfolio within the organization."

The Institute for Strategic Dialogue is far from unusual in this—indeed, the fact that Davey himself has built a consideration of the intersections with the manosphere into his work on far-right movements in many ways sets it ahead of other similar organizations. Davey believes it is an area in which the field is now playing catch-up. He said he was "seeing the transition—there has been a gap—behind the scenes, there's an increased awareness of this as its own unique thing...a burgeoning recognition." He pointed to the fact that the Southern Poverty Law Center only started to record male supremacist groups in its listing of operational hate groups in 2018. At the time, the Southern Poverty Law Center noted, "The vilification of women by these groups makes them no different than other groups that demean entire populations, such as the LGBTQ community, Muslims or Jews, based on their inherent characteristics."[6] But looking at most international organizations or task forces claiming to tackle "all forms" of extremism or terrorism, it is clear that this transition, if it is occurring, is still in its very early stages.

There are several reasons this may be the case. One is that there have been comparatively fewer acts of mass offline violence carried out in the name of this particular form of extremism. But this is not a good enough reason to omit male supremacy from the spectrum of extremist ideologies investigated, tracked, and tackled by antiextremist organizations. Especially when animal rights and environmental extremism are often included and have a far lower recent death toll. The number of murders and injuries racked up by the international incel community is by no means insignificant, particularly in light of the fact that as a coherent, online movement, it is a relatively recent phenomenon, and there is evidence to suggest it is quickly growing, attracting large numbers of new recruits and actively inciting an increasing number of violent hate crimes. Nor can it be separated in any meaningful way from the terrorist violence carried out in the name of far-right ideologies, including white supremacy and neo-Nazism, which we have seen to be suffused with and even, to a large degree, predicated on misogynistic extremism. Yet it fails to be mentioned or considered, even when those groups, rightly and relatively newly, are included in analyses of and policy responses to extremist and terrorist threats.

Furthermore, acts of mass violence are not the only ways in which extremist threats and ideologies manifest themselves, and there is a very serious risk that the enormous spread of misogynistic extremism and male supremacy online, if allowed to continue unchecked, could have a more subtle offline impact in the forms of violence against women, such as relationship abuse and rape, which already go largely unnoticed and unremarked upon within our society.

This in itself may be another major driver of our blind spot when it comes to male supremacy; in a society in which misogyny and violence against women are so widespread and so normalized, it is difficult for us to consider these things "extreme" or "radical," because they are simply not out of the ordinary. We do not leap to tackle a terrorist threat to women, because the reality of women being terrorized, violated, and murdered by men is already part of the wallpaper.

So the first major shift we need to see is for male supremacy and misogynist extremism to be included whenever organizations or governments are monitoring, legislating for, and tackling other forms of terrorism. (Domestic terrorism laws, for example, should be introduced or amended to ensure that these crimes can be treated with the same severity as other acts of violence driven by extremist hatred.) It is shocking that terrorist charges have only once been brought in an incel-related killing, by the Canadian authorities, and other countries must follow suit where these attacks fall clearly under the definition of terrorism. The second important shift we need to see is for that horrifyingly normal, everyday form of terrorism—domestic abuse—to be taken just as seriously too.

We can no longer allow ourselves to be deterred from confronting the existence of extremist misogyny just because of a squeamish distaste for identifying a problem that originates with the most powerful societal group: heterosexual, white men. Our tendency to provide members of this group with the benefit of the doubt, to afford them individuality and status far beyond that of women and minorities, has shielded extremists for too long from examination under a critical lens.

We are too afraid of being labeled "misandrists" or "man-haters," of encountering the traditional cry of "not all men." Yet this is laughably oversimplistic. Of course, it is possible to confront the reality of this threat and the existence of this movement without suggesting that it somehow implicates all men. Indeed, as we have already seen, one of the biggest threats it poses is to men themselves.

One of the most powerful antidotes to the manosphere is to take real, concerted action against the threats it poses to men. To challenge the stringent, hypermasculine stereotypes it blindly clings to, even as they stunt and suffocate its most devoted followers. To offer solutions to and practical support for the problems MRAs love to exploit as justification for their hatred but don't actually try to address. To confront the gender stereotypes that lead to assumptions about who should take on the majority of childcare.

To demand greater flexibility for working parents. To campaign for better shared parental leave rights. To tackle the stigma faced by male survivors of sexual violence and domestic abuse and ensure specialist support services are available to them without needing to attack female survivors or undermine their services in the process. To fund and highlight mental health services and find ways to make them more accessible to men, particularly young men. (A recent BBC Freedom of Information request revealed that just 31 percent of those accessing university counseling services were men.)[7]

There are innovative and effective ways to achieve this. But they require a united effort and funding. CALM (the UK-based Campaign Against Living Miserably), for example, has created a powerful movement against suicide, particularly focused on supporting men and boys. It offers frontline services, such as a confidential helpline and web chat, but it also encourages community engagement by facilitating supportive spaces in workplaces, universities, pubs, clubs, and prisons. It runs campaigns with popular figures, like celebrity comedians, to tackle male stereotypes and encourage "help-seeking behavior, using cultural touch points like art, music, sport and comedy." In other words, it adopts exactly the tactics of the manosphere, infiltrating cultural spaces and communities, but with a positive and constructive aim.

Many of those already most effectively leading this resistance are men themselves. Men who hate men who hate women.

The men's liberation movement of the 1970s began a powerful and positive tradition of men tackling misogyny, which continues to this day. Men who recognize the extreme harms posed to their gender by rigid stereotypes and patriarchal structures have not stopped battling to try to stem the tide of sexism, and they do so, crucially, within a feminist framework.

This work takes place across a spectrum so broad that it encompasses international charities carrying out male-focused interventions, small organizations delivering workshops to boys in schools, and individuals using their own platforms to stand up and speak out against misogyny and gender inequality in all its forms. Two of the biggest and most widely respected such organizations are Promundo, a leading global NGO founded in Brazil in 1997, which promotes gender justice and prevents violence by engaging men and boys, and the White Ribbon Campaign, the largest network of men working to end violence against women worldwide.

I spoke to Gary Barker, founder and CEO of Promundo, to see what lessons he could offer about how to tackle the threat of misogynistic extremism. He stressed the importance of interventions that don't rely on a self-selecting audience. "Put up a poster, a flyer, an e-blast that says, 'Come talk about how we as men overcome misogyny.' You get two and a half guys!" Instead, he said, we have to take "what we do to where young men and adult men are":

Make it part of the school session, make it part of the sports group they're in, make it part of the occupational safety course that their employer gives them. Guys aren't just going to walk in the door going "Hey, let me talk about misogyny and gender equality!" The guys who need it the most are not going to walk in the room, we've got to take the room to them.

Ultimately, in its most easily achievable and scalable form, that means incorporating these issues into mainstream education. Education has a vital role to play in tackling misogynistic extremism, preferably not as a responsive measure but as a preventative one: inoculating boys against the persuasive impact of online grooming and arming them with credible tools to confront the ideology of the manosphere *before* they encounter it, rather than trying to disentangle them from a web that already has them bound in its sticky threads. This is particularly important in light of the extent to which the far right, from manosphere groups to white supremacists, rely on misinformation and sowing distrust of reputable information sources, which makes it very difficult to extract recruits using logical argument once they have already become enmeshed.

The London teacher I interviewed, who shared her concerns about her students being radicalized by manosphere content, said,

> I've tried to counteract the 'it's just banter' argument by showing students the Pyramid of Sexual Violence (starting with sexist jokes and ending with violence), but I'm aware that, as a female teacher, it can be difficult to be taken seriously by students who are already engaging with men's rights arguments. I feel nervous that when I try to crack down on students' misogynistic views, I could end up reinforcing them.

As somebody on the frontline of trying to tackle the problem, she believes "there needs to be more teacher training about how to engage with students on these issues."

Education then—nationally mandated, properly funded, and supported with effective training—is another important part of the solution. This doesn't only mean directly educating young people about extreme misogyny. It also means providing them with basic tools and knowledge about issues like gender stereotypes and healthy relationships, sexual consent and respect—foundational ideas that will help to fortify young people against some of the toxic misconceptions they may encounter online later on.

Ben Hurst of the Good Lad Initiative emphasized that teaching young people to analyze and evaluate news sources must be high on the list of effective interventions. "The thing that makes it really dangerous is that, in school especially, kids are not taught to be critical of source materials—they're used to being in science, learning from a science textbook and not questioning what they're learning." He pointed out the irony that after exposure to the manosphere, many of the young men he works with become extremely resistant to accepting facts from robust sources, because they have been primed to consider them "fake news," even though the information that is actually skewed or outright fabricated comes from the manosphere itself.

Hurst's many years' practice facilitating these conversations directly with young men have given him a rich wealth of experience to draw on when making recommendations about how such education should most effectively be delivered. He reflected that the topic of masculinity is currently very underdiscussed in interventions, particularly at the school level, and that people find it "really hard to know how to navigate [those] conversations." He said,

> Parents don't know how to talk to kids, teachers don't know how to talk to kids, no one knows how to talk to kids, but also people don't know how to talk to each other about the male experience. It's hard to problematize it without it feeling like an attack, which means that people shut down really quickly.

So educating parents and teachers about the reality of what young people are confronted with online is a vital first step. A

2014 study found that the five most influential figures among Americans aged thirteen to eighteen are all YouTube stars.[8] Figures like PewDiePie and Logan Paul are major celebrities in the adolescent world, with hundreds of millions of followers. They shape and influence young people's lives, yet they are so completely unknown to adults that parents may not even recognize their names. That represents a massive disconnect between the world young people are living in and their parents' perceptions. So parents need to get online, explore some of the content young people are exposed to, and give themselves a foundation from which to start talking to their children.

Where to begin? YouTube, of course. Take a look at some of the content teenagers are stumbling across, like the endless "angry feminazi destroyed by…" compilations. Browse some of the manosphere videos like pickup tips and MGTOW rants. Let the algorithm pull you into the rabbit hole of increasingly misogynistic "facts." Spend half an hour immersing yourself in the comments; I promise they will be illuminating. Visit some bodybuilding forums or take a look at some of the more mainstream "red pill" content on Reddit. Sign up to some of the biggest meme accounts on Instagram and see what floods into your timeline. All this will give you a basic foundation in the sort of background noise teenagers are hearing every single day.

Look out for manosphere language cropping up in young people's conversations: any mention of being "blue pilled" or "cucked" is a telltale sign of derision toward those uninitiated into the manosphere. Words like *triggered* or *butthurt* suggest they've already been taught to mock anyone who objects to bigotry. *Feminazi, snowflake,* or *SJW* are terms to look out for too.

When a red flag crops up, challenge it. Challenge it again and again. The manosphere is an echo chamber. The very reason it is so persuasive is that the nature of its closed communities and algorithmically supported video loops totally indoctrinates. No opposing views are shared. So share them. Expose young people to other ideas, other options. Challenge and question manosphere assumptions. Explore the limits of the false facts and shoddy science young people might have been provided as "proof." Giving young people as much reliable information as possible and allowing them to draw their own conclusions is the best way to tackle this problem without alienating or patronizing them.

Instead of simply telling young people the information they have accessed online is bogus, Hurst said, it can be more productive to accept it as a starting point and then help them to engage in a process of examination that enables them to realize the limitations of such ideologies for themselves.

"My objective when I'm in a room is not to tell them the person they're listening to is chatting shit, but more to say, 'Okay, let's explore that together—where does it come from? What are the consequences of following that worldview or opinion to the logical conclusion?'" This, he suggested, is more likely to yield positive results, because it doesn't play into the hands of the manosphere ideologues who have already framed themselves as tragic Cassandra figures, daring the world to dismiss them as false prophets.

YouTube star Natalie Parrott, aka "Contra," who runs the hugely successful ContraPoints channel, is a brilliant example of how to approach these conversations. She meets the alt-right on their own turf, taking their bizarre, funny, stunt-driven tactics and replicating them in her own videos. ContraPoints disseminates robust but entertaining videos, countering everything from the manosphere idea of the "alpha male" to the portrayal of feminists as "social justice warriors." And it's working: while individual educators might be able to visit several schools a week, speaking to a few hundred students each time, Parrott is reaching over half a million subscribers with every video, many of them racking up millions of views. Her approach is a vital example of the need to update our tactics and the vehicles we use for messaging, which have, in many cases, become outdated and preachy, in contrast to the tech-savvy communication perfected by online extremists.

If we're going to try to protect boys (and, by extension, potential future victims) from the manosphere quagmire, we've got to understand what pulls them in in the first place. We have to recognize that our current societal version of masculinity is failing them. It leaves them isolated, forced to adopt a swaggering bravado that prevents them from talking about how they feel or forming mutually supportive relationships.

I am not particularly interested in a "redemption" narrative for incels. That is a question for those individuals to ponder. We do not implore the victims of other forms of terrorism to absolve and educate their tormentors. Nor do we require that other extremists be acknowledged as some kind of wounded, misunderstood victims. It is ironic that so much pressure is brought to bear on women to allow for the humanity and individuality of fallible men when it is precisely this courtesy that incels unfailingly refuse to pay to women.

But I am interested in the men in between. The boys who fall through the cracks. The "good" men who feel scared. The ones who went looking for help, because they felt frightened or sad or lonely, and haven't been able to disentangle themselves. The ones who just haven't heard about any of this yet. The ones who look the other way on the bus. Because we can't change anything without those men. So how do we reach them?

Hurst said, "My understanding of it is that, for most guys who engage in those movements, it comes from a place of pain and a place of hurt and a place of not being able to understand why they are not who they think they should be." He described the discovery of manosphere movements as a great release or soothing salve for such men. It "gives them a really easy out, because they can just blame a system or they can blame women and say, 'It's this person's fault, because they won't give me what I deserve.'"

"The demands and strictures of manhood are difficult for any man to live up to," added Michael Kaufman, cofounder of the White Ribbon Campaign. "Always be in control, never back down, be fearless, take the pain."

Barker agreed, pointing to the high percentage of boys who experience physical violence:

There is trauma, there is fear of other men, there is violence, there is undiagnosed depression—the list goes on in terms of what it means to be a victim of some kind of violence during childhood. If we don't make space for that, we don't help men and boys heal, we don't bring them on board to be the allies that they could be.

When boys bring up manosphere obsessions like false rape allegations, Hurst said,

[They] aren't talking about that stuff just to be difficult. They're talking about it because they're scared, and a big part of masculinity is not showing fear. So they're not going to say, "I'm really scared that if I try to have sex with someone, they'll say I raped them." They're more likely to say,

"Women lie about false rape." But essentially it's the same conversation.

Emotions are equated with shame, and boys are encouraged to hide them. Isolation breeds longing for community. Shame breeds desperation for prestige, for respect, for a sense of purpose. A sense of vulnerability, arising, in part, from the fact that boys are most at risk of being victims of violent crime, leads naturally to a desire for the security of a group allegiance. All these cravings are gleefully satisfied by manosphere communities, keen to seize upon disenfranchised, angry young men and fill their gaping holes with false promises, skewed logic, and hate.

So how do we prevent young men from becoming isolated in the first place? The answer is both social and political. We are reaping the fruit sown by local government cuts and community center closures: the gradual, systematic disappearance of real-life places for boys to hang out and socialize. So they turn to online hangouts instead. We need to provide meaningful, fulfilling offline spaces they can make their own.

But we also need to address the social divisions that are driven by stigma, prejudice, and absurd stereotypes. The low-level racism that allows white boys to grow up already thinking boys who don't look like them are different, threatening, invaders. The sexism that shames and sexualizes mixed-sex childhood friendships and leads to near-total gender segregation by the early teens. As simple as it sounds, if young men knew other people from different communities, if they had meaningful friendships with girls their own age, they wouldn't be so easy to trick into believing monstrous distortions about what those "other" groups represent. They would push back, because they would know better. I'm reminded of David

Sherratt, whose journey out of the manosphere was so simply facilitated by meeting a girl who talked to him.

Part of the problem with trying to protect young people from exploitation and grooming by extremist elements of the manosphere is that our understanding of exploitation and how to tackle it is still hopelessly out of touch. Dr. Firmin explained that the very hallmarks of adolescence that most attract young men to these online communities are also the ones least understood by traditional support mechanisms. During adolescence, young people prioritize belonging, self-autonomy, and independence. This, she said, is a period in which young people are struggling with intense emotions: they are "more inclined to take risks" and are particularly unlikely to think about "long-term consequences." As such, traditional support services are not well suited to this period, because they tend to be "targeted at individuals who don't like to take risks and will think about the long-term consequences of their behavior and will be generally emotionally stable."

While support structures struggle against these typical adolescent behaviors, Dr. Firmin explained, those who exploit young people "will tend to work *with*" them, offering children

> a sense of risk or going against the grain, focus on short-term gains, what it means in the here and now, and push aside the potential negative long-term consequences... They will provide means by which you can be very emotionally driven and passionate...and also validate those emotions as authentic when other adults are saying, "Don't get so worked up."

All this resonates powerfully with the tactics of the manosphere.

Young people are offered a highly emotive narrative and a sense of deep belonging and community. They are repeatedly encouraged, in incel forums, for example, to take violent action that would position them as countercultural disrupters without thinking too much about the consequences. "It's very easy to sell those ideas," Dr. Firmin added, in a community that boasts about "going against the norm." In the case of the manosphere, she said, that manifests as "pushing against this idea of new masculinity...or men's increased role in parenting... This narrative would push against all of that, push against #MeToo, so it's very easy then to sell it as a risk and sell it into this idea of wanting a sense of self, a sense of personal identity." In some respects, she said, given the current climate, the attractiveness of the manosphere to young men is "not very surprising at all."

In response to the ineffectiveness of traditional models of intervention when it comes to adolescents, Dr. Firmin has pioneered a model known as "contextual safeguarding." The theory emphasizes the importance of taking interventions and support to the environments in which young people spend their time, rather than assuming that harm only comes to young people within their own homes. "Individuals embody the rules of certain environments when they have spent time in them and engage with the rules at play in any given environment in order to navigate them and achieve status," her website explains. The framework has so far been applied to locations like shopping districts and public parks, pioneering the notion of cooperation with people who might not normally be involved in safeguarding work, from shopkeepers to park authorities. But it strikes me that it might also have a radically transformative impact online. After all, the online world, from the casual sexism of social media to the persuasive misogyny of manosphere forums, is the perfect example of an arena within which we haven't traditionally considered young people to be at risk of harm and against which effective intervention could be enormously valuable.

Dr. Firmin agrees that there may be positive applications of contextual safeguarding in the online world but stresses that far more research and strategizing would be necessary before it could be widely delivered in practice. She noted the importance of consent in a safeguarding relationship. ("The difference between a high street and an online place is that on a high street, young people know the youth worker is there.") Some of the most effective interventions Dr. Firmin has seen, she said, have involved detached youth workers: those who interact with young people in their own environment, rather than in an official session or office space. This involves the gradual build-up of a trusting relationship and, Dr. Firmin said, provides meaningful opportunities for disruption of misogynistic assumptions and extremist messaging. Though the practice is currently in its infancy, Dr. Firmin has heard about the use of detached youth workers online in some Scandinavian countries, and she described youth centers that have begun trying to create internet spaces for young people to interact, with the aim of establishing similar opportunities to disrupt internet misogyny. There are practical barriers, yes. But they are not insurmountable.

Based on my own experiences of speaking to young people about these issues, Dr. Firmin's words immediately resonated. The conversations I've had with young people in smaller groups, on their own turf, are almost universally more productive and revealing than those in settings like a whole-school assembly or a teacher-observed discussion session. Talking to Dr. Firmin about detached youth work, I was galvanized by the exciting prospect that here, at last, is a potential solution to the insidious infiltration of extremist misogyny into adolescent communities.

But perhaps to a greater extent even than other public services, funding for detached youth work has been decimated over the past decade. Between 2012 and 2016, more than 600 youth centers across the UK were closed, and council funding for youth services plummeted by 62 percent between 2009 and 2017. Experts like Leigh Middleton, chief executive officer of the National Youth Agency, suggest that the cuts are particularly likely to affect "lonely, isolated young people"—his description exactly matching those most inclined to be vulnerable to the pull of manosphere communities. Devastatingly, detached youth work (a long-term project involving one-to-one support) is exactly the kind of service that tends to be first in line to be cut. And as Dr. Firmin succinctly explained, "when you cut away opportunities for people to disrupt that narrative, it gives space for it to breed."

Yet these are precisely the services we need to invest in if we want to tackle the impact of the manosphere proactively and preventively. If my hundreds of school visits have taught me one strikingly clear lesson, it's that early intervention is far simpler and more effective than trying to change the minds of those already radicalized later on.

For those already in the grip of the manosphere, however, we also need a responsive solution. So we must be able to rely on law enforcement to tackle existing crimes rooted in extremist misogyny. To police what is already illegal sounds like a simple demand, yet the vast swathes of illegal activity currently undertaken by manosphere trolls with absolute impunity suggests otherwise. The disconnect between traditional policing and online crime is a massive barrier. In the UK, it is illegal to threaten to rape or kill someone online, just as it would be in real life. Yet hundreds, even thousands, of men get away with such acts every day online, with no punishment whatsoever.

We know that institutionalized prejudice is a problem within the police force. We know that women and certain groups—in particular, women of color and LGBTQ people—have not always had positive responses when reporting to the police. System-wide antibias training would help to tackle issues around victim blaming and the fact that these crimes are often not taken seriously. But this is not just an issue of individual failings. Indeed, many individual officers and forces are championing and supporting victims, but a widespread lack of funding and training hampers progress. Outside of specialist internet crime units, there is often little understanding or specialist knowledge to support officers in tackling these crimes, which, in my own experience, has repeatedly led to cases simply reaching dead ends and being closed.

When I first reported a spate of death and rape threats to the police, the local officers sent to take my statement arrived fresh from a dangerous-dog incident, pencils and notebooks in hand, and kept interrupting me to ask politely what a Twitter handle was. After they were unable to trace any of the hundreds of IP addresses I had provided or take any action against the online incitement of a mob to bombard me with targeted harassment (because the forum on which the attack was coordinated was registered overseas), the case was closed with no action taken.

The first time I arrived at a police station with a thick sheaf of printed-out death threats clutched in my fist, which I showed to the officer at the desk, I was met with a surprised look and asked, "Do you think they *will* track you down?"

A lack of understanding of the severity and real-life impact of online misogynistic extremism may be having a dire impact in other areas of policing as well. As I write, UK police have just announced plans to ask victims reporting rapes to hand over their cell phones to police or risk prosecutions not going ahead. A policy that makes victims feel like they are on trial, that risks reinforcing the notion of women lying about rape. Even though we know that in reality, in a seventeen-month period in which there were 5,651 prosecutions for rape in the UK, there were just 35 for making false allegations of rape.[9]

But how could the police possibly know, with their apparently limited awareness of misogynistic online crime, that in the manosphere forums I've spent the past year wading through, there are thousands of threads connected to conspiracy theories about widespread false rape claims, urging men to manipulate women the morning after a sexual assault? These messages specifically instruct men to send text messages the following day, designed to solicit responses that would weaken a woman's case if she tried to make an allegation of rape. Pressuring her to reply about the previous night, breezily referencing the great time had by all, doing everything that might coerce a traumatized victim into a placatory or ambivalent response. Of course, the police would know this if there were any police effort focused on looking into these online communities. But in all my research, I have come across none.

Then there are the ways in which online abuse, underestimated and repeatedly belittled, bleeds into offline abuse. It is a reality consistently ignored in the response from authorities. The lackluster reaction to online threats against female politicians. The dismissal of cyberstalking as a tool used by bullying ex-partners, until the escalation from online to offline violence proves fatal and intervention is too late. As case after case reveals that the police have missed opportunities to intervene before women are murdered by their stalkers, frequently failing to join the dots between multiple incidents and forms of harassment, these are very real concerns.

Davey believes that the adoption of misogyny as a hate crime category would help to shift the dial on the public and institutional perception of male supremacy and extremism, stressing the importance of acknowledging that gendered hatred can be as forceful a driver of criminal acts as other already existing strands, such as race and religion. Davey submitted his recommendation to the Home Affairs Select Committee on hate crime, and feminist activists have campaigned fiercely for the category to be introduced, but there has been a powerful and predictable backlash to the suggestion, from police sources and media alike, with tabloid headlines suggesting that the police would be inundated with reports of wolf whistling and senior police figures suggesting the issue would be a trivial distraction from the important "bread-and-butter" work of mainstream policing.

The next source we must look to if we are to meaningfully tackle these issues is social media platforms themselves. This book has explored the many ways in which these companies and their algorithms proffer space and persuasive recruitment tools for far-right extremists, enabling them to reach millions of men and groom and radicalize vulnerable young people, rewarding and actively promoting their content to exploit its financial value, providing revenue streams and propaganda platforms, facilitating mass attacks and cyberstalking, failing to protect victims, and avoiding accountability whenever possible.

For a while, these companies were able to feign credible ignorance. That is no longer the case. Yes, it is possible that the ways in which their technology aids and abets online extremists was originally unintentional. But that is no excuse at all for failing to take action to fix it once the problem has been made clear. Yet again and again, profit is prioritized over responsibility. In 2019, journalists alerted YouTube to a deeply disturbing trend: its algorithm was grouping together videos it automatically identified as footage of partially clothed, prepubescent children and recommending them to viewers who had watched similar content. Without intending to, the platform was serving long, unbroken chains of fodder to pedophiles, hundreds of whom would comment on the videos, recommending specific time stamps to other users, letting them know exactly when a crotch or nipple was accidentally revealed by an innocent child playing in their bathing suit. The algorithm was so accurate that it repeatedly swept up completely innocuous home movies in the trend. Families were suddenly alerted when the clips of their young daughters playing in the wading pool racked up hundreds of thousands of views in a matter of days.

Just like the facilitation of manosphere radicalization on the platform, the problem may have been completely unintentional, but the outcome was horrifying. What matters is that once YouTube was alerted to the issue, it was given a clear solution. Researchers suggested that the platform simply turn off its recommendation system on videos of children. It was a change that could have been implemented automatically and with ease. And it would have stopped the exploitation in its tracks. But YouTube declined to put it into practice. Why? Because recommendations are its biggest traffic driver, it told the *New York Times*, so turning them off "would hurt 'creators' who rely on those clicks." In other words, it would have hit YouTube's bottom line.[10]

If you think social media platforms are already doing all they can to avoid the victimization and exploitation of their most vulnerable users, you need to think again. We know that YouTube has a breathtakingly influential impact on young people. We know it unilaterally controls the content served to millions of people around the world every hour. It is not an exaggeration to describe it, as Zeynep Tufekci has, as "one of the most powerful radicalizing instruments of the 21st century."[11] So changes to its algorithm to prevent viewers from being deliberately nudged down the rabbit hole of extremism could be transformative.

Evidence suggests that social media platforms, like the media and government, approach different forms of extremism and radicalization in dramatically different ways. A 2016 study, comparing white nationalist versus ISIS-related social media networks, revealed that during the data collection period on Twitter, three white nationalist accounts and four Nazi accounts were suspended, compared with around 1,100 ISIS accounts.[12] This despite the fact that the same study revealed American white nationalist movements "outperform ISIS in nearly every social metric, from follower counts to tweets per day."

Recommendations for improvement in this area are not lacking. But the will to implement them is. The Data & Society report suggested, for example, that YouTube should take into account the influencers hosted by the platform, rather than just the channel's own content, when making moderation decisions.

Yes, freedom of speech is vital and valuable. But it is not infinite and unbounded. There are myriad examples where the use of these platforms by male supremacist movements already well exceeds the bounds of free speech in its active incitement to violence, its targeted, vitriolic harassment and doxxing, and its deliberate nurturing of division and hatred. When this bar is reached, social media platforms must be held accountable for the content they host and forced to concern themselves with the safety of their users. When the threshold is not reached, we need to see a mass mobilization of bystander action online, in the same way we frequently advocate in "real-life" spaces, to take collective responsibility for the atmosphere of our online world and the tenor of its debate, to support those with less of a platform, to denormalize the culture of online harassment and encourage the online equivalent of stepping in instead of crossing to the other side of the street. Here again is an opportunity for the men who declare themselves keen allies to step in and play a significant role.

Clearly, this is complex. In order to prosecute the perpetrators of online abuse, it is necessary to compel social media sites and other platforms to reveal users' IP addresses, which are then used to access their legal identities. Such compulsion is bound up in online anonymity and must be balanced with the rights of whistleblowers, dissidents, and others. Heavy-handed legislation risks abuse by governments and international actors. Yet it is possible to create complex legislation to deal with complex problems. This is not enough of an excuse not to take action.

Then there is the question of no-platforming (the decision to effectively remove a person's megaphone by banning them from a particular platform or social media website). Experts tend to express concern that simply shutting down entire extremist communities risks driving them further underground, particularly in light of the existence of platforms like Gab, generally perceived as the social network of the far right, which prides itself on enabling its users to bypass any form of what it describes as "rampant corporate censorship."[13] It has provided a safe haven for many a group after they have finally expressed sentiments violent or deplorable enough to be evicted from more mainstream social media spaces. Davey described it as a platform that "give[s] host to extremists with virtually no regulation or moderation whatsoever." The same might be said of platforms like 4chan and 8chan.

There is, of course, a risk of pushing these conversations further and further from the reach of challenge and debate and of playing into these communities' narratives of victimhood and persecution by being seen to tar entire groups with the same extremist brush. But there is hardly constructive dialogue happening on incel forums and subreddits at the moment. I'm reminded of Ellen Pao's conclusion that oxygen has simply allowed these communities to proliferate. And there is powerful evidence to suggest that no-platforming does work effectively when it comes to individuals—particularly the high-profile leaders and spokespeople of these groups, whose audience inevitably shrinks when they are forced out of mainstream online spaces, even if they do paint themselves as martyrs, and subsequently take refuge in more fringe forums.

Christian Picciolini has provided another powerful argument for the no-platforming of extremists—cutting off their funding:

These groups are generating revenue, for instance, through serving ads on some of their propaganda videos. If ads are being served on their videos, chances are good, depending on how many views, they're making ad revenue based on Google, Facebook, YouTube, serving ads against their content. So, in that sense, de-platforming is good. It does slow them down quite a bit.[14]

When social media companies have been brave enough to take these steps, the impact has been significant: Milo Yiannopoulos saw his influence and platform greatly reduced after his ban from Twitter, with reports of his finances plummeting and tours being canceled. "If you look at [far-right conspiracy theorist] Alex Jones, for example," Davey pointed out, "when he got de-platformed, he lost a zero off his regular viewing figures." As I wrote this chapter, the news came in that Facebook, having taken many months to pluck up the same courage as Twitter, had decided to permanently ban Yiannopoulos and Jones, alongside five other high-profile extremist figures. It subsequently announced plans to ban "praise, support and representation of white nationalism and separatism" on Facebook and Instagram.[15] In the very recent past, domain registrar GoDaddy has taken down Richard B. Spencer's alt-right website, and fundraising pages like Patreon have begun to prevent far-right extremists from using them as a revenue stream (though a number of controversial figures, including Jordan Peterson and Dave Rubin, immediately announced plans to launch an alternative crowdfunding platform, exemplifying the problem of what can amount to a game of online whack-a-mole). Nonetheless, the actions taken against prominent hate figures by social media platforms not only curtail their mainstream reach but also send a vital societal message about what we normalize and consider acceptable fodder for public "debate." This recent activity suggests that progress is finally starting to be made, in this area at least.

Yet governments remain remarkably reluctant to hold social media companies to account in any meaningful way. And their reluctance does not go unnoticed by extremists and trolls, who are well aware of the likelihood that they will continue to be able to operate with impunity. One breathtakingly clear example of this came in 2019 at a U.S. House Judiciary Committee hearing on the rise of hate crimes and white nationalism. The hearing was intended to give Congress the opportunity to grill representatives of major tech platforms like Facebook and Google (owner of YouTube) on their role in allowing such extremism to spread. But even as proceedings got under way, the comments section beneath the YouTube livestream of the event quickly flooded with white nationalist memes, anti-Semitic slurs, misogynistic comments, and complaints about "white genocide." Within an hour, YouTube moderators were forced to disable comments on the video altogether. Observers reported that the tech company representatives present "mostly sat back, fielding overly simple questions about whether Facebook allows people to report hate or how YouTube spots videos that violate its policies," while committee members failed to pin them down or hold them to account.[16]

Seyi Akiwowo, who experienced blistering racist and misogynistic online abuse after her speech at the European Parliament went viral, chose to respond by setting up Glitch, an ambitious not-for-profit organization with an intersectional lens, aimed at ending online abuse. The results have been impressive. Within just two years, the organization's digital citizenship workshop has provided over 3,500 young people with tools to navigate the online world and play an active role in confronting online harms, like bullying and abuse. It has also provided digital self-defense training to women with a public presence, including those in politics, resulting in a 55 percent increase in participants feeling safe to express themselves online.

But Akiwowo stresses the need for social media companies themselves to take responsibility in order to achieve real change in the atmosphere of "toxic online spaces." When I interviewed her, she said we need "investment in data gathering to identify patterns and join the dots between all forms of online abuse and 'in real life' attacks," plus investment in digital citizenship education and the inclusion of marginalized communities and voices in discussion and decision-making around online abuse. Pointing to the increased levels of abuse faced by women from Black and minority ethnic backgrounds online, she suggested social media companies widen the pool of experts with whom they work on these issues. "Not only is an intersectional approach to addressing online harms necessary, but also the inclusion of many diverse civil society groups working on online harms." Online users, she believes, should "have more of a stake and say in how their online spaces are governed."

This might also be extended to the actual funding of such groups, which is often woefully underprioritized. Sara Khan, UK lead commissioner for countering extremism, told me,

> Although not acknowledged enough, women continue to play a critical role in countering extremism and working to establish peace and security, both at a local and national level. Yet women's civil society groups often operate on a shoestring. This must change if we are to strengthen our counterextremism response.

Glitch has also taken the bold step of suggesting that tech giants themselves should fund action on online abuse, campaigning for 1 percent of the UK government's new digital services tax to be earmarked specifically for tackling the problem.

As social media has exploded into a billion-dollar industry with massive influence, women like Akiwowo have continued to act as the—often unheard—canaries in the coal mine, yet they are frequently the people best placed to suggest the changes that would make a real difference to issues such as online abuse.

A recent article highlighted a mass harassment and misinformation campaign launched by anonymous 4chan trolls in 2014 to undermine and damage the reputations of Black feminists.[17] Shortly before Father's Day, the trolls started a Twitter hashtag,

#EndFathersDay, using sock puppets and fake accounts purporting to belong to Black feminists, with offensive, exaggerated stereotypical language and tropes about angry Black women. The hashtag quickly began trending worldwide and picked up a maelstrom of media coverage from conservatives, ready to use it to pillory real Black women working for change.

The story, like so many in which the focus of vitriol has been a marginalized group, was largely forgotten, particularly in comparison with the greater weight and analysis given to a bigger campaign like Gamergate. And alongside it, we have also forgotten the smart, coordinated and tech-savvy campaign of resistance launched by the Black feminist movement in response. Women like Shafiqah Hudson and I'Nasah Crockett quickly uncovered the source of the hashtag, revealing it to be a deliberate hoax by MRAs, who had launched it on a forum thread (titled "#EndFathersDay Straw Feminist!") rife with racist language, rape jokes, and fake statistics, like the claim that "1 in 2 mothers will abuse their children."

Hudson then launched a new hashtag, #YourSlipIsShowing, which members of the Black feminist Twittersphere could use to flag and report sock puppets and fake accounts purporting to represent Black women, exposing those that were deliberately stirring up hatred and highlighting incidents in which photographs of real Black women were being used, without consent, by trolls. The anti-harassment campaign was significant, because it saw the victims of a mass trolling attack using similar electronic tactics and online coordination to retaliate against the perpetrators. Black women with large platforms helped to spread the word to their followers, and activists blocked users revealed to be trolls and shared their block lists widely with others, which then enabled them to report hundreds of perpetrator accounts to Twitter en masse, increasing the chance of action being taken (though the women at the forefront of the campaign told *Slate* that little was done to tackle the problem). These women uncovered the roots of mass harassment campaigns, the coordination of weaponized misinformation by trolls, and the use of forums to plan tactics long before the mainstream media had picked up on the problem. And they demonstrated a targeted, multifaceted, scalable response from which social media companies and other actors might have learned valuable lessons before the Gamergate catastrophe, if only anybody had been listening.

Alongside the immediate actions we might demand of social media platforms then, we might also urge more long-term investment in civil society groups leading the way on these issues, particularly those representing marginalized groups, and an investment in increasing diversity in STEM fields in order to change the dynamics of a sphere in which women and minorities face systemic harassment while playing little role in the processes designed to respond to that abuse. A 2018 report revealed that across the British technology sector, just 8.5 percent of senior leaders are from a minority background, and women make up just 12.6 percent of board members. Almost two-thirds of boards in the sector and more than 40 percent of senior leadership teams have no female representation at all.[18]

The next area in which we must see change, if we are to make meaningful progress, is the mainstream media. By amplifying and spreading the messages of those peddling hate in the service of controversy and clickbait, the media has provided vital offline oxygen to the vitriol of online bile. By framing hate speech as one side of "balanced debate," it has normalized and legitimized what should be acknowledged as extreme and unacceptable. By presenting a trivialized and exaggerated version of feminism to stoke controversial outrage, it has helped fuel the fire of misogynist conspiracy theorists and harassing mobs. By failing to recognize the extremist nature of violent attacks on women, it has obstructed us from recognizing and tackling misogynistic terrorism for what it really is. As such, it has, sometimes unintentionally, aided and abetted the spread of once-fringe extremist online communities into the center of acceptable discourse.

And yet the media also has one of the biggest opportunities to help us solve the problem instead of worsening it. Through responsible reporting, through editorial decisions driven by ethics, not eyeballs, the media has the capacity to help delegitimize and undermine hate-fueled extremist ideologies, evicting them from general conversation, rather than propelling them to greater prominence.

A 2018 report starkly described "the relationship between journalism and the amplification of harmful, polluted, or false information" around the 2016 U.S. presidential election and the ability of online extremists to deliberately target journalists with manipulative techniques, leading to the risk of "filter[ing] violent bigotries into mainstream discourse" and "catalyz[ing] the visibility of alt-right manipulators."[19]

Even the very fact of covering such antagonists as slavishly and repeatedly as the media did had a huge impact, wrote lead report author Whitney Phillips:

However critically it might have been framed, however necessary it may have been to expose, coverage of these extremists and manipulators gifted bad actors a level of visibility and legitimacy that even they could scarcely believe, as nationalist and supremacist ideology metastasized from culturally peripheral to culturally principal in just a few short months.

After interviewing dozens of reporters and newsroom employees, Phillips determined a host of recommendations for editorial best practice, designed "to minimize narrative hijacking by bad-faith actors," including reporting on objectively false information without creating a false equivalence. She also recommended avoiding personal details in reports on bigots and abusers, using the term *troll* as sparingly as possible, minimizing the inclusion of identifying information about victims, and avoiding the publication of euphemistic dog-whistle quotes.

But even at the most basic level, the media must surely learn lessons from the copycat nature of recent mass murderers whose manifestos overlap and echo one another, often having been given a massive platform in the international press. The *New York Times* published Rodger's manifesto and video statement, with its national editor, Alison Mitchell, defending the decision at the time: "In this case, the video and manifesto were so integral to understanding the motivation for the crimes [that had we not published them], we would have very consciously not have been telling a big part of the story."[20] Yet it is difficult to imagine such a justification being used for the publication of a jihadi terrorist manifesto in the wake of an ISIS massacre. And in the years since, as this book has detailed, mass killers have repeatedly cited Rodger as an inspiration. It is perfectly possible for the media to cover the crimes of these men without amplifying their instructional, propagandist screeds.

Ultimately, there are major changes that need to happen across a wide range of sectors, from government to tech companies, from media to education, if we are effectively to analyze and respond to the threat of online misogynistic extremism. But as men like Kaufman, Hurst, and Barker—men who hate men who hate women—suggested, there is also perhaps a need for a fundamental shift in our approach to the very idea of masculinity if we want this change to take hold at a mainstream, attitudinal level. This may seem several levels removed from the direct challenges of the manosphere itself, but just as male supremacists have become astonishingly adept at optimizing their ideologies to fluidly permeate the boundaries between on- and offline, so we must work on creating equally powerful narratives about masculinity that can flow the other way. Not least as a preventative measure to try to fill in the vacuum that risks leaving young men so vulnerable to the messaging of the manosphere in the absence of accessible alternatives.

As our society changes and shifts, men have lost their traditional, stereotypically prescribed means of asserting their maleness. But where we have been good at picking up on this, at critiquing those traditional requirements of masculinity and their potentially toxic effects, we have not necessarily been effective in our communication of that critique or in the provision of alternative, realistic, positive visions of masculinity.

When feminists talk about "toxic masculinity," we mean the enormous potential damage posed by an outdated version of what it means to be a man: showing strength and hiding weakness. Dominating and asserting control in all personal relationships. Never admitting vulnerability or emotions. Stoically bottling up fear or distress and avoiding support or communication at all costs. Assuming the role of household head, provider, and protector. Treating female spouses and children as vulnerable secondary dependents, extensions of the self or property, instead of equal partners and sources of support. Prioritizing strength, physical prowess, and sexual triumph over intellect, emotional intelligence, and friendship. Secretive self-flagellation and self-medication over admission of failure. Money and status over job satisfaction. Career over parental involvement. Society over self.

All this is true. But it is too often assumed that the potential damage we highlight is only damage to women and children, when the truth is that the damage toxic masculinity causes to men and boys is also enormous. The problem, I am repeatedly told by boys, men, and activists, is that when we say "toxic masculinity," people hear "toxic men."

Nowhere was this more painfully apparent than in the recent explosive response to the aforementioned Gillette advertisement that caused such extreme discomfort. The ad sought to tackle toxic forms of masculinity and encourage men to play an active role in addressing the problem. It was really a fairly tame video, showing men intervening to prevent harassment and including lines like "We believe in the best in men." Nonetheless, it sparked an enormous wave of vitriol that united manosphere communities, alt-right YouTubers, and the mainstream media alike, with the video instantly becoming the most disliked in YouTube history (with 1.4 million "down votes"). Men across the internet videotaped themselves snapping Gillette razors in half and burning other products made by the company. ("Got six cuts but it was worth it!" enthused one incel forum member after destroying his razor. "Fuck Gillette!")

As much as these might feel like (and are often portrayed as) very modern forms of unease, born out of gendered tension over the recent explosion of fourth-wave feminism and resentment that the #MeToo movement has somehow criminalized "maleness," the reality is that these conversations have been percolating for decades. In November 1958, in an article in *Esquire* magazine, the historian Arthur Schlesinger Jr. asked,

What has happened to the American male? For a long time he seemed utterly confident in his manhood, sure of his masculine role in society, easy and definite in his sense of sexual identity. Today men are more and more conscious of maleness not as a fact but as a problem. The ways by which American men affirm their masculinity are uncertain and obscure. There are multiplying signs, indeed, that something has gone badly wrong with the American male's conception of himself.[21]

So how do we provide those role models and create those positive new ideas about what it means to be a man? Hurst laughed as he remembered the advice he was given when he first started designing courses about masculinity to deliver to boys in school. "There were loads of people who were like: 'You need to take men into the woods and get boys to cut down trees, and that's how they'll get in touch with their masculinity.' But I was never that kind of kid—I liked art and music and drama."

Sitting across the table from him in a crowded London café, it struck me that Hurst himself epitomizes exactly the kind of role model we need. A young, charismatic, athletic man who arrives in a hoodie and effortlessly pulls off several items of jewelry, Hurst is about as far as you could get from the uptight feminist harridans teenage boys might be expecting to lambast them about sexism. He is, I suspect, likely to receive much more candid insight into their influences and opinions than I am. And as he told me about his journey to becoming involved in gender equality work, it occurred to me that there might be nobody more powerfully placed to win boys away from the lure of the involuntary celibates than a man like him, who quite literally represents the opposite. His career in intervention work only started after he was thrown out of theological college for having sex when he was supposed to be celibate.

Hurst emphasized the importance of diversity in our new ideas about what it means to be a man—of not replacing one stereotype with another:

> One of the really shit things about masculinity is that it's so prescriptive, so I don't ever want to walk into a room and say, "This list is out and we're now giving you a new list of what you need to be." Because inevitably, that's going to lead to more of the same stuff, like failing and feeling like you don't live up to the standards, and then rebelling against it or weaponizing it against other people. But giving people space to come up with their own alternatives is really important.

There are men quietly modeling a different, complex version of what it means to be a man. Barack Obama, with his willingness to cry publicly and his decision to make sexual violence on campus a central focus of his presidency. Andy Murray, who frequently, unshowily corrected reporters when they attributed to him records already broken by female tennis players like the Williams sisters. Men like Jordan Stephens of the hip-hop duo Rizzle Kicks, who sat next to me on a *Newsnight* panel discussion about #MeToo with a wreath of flowers in his hair and talked openly about the need for men to be allowed to breach constrictive stereotypes and experience intimacy with themselves and others.

These different and apparently "unusual" versions of masculinity can have an enormous impact on young people. Adam, the twenty-year-old student who told me how so many of his friends had been impacted by extreme online misogyny, credits his own recovery from serious mental health problems to one of his favorite bands. He said he had always struggled with societal pressure, having "never been a particularly outwardly masculine person," leading to teasing and name-calling at school. After coming out as pansexual at college and "trying to figure out who I am," he began to experience depression and anxiety, eventually reaching the point at which he barely felt able to leave the house. But Adam found solace in an unexpected place. He is a huge fan of the English rock band IDLES, whom he credits with rejecting the "performative macho bluster" more typical of male celebrities. Their single "Samaritans," released at the peak of Adam's depression, refers to the "mask of masculinity," describing the pressures on men to "man up...chin up...don't cry...just lie" and includes the lyrics "I'm a real boy/ Boy, and I cry." The potential impact of a band this prominent, nominated for British Breakthrough Act at the BRITs, choosing to discuss these issues so openly is massive, Adam said, particularly for their thousands of fans. "It allows us to start the conversation that maybe, in other circles or in other times in history, probably wouldn't have been had."

It might sound simple, but the impact of role models on opening up wider conversation is crucial, especially in an area in which discussion can be so deeply stigmatized. And it becomes critical to offer alternative spaces to talk about issues otherwise seized upon and jealously guarded by toxic online discourse. When I asked Jack Peterson, the former incel, about the appeal of such forums, he said,

> Part of the problem is that it's kind of taboo to talk about these things, you know, outside of an anonymous internet forum... I think the problem is that there are barriers

within our society to what we can talk about, and I think male loneliness is definitely one of those. There's definitely a barrier where most people don't want to hear stuff like that, and so these guys are just forced to either keep quiet or go on some of these online forums. I think, if we could just be more willing to discuss these issues as a society, then that would be a big improvement.

Adam pointed out that finding the physical space for such conversations to take place is as important as the emotional territory. He referred to the cutting of funding for youth clubs, without which, he said,

[Boys] don't have an outlet for their anger and their energy, so where else are they going to go but online? And that's where the flames start to appear, because they've got nothing else to do, so they'll go online, they'll find this outlet for their energy, they'll find this YouTube or this right-wing commentator that speaks to them, and then it just escalates from there.

The same warning is echoed by Picciolini, who told *The Atlantic*,

Thirty years ago, marginalized, broken, angry young people had to be met face-to-face to get recruited into a movement. Nowadays, those millions and millions of young people are living most of their lives online if they don't have real-world connections. And they're finding a community online, instead of in the real world, and having conversations about promoting violence.[22]

Individual men are often powerfully placed to be the ones to critique, challenge, and undermine the messaging of male supremacist extremism, on- and offline. For every good man who asks "what can I do?," there is an opportunity to join this chorus, speaking to the men around you and contributing to a wider ripple effect.

When the manosphere conspiracy theories about Katie Bouman began to overshadow the work she had done to capture the first image of a black hole, for example, the resistance was led by Andrew Chael, the same white male scientist MRAs were trying to credit with Bouman's achievement instead. "Once I realized that many online commentators were using my name and image to advance a sexist agenda to claim that Katie's leading role in our global team was invented, I felt I should say something to make it clear I rejected that view," Chael told CNN. He immediately took to Twitter to amplify his message in the same forum being used by the perpetrators, describing misogynistic attacks on his colleague as "awful and sexist," correcting false statistics being spread by the manosphere, and writing, "So while I appreciate the congratulations on a result that I worked hard on for years, if you are congratulating me because you have a sexist vendetta against Katie, please go away and reconsider your priorities in life."

Men like Matt McGorry, Patrick Stewart, Barack Obama, David Schwimmer, and many more continue to use their personal platforms to speak, write, and sing about the problem with prescriptive masculinity, exploring nuanced and new ways to examine being a man. We need the bulk of this work to come from men. If masculinity is the problem, it is men who must invent and drive new forms of manhood. The one thing everyone seems to agree on is that it is fairly fruitless for feminists to be seen to be telling boys the right way to be a man. That doesn't mean that the project of reforming masculinity has failed. It means that, as with so much of the heavy lifting of the pursuit of equality in our society, the hard work has been foisted on the wrong people.

We need to harness the energies of those men who are afraid of women because they have been misled by the lies and inflammatory rhetoric of other men. The men who have been sold the lie that they should fear women because women who report abuse risk tarring all men with the same brush. The truth is that it is abusive men who risk tarring all men with the same brush. So these are not really men who are afraid of women at all. They are men who hate men who hate women. They just don't know it yet.

Crucially, none of these interventions will work unless we see the problem for what it really is and take it seriously. You don't know what's out there until you look. We don't want to talk about a mass movement encouraging violent hatred of women. We would prefer not to confront it. It is much easier to paint sexism as a vague, perpetrator-free issue, hazily floating in the ether, waiting to affect women. It is much easier to dismiss or belittle manosphere communities than to tackle them. But the more we look away, the worse it gets.

It wasn't until I started researching the manosphere to write this book that I began to stumble across increasing numbers of casual forum discussions and chatroom threads dedicated to fantasizing about raping and murdering me specifically. As I worked my way through the different manosphere communities, I saw the way they treat women who have dared to write about them or even simply to make the briefest comments about them on social media. Borrowing the wording of jihadist terrorism, an incel message board contained an announcement about a female journalist who made a single YouTube video about incel message boards: "fatwa on this cunt. all incels have a duty to do her harm if they see her. INCELU AKBAR!!!!"

I'm scared about this book being published. Unlike some of the trolling victims I've interviewed, I have foreknowledge of what is to come. I have done everything I can to anticipate and mitigate it. In the years since the death threats started, I have moved several times, and I have restricted my personal details further and further from social media, taking care never to share anything specific about my family or friends. I have stopped writing about personal things. If I'm interviewed or photographed at home, I ask the journalist not to mention the area, persuade the photographer to make sure the street doesn't feature in the picture. It's an exhausting way to live. I don't know what's going to happen next. But in a way, I'm throwing down the gauntlet. The men from the groups I have described, if they become aware of this book, will be faced with something of a dilemma. They will claim it misrepresents and maligns their communities. But if they choose to deluge me with threats and abuse, as they have done countless times before, they will be proving me right. I like to think it will be a confusing moment for them.

So writing this book is scary, but it is also an act of resistance. We can't tackle a problem if people don't even know it exists. And once we do know, we all have a responsibility to answer a simple question: What are we going to do about it?

The shift we need to see is achievable. I know, because I've seen it firsthand.

In my experience, a school can be a very revealing microcosm of society. It has its cliques and communities, its leaders and citizens, its culture and norms. So observing different schools trying to come to terms with the infiltration of extreme misogyny has been extremely enlightening. I've watched as schools have attempted to yank the worm out too quickly, thinking it's possible to solve the problem with a single whole-school assembly, to tick the box and move on. I've seen them lop off the head, doling out a single punishment to a single ringleader, in the hope it will magically treat the deeper elements of the problem. And I've seen the putrefaction that follows as prejudice becomes more entrenched, victims face backlash, normalization fails to shift, and the cycle continues.

But I've also seen one school that did things differently. They had a major problem, and they knew it. To say that the attitudes I encountered on my first visit were deeply misogynistic would be an understatement. The girls were deathly silent. The boys shared classic manosphere tidbits. The atmosphere was toxic. But the school, galvanized by a small but determined group of teachers, had taken one vital first step: they had acknowledged the problem. What they did next was groundbreaking.

They thought about the many different possible approaches for solving the problem. And then they implemented all of them. They convened a student council so that the pupils themselves could work out what the issues were and make suggestions for fixing them. They had big assemblies, yes, but they were led by male members of staff and visibly supported by the entire senior leadership team. They sent the message that this was being taken seriously at every level. And they didn't leave it at that. They followed up the assemblies with tutor-group discussions, looking at a wide range of different subjects and going into depth about issues like gender stereotypes and mental health, looking at how young men were impacted, as well as their female peers. They gave the students a safe space to explore and discuss the problem. Where young people might have encountered misleading information online, they provided facts. And it wasn't just talk. The school started to take action, too, to tackle sexual harassment and to send a message that it was unacceptable. They appointed a counselor to offer mental health support. They worked with parents, inviting them to a talk to educate them about the issues facing their children and the online content they might be unaware of. They provided the tools, information, and confidence for parents to start vital conversations with their teenagers.

As time passed, the school invited me back again and again. Each year, they asked me to visit and deliver the same talk to a new freshman class. And so I watched things shift.

The second year I visited, the dial had moved just a little. A small, brave group of students had started a feminist society. There were fewer than ten of them, and they'd encountered some pretty stiff resistance from their peers, but they were determined to battle on. The atmosphere remained hostile, but there were fewer outright abusive comments from boys in my session. Misogyny no longer had a stranglehold. One or two girls even raised their hands.

The next year, the feminist society had doubled in size. There was a sense of openness to debate. There were still plenty of misogynistic ideas and a good amount of misinformation, but it no longer went completely unchallenged. Female staff no longer looked devastated during the question-and-answer session.

By the time I paid my final visit, five years on from that first difficult day, the school felt unrecognizable. We sat in the same classrooms, I spoke in the same assembly hall, but the atmosphere was transformed. It wasn't groupthink. Students still had different views, and of course, not everybody was magically convinced. There were still disruptive boys and difficult questions. But among a critical mass of students, something had shifted. The girls put up their hands. The place no longer felt infected.

It doesn't happen overnight, but it is possible—with enough effort, on enough different fronts, and enough willingness from male role models to take responsibility for the work.

That's how we get the whole worm.

# Reading Group Guide

1. In the introduction, Laura Bates declares, "You already live in [that misogynistic world]. But perhaps you didn't know, because we don't like to talk about it." How much of the material in the book were you familiar with before reading? What was the most surprising thing you learned?

2. Some argue that this problem will escalate if it is given the credence of attention and discussion. Bates disagrees. What do you think?

3. How does an "us versus them" mentality fuel online communities and contribute to indoctrination?

4. It is clear that the manosphere is not a homogeneous group. How do you think the network holds together despite the many points of difference between its members?

5. One of the things that decreases our ability to talk about the manosphere is the idea that the online world and the "real" world are completely distinct. How can we better understand the real-life consequences of discussions online?

6.  Many commenters across the manosphere mention "PC madness" offhandedly. What are they referring to, and how does their hatred of it dovetail with their extreme misogyny?

7.  Bates points out the conundrum of many online groups: "the special quality of being a group supposedly exclusively devoted to men whose near-total focus is women." How do members reconcile this contradiction? How would they be different if their focus really was on supporting men?

8.  What effect do female MRAs like Karen Straughan and Janet Bloomfield have on the movement at large? What benefits do Straughan and Bloomfield gain from espousing these views?

9.  When trolls—even those sending violent threats—are reported, people are often told that a platform's community guidelines have not been explicitly violated. How can we hold social media platforms accountable for ensuring safety on their sites?

10. How did you feel about the parallel that Bates draws between terrorism and domestic abuse? What does that comparison tell us about how we should approach both problems?

11. The effects of media coverage are discussed in multiple chapters of the book. What was your greatest takeaway on the effects of media on extreme misogyny?

12. Based on the stories in the chapter "Men Who Don't Know They Hate Women," do you think intervention works? What

are the most effective methods for educating young people and helping them sort through toxic manosphere rhetoric?

13. Bates emphasizes that extremist misogyny is not investigated in the same way as other terrorist movements. How do you think this oversight has persisted?

14. One thing that can help, especially for young men, is increased visibility of positive role models. Who comes to mind when you think of men who represent nontoxic masculinity? What qualities do you think they offer people who look up to them?

15. How did you feel at the end of the book? Were you encouraged or frustrated?

# Notes

All quotes from Tim Squirrell are from an email to the author on December 20, 2018. All quotes from Dr. Lisa Sugiura are from an interview with the author conducted on April 1, 2019. All quotes from Jacob Davey are from an interview with the author conducted on April 4, 2019. All quotes from Jack Peterson (except those with individual citations) are from an interview with the author conducted on December 12, 2018. All quotes from Brydie Lee-Kennedy are from an interview with the author conducted on April 17, 2019. All quotes from Seyi Akiwowo are from an email message to the author on April 24, 2019. All quotes from Michael Kaufman are from an interview with the author conducted on April 11, 2019. All quotes from Ben Hurst are from an interview with the author conducted on March 27, 2019. All quotes from Gary Barker are from an interview with the author conducted on March 21, 2019. All quotes from Alex are from an interview with the author conducted on March 31, 2019. All quotes from Tom are from an interview with the author conducted on March 31, 2019. All quotes from Adam are from an interview with the author conducted on April 4, 2019. All quotes from Dr. Carlene Firmin, MBE, are from an interview with the author conducted on September 23, 2019. All quotes from the unnamed female teacher in chapter 9 are from an email sent to the author on November 10, 2019. All quotes from Sara Khan are from an email sent to the author on May 13, 2019. All quotes from manosphere forums and groups were accessed between November 10, 2018, and June 9, 2020. All quotes have been reproduced faithfully, with spelling, grammar, and punctuation unedited, but citations are not provided to avoid promoting extremist individuals and platforms.

## INTRODUCTION

1    Chris Smyth, "Nearly Half of Girls Have Self-Harmed," *Times* (London), March 1, 2018, https://www.thetimes.co.uk/article/nearly-half-of-girls-have-self-harmed -rjp50vww6; Chris Smyth, "Quarter of Girls Are Depressed at 14 in Mental Health Crisis," *Times* (London), September 20, 2017, https://www.thetimes.co.uk/article /quarter-of-girls-are-depressed-at-14-in-mental-health-crisis-ptmdsdzlr.

## CHAPTER 1: MEN WHO HATE WOMEN

1    Ashifa Kassam, "Woman behind 'Incel' Says Angry Men Hijacked Her Word as 'Weapon of War,'" *Guardian*, April 25, 2018, https://www.theguardian.com /world/2018/apr/25/woman-who-invented-incel-movement-interview-toronto -attack.

2    Luke O'Brien, "The Making of an American Nazi," *The Atlantic*, December 2017, https://www.theatlantic.com/magazine/archive/2017/12/the-making-of-an -american-nazi/544119/.

3    Erin Corbett, "Inside the Alt-Right's Violent Obsession with 'White Sharia War Brides,'" *Vice*, April 3, 2018, https://www.vice.com/en_ca/article/d35z5a/inside-the -alt-rights-violent-obsession-with-white-sharia-war-brides.

4    "Teenage Neo-Nazis Jailed over Terror Offenses," BBC, June 18, 2019, https://www .bbc.com/news/uk-48672929.

5    Jesselyn Cook and Andy Campbell, "Congressional Candidate in Virginia Admits He's a Pedophile," *HuffPost*, May 31, 2018, https://www.huffingtonpost.ca/entry /nathan-larson-congressional-candidate-pedophile_n_5b10916de4b0d5e89e1e48 24?ri18n=true.

6    Ellen Pao, "The Perverse Incentives That Help Incels Thrive in Tech," *Wired*, June 19, 2018, https://www.wired.com/story/ellen-pao-the-perverse-incentives -that-help-incels-thrive-in-tech/.

7    Nicky Woolf, "Chilling Report Details How Elliot Rodger Executed Murderous Rampage," *Guardian*, February 20, 2015, https://www.theguardian.com/us-news/2015 /feb/20/mass-shooter-elliot-rodger-isla-vista-killings-report.

8    Megan Garvey, "Transcript of the Disturbing Video 'Elliot Rodger's Retribution,'" *Los Angeles Times*, May 24, 2014, https://www.latimes.com/local/lanow/la-me-ln -transcript-ucsb-shootings-video-20140524-story.html.

9    Sean D. Hamill, "Blog Details Shooter's Frustration," *New York Times*, August 5, 2009, https://www.nytimes.com/2009/08/06/us/06shoot.html.

10   Lee Ferran, Chris Cuomo, Sarah Netter, and Lindsay Goldwert, "Pa. Gunman 'Hell-Bent' on Killings, Had 4 Guns," ABC, August 5, 2009, http://www.source.ly/10lnO# .Xxbqrp5KjIU.

11   "Full Text of Gym Killer's Blog," *New York Post*, August 5, 2009, https://nypost .com/2009/08/05/full-text-of-gym-killers-blog/.

12   "Virgin Teenager Ben Moynihan 'Stabbed Women in Revenge,'" BBC, January 13, 2015, https://www.bbc.com/news/uk-england-hampshire-30803039.

13   Heather Saul, "Teenager Ben Moynihan Sentenced to 21 Years for Attempted Murder of Three Women Because He Could Not Lose His Virginity," *Independent*, March 6, 2015, https://www.independent.co.uk/news/uk/crime

/teenager-ben-moynihan-sentenced-to-21-years-for-attempted-murder-of-three
-women-because-he-could-not-10091277.html.

14   Kevin Johnson, Trevor Hughes, and Aamer Madhani, "Oregon Community
     College Shooter Was Bitter," *USA Today*, October 2, 2015, https://www.usatoday
     .com/story/news/2015/10/02/oregon-community-college-shooter-christopher
     -harper-mercer/73206986/.

15   Allison Tierney, "Edmonton Man Uses 'Involuntary Celibacy' as Excuse in Stomping
     Death," *Vice*, August 30, 2018, https://www.vice.com/en_ca/article/ev8ekp/edmonton
     -man-uses-involuntary-celibacy-as-excuse-in-stomping-death.

16   Keegan Hankes and Alex Amend, "The Alt Right Is Killing People," Southern
     Poverty Law Center, February 5, 2018, https://www.splcenter.org/20180205/alt-right
     -killing-people.

17   Ben Collins and Brandy Zadrozny, "After Toronto Attack, Online Misogynists Praise
     Suspect as 'New Saint,'" NBC, April 24, 2018, https://www.nbcnews.com/news/us-news
     /after-toronto-attack-online-misogynists-praise-suspect-new-saint-n868821.

18   Audra D. S. Burch and Patricia Mazzei, "Death Toll Is at 17 and Could Rise in
     Florida School Shooting," *New York Times*, February 14, 2018, https://www.nytimes
     .com/2018/02/14/us/parkland-school-shooting.html.

19   Gabrielle Fonrouge and Ruth Brown, "Alleged School Shooter Was Abusive to Ex-
     Girlfriend: Classmate," *New York Post*, February 15, 2018, https://nypost.com/2018
     /02/15/alleged-school-shooter-was-abusive-to-ex-girlfriend-classmate/.

20   Madeleine Aggeler, "Inside the Misogynistic Philosophy Behind the Toronto Killer's Attack,"
     *The Cut*, April 25, 2018, https://www.thecut.com/2018/04/what-is-incel-rebellion
     -toronto-van-attack-alex-minassian.html.

21   Leyland Cecco, "Toronto Van Attack Suspect Says He Was 'Radicalized' Online by
     'Incels,'" *Guardian*, September 27, 2019, https://www.theguardian.com/world/2019
     /sep/27/alek-minassian-toronto-van-attack-interview-incels.

22   Madeline Holcombe, Nicole Chavez, and Marlena Baldacci, "Florida Yoga Studio
     Shooter Planned Attack for Months and Had 'Lifetime of Misogynistic Attitudes,'
     Police Say," CNN, February 13, 2019, https://www.cnn.com/2019/02/13/us/tallahassee
     -yoga-studio-shooting/index.html.

23   Orion Donovan-Smith, "He Pledged to Kill 'As Many Girls as I See' in Mass Shooting.
     After Second Chances, He's Going to Prison," *Washington Post*, May 24, 2019, https://
     www.washingtonpost.com/crime-law/2019/05/24/he-pledged-kill-many-girls-i-see
     -mass-shooting-after-second-chances-hes-going-prison/.

24   Harold Carmichael, "Troubled Sudbury Man to Undergo Psychiatric Assessment,"
     *Sudbury Star*, August 17, 2020, https://www.thesudburystar.com/news/local-news
     /troubled-sudbury-man-to-undergo-psychiatric-assessment.

25 Elisha Fieldstadt, Brandy Zadrozny, and Ben Collins, "Gunman Dead after Shootout with Police Outside Dallas Court Building," NBC, June 17, 2019, https://www.nbcnews.com/news/us-news/suspected-gunman-shot-after-opening-fire-outside-dallas-court-building-n1018251.

26 "Updated Charge, Young Person Charged with First-Degree Murder and Attempted Murder, Updated to First-Degree Murder – Terrorist Activity and Attempted Murder – Terrorist Activity, Homicide #12/2020, Dufferin and Wilson Avenue," May 19, 2020, Royal Canadian Mounted Police. https://www.newswire.ca/news-releases/updated-charge-young-person-charged-with-first-degree-murder-and-attempted-murder-updated-to-first-degree-murder-terrorist-activity-and-attempted-murder-terrorist-activity-homicide-12-2020-dufferin-and-wilson-avenue-867108947.html.

27 "The FBI Says a Guy Blew His Hand Off with a Bomb Possibly Planned for an Attack on 'Hot Cheerleaders,'" BuzzFeed, June 6, 2020. https://www.buzzfeednews.com/article/davidmack/incel-bomber-blows-hand-off-cheerleaders.

28 Tim Walker, "California Drive-By Shootings: Elliot Rodger Kills Six Near Santa Barbara University," Independent, May 24, 2014, https://www.independent.co.uk/news/world/americas/california-drive-by-shootings-seven-dead-after-gunman-goes-on-rampage-in-santa-barbara-9430598.html.

29 Martin Pengelly and Martin Williams, "Seven Dead Including Gunman in 'Mass Murder' California Shooting," Guardian, May 24, 2014, https://www.theguardian.com/world/2014/may/24/drive-by-shooting-near-uc-santa-barbara-leaves-seven-dead.

30 Gavon Laessig and Jim Dalrymple II, "'Mass Murder' in California, 7 Killed by 'Disturbed' Man," BuzzFeed, May 24, 2014, https://www.buzzfeednews.com/article/gavon/mass-murder-in-california-7-dead-in-drive-by-rampage.

31 Walker, "California Drive-By Shootings."

32 Pengelly and Williams, "Seven Dead Including Gunman."

33 Kashmir Hill, "The Disturbing Internet Footprint of Santa Barbara Shooter Elliot Rodger," Forbes, May 24, 2014, https://www.forbes.com/sites/kashmirhill/2014/05/24/the-disturbing-internet-footprint-of-santa-barbara-shooter-elliot-rodger/#286fb10477c3.

34 Chris Ferguson, "Misogyny Didn't Turn Elliot Rodger into a Killer," Time, May 25, 2014, https://time.com/114354/elliot-rodger-ucsb-misogyny/.

35 Bill Brown, "Isla Vista Mass Murder May 23, 2014: Investigative Summary," Santa Barbara County Sheriff's Office, February 18, 2015, https://web.archive.org/web/20150220034256/http://www.sbsheriff.us/documents/ISLAVISTAINVESTIGATIVESUMMARY.pdf.

36 Ian Austen and Liam Stack, "Toronto Van Driver Kills at Least 10 People in 'Pure Carnage,'" New York Times, April 23, 2018, https://www.nytimes.com/2018/04/23/world/toronto-van.html.

37    Cecco, "Toronto Van Attack Suspect."

38    Marni Soupcoff, "What Should We Do about Dangerous 'Incels'? Maybe Help Them,"
      *National Post*, April 24, 2018, https://nationalpost.com/opinion/marni-soupcoff
      -what-should-we-do-about-dangerous-incels-maybe-help-them.

39    "So-Called 'Incels' Celebrate Toronto Van Attack, Praise Alleged Driver Alek Minassian,"
      *Global News*, April 25, 2018, https://globalnews.ca/news/4167272/incels-celebrate
      -toronto-van-attack-praise-alek-minassian/.

40    David Lawler and Rob Crilly, "Oregon Shooting: Gunman Kills Nine," *Daily Telegraph*,
      October 1, 2015, https://www.telegraph.co.uk/news/worldnews/northamerica/usa
      /11906116/Oregon-shooting-Gunman-kills-nine-as-it-happened-on-Thursday
      -October.html.

41    Adam Nagourney, Michael Cieply, Alan Feuer, and Ian Lovett, "Before Brief, Deadly
      Spree, Trouble Since Age 8," *New York Times*, June 1, 2014, https://www.nytimes
      .com/2014/06/02/us/elliot-rodger-killings-in-california-followed-years-of
      -withdrawal.html.

## CHAPTER 2: MEN WHO PREY ON WOMEN

1    Myles Bonnar, "Inside Britain's 'Seduction Boot Camps' Teaching Men How to Pick Up
     Women," *Daily Telegraph*, October 7, 2019, https://www.telegraph.co.uk/women/life
     /inside-britains-seduction-bootcamps-teaching-men-pick-women/.

2    Neil Strauss, *The Game: Penetrating the Secret Society of Pickup Artists* (New York:
     ReganBooks, 2005), 398.

3    James Bloodworth, "The Game and Real Social Dynamics: Is the Seduction Community
     Pushing the Idea that 'No' Just Means 'Not Yet'?," *Independent*, January 24, 2013,
     https://www.independent.co.uk/voices/comment/the-game-and-real-social-dynamics
     -is-the-seduction-community-pushing-the-idea-that-no-just-means-not-8463333
     .html.

4    Brandy Zadrozny, "The Secret World of Pickup Artist Julien Blanc," *Daily Beast*, December 1,
     2014, https://www.thedailybeast.com/the-secret-world-of-pickup-artist-julien-blanc.

5    Eric Weber, *How to Pick Up Girls!: The Fool-Proof Guide to Meeting Women without a
     Formal Introduction* (New York: Symphony Press, 1970).

6    Glenn Whipp, "395: The Number of Women Who Have Contacted the *Times* with
     Allegations of Sexual Harassment against James Toback," *Los Angeles Times*, January
     7, 2018, https://www.latimes.com/entertainment/la-et-mn-james-toback-women
     -sexual-harassment-breaking-silence-20180107-story.html.

7    Duncan Campbell, "Dating Game Turns Ugly," *Guardian*, January 16, 2000, https://
     www.theguardian.com/world/2000/jan/16/uk.duncancampbell.

8   Kathy Gilsinan, "*The Game* at 10: Reflections from a Recovering Pickup Artist," *The Atlantic*, October 13, 2015, https://www.theatlantic.com/entertainment/archive /2015/10/neil-strauss-the-game/409789/.

9   Patrick McGuire, "This Canadian Pick-Up Artist Bragged about Forcing Sex On a 'Slut Whore,'" *Vice*, November 12, 2014, https://www.vice.com/en_ca/article/av4xea /this-canadian-pick-up-artist-bragged-about-forcing-sex-on-a-slut-whore-bitch-297.

10  Antonia Molloy, "Julien Blanc 'Apologizes' in CNN Interview: 'I Am the Most Hated Man in the World,'" *Independent*, November 18, 2014, https://www.independent.co.uk/news /people/julien-blanc-apologises-in-cnn-interview-im-the-most-hated-man-in-the -world-9867780.html.

11  Tareq Haddad, "California Pick-Up Artist Who Raped Woman and Blogged about It Jailed for 8 Years," *International Business Times*, December 14, 2016, https://www.ibtimes.co.uk /california-pick-artist-who-raped-woman-blogged-about-it-jailed-8-years-1596379.

12  Brandy Zadrozny, "The Pickup Artist Rape Ring," *Daily Beast*, September 21, 2016, https://www.thedailybeast.com/pickup-artists-preyed-on-drunk-women -brought-them-home-and-raped-them.

13  Brandy Zadrozny, "Pickup Artist: I'm Autistic and Didn't Know Rape Was Bad," *Daily Beast*, October 6, 2017, https://www.thedailybeast.com/pickup-artist-rapist-has -a-new-champion-the-unabombers-lawyer.

14  Bloodworth, "The Game and Real Social Dynamics."

15  Peter Jacobs, "Ohio State University Students Have Come Together to Shame a Notoriously Creepy 'Pick-Up Artist,'" *Business Insider*, October 31, 2013, https://www .businessinsider.in/ohio-state-university-students-have-come-together-to-shame-a -notoriously-creepy-pick-up-artist/articleshow/25013609.cms.

16  "Shh...No Talking: LGBT-Inclusive Sex and Relationships Education in the UK," Terrence Higgins Trust, July 2016, https://www.tht.org.uk/sites/default/files/2018–07 /Shh%20No%20talking%20LGBT%20inclusive%20SRE%20in%20the%20UK.pdf.

17  Katie J. M. Baker, "Prominent Pick-Up Artist Drives a 'Rape Van' and Harasses Women on OkCupid," *Jezebel*, February 1, 2013, https://jezebel.com/prominent-pick-up-artist -drives-a-rape-van-and-harasses-5980600.

18  Jon Levine, "The Fall of the Pickup Artist," *Mic*, April 7, 2016, https://www.mic.com /articles/135918/the-fall-of-the-pickup-artist-inside-the-world-of-the-world-s-most -misunderstood-men.

19  Roosh Valizadeh, *Game: How to Meet, Attract, and Date Attractive Women* (n.p.: Kings Media, 2018).

20  Roosh Valizadeh, *Lady: How to Meet and Keep a Good Man for Love and Marriage* (n.p.: Kings Media, 2019).

## CHAPTER 3: MEN WHO AVOID WOMEN

1   James McCarthy, "David Sherratt, 18, Is a Men's Rights Activist Who Won't Have Casual
    Sex in Case He Is Falsely Accused of Rape," *WalesOnline*, November 22, 2015, https://
    www.walesonline.co.uk/news/wales-news/david-sherratt-18-mens-rights-10480411.

2   Rebecca Greenfield, "Powerful Men Have Changed Their Behavior at Work Since #MeToo,"
    *Bloomberg*, October 4, 2018, https://www.bloomberg.com/news/articles/2018-10-04
    /powerful-men-have-changed-their-behavior-at-work-since-metoo.

3   Claire Cain Miller, "Unintended Consequences of Sexual Harassment Scandals," *New
    York Times*, October 9, 2017, https://www.nytimes.com/2017/10/09/upshot/as-sexual
    -harassment-scandals-spook-men-it-can-backfire-for-women.html.

4   Maggie Astor, "Austin Official Is Reprimanded for Avoiding Meetings with Women,"
    *New York Times*, September 15, 2017, https://www.nytimes.com/2017/09/15/us/austin
    -william-manno-sxsw.html.

5   Katrin Bennhold, "Another Side of #MeToo: Male Managers Fearful of Mentoring
    Women," *New York Times*, January 27, 2019, https://www.nytimes.com/2019/01/27/world
    /europe/metoo-backlash-gender-equality-davos-men.html.

6   Bess Levin, "Wall Street Goes Full Mike Pence to Avoid #MeToo Accusations,"
    *Vanity Fair*, December 3, 2018, https://www.vanityfair.com/news/2018/12/wall-street
    -goes-full-mike-pence-to-avoid-metoo-accusations.

7   Gillian Tan and Katia Porzecanski, "Wall Street Rule for the #MeToo Era: Avoid Women
    at All Cost," *Bloomberg*, December 3, 2018, https://www.bloomberg.com/news/articles
    /2018-12-03/a-wall-street-rule-for-the-metoo-era-avoid-women-at-all-cost.

8   Soraya Chemaly, "Do People Understand That the Pence Rule Is Illegal at Work?,"
    *Medium*, November 18, 2019, https://medium.com/swlh/do-people-understand-that
    -the-pence-rule-is-illegal-at-work-a99c4c4362b5.

## CHAPTER 4: MEN WHO BLAME WOMEN

1   "Men's Rights Movement: Why It Is So Controversial?," *The Week*, February 19,
    2015, https://www.theweek.co.uk/people/62607/mens-rights-movement-why
    -it-is-so-controversial.

2   Ruth Picardie, "Champions of the Downtrodden Male," *Independent*, January 28,
    1994, https://www.independent.co.uk/life-style/champions-of-the-downtrodden
    -male-1403072.html.

3   Alice E. Marwick and Robyn Caplan, "Drinking Male Tears: Language, the
    Manosphere, and Networked Harassment," *Feminist Media Studies* 18, no. 4 (March
    26, 2018): 543–559, https://doi.org/10.1080/14680777.2018.1450568.

4   Warren Farrell, *The Myth of Male Power: Why Men Are the Disposable Sex* (New York:
    Simon & Schuster, 1993).

5    Picardie, "Champions of the Downtrodden Male."

6    Marwick and Caplan, "Drinking Male Tears."

7    Mariah Blake, "Mad Men: Inside the Men's Rights Movement—and the Army of Misogynists and Trolls It Spawned," *Mother Jones*, January 2015, https://www.motherjones.com /politics/2015/01/warren-farrell-mens-rights-movement-feminism-misogyny-trolls/.

8    Jill Filipovic, "Why Is an Anti-Feminist Website Impersonating a Domestic Violence Organization?," *Cosmopolitan*, October 24, 2014, https://www.cosmopolitan.com/politics /news/a32452/antifeminist-site-white-ribbon/.

9    Brett Stevens, "Interview with Matt Forney," *Amerika*, November 3, 2017, http://www .amerika.org/politics/interview-with-matt-forney/.

10   Jaclyn Friedman, "A Look Inside the 'Men's Rights' Movement That Helped Fuel California Alleged Killer Elliot Rodger," *American Prospect*, October 24, 2013, https:// prospect.org/power/look-inside-men-s-rights-movement-helped-fuel-california -alleged-killer-elliot-rodger/.

11   Catherine Bennett, "Justice for Men and Boys' Hatred of Feminism Eclipses Its Remit to Help Men," *Guardian*, January 18, 2015, https://www.theguardian.com/commentisfree /2015/jan/18/justice-for-men-and-boys-feminists-backlash.

12   Amanda Marcotte, "A Fond Salute to 'Honey Badgers,' the Ladies' Auxiliary of Online Anti-Feminism," *Slate*, September 23, 2015, https://slate.com/human-interest/2015/09 /honey-badgers-misogyny-the-ladies-wing-of-online-anti-feminism.html.

13   Alex Brook Lynn, "The Women of the Men's Rights Movement," *Vice*, August 4, 2014, https://www.vice.com/en_ca/article/znwwva/the-women-of-the-mens-rights -movement-751.

14   Marcotte, "A Fond Salute."

15   Mariah Blake, "The Men's Rights Movement and the Women Who Love It," *Mother Jones*, August 11, 2014, https://www.motherjones.com/politics/2014/08/mens -rights-movement-women-who-love-it/.

16   Alexandra Topping, "Maternity Leave Discrimination Means 54,000 Women Lose Their Jobs Each Year," *Guardian*, July 24, 2015, https://www.theguardian .com/money/2015/jul/24/maternity-leave-discrimination-54000-women-lose-jobs -each-year-ehrc-report.

17   Samara McPhedran, "FactCheck: Are 'Up to 21 Fathers' Dying by Suicide Every Week?," *The Conversation*, November 14, 2017, https://theconversation.com/factcheck-are -up-to-21-fathers-dying-by-suicide-every-week-87308.

18   Rebecca Watson, "Do 21 Fathers Commit Suicide Each Week Over Custody Issues?," *Skepchick*, February 21, 2019, https://skepchick.org/2019/02/do-21-fathers-commit -suicide-each-week-over-custody-issues/.

19   Jonathan M. Raub, Nicholas J. Carson, Benjamin L. Cook, Grace Wyshak, and Barbara
     B. Hauser, "Predictors of Custody and Visitation Decisions by a Family Court Clinic,"
     *Journal of the American Academy of Psychiatry and the Law* 41, no. 2 (2013): 206–218,
     http://jaapl.org/content/jaapl/41/2/206.full.pdf.

20   "Study Finds English and Welsh Family Courts Not Discriminating against Fathers,"
     University of Warwick, https://warwick.ac.uk/newsandevents/pressreleases/study
     _finds_english/.

21   Nico Trocmé and Nicholas Bala, "False Allegations of Abuse and Neglect When
     Parents Separate," *International Journal of Child Abuse & Neglect* 29, no. 12 (December
     2005): 1333–1345, https://doi.org/10.1016/j.chiabu.2004.06.016.

22   A. J. Kposowa, "Divorce and Suicide Risk," *Journal of Epidemiology and Community
     Health* 57, no. 12 (2003): 993–995, http://dx.doi.org/10.1136/jech.57.12.993.

23   Watson, "Do 21 Fathers Commit Suicide."

24   "Male Supremacy," Southern Poverty Law Center, https://www.splcenter.org/fighting
     -hate/extremist-files/ideology/male-supremacy.

25   Nick Arnold, "How This Feminist Found Herself Sympathising with the Men's Rights
     Movement," BBC, March 8, 2017, https://www.bbc.co.uk/bbcthree/article/55285fcb
     -81a4–424b-92ab-6c10278b5ab5.

26   Milo Yiannopoulos, "Dear Cassie Jaye, Sorry for Manspreading Your 'Red Pill'
     Kickstarter," *Breitbart*, October 29, 2015, https://www.breitbart.com/tech/2015/10/29/dear
     -cassie-jaye-sorry-for-manspreading-your-red-pill-kickstarter/.

27   Paul Elam, interview by Monique Wright and Andrew O'Keefe, *Morning Sunrise*, July
     5, 2014, https://www.youtube.com/watch?v=dxcXldIFsbQ.

28   Jamie Ross, "An Anti-Feminist Party Is Standing in the General Election," *BuzzFeed*,
     January 14, 2015, https://www.buzzfeed.com/jamieross/an-anti-feminist-party-is
     -standing-in-the-general-election.

29   "Donald Trump: 'It's a Very Scary Time for Young Men in America'—video," *Guardian*,
     October 2, 2018, https://www.theguardian.com/us-news/video/2018/oct/02/donald
     -trump-its-a-very-scary-time-for-young-men-in-america-video.

30   Ben Graham, "Inside Men's Rights Meeting: 'There's Going to Be Civil War," *New Zealand
     Herald*, September 1, 2018, https://www.nzherald.co.nz/lifestyle/news/article.cfm?c
     _id=6&objectid=12117547.

31   Corey Kilgannon, "One Man's Losing Fight Against Ladies' Nights," *New York Times*,
     January 13, 2011, https://cityroom.blogs.nytimes.com/2011/01/13/one-mans-odd
     -fight-against-ladies-nights/.

32   Eric Levenson, Paul P. Murphy, and Katelyn Polantz, "Suspect in Fatal Shooting
     at Home of Judge Esterh Salas Described Himself as an 'Anti-Feminist' Lawyer,

Once Argued a Case Before the Judge," CNN, July 21, 2020, https://edition.cnn.com/2020/07/20/us/suspect-shooting-at-judge-salas-home/index.html.

33  Stephanie Pappas, "APA Issues First-Ever Guidelines for Practice with Men and Boys," *Monitor on Psychology* 50, no. 1 (2019), 34, https://www.apa.org/monitor/2019/01/ce-corner.

34  Jordan Peterson, "It's Ideology vs. Science in Psychology's War on Boys and Men," *National Post*, February 1, 2019, https://nationalpost.com/opinion/jordan-peterson-its-ideology-vs-science-in-psychologys-war-on-boys-and-men/wcm/4ae1f32d-5c4d-4781-8e44-c527bb985e13/.

## CHAPTER 5: MEN WHO HOUND WOMEN

1   Nelli Ferenczia, Tara C. Marshall, and Kathrine Bejanyan, "Are Sex Differences in Antisocial and Prosocial Facebook Use Explained by Narcissism and Relational Self-Construal?," *Computers in Human Behavior* 77, no. C (2017): 25–31, https://doi.org/10.1016/j.chb.2017.08.033.

2   Alex Hern, "Feminist Games Critic Cancels Talk after Terror Threat," *Guardian*, October 15, 2014, https://www.theguardian.com/technology/2014/oct/15/anita-sarkeesian-feminist-games-critic-cancels-talk.

3   Marwick and Caplan, "Drinking Male Tears."

4   Taylor Wofford, "Is GamerGate about Media Ethics or Harassing Women? Harassment, the Data Shows," *Newsweek*, October 25, 2014, https://www.newsweek.com/gamergate-about-media-ethics-or-harassing-women-harassment-data-show-279736.

5   Aja Romano, "Milo Yiannopoulos's Twitter Ban, Explained," *Vox*, July 20, 2016, https://www.vox.com/2016/7/20/12226070/milo-yiannopoulus-twitter-ban-explained.

6   Damien Gayle, "Man Who Harassed MP Luciana Berger Online Is Jailed for Two Years," *Guardian*, December 8, 2016, https://www.theguardian.com/uk-news/2016/dec/08/man-joshua-bonehill-paine-harassed-mp-luciana-berger-online-jailed-two-years.

7   Hilary Whiteman, "I Will Not Be Silenced: Australian Muslim Fights Twitter 'Troll Army,'" CNN, February 27, 2015, https://www.cnn.com/2015/02/27/asia/australia-muslim-twitter-campaign/index.html.

8   Casey Johnston, "Chat Logs Show How 4chan Users Created #GamerGate Controversy," *Ars Technica*, September 9, 2014, https://arstechnica.com/gaming/2014/09/new-chat-logs-show-how-4chan-users-pushed-gamergate-into-the-national-spotlight/.

9   Ainsley Harris, "Visualizing the Two Sides of #Gamergate's Twitter Debate," *Fast Company*, October 28, 2014, https://www.fastcompany.com/3037713/analyzing-gamergate-on-twitter-polarized-debate-anonymous-voices.

10  Milo Yiannopoulos, "Feminist Bullies Tearing the Video Game Industry Apart," *Breitbart*, September 1, 2014, https://www.breitbart.com/europe/2014/09/01/lying-greedy-promiscuous-feminist-bullies-are-tearing-the-video-game-industry-apart/.

11  Sarah Jeong, "If We Took 'Gamergate' Harassment Seriously, 'Pizzagate' Might Never Have Happened," *Washington Post*, December 14, 2016, https://www.washingtonpost.com/posteverything/wp/2016/12/14/if-we-took-gamergate-harassment-seriously-pizzagate-might-never-have-happened/.

12  Andrew Marantz, "Trolls for Trump," *New Yorker*, October 24, 2016, https://www.newyorker.com/magazine/2016/10/31/trolls-for-trump.

13  Mike Cernovich, "When in Doubt, Whip It Out," *Danger & Play*, February 27, 2012, https://web.archive.org/web/20160318163008/http://www.dangerandplay.com/2012/02/27/when-masturbation-leads-to-a-close/.

14  Rex Sorgatz, "Macroanonymous Is the New Microfamous," *Fimoculous*, February 18, 2009, http://fimoculous.com/archive/post-5738.cfm.

15  Lorna Hughes, "Man Admits Sending Sickening Death Threats to MP Angela Eagle," *Liverpool Echo*, October 19, 2016, https://www.liverpoolecho.co.uk/news/liverpool-news/man-admits-sending-sickening-death-12048741.

16  Martin Daubney, "Britain's Vilest Troll: 'I'm Here to Expose Hypocrisy,'" *Daily Telegraph*, February 5, 2015, https://www.telegraph.co.uk/men/thinking-man/11390745/Britains-vilest-troll-Im-here-to-expose-hypocrisy.html.

17  Jacob Dirnhumber and Paul Sims, "Britain's Worst Troll: We Expose Dad-of-Two Youth Football Coach Living Double Life as UK's Sickest Troll—Targeting Celebs Including Katie Price with Barrage of Vile Racist Tweets," *Sun* (UK), February 21, 2018, https://www.thesun.co.uk/news/5631052/uk-worst-troll-josh-maddison-katie-price-harvey-celebrities-victims/.

18  Cindy Tran, "Heavily Pregnant Woman's Bold Response to a Man Who Refused to Let Her Sit Down on a Bus Is Taking the Internet by Storm," *Daily Mail*, September 10, 2018, https://www.dailymail.co.uk/femail/article-6150059/Eight-months-pregnant-Brydie-Lee-Kennedy-sits-mans-HAND-bus-refuses-it.html.

19  "Online Abuse and Harassment," Ipsos MORI, November 20, 2017, https://www.ipsos.com/ipsos-mori/en-uk/online-abuse-and-harassment.

20  "Review of the Committee on Standards in Public Life into the Intimidation of Parliamentary Candidates," National Democratic Institute for International Affairs, September 8, 2017, https://www.ndi.org/publications/review-committee-standards-public-life-intimidation-parliamentary-candidates.

21  "Sexism, Harassment and Violence against Women Parliamentarians," Inter-Parliamentary Union, October 2016, http://archive.ipu.org/pdf/publications/issuesbrief-e.pdf.

22  Jessica Elgot, "Diane Abbott More Abused than Any Other Female MP during Election," *Guardian*, September 5, 2017, https://www.theguardian.com/politics/2017/sep/05/diane-abbott-more-abused-than-any-other-mps-during-election.

23  Susan Devaney, "Alexandria Ocasio-Cortez Opens Up about the Online Death Threats She Receives from Men," *Vogue*, May 30, 2019, https://www.vogue.co.uk/article /alexandria-ocasio-cortez-death-threats-video-twitter; Michael Brice-Saddler, "He Easily Found Hundreds of Death Threats against Rep. Ilhan Omar. He Wants Twitter to Stop Them," *Washington Post*, April 16, 2019, https://www.washingtonpost.com /technology/2019/04/16/he-easily-found-hundreds-death-threats-against-rep-ilhan -omar-he-wants-twitter-stop-them/.

24  Brendan I. Koerner, "It Started as an Online Gaming Prank. Then It Turned Deadly," *Wired*, October 23, 2018, https://www.wired.com/story/swatting-deadly-online-gaming -prank/.

25  Delyth Jewell, "Violence against Women in Politics Case Study: The United Kingdom," Westminster Foundation for Democracy, August 6, 2018, https://www.wfd.org /2018/08/06/violence-against-women-in-politics-case-study-united-kingdom/.

26  Frances Perraudin and Simon Murphy, "Alarm over Number of Female MPs Stepping Down after Abuse," *Guardian*, October 31, 2019, https://www.theguardian.com/politics /2019/oct/31/alarm-over-number-female-mps-stepping-down-after-abuse.

27  Lizzie Dearden, "Jo Cox Death: Labor MP Reported 'Malicious Communications' to Police before Attack amid Concerns for Security," *Independent*, June 17, 2016, https:// www.independent.co.uk/news/uk/crime/jo-cox-death-killing-labour-mp-malicious -communications-police-attack-concerns-for-security-a7086921.html.

28  Ian Cobain and Matthew Taylor, "Far-Right Terrorist Thomas Mair Jailed for Life for Jo Cox Murder," *Guardian*, November 23, 2016, https://www.theguardian.com/uk-news /2016/nov/23/thomas-mair-found-guilty-of-jo-cox-murder.

29  "The *Guardian* view on the Jo Cox Murder Trial: A Killing of Our Times," *Guardian*, November 23, 2016, https://www.theguardian.com/commentisfree/2016/nov/23/the -guardian-view-on-the-jo-cox-trial-a-killing-of-our-times.

30  "Jo Cox Murder: Judge's Sentencing Remarks to Thomas Mair," BBC, November 23, 2016, https://www.bbc.com/news/uk-38076755.

31  Pao, "Perverse Incentives."

32  Rebecca Taylor, "Why Are White Men Carrying Out More Mass Shootings?," *Sky*, August 6, 2019, https://news.sky.com/story/why-are-white-men-more-likely-to-carry-out -mass-shootings-11252808.

33  "Not a Classical Neo-Nazi": What We Know About the German Hookah Bar Terrorist', *Vice*, February 21, 2020. https://www.vice.com/en/article/n7jdak/race-hate-mind -control-and-incel-ideology-what-we-know-about-the-german-hookah-bar-shooter.

34  Casey Quinlan, "It's No Coincidence the Synagogue Shooter Posted about the 'Red Pill' Movement," *ThinkProgress*, April 30, 2019, https://archive.thinkprogress.org/no

-coincidence-california-synagogue-shooter-john-earnest-posted-about-the-red-pill
-movement-aa46b31c01ad/.

## CHAPTER 6: MEN WHO HURT WOMEN

1   "Global Study on Homicide: Gender-Related Killing of Women and Girls," United
    Nations Office on Drugs and Crime, 2018, https://www.unodc.org/documents/data-and
    -analysis/GSH2018/GSH18_Gender-related_killing_of_women_and_girls.pdf.

2   Teresa K. Sourour, "Report of Coroner's Investigation," May 10, 1991, https://web.archive
    .org/web/20160303180531/http://www.diarmani.com/Montreal_Coroners_Report.pdf.

3   Donna Riley and Gina-Louise Sciarra, "'You're All a Bunch of Fucking Feminists':
    Addressing the Perceived Conflict between Gender and Professional Identities Using the
    Montreal Massacre," (conference paper, 36th Annual Frontiers in Education Conference,
    San Diego, CA, December 2006), https://doi.org/10.1109/FIE.2006.322741.

4   Bianca Dekel, Naeemah Abrahams, and Michelle Andipatin, "Exploring the
    Intersection between Violence against Women and Children from the Perspective
    of Parents Convicted of Child Homicide," *Journal of Family Violence* 34, no. 2 (2018):
    9–20, https://doi.org/10.1007/s10896-018-9964-5.

5   Anna Duff, "Student's Lip Was Bitten Off by Her Ex...Because He Wanted to 'Leave
    His Mark' for Her Next Boyfriend," *Sun* (UK), April 8, 2019, https://www.thesun.co.uk
    /fabulous/7594201/students-lip-bitten-off-ex-leave-his-mark/.

6   Lizzie Dearden, "London Attack: Rachid Redouane's Wife Says She Is 'Numbed' by
    His Actions amid Reports of Domestic Abuse," *Independent*, June 7, 2017, https://www
    .independent.co.uk/news/uk/home-news/london-attack-rachid-redouane-wife
    -domestic-abuse-numbed-response-bridge-borough-market-isis-a7778041.html.

7   Lizzie Dearden, "Westminster Attack Inquests: Khalid Masood's Mother 'Feared He
    Would Kill' Because of Extreme Violence and Crime," *Independent*, September 19, 2018,
    https://www.independent.co.uk/news/uk/crime/westminster-attack-khalid-masood
    -mother-terrorism-extreme-violence-crime-a8545436.html.

8   Erin Marie Saltman, "Orlando and Nice Attacks: Domestic Violence Links to
    Radicalization," BBC, July 22, 2016, https://www.bbc.com/news/world-36861840.

9   Jack Healy, "Sitora Yusufiy, Ex-Wife of Orlando Suspect, Describes Abusive Marriage,"
    *New York Times*, June 13, 2016, https://www.nytimes.com/2016/06/14/us/sitora-yusufiy
    -omar-mateen-orlando-shooting.html.

10  Melissa Davey, "Man Haron Monis 'Would Not Have Been on Bail If Domestic
    Violence Was Taken as Seriously as Terrorism,'" *Guardian*, December 17, 2014, https://
    www.theguardian.com/australia-news/2014/dec/17/man-haron-monis-bail-domestic
    -violence-taken-seriously-terrorism.

11    Alan Blinder, Dave Philipps, and Richard A. Oppel Jr., "In 2012 Assault, Texas Gunman
      Broke Skull of Infant Stepson," *New York Times*, November 6, 2017, https://www.nytimes
      .com/2017/11/06/us/devin-patrick-kelley-texas.html.

12    Phil McCausland, "Gun Used by Airport Shooting Suspect Was Once Taken Away
      from Him—Then Returned," NBC, January 8, 2017, https://www.nbcnews.com/news
      /us-news/gun-used-airport-shooting-suspect-was-once-taken-away-him-n704501.

13    Mark Follman, "Armed and Misogynist: How Toxic Masculinity Fuels Mass Shootings,"
      *Mother Jones*, May/June 2019, https://www.motherjones.com/crime-justice/2019/06
      /domestic-violence-misogyny-incels-mass-shootings/.

14    "Ten Years of Mass Shootings in the United States," Everytown for Gun Safety, November
      21, 2019, https://everytownresearch.org/massshootingsreports/mass-shootings-in
      -america-2009–2019/.

15    Rachel Pain, "Everyday Terrorism: Connecting Domestic Violence and Global Terrorism,"
      *Progress in Human Geography* 38, no. 4 (August 1, 2014): 531–550, https://doi.org/10.1177
      /0309132513512231.

16    J. Pete Blair and Katherine W. Schweit, "A Study of Active Shooter Incidents in the United
      States Between 2000 and 2013," Texas State University and Federal Bureau of Investigation,
      U.S. Department of Justice, 2014, https://www.fbi.gov/file-repository/active-shooter
      -study-2000-2013-1.pdf/view.

17    Erin M. Kearns, Allison E. Betus, and Anthony F. Lemieux, "Why Do Some Terrorist
      Attacks Receive More Media Attention Than Others?," *Justice Quarterly* 36, no. 6
      (2019): 985–1022, https://doi.org/10.1080/07418825.2018.1524507.

18    Travis L. Dixon and Charlotte L. Williams, "The Changing Misrepresentation of
      Race and Crime on Network and Cable News," *Journal of Communication* 65, no. 1
      (February 2015): 24–39, https://doi.org/10.1111/jcom.12133.

19    Kimberly A. Powell, "Framing Islam: An Analysis of U.S. Media Coverage of Terrorism
      Since 9/11," *Communication Studies* 62, no. 1 (2011): 90–112, https://doi.org/10.1080
      /10510974.2011.533599.

20    Bryan Arva, Muhammed Idris, and Fouad Pervez, "Almost All News Coverage of the
      Barcelona Attack Mentioned Terrorism. Very Little Coverage of Charlottesville Did,"
      *Washington Post*, August 31, 2017, https://www.washingtonpost.com/news/monkey
      -cage/wp/2017/08/31/almost-all-news-coverage-of-the-barcelona-attack-mentioned
      -terrorism-very-little-coverage-of-charlottesville-did/.

21    Jennifer Calfas, "Charlottesville Attack Driver James Fields Sentenced to Life in
      Prison," *Wall Street Journal*, June 28, 2019, https://www.wsj.com/articles/charlottesville
      -attack-driver-sentenced-to-life-in-prison-11561748867.

22    "The FBI Says a Guy Blew His Hand Off with a Bomb Possibly Planned for an Attack on 'Hot Cheerleaders,'" *BuzzFeed*, June 6, 2020. https://www.buzzfeednews.com/article /davidmack/incel-bomber-blows-hand-off-cheerleaders.

23    Trevor Aaronson, "Terrorism's Double Standard," *The Intercept*, March 23, 2019, https://theintercept.com/2019/03/23/domestic-terrorism-fbi-prosecutions/.

24    Katie Rogers, Jonathan Martin, and Maggie Haberman, "As Trump Calls Protesters 'Terrorists,' Tear Gas Clears a Path for His Walk to a Church," *New York Times*, June 1, 2020, https://www.nytimes.com/2020/06/01/us/politics/trump-governors.html.

25    "Western Tabloids Condemned for 'Humanizing' NZ Mosque Attacker," *Al Jazeera*, March 17, 2019, https://www.aljazeera.com/news/2019/03/zealand-tabloids-condemned -humanising-mosque-attacker-190316081740694.html.

26    Matthew Young, "Boy Who Grew into Evil Far-Right Mass Killer as 49 Murdered at Prayers," *Daily Mirror*, March 15, 2019, https://www.mirror.co.uk/news/world-news/new-zealand -shooting-brenton-tarrant-14142703.

27    "'Angelic' Terrorist? Tabloid Treatment of Christchurch Shooter Slammed on Social Media," *RT*, March 16, 2019, https://www.rt.com/news/454013-media-criticized -christchurch-coverage-killer/.

28    Nagourney et al., "Before Brief, Deadly Spree."

29    Hamill, "Blog Details Shooter's Frustration."

30    Dennis Chong and James N. Druckman, "Dynamic Public Opinion: Communication Effects over Time," *American Political Science Review* 104, no. 4 (2010): 663–680, https:// doi.org/10.1017/S0003055410000493.

31    Mike Sullivan, Alex West, Gary O'Shea, and Caroline Grant, "'I've Killed the Kids,'" *Sun*, February 15, 2011, https://www.thesun.co.uk/archives/news/372289/ive-killed -the-kids.

32    Amy Murphy, "Man Killed Wife and Kids before Jumping from Anglesey Cliff Where He'd Proposed to Her," *North Wales Live*, March 5, 2019, https://www.dailypost.co.uk/news /north-wales-news/man-killed-wife-kids-before-15920753.

33    Laura Bates, "A Cycle of Violence: When a Woman's Murder Is Called 'Understandable,'" *Guardian*, July 26, 2016, https://www.theguardian.com/lifeandstyle/womens-blog /2016/jul/26/womans-murder-called-understandable-lance-hart.

34    John Shammas and Gemma Mullin, "Spalding Shooting: Recap after Man Kills Wife and Daughter with Shotgun then Kills Himself Outside Swimming Pool," *Mirror*, July 20, 2016, https://www.mirror.co.uk/news/uk-news/spalding-shooting -live-updates-three-8446975.

35    Martin Evans, "Builder Shoots Wife and Daughter before Turning the Gun on Himself in Spalding," *Telegraph*, July 19, 2016, https://www.telegraph.co.uk/news/2016/07/19 /three-people-killed-in-shooting-at-swimming-pool/.

36    Rossalyn Warren, "'We Didn't Recognise That He Was Dangerous': Our Father Killed Our Mother and Sister," *Guardian*, June 17, 2017, https://www.theguardian.com /society/2017/jun/17/we-didnt-recognise-that-he-was-dangerous-our-father-killed -our-mother-and-sister.

37    Sarah Shaffi, "UK Judge Tells Convicted Abuser That There Are 'Lots More Fishes in the Sea,'" *Stylist*, May 8, 2019, https://www.stylist.co.uk/life/uk-judge-tells-convicted -abuser-that-there-are-lots-more-fishes-in-the-sea/265667.

38    Paula Chin, "A Texas Massacre," *People*, November 4, 1991, https://people.com/archive /a-texas-massacre-vol-36-no-17/.

## CHAPTER 7: MEN WHO EXPLOIT OTHER MEN

1    Michael A. Cohen, "Trump Has Turned the Racial Dog Whistle into a Steam Whistle," *Boston Globe*, July 19, 2019, https://www.bostonglobe.com/opinion/2019/07/19/trump -has-turned-racial-dog-whistle-into-steam-whistle/oxjaxnNaShQmLg71sHCsSK /story.html.

2    Kevin Breuninger, "Trump Condemns 'Racism, Bigotry and White Supremacy' in Speech after Mass Shootings Kill 31," CNBC, August 5, 2019, https://www.cnbc.com/2019 /08/05/trump-condemns-racism-bigotry-and-white-supremacy.html.

3    Joseph Bernstein, "Here's How *Breitbart* and Milo Smuggled White Nationalism into the Mainstream," *BuzzFeed*, October 5, 2017, https://www.buzzfeednews.com/article/joseph bernstein/heres-how-breitbart-and-milo-smuggled-white-nationalism; Tina Nguyen, "The Movement Formerly Known as the Alt-Right Tries to Evolve," *Vanity Fair*, April 20, 2017, https://www.vanityfair.com/news/2017/04/alt-right-movement-evolution.

4    Scaachi Koul, "Pickup Artists Are Still a Thing. And They Want You to Know They've Evolved," *BuzzFeed*, September 22, 2018, https://www.buzzfeednews.com/article /scaachikoul/pickup-artists-manosphere-incels-the-game-mras.

5    Bernstein, "*Breitbart* and Milo."

6    Adam Serwer and Katie J. M. Baker, "How Men's Rights Leader Paul Elam Turned Being a Deadbeat Dad into a Moneymaking Movement," *BuzzFeed*, February 6, 2015, https://www.buzzfeed.com/adamserwer/how-mens-rights-leader-paul-elam-turned -being-a-deadbeat-dad.

7    Pankaj Mishra, "Jordan Peterson & Fascist Mysticism," *New York Review of Books*, March 19, 2018, https://www.nybooks.com/daily/2018/03/19/jordan-peterson-and -fascist-mysticism/.

8    O'Brien, "Making of an American Nazi."

9    Ashley Feinberg, "This Is the Daily Stormer's Playbook," *HuffPost*, December 13, 2017, https://www.huffingtonpost.ca/entry/daily-stormer-nazi-style-guide_n_5a2ece19e4 b0ce3b344492f2?ri18n=true.

10    Serwer and Baker, "Deadbeat Dad."

11    Philip Bump, "Trump's Rationalization for Calling Women 'Dogs' Helped Define
      His Campaign," *Washington Post*, August 14, 2018, https://www.washingtonpost
      .com/news/politics/wp/2018/08/14/trumps-rationalization-for-calling-women
      -dogs-helped-define-his-campaign/.

12    Andrew Buncombe, "Controversial Pick-Up Artist Roosh V Celebrates Donald Trump's
      Victory: 'If the President Can Say It Then You Can Say It,'" *Independent*, November
      16, 2016, https://www.independent.co.uk/news/people/controversial-pick-up-artist
      -roosh-v-celebrates-donald-trump-s-victory-if-the-president-can-say-it-a7421161.html.

13    Michelle Ye Hee Lee, "Donald Trump's False Comments Connecting Mexican
      Immigrants and Crime," *Washington Post*, July 8, 2015, https://www.washingtonpost
      .com/news/fact-checker/wp/2015/07/08/donald-trumps-false-comments-connecting
      -mexican-immigrants-and-crime/.

14    Gregory Korte and Alan Gomez, "Trump Ramps Up Rhetoric on Undocumented
      Immigrants: 'These Aren't People. These Are Animals.,'" *USA Today*, May 16, 2018, https://
      www.usatoday.com/story/news/politics/2018/05/16/trump-immigrants-animals
      -mexico-democrats-sanctuary-cities/617252002/.

15    Vivian Salama, "Trump Claims Women 'Are Raped at Levels Never Seen Before'
      during Immigrant Caravan," NBC, April 5, 2018, https://www.nbcnews.com
      /politics/white-house/trump-claims-women-immigrant-caravan-being-raped-levels
      -never-seen-n863061.

16    Tom McCarthy, "Trump Mocks Christine Blasey Ford at Mississippi Rally as
      Supporters Cheer," *Guardian*, October 2, 2018, https://www.theguardian.com/us
      -news/2018/oct/02/trump-mocks-christine-blasey-ford-at-mississippi-rally.

17    Tony Romm, "Trump Jr. Accuses Facebook of Silencing Conservatives Day After It Bans
      Some Far Right Users," *Washington Post*, May 3, 2019, https://www.washingtonpost
      .com/technology/2019/05/03/trump-jr-accuses-facebook-silencing-conservatives
      -day-after-it-bans-some-far-right-users/.

18    Brian F. Schaffner, "Trump, the 2016 Election, and Expressions of Sexism" (pre-
      sentation at the Annual Meeting of the American Political Science Association,
      Boston, MA, August 30–September 2, 2018), https://tufts.app.box.com/s
      /wrth10sv6yv7gls8o7q3i61tanoqkss4.

19    "The State of the Union on Gender Equality, Sexism, and Women's Rights," Planned
      Parenthood, January 17, 2017, https://www.plannedparenthoodaction.org/uploads
      /filer_public/c9/ba/c9ba8d51-2719-4267-8784-ada24f047adc/perryundem_gender
      _equality_report_1.pdf.

20    Equality and Diversity (Reform) Bill 2010–12, UK Parliament, 2011, https://services
      .parliament.uk/Bills/2010–12/equalityanddiversityreform.html.

21  Jamie Grierson, "Feminist Zealots Want Women to Have Their Cake and Eat It, Says Tory MP," *Guardian*, August 12, 2016, https://www.theguardian.com/politics/2016/aug/12/tory-mp-philip-davies-claims-uk-legal-system-favours-women-at-mens-rights-event.

22  Peter Walker, "Tory MP Philip Davies to Speak at US Men's Rights Conference," *Guardian*, April 26, 2019, https://www.theguardian.com/politics/2019/apr/26/tory-mp-philip-davies-to-speak-at-us-mens-rights-conference.

23  Katy Balls, "Philip Davies Interview: I Don't Like Being Bullied," *Spectator*, January 6, 2017, https://www.spectator.co.uk/article/philip-davies-interview-i-don-t-like-being-bullied.

24  "Men's Rights MP Philip Davies: Gender Must Be Irrelevant," BBC, December 14, 2016, https://www.bbc.com/news/uk-politics-38313555.

25  Rowena Mason, "Conservative MP Tries to Derail Bill Protecting Women against Violence," *Guardian*, December 16, 2016, https://www.theguardian.com/politics/2016/dec/16/philip-davies-anti-feminist-tory-mp-filibuster-women-violence-bill.

26  Nick Duffy, "Tory MPs Filibuster Plans for LGBT-Inclusive Sex Education," *Pink News*, January 23, 2017, https://www.pinknews.co.uk/2017/01/23/tory-mps-filibuster-plans-for-lgbt-inclusive-sex-education/.

27  Sarah Martin, "Pauline Hanson Sparks Fury with Claim Domestic Violence Victims Are Lying to Family Court," *Guardian*, September 18, 2019, https://www.theguardian.com/australia-news/2019/sep/18/pauline-hanson-sparks-fury-with-claims-domestic-violence-victims-are-lying-to-family-court.

28  Melissa Davey, "One in Seven Young Australians Say Rape Justified If Women Change Their Mind, Study Finds," *Guardian*, May 21, 2019, https://www.theguardian.com/australia-news/2019/may/22/one-in-seven-young-australians-say-justified-if-women-change-their-mind-study-finds.

29  James Purtill and Shalailah Medhora, "Brothers & Blokes: The Men Behind One Nation's Domestic Violence Policy," ABC, November 24, 2017, https://www.abc.net.au/triplej/programs/hack/queensland-election-men-behind-one-nation-policy/9190984.

30  McPhedran, "Are 'Up to 21 Fathers' Dying."

31  Christina Cauterucci, "Betsy DeVos Plans to Consult Men's Rights Trolls about Campus Sexual Assault," *Slate*, July 11, 2017, https://slate.com/human-interest/2017/07/betsy-devos-is-asking-mens-rights-trolls-to-advise-her-on-campus-sexual-assault.html.

32  "Misogyny: The Sites," Southern Poverty Law Center, March 1, 2012, https://www.splcenter.org/fighting-hate/intelligence-report/2012/misogyny-sites.

33  Adam Bienkov, "Boris Johnson Called Gay Men 'Tank-Topped Bumboys' and Black People 'Piccaninnies' with 'Watermelon Smiles,'" *Business Insider*, June 9, 2020, https://www.businessinsider.com/boris-johnson-record-sexist-homophobic-and-racist-comments-bumboys-piccaninnies-2019-6?r=US&IR=T.

34    Boris Johnson, "Denmark Has Got It Wrong. Yes, the Burka Is Oppressive and Ridiculous—but That's Still No Reason to Ban It," *Telegraph*, August 5, 2018, https://www.telegraph.co.uk/news/2018/08/05/denmark-has-got-wrong-yes-burka -oppressive-ridiculous-still/.

35    "Boris Johnson: I Compared Muslim Women to Letterboxes to 'Defend Their Right to Wear Burqas,'" *Guardian*, July 6, 2019, https://www.theguardian.com/politics/video /2019/jul/06/boris-johnson-i-compared-muslim-women-to-letterboxes-to-defend -their-right-to-wear-burqas-video.

36    "Steve Bannon: Five Things to Know," ADL, https://www.adl.org/resources /backgrounders/steve-bannon-five-things-to-know.

37    Sarah Posner, "How Donald Trump's New Campaign Chief Created an Online Haven for White Nationalists," *Mother Jones*, August 22, 2016, https://www.motherjones .com/politics/2016/08/stephen-bannon-donald-trump-alt-right-breitbart-news/.

38    Stephen Piggott, "White Nationalists Rejoice at Trump's Appointment of Breitbart's Stephen Bannon," Southern Poverty Law Center, November 14, 2016, https://www .splcenter.org/hatewatch/2016/11/14/white-nationalists-rejoice-trumps-appointment -breitbarts-stephen-bannon.

39    Matthew d'Ancona, "The Horror, the Horror," *Tortoise*, April 3, 2019, https://members .tortoisemedia.com/2019/04/03/boris-johnson/content.html.

40    Boris Johnson, "Only a Proper Brexit Can Spare Us from This Toxic Polarisation," *Daily Telegraph*, April 15, 2019, https://www.telegraph.co.uk/politics/2019/04/14/proper -brexit-can-spare-us-toxic-polarisation/.

41    Carole Cadwalladr, "Steve Bannon: 'We Went Back and Forth' on the Themes of Johnson's Big Speech," *Guardian*, June 22, 2019, https://www.theguardian.com/politics/2019/jun /22/boris-johnson-steve-bannon-texts-foreign-secretary-resignation-speech.

42    Cadwalladr, "Steve Bannon."

43    "MPs' Fury at Boris Johnson's 'Dangerous Language,'" BBC, September 25, 2019, https:// www.bbc.com/news/uk-politics-49833804.

44    Jamie Grierson, "Man Arrested outside Office of Labour MP Jess Phillips," *Guardian*, September 26, 2019, https://www.theguardian.com/politics/2019/sep/26/man -arrested-outside-office-of-labour-mp-jess-phillips.

45    David Jackson, "Trump Defends Response to Charlottesville Violence, Says He Put It 'Perfectly' with 'Both Sides' Remark," *USA Today*, April 26, 2019, https:// www.usatoday.com/story/news/politics/2019/04/26/trump-says-both-sides -charlottesville-remark-said-perfectly/3586024002/.

46    "Dominic Cummings: Anger at MPs 'Not Surprising,' PM's Adviser Says," BBC, September 27, 2019, https://www.bbc.com/news/uk-politics-49847304.

47    Kevin Rawlinson, "Labour MP Calls for End to Online Anonymity after '600 Rape Threats,'" *Guardian*, June 11, 2018, https://www.theguardian.com/society/2018/jun /11/labour-mp-jess-phillips-calls-for-end-to-online-anonymity-after-600-threats.

48    Peter Walker, "UKIP MEP Candidate Blamed Feminists for Rise in Misogyny," *Guardian*, April 22, 2019, https://www.theguardian.com/politics/2019/apr/22/ukip -mep-candidate-carl-benjamin-blamed-feminists-for-rise-in-male-violence.

49    Rajeev Syal, "Police Investigate UKIP Candidate over Jess Phillips Rape Comments," *Guardian*, May 7, 2019, https://www.theguardian.com/politics/2019/may/07/police -investigating-ukip-candidate-youtube-carl-benjamin-jess-phillips-comments.

50    Alex Spence and Mark Di Stefano, "Under Siege for His Comments about Rape, UKIP's Star Candidate Carl Benjamin Has Recruited Milo Yiannopoulos to Join His Campaign," *BuzzFeed*, May 8, 2019, https://www.buzzfeed.com/alexspence/ukips -european-election-campaign-has-a-new-recruit-milo.

51    Sam Jones, "Far Right Breakthrough in Andalucía Send Shockwave through Spanish Politics," *Guardian*, December 9, 2018, https://www.theguardian.com/world/2018/dec /09/far-right-andalucia-seville-vox-party-shockwave-spanish-politics.

52    Tareq Haddad, "Steve Bannon Targeted 'Incels' Because They Are 'Easy to Manipulate,' Cambridge Analytica Whistleblower Says," *Newsweek*, October 29, 2019, https:// www.newsweek.com/steve-bannon-targeted-incels-manipulate-cambridge-analytica -whistleblower-christopher-wylie-1468399.

53    Aja Romano, "Reddit's TheRedPill, Notorious for Its Misogyny, Was Founded by a New Hampshire State Legislator," *Vox*, April 28, 2017, https://www.vox.com/culture /2017/4/28/15434770/red-pill-founded-by-robert-fisher-new-hampshire.

54    Bonnie Bacarisse and Brandy Zadrozny, "Red Pill Boss: All Feminists Want to Be Raped," *Daily Beast*, November 29, 2017, https://www.thedailybeast.com/red-pill-boss-all -feminists-want-to-be-raped.

55    Brandy Zadrozny and Bonnie Bacarisse, "New Hampshire State Rep Who Created Reddit's 'Red Pill' Resigns," *Daily Beast*, May 22, 2017, https://www.thedailybeast.com /new-hampshire-state-rep-who-created-reddits-red-pill-resigns.

56    Mishra, "Jordan Peterson & Fascist Mysticism."

57    Cathy Young, "Op-Ed: Hate on Jordan Peterson All You Want, but He's Tapping into Frustration That Feminists Shouldn't Ignore," *Los Angeles Times*, June 1, 2018, https://www.latimes.com/opinion/op-ed/la-oe-young-peterson-20180601-story .html.

58    Tom Yun, "Jordan Peterson: 'I Don't Think That Men Can Control Crazy Women,'" *Varsity*, October 8, 2018, https://thevarsity.ca/2017/10/08/jordan-peterson -i-don't-think-that-men-can-control-crazy-women/.

59    Conor Friedersdorf, "Why Can't People Hear What Jordan Peterson Is Saying?," *The Atlantic*, January 22, 2018, https://www.theatlantic.com/politics/archive/2018/01/putting-monsterpaint-onjordan-peterson/550859/.

60    Mishra, "Jordan Peterson & Fascist Mysticism."

61    Nellie Bowles, "Jordan Peterson, Custodian of the Patriarchy," *New York Times*, May 18, 2018, https://www.nytimes.com/2018/05/18/style/jordan-peterson-12-rules-for-life.html.

62    Mishra, "Jordan Peterson & Fascist Mysticism."

63    Zack Beauchamp, "Jordan Peterson, the Obscure Canadian Psychologist Turned Right-Wing Celebrity, Explained," *Vox*, May 21, 2018, https://www.vox.com/world/2018/3/26/17144166/jordan-peterson-12-rules-for-life.

64    "U of T Profs Alarmed by Jordan Peterson's Plan to Target Classes He Calls 'Indoctrination Cults,'" CBC, November 10, 2017, https://www.cbc.ca/radio/asithappens/as-it-happens-Friday-edition-1.4396970/u-of-t-profs-alarmed-by-jordan-peterson-s-plan-to-target-classes-he-calls-indoctrination-cults-1.4396974.

65    Bowles, "Jordan Peterson."

66    Beauchamp, "Jordan Peterson."

67    Yun, "Jordan Peterson."

68    Bowles, "Jordan Peterson."

69    J. Oliver Conroy, "What the Left Gets Wrong about Jordan Peterson," *Guardian*, June 22, 2018, https://www.theguardian.com/commentisfree/2018/jun/22/what-the-left-gets-wrong-about-jordan-peterson.

70    Nosheen Iqbal, "Cathy Newman: 'The Internet Is Being Written by Men with an Agenda,'" *Guardian*, March 19, 2018, https://www.theguardian.com/media/2018/mar/19/cathy-newman-the-internet-is-being-written-by-men-with-an-agenda.

71    Jamie Doward, "'Back Off,' Controversial Professor Urges Critics of Channel 4's Cathy Newman," *Guardian*, January 21, 2018, https://www.theguardian.com/media/2018/jan/21/no-excuse-for-online-abuse-says-professor-in-tv-misogyny-row.

72    Alex Hern, "The Rise of Patreon—the Website That Makes Jordan Peterson $80K a Month," *Guardian*, May 14, 2018, https://www.theguardian.com/technology/2018/may/14/patreon-rise-jordan-peterson-online-membership.

73    Catherine Hakim, "Academic Who Says Wives Who Deprive Husbands of Sex Are Wrecking Society," *Daily Mail*, February 15, 2017, https://www.dailymail.co.uk/femail/article-4228560/Hidden-toll-starved-sex-husbands.html.

74    Lucy Vine, "Why Is Piers Morgan So Threatened by Feminism?," *Grazia*, January 23, 2017, https://graziadaily.co.uk/life/opinion/piers-morgan-feminism/.

75    Sarah Young, "Piers Morgan Calls Daniel Craig an 'Emasculated Bond' for Using a Baby Carrier," *Independent*, October 16, 2018, https://www.independent.co.uk/life-style

/piers-morgan-daniel-craig-baby-carrier-james-bond-emasculated-papoose-twitter
-reaction-a8585836.html.

76   Piers Morgan, "I'm So Sick of This War on Masculinity and I'm Not Alone—With Their
     Pathetic Man-Hating Ad, Gillette Have Just Cut Their Own Throat," *Daily Mail*, January
     15, 2019, https://www.dailymail.co.uk/news/article-6594295/PIERS-MORGAN
     -Im-sick-war-masculinity-Gillette-just-cut-throat.html.

77   Sian Norris, "Piers Morgan's Campaign for Men Is Straight Out of the MRA and
     Incel Playbooks," *New Statesman*, September 20, 2018, https://www.newstatesman
     .com/politics/feminism/2018/09/piers-morgan-s-campaign-men-straight-out-mra
     -and-incel-playbooks.

78   Marantz, "Trolls for Trump."

## CHAPTER 8: MEN WHO ARE AFRAID OF WOMEN

1    Koul, "Pickup Artists."

2    Audrey Carlsen et al., "#MeToo Brought Down 201 Powerful Men. Nearly Half of Their
     Replacements Are Women," *New York Times*, October 23, 2018, https://www.nytimes
     .com/interactive/2018/10/23/us/metoo-replacements.html.

3    Eliza Relman, "The 25 Women Who Have Accused Trump of Sexual Misconduct,"
     *Business Insider*, October 9, 2019, https://www.businessinsider.com/women-accused
     -trump-sexual-misconduct-list-2017–12.

4    Ryan Mac and Davey Alba, "These Tech Execs Faced #MeToo Allegations. They All Have
     New Jobs.," *BuzzFeed*, April 16, 2019, https://www.buzzfeednews.com/article/ryanmac
     /tech-men-accused-sexual-misconduct-new-jobs-metoo.

5    Giles Coren, "A Couple of XX's Could End My Glorious Career," *Times* (London), October
     21, 2017, https://www.thetimes.co.uk/article/a-couple-of-misplaced-kisses-could
     -end-my-career-plwzh6n3l.

6    "Still Just a Bit of Banter? Sexual Harassment in the Workplace in 2016," TUC, August
     10, 2016, https://www.tuc.org.uk/research-analysis/reports/still-just-bit-banter/.

7    Lauren Aratani, "The Six Women Who Accused Harvey Weinstein at His Trial, and
     What They Said," *Guardian*, March 11, 2020, https://www.theguardian.com/film
     /2020/feb/24/weinstein-accusers-what-they-said-accusations.

8    James Damore, "Google's Ideological Echo Chamber: How Bias Clouds Our Thinking
     about Diversity and Inclusion," July 2017, https://www.documentcloud.org/documents
     /3914586-Googles-Ideological-Echo-Chamber.html.

9    Matthew Kassel, "The Annie Leibovitz of the Alt-Right," *New York Times*, July 20,
     2017, https://www.nytimes.com/2017/07/20/magazine/the-annie-leibovitz-of-the-alt
     -right.html.

10    Richard A. Oppel Jr., "Ohio Teenagers Guilty in Rape That Social Media Brought to Light," *New York Times*, March 17, 2013, https://www.nytimes.com/2013/03/18/us /teenagers-found-guilty-in-rape-in-steubenville-ohio.html.

11    Mallory Ortberg, "CNN Reports on the 'Promising Future' of the Steubenville Rapists, Who Are 'Very Good Students,'" *Gawker*, March 17, 2013, https://gawker.com /5991003/cnn-reports-on-the-promising-future-of-the-steubenville-rapists-who-are -very-good-students.

12    Tara Culp-Ressler, "George Will Defends Controversial Column on Campus Sexual Assault," *ThinkProgress*, June 21, 2014, https://archive.thinkprogress.org/george -will-defends-controversial-column-on-campus-sexual-assault-9583acdacb0c/.

13    Anita Singh, "Jeremy Clarkson: BBC Won't Give Jobs to Men Anymore, So No Wonder Nick Robinson Didn't Get Question Time Role," *Daily Telegraph*, January 7, 2019, https://www.telegraph.co.uk/news/2019/01/07/jeremy-clarkson-bbc-wont -give-jobs-men-no-wonder-nick-robinson/.

14    "DJ Paul Gambaccini and Sir Cliff Richard behind Petition Urging Anonymity in Sex Offense Arrests," *Press Gazette*, July 1, 2019, https://www.pressgazette.co.uk/dj-paul -gambaccini-and-sir-cliff-richard-behind-petition-urging-anonymity-in-sex-offence -arrests/.

15    Georgina Lee, "FactCheck: Men Are More Likely to Be Raped Than Falsely Accused of Rape," Channel 4, October 12, 2018, https://www.channel4.com/news/factcheck /factcheck-men-are-more-likely-to-be-raped-than-be-falsely-accused-of-rape.

16    "An Overview of Sexual Offending in England & Wales," Office for National Statistics, January 10, 2013, https://assets.publishing.service.gov.uk/government/uploads /system/uploads/attachment_data/file/214970/sexual-offending-overview-jan-2013 .pdf.

17    Owen Bowcott and Caelainn Barr, "Just 1.5% of All Rape Cases Lead to Charge or Summons, Data Reveals," *Guardian*, July 26, 2019, https://www.theguardian.com/law /2019/jul/26/rape-cases-charge-summons-prosecutions-victims-england-wales.

18    Elizabeth Plank, "The Daily Mail Used the Term 'Cried Rape' in 54 Headlines in the Last Year," *Mic*, April 1, 2013, https://www.mic.com/articles/32159/the-daily-mail-used -the-term-cried-rape-in-54-headlines-in-the-last-year.

19    Keir Starmer, "False Allegations of Rape and Domestic Violence Are Few and Far Between," *Guardian*, March 13, 2013, https://www.theguardian.com/commentisfree /2013/mar/13/false-allegations-rape-domestic-violence-rare.

20    Ross Douthat, "The Redistribution of Sex," *New York Times*, May 2, 2018, https:// www.nytimes.com/2018/05/02/opinion/incels-sex-robots-redistribution.html.

21    Robin Hanson, "Two Types of Envy," *Overcoming Bias* (blog), April 26, 2018, https:// www.overcomingbias.com/2018/04/two-types-of-envy.html.

22    Toby Young, "What Every Incel Needs: A Sex Robot," *Spectator*, May 3, 2018, https://www.spectator.co.uk/article/what-every-incel-needs-a-sex-robot.

23    Douthat, "Redistribution of Sex."

24    Soupcoff, "What Should We Do."

25    Coren, "A Couple of XX's."

26    "Still Just a Bit."

27    Irin Karmon, "How the Kavanaugh Hearings Changed American Men and Women," *The Cut*, April 16, 2019, https://www.thecut.com/2019/04/new-study-reveals-how-kavanaugh-hearings-changed-americans.html.

28    Lee, "Men Are More Likely."

29    Katy Steinmetz, "Nearly Half of Men Believe the Pay Gap Is 'Made Up,' Survey Finds," *Time*, April 2, 2019, https://time.com/5562171/pay-gap-survey-equal-pay-day/.

## CHAPTER 9: MEN WHO DON'T KNOW THEY HATE WOMEN

1    Monica Anderson and Jingjing Jiang, "Teens, Social Media & Technology 2018," Pew Research Center, May 31, 2018, https://www.pewresearch.org/internet/2018/05/31/teens-social-media-technology-2018/.

2    Charles Hymas and Laurence Dodds, "Thousands of Teenagers Spending More Than Eight Hours a Day Online at Weekends, Ofcom Figures Show," *Daily Telegraph*, July 12, 2018, https://www.telegraph.co.uk/news/2018/07/12/thousands-teenagers-spending-eight-hours-day-online-weekends/.

3    "BBC Three Survey Reveals One in Four Young People First View Porn at Age 12 or Under," BBC, April 10, 2014, https://www.bbc.co.uk/mediacentre/latestnews/2014/porn-whats-the-harm.

4    Charles Hymas, "A Fifth of 16–24 Year Olds Spend More Than Seven Hours a Day Online Every Day of the Week, Exclusive Ofcom Figures Reveal," *Daily Telegraph*, August 11, 2018, https://www.telegraph.co.uk/news/2018/08/11/fifth-16-24-year-olds-spend-seven-hours-day-online-every-day/.

5    Anderson and Jiang, "Teens, Social Media & Technology 2018."

6    Paul Lewis, "Fiction Is Outperforming Reality: How YouTube's Algorithm Distorts the Truth," *Guardian*, February 2, 2018, https://www.theguardian.com/technology/2018/feb/02/how-youtubes-algorithm-distorts-truth.

7    Cam Cullen, "The Mobile Internet Phenomena Report," Sandvine, February 2019, https://www.sandvine.com/press-releases/sandvine-releases-2019-mobile-internet-phenomena-report.

8    John Herrman, "For the New Far Right, YouTube Has Become the New Talk Radio," *New York Times*, August 3, 2017, https://www.nytimes.com/2017/08/03/magazine/for-the-new-far-right-youtube-has-become-the-new-talk-radio.html.

9    Rebecca Lewis, "Alternative Influence: Broadcasting the Reactionary Right on YouTube," Data & Society, September 18, 2018, https://datasociety.net/library/alternative -influence/.

10   Joan E. Solsman, "YouTube's AI Is the Puppet Master over Most of What You Watch," CNET, January 10, 2018, https://www.cnet.com/news/youtube-ces-2018-neal-mohan/.

11   Zeynep Tufekci, "YouTube, the Great Radicalizer," *New York Times*, March 10, 2018, https://www.nytimes.com/2018/03/10/opinion/Sunday/youtube-politics-radical .html.

12   Jack Nicas, "How YouTube Drives People to the Internet's Darkest Corners," *Wall Street Journal*, February 7, 2018, https://www.wsj.com/articles/how-youtube-drives -viewers-to-the-internets-darkest-corners-1518020478.

13   Kevin Roose, "YouTube's Product Chief on Online Radicalization and Algorithmic Rabbit Holes," *New York Times*, March 29, 2019, https://www.nytimes.com/2019/03/29 /technology/youtube-online-extremism.html.

14   "Google Diversity Annual Report 2020," Google, 2020, https://kstatic.googleusercontent .com/files/25badfc6b6d1b33f3b87372ff7545d79261520d821e6ee9a82c4ab2de42a 01216be2156bc5a60ae3337ffe7176d90b8b2b3000891ac6e516a650ecebf0e3f866.

15   Kelly Weill, "How YouTube Built a Radicalization Machine for the Far-Right," *Daily Beast*, December 19, 2018, https://www.thedailybeast.com/how-youtube-pulled-these -men-down-a-vortex-of-far-right-hate.

16   Paul Lewis and Erin McCormick, "How an Ex-YouTube Insider Investigated Its Secret Algorithm," *Guardian*, February 2, 2018, https://www.theguardian .com/technology/2018/feb/02/youtube-algorithm-election-clinton-trump -guillaume-chaslot.

17   Lewis and McCormick, "Ex-YouTube Insider."

18   Robert Evans, "From Memes to Infowars: How 75 Fascist Activists Were 'Red-Pilled,'" *Bellingcat*, October 11, 2018, https://www.bellingcat.com/news/americas/2018/10/11 /memes-infowars-75-fascist-activists-red-pilled/.

19   Adrienne Massanari, "#Gamergate and The Fappening: How Reddit's Algorithm, Governance, and Culture Support Toxic Technocultures," *New Media & Society* 19, no. 3 (2015): 329–346, https://doi.org/10.1177/1461444815608807.

20   Romano, "Milo Yiannopoulos's Twitter Ban, Explained."

21   Andrew Perrin, "5 Facts about Americans and Video Games," Pew Research Center, September 7, 2018, https://www.pewresearch.org/fact-tank/2018/09/17/5-facts -about-americans-and-video-games/.

22   Anya Kamenetz, "Right-Wing Hate Groups Are Recruiting Video Gamers," NPR, November 5, 2018, https://www.npr.org/2018/11/05/660642531/right-wing-hate -groups-are-recruiting-video-gamers.

23 David Barrett, "Drunk or Flirty Rape Victims Often 'to Blame,' Says Survey," *Daily Telegraph*, February 12, 2015, https://www.telegraph.co.uk/news/uknews/crime /11409210/Drunk-or-flirty-rape-victims-often-to-blame-says-survey.html.

## CHAPTER 10: MEN WHO HATE MEN WHO HATE WOMEN

1 Farhad Manjoo, "A Hunt for Ways to Combat Online Radicalization," *New York Times*, August 23, 2017, https://www.nytimes.com/2017/08/23/technology/a-hunt-for-ways-to -disrupt-the-work-of-online-radicalization.html.

2 "Countering Violent Extremism: Actions Needed to Define Strategy and Assess Progress of Federal Efforts," U.S. Government Accountability Office, April 2017, https:// www.gao.gov/assets/690/683984.pdf.

3 Joshua D. Freilich, Steven M. Chermak, Roberta Belli, Jeff Gruenewald, and William S. Parkin, "Introducing the United States Extremist Crime Database (ECDB)," *Terrorism and Political Violence* 26, no. 2 (2014): 372–384, https://doi.org/10.1080/09546553 .2012.713229.

4 Cecco, "Toronto Van Attack Suspect."

5 Molly Hayes, "Years before Toronto Van Attack, Alek Minassian Says He Connected Online with Misogynistic Radicals," *Globe and Mail*, September 27, 2019, https://www .theglobeandmail.com/meric/merica/article-years-before-toronto-van-attack-alek -minassian-says-he-connected/.

6 "The Year in Hate: Trump Buoyed by White Supremacists in 2017, Sparking Backlash among Black Nationalist Groups," Southern Poverty Law Center, February 21, 2018, https:// www.splcenter.org/news/2018/02/21/year-hate-trump-buoyed-white-supremacists -2017-sparking-backlash-among-black-nationalist.

7 Chris Hemmings, "How Can Universities Get Men to Talk about Mental Health?," BBC, August 1, 2019, https://www.bbc.com/news/education-49157596.

8 Susanne Ault, "Survey: YouTube Stars More Popular Than Mainstream Celebs Among U.S. Teens," *Variety*, August 5, 2014, https://variety.com/2014/digital/news/survey -youtube-stars-more-popular-than-mainstream-celebs-among-u-s-teens-1201275245/.

9 Starmer, "False Allegations."

10 Max Fisher and Amanda Taub, "On YouTube's Digital Playground, an Open Gate for Pedophiles," *New York Times*, June 3, 2019, https://www.nytimes.com/2019/06/03/world /americas/youtube-pedophiles.html.

11 Tufekci, "YouTube, the Great Radicalizer."

12 J. M. Berger, "Nazis vs. ISIS on Twitter: A Comparative Study of White Nationalist and ISIS Online Social Media Networks," GW Program on Extremism, September 2016, https://extremism.gwu.edu/sites/g/files/zaxdzs2191/f/downloads/Nazis%20v .%20ISIS.pdf.

13    David Gilbert, "Users of Far-Right Social Network Gab Can Now Comment on the Entire Internet," *Vice*, February 17, 2019, https://www.vice.com/en_ca/article/nexq9d/gab-far -right-social-network-comments.

14    Yara Bayoumy and Kathy Gilsinan, "A Reformed White Nationalist Says the Worst Is Yet to Come," *The Atlantic*, August 6, 2019, https://www.theatlantic.com/politics /archive/2019/08/conversation-christian-picciolini/595543/.

15    Donie O'Sullivan, "Facebook Bans White Nationalism Two Weeks after New Zealand Attack," CNN, March 28, 2019, https://www.cnn.com/2019/03/27/tech/facebook-white -nationalism-ban/index.html.

16    Issie Lapowsky, "In Congressional Hearing on Hate, the Haters Got Their Way," *Wired*, September 4, 2019, https://www.wired.com/story/house-hearing-hate-crimes -white-nationalism/.

17    Rachelle Hampton, "The Black Feminists Who Saw the Alt-Right Threat Coming," *Slate*, April 23, 2019, https://slate.com/technology/2019/04/black-feminists-alt-right -twitter-gamergate.html.

18    Alex Hern, "'Worrying' Lack of Diversity in Britain's Tech Sector, Report Finds," *Guardian*, November 14, 2018, https://www.theguardian.com/technology/2018/nov/14 /worrying-lack-of-diversity-in-britains-technology-sector-race-gender-report-finds.

19    Whitney Phillips, "The Oxygen of Amplification: Better Practices for Reporting on Extremists, Antagonists, and Manipulators Online," Data & Society, May 2018, https://datasociety.net/wp-content/uploads/2018/05/FULLREPORT_Oxygen _of_Amplification_DS.pdf.

20    Margaret Sullivan, "Giving Killers Coverage, Not Platforms," *New York Times*, June 1, 2014, https://www.nytimes.com/2014/06/01/public-editor/giving-killers-coverage -not-platforms.html.

21    Michael Kimmel, *Manhood in America*, 4th ed. (Oxford: Oxford University Press, 2018).

22    Bayoumy and Gilsinan, "Reformed White Nationalist."

# Index

# Acknowledgments

I have been immensely lucky to be surrounded by a supportive and brilliant team that has championed this book from its inception. No one more so than Abigail Bergstrom, who by a strange twist of fate, both commissioned it during her former tenure as my editor at Simon & Schuster and cheered it over the finish line as my wonderfully supportive agent at Gleam Titles. I am so grateful to her, Megan Staunton, and everyone at Gleam for their hard work and kindness.

I am so lucky to work with the fantastic team at Sourcebooks, whose support, hard work, and attention to detail are hugely appreciated.

I am deeply grateful to all the interviewees who gave so generously of their time and expertise in the course of my research for this book and to the young people at schools all over the country who bravely offered me a window into their world.

I owe a great debt of thanks to all those who supported the book through background conversations and early reading or who offered me general support and encouragement during the writing period, including Hugh, Hayley, Aileen, Eileen, Lucy, Emma, Rachael, Brenna, Sarah, Charlotte, and Joe. And to my family, who have supported my career, even when the attendant backlash must have seemed disproportionate and bewildering and there appeared to be easier routes to take.

It makes me smile when people ask me, as they already have, whether you have to be a woman who hates men to write a book about men who hate women. It is certainly the stereotype that the members of the manosphere would have you believe. In reality, the opposite is true. I don't think it would have been possible to write this book without a real understanding of the impact and power of men who love women. The men who champion them tirelessly. The men who understand the real impact of misogyny and work hard, in their own quiet way, in their individual spheres, to do all they can to mitigate it. Men like that have supported my cause, and I have them to thank for many elements of my career. In very different ways, they all played a part in leading to this book.

Men like Bob Currie, who supported me to believe (to paraphrase Alice) that I could do any number of impossible things before lunchtime. Dr. Michael Hurley, whose calm evisceration of linguistic gender inequality first sparked my awareness of the systemic nature of sexism. James Bartlett, whose quiet generosity and kindness have enabled the Everyday Sexism Project to flourish since its earliest origins, and Tom Livingstone, who helped me to believe in the value of my own time. Men like Peter Florence and Stephen Dunbar-Johnson, who do not just talk the talk but also work hard and unostentatiously in their professional fields to advance gender equality.

Most of all, I owe a debt of enormous gratitude to Nick, my partner, accomplice, and best friend. He is the kind of man whose beliefs and behaviors are anathema to the men described in this book. The kind of man whose encouragement of my budding interest in feminism helped to spark the Everyday Sexism Project and whose endless support has enabled me to continue ever since. Who does not pontificate about pioneering new gender roles but simply lives them, doesn't lecture on shared labor but shoulders it, doesn't expect accolades for providing endless help but offers it freely. He is proof that a different world is possible, that talk of biological imperatives for machismo are nonsense, that #NotAllMen...

In the course of supporting me to do this work, he has remained steadfast throughout career compromises, the contempt of strangers, and extreme abuse from trolls.

While it seems absurd even to have to address it, when I am faced with the ubiquitous questions about whether or not I hate men, he is the answer. And whenever I have questioned myself, struggled with this work, or been overwhelmed by abuse, he has been the answer too.

Thank you, Nick. I love you.

# About the Author

Laura Bates is the founder of the Everyday Sexism Project, a crowdsourced collection of stories from women around the world about their experiences with gender inequality. Laura has received the British Empire Medal in the Queen's Birthday Honours, the WMC Digital Media Award from the Women's Media Center, and the Georgina Henry prize; has been named in the BBC Woman's Hour Power List Game Changers; and has won *Cosmopolitan's* Ultimate Woman of the Year Award. She was also named in CNN's 10 Visionary Women List. Follow her efforts on Twitter @everydaysexism.